COLD WAR WORKERS

COLD WAR WORKERS

Labour, Family, and Community in a Nuclear State

EDITED BY
ISABEL CAMPBELL

McGill-Queen's University Press
Montreal & Kingston · London · Chicago

ISBN 978-0-2280-2440-8 (paper)
ISBN 978-0-2280-2441-5 (ePDF)
ISBN 978-0-2280-2442-2 (ePUB)

Legal deposit second quarter 2025
Bibliothèque nationale du Québec

Printed in Canada on acid-free paper that is 100% ancient forest free (100% post-consumer recycled), processed chlorine free

This book has been published with the help of a grant from the Federation for the Humanities and Social Sciences, through the Awards to Scholarly Publications Program, using funds provided by the Social Sciences and Humanities Research Council of Canada. Funding was also received from the Royal Canadian Air Force Heritage Fund.

Funded by the Government of Canada | Financé par le gouvernement du Canada | Canada | Canada Council for the Arts | Conseil des arts du Canada

We acknowledge the support of the Canada Council for the Arts.
Nous remercions le Conseil des arts du Canada de son soutien.

McGill-Queen's University Press in Montreal is on land which long served as a site of meeting and exchange amongst Indigenous Peoples, including the Haudenosaunee and Anishinabeg nations. In Kingston it is situated on the territory of the Haudenosaunee and Anishinaabek. We acknowledge and thank the diverse Indigenous Peoples whose footsteps have marked these territories on which peoples of the world now gather.

LIBRARY AND ARCHIVES CANADA CATALOGUING IN PUBLICATION

Title: Cold War workers : labour, family, and community in a nuclear state / edited by Isabel Campbell.
Names: Campbell, Isabel (Historian), editor
Description: Includes bibliographical references and index.
Identifiers: Canadiana (print) 20240494652 | Canadiana (ebook) 20240495365 | ISBN 9780228024408 (paper) | ISBN 9780228024415 (ePDF) | ISBN 9780228024422 (ePUB)
Subjects: LCSH: Cold War—War work—Canada. | LCSH: Cold War—Social aspects—Canada.
Classification: LCC FC603 .C65 2025 | DDC 971.064—dc23

This book was designed and typeset by Garet Markvoort, zijn digital, in 9.5/14 Baskerville 10 Pro with Obviously and Univers Next Pro.
Copyediting by Shelagh Plunkett.

Contents

Figures

Acknowledgments

This edited volume owes a great deal to Warren Sinclair, Sue Heffernan, Stacey Fritz, Matthew S. Wiseman, Frances Reilly, and Sarah Hogenbirk, the primary authors of the six chapters. I could not have asked for a more patient, generous, and intelligent group of contributors. The two anonymous peer reviewers of my original manuscript made constructive suggestions and improved my framing of the chapters immensely. Kyla Madden, my editor at McGill-Queen's University Press, encouraged and supported me as I edited the chapters and worked on the framing of these diverse pieces. Crystal Fraser provided helpful feedback on chapter 1 and offered kindness on other occasions. Stella McTaggart improved the references.

Sincere thanks to Alison Campbell, Raphael Sandovel, Corporal Michael Creech, Stefan Heratsuka, Brian Jeffrey, the late Larry Wilson, and others at Library and Archives Canada who helped improve and select the illustrations and also gave permissions for publication. Thanks especially to Warren Sinclair who contributed so many of his own family photos, kindly illustrating his family's intimate and proud moments.

During the years I worked on this edited volume, I received love and support from dear family members, including Michael, Luke, Nora,

Madeleine, Juliette, and Elyse Barre, Matt Feldman, Eddy, Norm, and Rod Campbell, and Alice Hinther. Beloved friends, Karla Weys, Anne Northcott, Kim Rogers, Lyna Champagne, Bruce Miller, Cecily Strickland, Colleen McKee, Maggie Ring, Sharon McMillan, Don Lavic, and others propped me up when my marriage disintegrated as the volume reached its final stages.

My colleagues and friends at the Directorate of History and Heritage at National Defence also encouraged and supported me. Melissa Davidson, Adam Coombs, Jason Delaney, Ken Ingram, Jim McKillip, Yves Tremblay, Sarah Williams, Emilie Fortier, Steve Harris, Dara Price, and especially Chaplain Tom Hamilton and others are thanked for their kindnesses. These people at National Defence are helping to implement important cultural changes regarding gender, sexuality, and racial diversity and inclusion as we learn how to be better at what we do. They give me faith in redemption and hope for a better future.

Over the course of my career as an archivist and historian, I have come to appreciate the term "it takes a village." The village has helped me, but I take full responsibility for any remaining errors of fact or interpretation here. Thanks, everyone, for being there for me.

Abbreviations

APA – American Psychiatric Association
ATG – Alaska Territorial Guard
CAS – Chief of the Air Staff
CIA – Central Intelligence Agency
CFS – Canadian Forces Station
DEW Line – Distant Early Warning Line (the most northerly radar line across North America)
DND – Department of National Defence (Canadian)
DRB – Defence Research Board
DRML – Defence Research Medical Laboratories
DSM – *Diagnostic and Statistical Manual of Mental Disorders*
GI – American slang for Ground Infantry
HBC – Hudson Bay Company
MCL – Mid-Canada Line (a radar line that ran along the 55th parallel between the Pinetree Line to the south and the DEW Line to the north)
MDAB – Moosonee Development Area Board (appointed by the Province of Ontario in 1968 under legislation passed in 1966)
MTDB – Moosonee Townsite Development Board (formed by town residents in 1963)

NATO – North Atlantic Treaty Organization
NORAD – North American Air Defense Command (formed in 1958 and renamed North American Aerospace Command in 1981)
NSO – Northern Service Officer
NWT – North West Territory (formerly this territory included what is now part of Nunavik). It is separate from the Yukon.
ONR – Ontario Northland Railway
PCB – Polychlorinated Bipheny
PMQ – Permanent Married Quarters
PPCLI – Princess Patricia's Canadian Light Infantry
PTSD – Post Traumatic Stress Disorder
RCAF – Royal Canadian Air Force
RCMP – Royal Canadian Mounted Police
SRFN – Serpent River First Nation
TPH – Toronto Psychiatric Hospital
UNEF – United Nations Emergency Force

COLD WAR WORKERS

Introduction

Early Cold War Transformations in Labour, Family, and Communities

ISABEL CAMPBELL

Growing up as the son of a DEW Line Inuvialuk employee, Sammy Lennie spoke about the benefits of his dad's work. "Yeah, in a way I could say he was lucky to have that job because it was either that or go trapping. At that time anyway when we moved to Tuk – no roads, no housing, everybody was trappers, everybody lived strictly off the land ... we had the advantage, we had all this other stuff, you know, more, better, fresher groceries." Later, he recalled the horrific environmental effects of these radar developments in the far north. "I remember seeing 'Caution: Radiation,' but I didn't know what it was. Especially around the big radar dishes ... But you see, that was our playground."[1]

During the 1950s, the American and Canadian governments constructed three northern radar lines, the Pinetree Line (the most southerly one, frequently built close to small towns), the Mid-Canada Line, and the DEW Line (the Distant Early Warning line which was furthest north and extended from Alaska to Greenland) to provide warning of a possible atomic attack.[2] Military and diplomatic historians and political scientists have studied the diplomatic, strategic, and economic aspects of these developments, acknowledging the unequal relationship between Canada and the United States, while drawing upon government sources.[3] The Americans, who had experienced a surprise attack on Pearl Harbour on 7 December 1941, insisted upon northern warning systems and air defence as priority in joint defence plans.[4] After the Soviets exploded an atomic bomb in 1949 and with the outbreak of combat in Korea in 1950, some security experts focused upon the threat of a nuclear attack on North America which justified these northern defence projects. Much depended upon who defined security. For the most part, elite white men dominated government discussions and the historical studies of these developments. Ann Denholm Crosby, one of a few women security scholars, criticized the "unanticipated militarism" resulting from the intertwining professional ties and integrated defence production relationships between the United States and Canada.[5] For the most part, scholars of this topic have not deeply analyzed the labour required to support these defence topics. Labour historians, for their part, have focused predominantly upon union work, aspects of the Red Scare, and leftist politics.[6]

As this volume will show, the Cold War created global and Canadian demands for new technological, scientific, construction, and other labour which affected many non-unionized workers. Labour is thus defined broadly in this volume, from those serving in the military, as well as civilian construction and maintenance workers to professionals such as scientists, psychologists, and psychiatrists. This book explores how Cold War labour in Canada transformed the lives of these individuals, their families, and their communities in ways that were both predictable and surprising, and both beneficial and harmful. It contributes to the Canadian historiography on the early Cold War by revealing and contrasting the experiences of marginalized peoples (Indigenous, women, gays, lesbians, and northerners) and elite white men (scientists and psychiatrists) that are seldom brought together in a single volume.

Because Canada's Cold War society did not use "forced labour" in the legal sense, workers and their families had some influence over decision-making processes.[7] When people left jobs in large enough numbers, policies changed.[8] Yet, as the quotes above reveal, employment choices were often limited and military developments went ahead regardless of whether individuals decided to take the jobs or not. Some workers and their families lobbied for community and lifestyle improvements to offset the militarization of their lives; others sometimes questioned work practices, and a few engaged in defiant behaviours. The relationship between employers and workers was not static, rather workers and their families sometimes altered work practices, even as early Cold War employment opportunities transformed and changed their lives in profound and unexpected ways.

Militarization in this volume refers to the "gradual encroachment of military ideas, values, and structures into the civilian domain."[9] The militarization (and colonization) of Indigenous lives and lands is a key theme in the first part of the book, while the second part exposes how Cold War security influenced scientific and psychiatric research and induced the Canadian services to promote the idea of a single career woman in the 1950s.[10] Both parts of this work reveal elements of intersectionality, that is, how factors such as race, class, and gender intersect to create multiple forms of exclusion within individual lives. Collectively, the chapters in this volume also contrast the lives of marginalized and privileged workers.[11] Readers of this volume may compare diversified stories about how race, gender, class, and sexuality intersected in the lives of individuals and of how Cold War labour affected workers and their families in contrasting and contradictory ways.

Global Cold War scholarship has blossomed over the past few decades, complicating an earlier predominant picture of two superpowers (the US and the USSR) utilizing militarized science and technology to challenge each other, while conquering nature and subduing other peoples. European and Canadian scholars have shed new light on small power influence and the roles of economic and cultural diplomacy, as well as military labour.[12] Internationally, nuanced studies demonstrate the global reach of the Cold War, while exposing multiple layers of interactions among the smaller sovereign powers and their diverse populations who became aligned or entangled with the West or East in this prolonged conflict. For American diplomatic historian Thomas Zeiler, such new approaches threaten to obscure how power functions at home and abroad.[13] While acknowledging the predominance of American power, other international historians have analyzed ideological, labour, gender, sexuality, technological, environmental, economic, and cultural aspects of international history. While some scholars shed new light on how elite white men dominated the global power structures, nuanced national and local studies expose challenges to that dominance and create a robust and more inclusive picture of Cold War experiences.[14]

In Canada, the 1990s history wars and the predominant American influence resulted in diplomatic, military, and naval historians focusing upon sovereignty, the inter-play with American and allied powers, and political or economic factors. As Adam Chapnick points out, the research on these topics and on the role of the Canadian north in the strategic calculations of foreign policy is not finished.[15] Recent interpretation reveals how influential American officials defined and practiced a westernized masculine conception of security, characterizing and dismissing the alternative views of lesser allies as "neurotic or emasculated."[16] Apart from these insights, Canadian historians have long studied social, cultural, and economic history and now reach past national boundaries, including intersectional and other lenses to expose discriminatory global and national practices.[17] This volume, which includes chapters about professional men who exercised power over others through their work and marginalized people who coped with the massive changes wrought by Cold War security projects (like the northern radar lines), demonstrates the value of bringing these contrasting pieces together in a single book.

Other historians have explored how American power and especially its nuclear strategies influenced Canada. Monographs by Andrew Burtch, Tarah Brookfield, and others have expanded our understanding of how global Cold War strategy filtered down at the national and local levels, with feminist and anti-nuclear groups protesting the dangers posed by nuclear weapons, while others sought protective measures in the case of a nuclear holocaust.[18] As we will see in this volume, the nuclear threat created a host of new military and civilian jobs, including scientific research, military posts for women, jobs in Indigenous occupied territories, and later activist work to address the environmental and other issues created by Cold War militarization.

If some welcomed new technological and scientific opportunities, others questioned conventional ideas about security in a world transformed by the atomic bomb.[19] In the face of this new threat, Alex Souchen and Matthew S. Wiseman argue that Canada leveraged "military and defence expenditures to fund domestic industries, bolster employment, and support science, and technology," concluding that this sponsorship had uneven patterns of influence.[20] Their edited volume focuses upon the "symbiotic relationship" among Canada's military, political, economic, and research institutions, with attention to environmental issues as well as other political, economic, and social developments.[21] Their work exposes inter-relationships among power, funding, and employment demonstrating Cold War security influence upon industries and university research in Canada. They focus upon a military-industrial complex closely intertwined with American interests and dominated by elite white men who defined security in traditional narrow terms.

At the global level, the Cold War created insecurity and significant physical and cultural displacements and hardships for vulnerable people. As Dominique Marshall pointed out in a review of David Meren's article, "The Tragedies of Canadian International History," Canadian historians have studied humanitarian aid, refugee policies, international adoptions, and the promotion of human rights for decades.[22] These studies broaden traditional definitions of security to emphasize the protection of displaced and vulnerable peoples. More recently, in *Undiplomatic History: The New Study of Canada and the World*, Asa McKercher and Philip Van Huizen highlight how race, gender, religion, identity, and other factors intersect, especially with respect to the role of non-state actors.[23] They sought to "move away from an exclusive focus on diplomatic history, viewed (rightly, in certain ways) as hidebound, elitist, and overly concerned with the state and the small group of white males who dominated it." The thirteen chapters of *Undiplomatic History* address the roles of non-state actors in influencing domestic and international relations in diverse areas including missionary work, the measurement of time, natural birth control methods, human environmental concerns, and human rights. While the editors of that volume do not frame these historical actors as performing labour, much of their domestic and international work may be analyzed in that way. This slight re-framing creates a deeper appreciation of the contradictions and diversity of Canada's labourers viewed through a holistic and inclusive perspective.

Laura Madokoro's *The Dominion of Race: Rethinking Canada's International History* brings in a decolonization perspective, with varied chapters analysing the interplay between the domestic and the international spheres and the processes of "exclusion, marginalization, and disempowerment of some racially determined Canadians."[24] The chapters in *The Dominion of Race* also make compelling arguments for intersectionality with stories of individuals experiencing multiple layers of racialized, sexualized, and gendered experiences during the early Cold War.[25] That volume also may be slightly reframed to consider historical actors as labourers, with consideration of Asian Canadians who served in the First World War and five thousand Chinese labourers who moved across Canada under armed guard during the war among others.[26]

Internalized racialized thinking created hierarchies within labouring communities, including the academic communities that structure our thinking about Canada and its place in the world. The emerging historiography highlights how Cold War employment displaced people as will be apparent in part one of this volume, which focuses upon varied Indigenous experiences. Cold War military, industrial, and mining developments displaced people across the globe and further justified the processes of colonialism and militarization that had already deprived Indigenous Peoples of traditional lands.[27] Militarization of Indigenous Peoples began much earlier. *A Commemorative History of Aboriginal People in the Canadian Military* describes "the long and proud Aboriginal traditions of alliance with the Crown, of loyalty in times of trial, and of military service in defence of the nation and its interests abroad."[28] The Indigenous–military alignment which displaced and disrupted traditional cultures is apparent in the current literature and in chapters one to three of this work.

During the Second World War and the early Cold War, these processes intensified. P. Whitney Lackenbauer examines the close intertwining of ideas about gender, race, and sexuality evident in government concerns about potential relations between African American service men stationed in the North and Inuit women.[29] Lackenbauer draws upon Sarah Carter's seminal work to argue that these "representations of women (and concomitant racial hierarchies) entrenched cultural presumptions [of white cultural morality] ... and maintained distinctions between dominant and subordinate populations" in an earlier period.[30] The varieties of Cold War construction and technical labour further disrupted communities and their norms and also contest the ubiquitous 1950s picture of a white middle class suburban family headed by a father/bread-winner.[31] What emerges, from new studies and this volume, are more complex pictures of how Cold War labour influenced work, family, and community life in other settings. These stories challenge the narrative of Canada as a land of progressive opportunities and consensus-based decision making.[32]

Indigenous scholar Brittany Luby discusses how her book *The Damned: The Politics of Loss and Survival in Anishinaabe Territory* "disrupts popular narratives of Canada as an affluent society after 1945." *The Damned* questions the optimistic historiographical picture of Canada as a land of opportunity and security. A progressive narrative of continuous improvements in life and choices dominated our understanding of the early Cold War and silenced negative experiences.[33] She is right. This theme is particularly evident in the first three chapters of this work which focus upon Indigenous experiences. Militarization resulted in losses of Indigenous lands, languages, and traditions even as it offered attractive employment.

The final three chapters reflect on the dominance of that early masculinized vision and the challenges to that vision that permeated the work of professional men, who were forced to question their prior assumptions and (in the Canadian military) make way for women as service members. The construction of an unmarried service career woman analyzed in the last chapter exemplifies how Cold War labour created lifestyle alternatives to the idealized nuclear family. The very workers who supported Cold War militarization and benefited from it sometimes sowed the seeds of change, especially when they were faced with recruitment issues, public disclosures of harms, or outside activism.

Lianne C. Leddy's *Serpent River Resurgence: Confronting Uranium Mining at Elliot Lake* demonstrates how twentieth-century colonialism and Cold War militarism justified systematic invasions and appropriation of Indigenous lands. Elders within the Serpent River First Nation eventually succeeded in drawing attention to the profound environmental and health devastation of uranium mining on their traditional territories.[34] Chapters one to three of this book challenge narrow definitions of security, forcing us to think more holistically about what security means when "traditional pursuits such as fishing, hunting, and trapping are no longer tenable and new opportunities for waged labour are fleeting and unsafe."[35] The new forms of employment often wiped out the old ways.

These studies expose how security meant different things to different people. Parks Canada historian David Neufeld undertook extensive oral histories at the end of the Cold War, documenting how the Indigenous people who had worked on the DEW Line endured "pervasive and continuing contact," which "undermined their own sense of identity."[36] He and other scholars recognized that increasing militarization threated Indigenous cultures, profoundly altering the lives of workers, their families, and their communities.

COLD WAR LABOUR, DIVERSITY, AND CONTRASTING METHODOLOGIES

The three chapters in the first half of this edited volume reflect these historiographical insights, including the contrasting experiences associated with earlier colonization. Indigenous labour for the Cold War security state further transformed individuals, their families, and their communities. The labourers we will encounter in these chapters include Elmer Sinclair, a residential school survivor who took great pride in his military technological accomplishments; Cree, military, and other community members who worked to build and maintain the Pinetree Line radar station at Moosonee, Ontario; and Inuit construction labourers who were brought into assist with the building of the 1950s DEW Line stations across the far north. The analysis in all three cases goes beyond individual workers to consider how different forms of labour transformed family and community life, sometimes resulting in acts of resistance and activism.[37] The primary authors of these chapters (Warren Sinclair, Sue Heffernan, and Stacey Fritz) draw upon their own lived experiences and personal connections with the people being studied. This approach is a vital aspect of this first part of the volume and differs from the more academic and literature-based approach found in the second half.

The first three chapters share other thematic and methodological common ground. All of them argue that Cold War militarization intensified and deepened the colonization processes which had begun much earlier. These chapters include childhood recollections seen from the distance of adult memory but intermingled with the stories of other family and community members. These stories add to the growing scholarship about the experiences of children in war, utilizing different tools and means to highlight how wars "created new patterns of mobility and family separation."[38] In contrast to the second half of the book, they rely more on oral testimony – a methodology that draws upon Indigenous traditions and challenges the notion of the written word as the most authoritative form of historical evidence.[39] Yet the stories told here are in English rather than Cree, Saulteaux, or Inuktitut and they are told through the medium of a scholarly study rather than simply shared within families and communities. The voices heard in these three chapters reflect uncomfortable moments of confusing, melding, and changing identities as Indigenous people lost languages and other elements of traditional cultures but actively sought new skills, better employment, and lobbied for changes that mattered to them. To work and to lobby for change often meant communicating through colonizing means.

These oral testimonies also reflect contrasting generational and cultural experiences in different geographical locations. For some, the Cold War was just that – a war upon the environments and lifestyles they treasured and sought to preserve. Others like Elmer Sinclair, a residential school survivor (whose story appears in the volume's first chapter), embraced Cold War technological opportunities, married a white woman, and did not regret his loss of Indigenous language. He advocated for Indigenous rights and recognitions within a militarized framework that honoured sacrifices for the Canadian state. In each of the first three chapters, Indigenous people fought for opportunities, rights, and recognitions that were important to them, even as their experiences and desires varied widely.

The placement of Warren Sinclair's chapter about his father, Elmer, at the beginning of this volume honours their courageous acts of truth-telling which came after decades of anguished silence. This placement signals recognition that historical agency is precarious, if essential for activism and reforms. We have begun to hear from military families, but few stories have been published from the unique perspectives of Indigenous service families. This chapter sits at the intersection between two scholarships: one about residential school survivors and the other about Cold War service people and their families.[40]

As an Indigenous military archivist and historian, Warren Sinclair exercised agency by writing about his father's life and ensuring that his father's voice is heard and preserved for his own family and for future generations. His interpretation combines the commemorative military history associated with white masculine privileging and the Indigenous rights activism that challenges this privileging. Warren illustrates how his father endured the extremes of residential school abuses in a nation-wide effort to eliminate varied Indigenous cultures. These childhood memories contrast with those recounted by Inuvialuk Sammy Lennie in chapter three; Lennie highlighted his years of living with his family on the DEW Line, adventuresome games with his brother, and only briefly mentioned the damages inflicted by short residential school incarcerations. In contrast, from the age of seven, Elmer Sinclair was trained to function as a labourer, spending half of every day on arduous work. As Jean Barman observed, unlike their white counterparts in private religious schools, these children functioned as "servants" and that "[t]o be of Indian descent was to be on the other side of an abyss which could not be bridged."[41] Residential schools trained children for jobs in the lowest tiers of Canada's employment hierarchy as well as forcing them to adopt white cultural practices and values.

Elmer Sinclair rejected that unequal path and chose instead to become a highly trained radio operator. The promotion and control of technology is associated with modern western masculine class dominance.[42] His status rose as he became a non-commissioned officer.[43] He remained proud of his service *and* his Indigenous heritage, combining two different identities into a single masculine performance which incorporated Cold War technological elite values. He refused to rely solely upon his impressive sharp-shooting skills, and he left behind important aspects of his Indigenous culture. Elmer Sinclair learned English at an early age at his mother's instigation. Although his mother spoke three languages, she and her son internalized the negative attitudes the residential school system had imposed upon them.

Elmer Sinclair's testimony ties into the observations made by historians John MacFarlane and John Moses in their analysis of sixty oral history interviews with Indigenous veterans. They found that nearly all those interviewed believed "that they are better in the military than in Canadian society." The younger groups "emphasized their Aboriginal culture ... [while] earlier groups referred to advantages of their background as snipers, as scouts, and during survival activities but seemed to value being treated equally more than having their distinctiveness recognized."[44] Elmer Sinclair was unique among the older group. Despite impressive sharp-shooting skills, he welcomed and mastered technology. Like other older veterans, Elmer insisted on equality and denied any discrimination within the military, while advocating for Indigenous recognitions in his retirement years. He nurtured close family relationships and Indigenous community connections throughout his life. Elmer's internal contradictions and changing perceptions form a theme found in other chapters of this work.

Towards the end of life, when he was in his nineties, Elmer Sinclair testified at the Truth and Reconciliation Commission. Warren Sinclair describes in his chapter how the early historiography of the residential schools encouraged long silences. It was only after others revealed their abusive experiences that gradually stories like Elmer Sinclair's emerged. History matters. In this chapter, Warren Sinclair demonstrates the importance of public history and activism in personal life journeys. Near the end of his life, Elmer Sinclair came to terms with his darkest childhood secrets and recognized that he was not alone. His life came full circle when Canadian society finally began to recognize the wrongs it had inflicted on Indigenous Peoples. For Elmer, this meant he could finally talk about the abuse he suffered.

The Sinclair narrative hints at the costs of an equality achieved through a silent distant masculine soldierly performance. At special moments, Warren and his father had "tears in our eyes, but no hugs." Like many military fathers, Elmer Sinclair repressed physical affection and warmth, enforcing a silence and a militarized discipline upon his own children.[45] The residential school experience also reinforced Indigenous identity, creating a common ground among diverse groups, even as it cruelly eliminated cultural practices, Indigenous languages, and attempted unsuccessfully to cut family ties. Not one of Elmer's seven sons has recorded their own memories of life as the children of a residential school survivor and a Cold War military member. Instead, these stoical individuals have set aside their own unique accounts to remember and to celebrate their father as proudly as they can. This is a different sort of silence. In general, we have heard little from the offspring of residential school survivors whose lives were further transformed by Cold War military labour, but their experiences are worth sharing, if and when those individuals wish to do so.[46] At the heart of this research is respect for diversity of experience, including a respect for the silences that reflect the trauma of lived experiences.

This Sinclair family story ties into the narratives of other Indigenous families across the country, but it is certainly not representative of most experiences. The first half of this volume highlights the historical value in exploring unique, contradictory, and diverse experiences and rejects the notion of any single representative Indigenous story. Cold War labour created varying opportunities and transformations. The Sinclair story leads into the next chapter by Sue Heffernan, which reveals contrasting experiences in the community of Moosonee, a small community located just south of James Bay, in Ontario.

Moosonee was one of several partly Cree communities in northern Ontario, where radar stations were established as part of the most southerly radar line, the Pinetree Line. Many small communities experienced first an influx of military members and workers, then several decades of co-existence with a military station and its shifting population of military members and support workers, followed by the aftermath of station closures. Readers of Steven High's *Base Colonies in the Western Hemisphere, 1940–1967* will recognize the similar pattern of transformations that occurred in American base communities.[47] The Moosonee case forms part of a larger global phenomena. Heffernan's close analysis helps us understand how these Cold War developments had positive and negative consequences for the labour force and the Moosonee area itself.

Heffernan notes that her ancestors came to this land not as "settlers" but "as the servants of settlers." As a young child, she listened to her Irish grandmother's tales about her work as a maid for English families. Later she learned that her grandfather served as a batman (servant) to a British officer. Heffernan acknowledges that Irish immigration was a part of a larger colonial process which deprived Indigenous Peoples of lands but carefully delineates how her ancestors served as cheap labour for landowners, rather than becoming landowners themselves. Such reflexivity or self-awareness points to an important distinction in the hierarchies of labour and privilege.[48] Heffernan worked closely with the people of Moosonee in her career as an Ontario government planner for more than a decade before she retired and began her doctorate in human studies. She interviewed Cree elders and community leaders, ensuring their voices were heard first in the provincial planning process and then later within the academic community. Her feminist environmental perspective, her intimate community knowledge, and her insistence upon using oral testimony to balance official accounts lends authority to her narrative. Her chapter on Moosonee represents a part of her own life journey and draws upon her awareness of the environmental issues and racial inequities that existed in this small community.

Heffernan demonstrates three distinct divisions which developed in Moosonee during the 1950s and 1960s. The first, a division between the military and civilians, reinforces Warren Sinclair's finding that military service provided a path to equality for men but demanded a type of masculine performance that was vastly different from the traditional Cree way of life. The second division reflected gender. As Sarah Hogenbirk's later chapter also demonstrates, during the early Cold War, a path to equality was never extended to any woman, regardless of race, class, education, service in the military, or other performances.[49] Rather, Heffernan observes that women in Moosonee were often dismissed as "housewives" by the very system that discouraged their participation in the paid labour market.[50] Thirdly, migration for the radar line work divided civilian communities with white people dominating in the original "town" site and northern Cree from the James Bay area moving to the "village" (just south of the town) with inadequate housing.

Despite these inequities, employment on the radar station taught people new skills, including water and sewage treatment. Activists, drawn from the town and village, including Indigenous "housewives," forced different levels of government to address their environmental, educational, health, family, and other community concerns.[51] Heffernan draws upon direct oral testimony from Cree elders, comparing them with official records. When the station closed, the community negotiated its transformation into a regional high school – the first such institution in the James Bay area. This nuanced examination of Moosonee allows specific failures and accomplishments to be explored, demonstrating how individuals gained technical and practical skills which they then used to benefit the wider community after the station closed.

The University of Calgary has supported Whitney Lackenbauer, Sheila Grant, and other northern scholars in making their studies and copies of official documents about security and sovereignty available on the internet.[52] Yet as Brian Calliou and others point out, oral history offers an essential tool for accessing Indigenous stories and attempting to hear specific voices that have been silenced.[53] Emerging scholars, like Crystal Fraser, offer new insights into the relationships among power structures, education, and colonization in the far north, drawing upon oral testimony and personal connections with the people she studied.[54] The third chapter is based upon the work of Stacey Fritz, an Alaskan settler and applied anthropologist of northern infrastructure whose doctoral work drew upon Inupiat, Inuvialuit, Gwich'in, and White peoples' oral testimony about the effects of DEW Line construction work. Her thesis research crosses the American and Canadian boundaries, revealing how work on the DEW Line created a host of changes in every-day Inuit life, including closer contact with southern influences, difficulties in obtaining traditional food, and disruptions in traditional gender performances, and family activities.

Fritz sailed and paddled the western Arctic coast for two summers to interview elders in remote communities, including those who had grown up as children near DEW Line stations. Despite the monolithic nature of these radar stations, her analysis highlights nuanced differences in each place as Inuit families and communities were transformed by this development. Her interpretation reinforces this volume's theme of contrasting Cold War transformations that influenced not only workers but also their families and communities. Her chapter contains detailed findings on environmental degradation and labour transformations that tie closely to those described in Heffernan's chapter, as well as those described in the works of Liane Leddy and Brittany Luby.[55] We delayed the volume to ensure that her original scholarship was included. Eventually, Fritz invited me, as editor, to become co-author; I agreed on the basis that she remain the primary author. Like the other authors in the first half of this volume, she has an intimate relationship with the subject.[56]

Our chapter focuses on Fritz's in-depth interviews with Sammy Lennie about his childhood growing up on the DEW Line sites where his father was employed, supplemented with other interviews. Her approach allows Lennie's unique voice to be heard, including his awe at the natural beauty surrounding these sites, the "millions of yellow berries," and the continuation of traditional hospitality when Inuit visitors stayed a few days with his family from time to time. Because the DEW Line "was his playground," he did not experience a traditional Inuk childhood. At this site, his father and other adult men drank heavily and rarely took part in hunting, trapping, and fishing, and he was never taught traditional survival skills.[57] Other scholars have noted that excessive drinking was a serious issue at Cold War military sites and observed that fathers who worked on those sites often became emotionally and physically distant from their wives and children.[58] Lennie's mother was especially isolated. His happiest memories reflected many hours of play with his brother on the radar station.

This chapter reveals a major transformation of labour in the north, the loss of Inuit and Gwich'in culture, widespread environmental degradation, and lengthy separations from extended family and friends. For these northern DEW Line workers, hard-won construction skills mattered little when the sites became automated and no longer required their labour. They lost traditional skills without any compensating employment, were no longer part of close-knit family and community support networks, and often developed harmful addictions. The automated DEW Line sites did not become available for community needs as had happened in Moosonee.

The Canadian government attempted to mold Inuit into northern citizens whose labour would contribute to Canada's security requirements. Despite measures to protect the Inuit way of life, DEW Line employment created harmful upheavals among Inuit families and communities. Some Inuit describe how their awareness of site contamination propelled them to become environmental activists. The DEW Line project first created a labour force to construct the stations, then a labour force to operate them, and finally a labour force which lobbied to clean up the sites after they were automated. These transformations mirror global de-industrialization changes and especially the transformation of the children of labourers into activists in the face of the collapse of a particular set of jobs as portrayed by the work of Steven High and others.[59] In this case, they also reflect the unique geography and the varied cultures of the peoples who first came to these northern lands.

These diverse Indigenous experiences of Cold War militarization and security work set the scene for the second half of the book, which explores the impact of Cold War security labour on other groups, including elite as well as marginalized populations. The early Cold War is associated with rapid technological development, with faith in the ability of masculinized western science to offer solutions to humanity's gravest problems. Early Cold War writings often reflected this positivist spirit. Yet as the second half of this volume demonstrates, the questioning or darker experiences of elites, experts, and service people were often silenced in the process. At times, persistent questioning and uneasiness helped create changes in scientific and medical practices and in discriminations against serving women. More often, outside activism influenced those transformations.

Cold War security priorities created the need for a labour force able to withstand the extreme isolation of northern radar sites. At the same time, Cold War anxiety about masculine and feminine gender roles influenced ideas about security, sexuality, and family life. In chapter 4, Matthew Wiseman focuses on how the requirement for labour on the radar lines resulted in scientific experimentation upon human subjects in southern Canada. In chapter 5, Frances Reilly writes about the nomenclature used in the psychiatric treatment of gay men. Together these chapters demonstrate how security concerns framed the research of scientists and medical personnel who gradually became less comfortable with their work. Ethical issues arose when activism exploded during the late sixties and seventies. Their chapters use professional publications to analyze how Cold War security concerns influenced scientific and medical practices and how those changed as researchers, practitioners, and others questioned professional orthodoxies. Their work also fits into an international historiographical framework with temporal links to research which emerged following Germany's use of gas during the First World War. In *Secret Science: A Century of Poison Warfare and Human Experiments,* Ulf Schmidt analyzes how the former allied powers (Britain, Canada, and the United States) continued to carry out nuclear, chemical, and biological weapons research on animals and humans during and after the Second World War, concluding that medical ethics "evolved inconsistently and at times unpredictably."[60] Not surprisingly, the American literature about Cold War military funded experimentation on human subjects is larger and richer.[61]

Matthew Wiseman addresses three different types of masculine labour: the scientists who attempted to create screening mechanisms for northern technical employees to work on the radar lines; the northern workers; and the paid volunteers, usually students, who participated in scientific studies designed to create those screening mechanisms and to study the effects of sensory deprivation. Here, the state's perceived needs affected different labour markets, beginning with the scientific community, its funding, and the formation of its research work at academic institutions, then the workers and their working and living conditions, and finally the paid volunteers who were studied – all in a defence-funded scientific attempt to create a psychological profile for the best workers able to withstand the extreme monotony of life on isolated radar stations.

This testing targeted southerners perceived to have the technical skills to monitor radar stations in the high north rather than northerners who might be recruited for radar work. Additionally, these studies focused on the more extreme conditions of the Mid-Canada and DEW Lines, rather than the Pinetree Line. The Pinetree Line postings, like Moosonee, usually included families and had an engaged community life, as described in Sue Heffernan's chapter. While the Pinetree communities were small, they were not in the far north. Some were located within commuting distance of major centres. While there are very good studies about the DEW Line,[62] we know little about the thousands of civilians and military people who worked in isolated postings during the Cold War and even less about how these labouring conditions influenced their family and community lives.[63]

Wiseman details how Defence Research Board grant money permitted scientists to study the effects of extreme isolation on humans with little to no concern expressed over the potential long-term harm to those taking part in the experimental tests. As he notes, Cold War anxiety and a corresponding faith in science and technology fuelled government and scientific curiosity about the human mind.[64] Academics and students voluntarily participated in the state's projection of western masculine power into Canada's north, but they did not necessarily understand and agree with all the uses their work eventually had. His examination of isolation research extends into the uncomfortable Cold War topic of "brainwashing" and the deliberate construction of testing that went beyond exploring the effects of isolation, by also attempting to measure how isolation might be utilized as a means of exerting "mind control" over subjects. These experiments focused upon testing men's performances in extreme conditions, but Wiseman's chapter briefly highlights one specific but important instance when a woman volunteer appeared to perform better than the men, reinforcing masculinized ideas about women's suitability for boring repetitive work.[65]

In the final chapter of this volume by Sarah Hogenbirk, we will see how the shortage of military members for radar line and other early Cold War work justified the recruitment of women military members, while their participation created fear and gender role tensions. For the most part, these isolation studies reflected idealized notions of masculine endurance and assumptions about a natural masculine white superiority and responsibility for security (defined in narrow terms) – all of which justified human experimentation even as these scientists acknowledged the possible harms to their subjects. Wiseman observes how broader western constructions of masculinity venerated those who opened the frontiers of the north, of technology, and of science, pushing ambitious scientists to discover more. By the 1970s, political and student activism put this research under critical scrutiny and scientists themselves began to question this testing. Wiseman demonstrates how changing public perceptions influenced scientific practices and exposes how multiple tiers of labour were influenced by security concerns and public ideas about legitimate scientific and security practices.

Frances Reilly's focus on psychiatric nomenclature in the fifth chapter helps us see the power of words, especially specialist labels to police human behaviours and to discourage expressions of sexual practices outside of heterosexual marriages as a means of promoting a particular version of masculine labour. This idealized type of labour revolved around a working father who supported a nuclear family. Gay men were targeted with psychiatric labelling, partly because Cold War-driven security sought to enforce and police an idealized masculine performance as normative for all men.[66] Global anxiety about sexual normalcy increased after the Second World War, especially because women's wartime labour had disrupted traditional gender and sexual relations. Over time, psychiatrists questioned these norms, gradually reforming their nomenclature as gay activists protested the medicalization of their sexuality – through a terminology that defined gay sex as a form of mental illness.[67]

Reilly focuses on Canadian psychiatrist and pioneer of forensic psychiatry Robert E. Turner (1926–2006) and his work at a Toronto Forensic Clinic, especially his study of "homosexuality" as a psychiatric condition.[68] Instead of receiving treatment by court order, as was typical for others at this clinic, gay men largely volunteered for psychiatric treatment. This chapter explores the psychiatric devotion to a nomenclature for "homosexuality" despite growing evidence indicating that this orientation of sexuality was not an illness. Like the servicewomen studied in the sixth chapter, society denied gay men equality, regardless of their class, race, and education. However, as Reilly demonstrates, unlike the servicewomen, most of the clients at the Toronto Forensic Clinic were like the psychiatrists treating them: white, male, educated, and of a similar socio-economic class.

These gay men displayed normative, western, masculinities, except for their sexual orientation, and their normative appearances and performances created discomfort, eventually influencing psychiatric thinking about their supposed disorder. Reilly's chapter highlights the dominance of white masculine heterosexual performance as a normative behavioural standard, which is a recurring theme across the chapters. Early Cold War perceptions reinforced the notion that deviations from rigid sexual and gender roles equalled a security risk. Activism within the gay community helped to transform psychiatry by challenging the notion that gay men were any sort of a threat, but sexuality remained closely tied to gender and gender performance. As the final chapter of the book will demonstrate, the Canadian forces opened its doors to women but policed their gender performances and actively discriminated against them throughout the early Cold War.

The Cold War generated a rich global scholarship relating to the role of women in the armed services. The American feminist theorist Cynthia Enloe exposed the relationship between masculinity and militarism in *Does Khaki Become You? The Militarization of Women's Lives*, published in 1988, demonstrating how service people, their spouses, workers in defence industries, and others support a patriarchal militarized society. Later, in *Bases, Beaches, and Bananas*, she analyzed the complex interplay among social, cultural, economic, and political forces in supporting American global militarism. Her feminist lens highlights how power operates, regulating sexuality and opportunities but also how small personal actions disrupt the global, militarized, patriarchal system.[69]

This volume sits at the intersection of feminist theory about patriarchal systems and the activism which at moments may moderate and influence those systems, working from within and outside of them. It is certainly not the first Canadian history to be situated this way. Ruth Roach Pierson's feminist analysis of Canadian women's participation in the Second World War preceded Enloe's theoretical insights but nonetheless highlighted how servicewomen faced systematic discriminations, whispering campaigns, and enforced demobilization at the war's end.[70] In contrast, Tarah Brookfield concludes that women's collective contributions to the First World War overcame opposition to women's voting rights, though the war itself produced ruptures within the suffrage community.[71] Yet, in a *Sisterhood of Suffering and Service. Women and Girls of Canada and Newfoundland During the First World War*, editors Sarah Glassford and Amy Shaw stress the uniqueness of each woman's experience of war. The twelve chapters in their work reach contradictory conclusions about the effect of war upon women, suggesting that gender alone does not produce any unifying wartime experience.[72]

Consideration of intersectionality, that is, how race, class, gender, sexuality, and other factors intersect to create multiple forms of exclusion in individual lives, is also relevant to the historiography about women and service.[73] Canadian feminist historians, including Kathryn MacPherson, Cynthia Toman, Mary Jane McCallum, and Karen Flynn, have exposed how the nursing profession, associated with white imperialistic forces, gradually reformed its practices to become more inclusive due to the activism of "others" over time.[74]

The sixth and final chapter by Sarah Hogenbirk fits into this framework. Because of the increased threat during the Korean Conflict, Canada's three armed services recruited women into full and part time service roles. Hogenbirk explores the creation of the feminine military career as an alternative to the traditional gendered roles of wife and mother and how official publicity surrounding this notion trumpeted feminine care-giving roles within the military. The services rigidly limited women's participation, restricting women to trades that lacked sufficient men. However, servicewomen had their own plans and sought to create and increase the space for women in the three services. Drawing upon internal military documents, Hogenbirk highlights how women sought to influence policies that were designed to restrict their employment and status. As she points out, women's participation in the forces was closely linked to their fight for political equality as well as equality within the workplace.

Her chapter reinforces Joan Sangster's arguments that feminism does not necessarily fit neatly into "waves." Feminists, and others who did not identity as feminists, pushed for changes throughout the twentieth century, even when the dominant post-war ideology defined a woman's place in the home. Sangster argues that Cold War anticommunism silenced dissent.[75] Although Sangster's definition of labour and the boundaries of her studies are different from this work, her conclusion that there were "subtle changes that occurred in the twenty-five years after the war" is supported by Hogenbirk's study of the career servicewoman.[76] That a conservative Cold War institution like the Canadian services created long term careers with pensions for single women points to the importance of their labour in supporting the Cold War agenda.

Within the forces, Indigenous men like Elmer Sinclair proudly declared their equality, while all servicewomen submitted to systematic barriers that restricted their employment and numbers. Women were assumed to be physically and mentally inferior to men, even when they met high service standards or displayed athletic prowess. The forces formulated an idealized feminine gender performance to restrict women's space within this traditional masculine sphere. Like other nations, Canada did not consider combat participation for women, and leaders used that prejudice to justify limiting the number of women in the services. Another factor against women's participation was their high rate of attrition, blamed upon marriage and pregnancy. Hogenbirk points out that, despite these constraints, the forces offered an attractive alternative career path for women, including at least a few visible minority, Indigenous, and lesbian or gay women, among others.[77] This construction of "respectability" assumed feminine celibacy, echoing the dominant scientific and masculine view that treated women as mere recipients of heterosexual attention rather than as human beings with their own desires. This dominant construction also denied women meaningful rights to equality in the workplace. Hogenbirk traces acts of deliberate defiance and changes in personnel policies over time, along with publicity that promised women challenging careers and an independent income in contrast to a domestic suburban ideal. Her scholarship highlights how defence publicity celebrated spinsters who had retired from the forces, demonstrating how women service members created an acceptable public space for alternative and professional feminine performances.

Taken together, all six chapters raise questions about the influence of western (settler-colonial) masculine institutional values on specific groups and individuals who laboured for the Cold War state and society. Individuals and groups exercised agency, seeking opportunities to improve their prospects, though they were often constrained by factors beyond their control. They alternatively challenged and accepted constraints and limitations. A theme throughout the volume is the role of silences. We hear little from the earlier generations of servicewomen about sexual and physical assaults and harassment and only limited amounts about lesbian and heterosexual feminine desires. New scholarship and the "me too" movement has helped uncover the hidden aspects of women's participation in traditional masculine spheres. It is not surprising that generations of women protected themselves from further harm, retribution, and damage to their reputations by remaining silent. Activists for survivors of sexual assault point out that survivor testimonies may be "turned into fodder for ... trauma porn." As a result, a foremost scholar of gender and the military, Megan MacKenzie, refuses to utilize detailed descriptions of militarized sexual violence in her published analysis on this topic.[78] Drawing upon the work of Black feminist scholars, she argues that sexual violence, is used to gain "masculine capital" and "to put those not at the top ... particularly women and marginalized groups – in their place."[79] The rhetoric around rape culture draws upon respectable women's statements, distancing themselves from rape victims and "others" – that is any women whose sexuality threatened the feminine respectable ideal. And perhaps similarly to Elmer Sinclair, some survivors may have not realized that they were not alone in their suffering or insisted upon a dignified privacy to protect this sensitive area of their personal lives.[80]

This volume highlights diversities and intersections with respect to early Cold War labour and demonstrates the importance of different types of scholarship in creating a place for unique voices to be heard. Academic publication requires so much dedicated time and effort that many of those with other demanding responsibilities cannot take part. Precarity of scholarly employment is not a new issue, but it is relevant here. Five of the authors in this work – Sue Heffernan, Stacey Fritz, Matthew Wiseman, Frances Reilly, and Sarah Hogenbirk – completed doctorates in the last two decades; yet none of these scholars have tenure track posts. All drew upon their doctoral research, sometimes writing chapters in this midst of other responsibilities or in precarious employment. Warren Sinclair, a recently retired Indigenous archivist, wrote his chapter about his father's life on his own time, while working as the chief archivist at the Directorate of History and Heritage. His work required personal courage as well as diligence.

As a settler scholar of a certain age and as an editor, it was a tremendous privilege to read these chapters and to see them evolve separately and together. I hope that readers will learn as much as I did.

NOTES

1 Samuel Lennie, interview with Stacey Fritz, Fairbanks, Alaska, 3 April 2009. The Inuvialuit are Inuit people living in Alaska and the Western Canadian Arctic.

2 The conclusion of this work contains more information on the Northern Warning System, an automated system which replaced the DEW Line at the end of the Cold War.

3 Joseph Jockel, *No Boundaries Upstairs: Canada, the United States, and the Origins of the North American Air Defence, 1945–1958* (Vancouver: UBC Press, 1987); Andrew

Richter, *Avoiding Armageddon: Canadian Military Strategy and Nuclear Weapons, 1950–1963* (Vancouver: UBC Press, 2002); Jeffrey Noakes, "Under the Radar: Defence Construction (1951), Limited and Military infrastructure in Canada, 1951–1965" (PhD diss., Carleton University, 2005).

4 Isabel Campbell, "A Tale of Submarine Sightings and a Golden Goose: American–British–Canadian Intelligence Sharing in the Early Cold War," *Journal of Military History* 85, no. 4 (October 2021): 980.

5 Ann Denholm Crosby, *Dilemmas in Defence Decision-Making: Constructing Canada's Role in NORAD, 1958–1996* (New York: St Martin's Press, 1998); Ann Denholm Crosby, "A Middle-Power Military in Alliance: Canada and NORAD," *Journal of Peace Research* 32, no. 1 (February 1997): 1–115.

6 Gary Marcuse, "Labour's Cold War. The Story of a Union That Was Not Purged," *Labour/Le Travailleur* 22 (1988): 199–210; Craig Heron, *Canadian Labour Movement: A Short History*, 2nd ed. (Toronto: Lorimer, 1996); Merk Leier, *Red Flags and Red Tape* (Toronto: University of Toronto Press, 1995); Robert McDonald, *Making Vancouver* (Vancouver: UBC Press, 1996); Ian McKay, *Rebels, Reds, Radicals: Rethinking Canada's Left History* (Toronto: Between The Lines, 2005); Judy Fudge and Eric Tucker, *The Regulation of Workers' Collective Action in Canada, 1900–1948* (Toronto: University of Toronto Press, 2004); Bryan Palmer and Joan Sangster, eds, *Labouring Canada: Class, Gender, and Race in Canadian Working-Class History* (Oxford: Oxford University Press, 2008).

7 Anne-Charlotte Martineau, "Forced Labour," in *International Law and the Cold War*, ed. Matthew Craven, Sundhya Pahuja, and Gerry Simpson (Cambridge: Cambridge University Press, 2020), 272–86. Martineau examines Cold War changes to international law to define and restrict forms of forced labour. She notes that the Soviet Union argued that poorly paid workers in the west (and especially in colonies) were no better than wage slaves. The United Nations Social and Economic Council found evidence of poorly paid and illegal labour in the west but although the Soviets refused inspections of their labour camps, the council discovered evidence of appalling conditions in those camps.

8 Isabel Campbell, *Unlikely Diplomats: The Canadian Brigade in Germany* (Vancouver: UBC Press, 2013), 139, shows how Canadian service people influenced the Canadian government decision to send families to Europe with units, by leaving the forces in droves in the early 1950s and taking their families with them without permission, and then influenced defence spending away from weapons to support an idealized vision of Canadian family life in Europe.

9 Laura McEnaney, *Civil Defense Begins at Home: Militarization Meets Everyday Life in the Fifties* (Princeton, NJ: Princeton University Press, 2000), 6. McEnaney rightly notes that the militarization created blurry lines and affected popular

culture and even social reform in the United States. Thanks to Matthew Wiseman for this helpful reference.

10 The three services consisted of the Royal Canadian Navy, the Canadian Army, and the Royal Canadian Air Force until February 1968 when they were unified into the Canadian Armed Forces. In August 2011, Canada restored the historical names of the services without separate legal status.

11 Sumi Chan, Kimberle Williams Crenshaw, and Leslie McCall, "Towards a Field of Intersectionality Studies: Theory, Applications, and Praxis," *Signs. Journal of Women in Culture and Studies* 38, no. 4 (2013): 785–810. The editor is grateful to peer reviewers for nuancing their understanding of intersectionality as defined by Crenshaw.

12 Laurien Crump and Susanna Erlandsson, eds, *Margins for Manoeuvre in Cold War Europe: The Influence of Smaller Powers* (London: Routledge, 2019); Pál Germuska, *Unified Military Industries of the Soviet Bloc: Hungary and the Division of Labor in Military Production* (Lanham: Lexington, 2015). John Ferris calls attention to how the author's *Unlikely Diplomats: The Canadian Brigade in Germany* sheds light on small power influence in the H-Diplo round table with reviews by John Ferris, Scott Bertinetti, Ruth Compton Bower, and Kim Nossal, February 2016. H-Diplo Roundtable XVII, 11 on *Unlikely Diplomats: The Canadian Brigade in Germany, 1951–64* (18 January 2016).

13 Thomas Zeiler, "The Diplomatic History Bandwagon: A State of the Field," *Journal of American History* 95, no. 4 (2009): 1053.

14 Jessica C.E. Gienow-Hecht, "What Bandwagon? Diplomatic History Today," *Journal of American History* 95, no. 4 (2009): 1086.

15 Adam Chapnick, "Where Have All of Canada's Diplomatic Historians Gone?" *International History* 65, no. 3 (Summer 2010): 726, stresses the continued relevance of diplomatic history. Examples of relevant recent studies include Corbin Williamson, *The U.S. Navy and its Cold War Alliances, 1945–1953* (Lawrence: University of Kansas Press, 2020); Richard Goette, *Sovereignty and Command in Canada-US Continental Air Defence, 1940–1957* (Vancouver: UBC Press, 2018). The 1990s history wars are closely associated with Jack Granatstein's *Who Killed Canadian History* (Toronto: HarperCollins, 1998) which criticized social historians. Penney Clark, "Introduction," in *New Possibilities for Shaping the Past. Shaping History Education in Canada*, ed. Penney Clark (Vancouver: UBC Press, 2011), 2–6.

16 Stephen Azzi, "The Problem Child: Diefenbaker and Canada in the Language of Kennedy Administration," in *Reassessing the Rogue Tory and His Times: New Perspectives on the Diefenbaker Era in Canadian Foreign Relations*, ed. Janice Cavell and Ryan Tovey (Vancouver: UBC Press, 2018), 104.

17 Margaret Conrad, "A Brief Survey of Canadian Historiography" in *New Possibilities for Shaping the Past* points out that social history was studied over a century ago with the blossoming of a new social history in the 1960s and 1970s. Shirley Tillotson, "The *Canadian Historical Review* at One Hundred Years," *Canadian Historical Review* 100, no. 3 (September 2019): 327–8, calls attention to nationalism, critiques of that approach, and trans-nationalism. Steven High, "Contesting Clio's Craft. Activists, True Professionals, and the Debate Over Genocide Recognition in Canada," *Canadian Issues* (Spring/Summer 2022): 44–9, tells us about more recent controversies.

18 Tarah Brookfield, *Cold War Comforts: Canadian Women, Child Safety and Global Insecurity* (Waterloo: Wilfrid Laurier University Press, 2012); Andrew Burtch, *Give Me Shelter. The Failure of Canada's Cold War Civil Defence* (Vancouver: UBC Press, 2012).

19 On 21 September 1945, W.G. Mills, the deputy minister of Naval Services wrote to C.J. Mackenzie, the president of Canada's National Research Council worried that the new atomic weapons, might render "the present methods of warfare obsolete." Some speculated that conventional forces were no longer relevant. Mills to Mackenzie, 21 September 1945, LAC, RG 24, 83-84/167, box 2039 NSS 5151-25. The American strategist Bernard Brodie argued that the chief purpose of the military establishment was no longer to "win wars" but "to avert them." In Bernard Brodie, *The Absolute Weapon: Atomic Power and World Order* (New York: Harcourt, 1946), 74.

20 Matthew S. Wiseman and Alex Souchen, eds, *Silent Partners: The Origins and Influence of Canada's Industrial Complex* (Vancouver: UBC Press, 2023), 14.

21 Ibid., 14, 17.

22 David Meren, "The Tragedies of Canadian International History," *Canadian Historical Review* 96, no. 4 (December 2015); Dominique Marshall, "Réponse à 'The Tragedies of Canadian International History,'" *Canadian Historical Review* 96, no. 4 (December 2015): 585. Marshall's own work covers these and other important initiatives, such as the rights of children.

23 *Undiplomatic History: The New Study of Canada and the World*, ed. Asa McKercher and Philip Van Huizen (Montreal and Kingston: McGill-Queen's University Press, 2019), 3–21.

24 Laura Madokoro, Francine McKenzie, and David Merin, eds, *The Dominion of Race: Rethinking Canada's International History* (Vancouver: UBC Press, 2017), 15–16.

25 David Merin, "Conclusion: Race and the Future of Canadian International History," in Ibid., 291.

26 John Price, "Asian Canadians and the First World War: Challenging White Supremacy," and Francine McKenzie, "Race, Empire, and World Order: Robert

Borden and Racial Equality at the Paris Peace Conference of 1919," in Ibid., 54–93.

27 In this volume, the term "Indigenous Peoples" is preferred and is used to refer to all people who trace their ancestry back to the original populations of this continent. First Nations refers to those diverse peoples once known as Indians, Métis and Inuit are the two other major groupings of Indigenous Peoples. Warren Sinclair's chapter carefully traces the diverse ancestry of his family, while Sue Heffernan's chapter utilizes and defines other specific historical terms used during the early Cold War for bureaucratic purposes. In chapter 3, Stacey Fritz distinguishes among Inuit (Inupiat and Inuvialuit) living in the western Arctic. Her interviews included Gwich'in and White peoples. The historic term "Eskimo" appears in quotes or where it is part of the proper name of a body, in the title of a document or published work reflecting the practices of the time. In general, the term Aboriginal refers to legal concepts, but in this volume, it also reflects a historical broader usage. These definitions are derived in part from Myra Rutherdale, Kerry Abel and P. Whitney Lackenbauer, eds, *Roots of Entanglement: Essays in the History of Native–Newcomer Relations* (Toronto: University of Toronto Press, 2018), xi.

28 P. Whitney Lackenauer, with John Moses, R. Scott Sheffield, and Maxime Gohier, *A Commemorative History of Aboriginal People in the Canadian Military* (Ottawa: National Defence, 2009), 185.

29 P. Whitney Lackenbauer, "Race, Gender, and International 'Relations': African Americans and Aboriginal People on the Margins of Canada's North, 1942–1948," in *The Dominion of Race*, 113. The original quote uses the term "male." In this work, we have preferred the binary terms men and women in preference to male and female because some find the latter terms offensive, especially in a racialized context. However, the terms male and female appear in quotes and also where they reflect the terms used at the time. Chapter 5 also describes some transgender experiences.

30 Ibid., 114; Sarah Carter, *Aboriginal People and Colonizers of Western Canada to 1900* (Toronto: University of Toronto Press, 1999).

31 Robert Rutherdale, "New 'Faces' for Father. Memory, Life-writing, and Fathers as Providers in the Postwar Consumer Era," in *Creating Post War Canada: Community, Diversity, and Dissent, 1945–1975*, ed. Magda Fahrni and Robert Rutherdale (Vancouver: UBC Press, 2008), 241–67. Rutherdale examines a variety of fathering models, emphasizing a return to the dominant pre-Second World War provider role.

32 Brittany Luby, *The Damned: The Politics of Loss and Survival in Annishinaabe Territory* (Winnipeg: University of Manitoba Press, 2020), 28–33. Luby critiques general post-war histories of Canada, noting that statistically measured

affluence has based upon benefits to individuals of European descent, extracting resources from Indigenous lands. *The Dominion of Race*, 16, similarly critiques the "notions of emancipation" in the narrative of decolonization in Canada.

33 Luby, *The Damned*, 10.

34 Lianne C. Leddy, *Serpent River Resurgence: Confronting Uranium Mining at Elliot Lake* (Toronto: University of Toronto Press, 2022).

35 Ibid., 136.

36 David Neufeld, "Commemorating the Cold War in Canada. Considering the DEW Line," *Public Historian* 20, no. 1 (1998): 9–19. David Neufeld passed away while this work was in progress. Chapter 3 owes much to his encouragement and provision of relevant documents.

37 Isabella Sun recently argued that the skills gained during Second World War military service helped American and Canadian servicewomen become activists for their communities after they left the services in the postwar era. Isabella Sun, "Indigenous and Native American Servicewomen: How the Second World War Propelled Activism Forward," *Journal of Military and Strategic Studies* 22, no. 4 (2024).

38 Barbara Lorenzkowski, Kristine Alexander, and Andrew Burtch, eds, *Small Stories of War: Children, Youth, and Conflict in Canada and Beyond* (Montreal and Kingston: McGill-Queen's University Press, 2023), 4.

39 Michael Marker, "Teaching History from an Indigenous Perspective. Four Winding Paths up the Mountain," in *New Possibilities for Shaping the Past* notes the 1997 Delgamuukw decision of the Supreme Court of Canada which afforded oral testimony equal weight to written evidence in regard to the Indigenous occupation of land. Oral testimony is an important means to decolonize public narratives.

40 Isabel Campbell, "Deconstructing a Canadian Military Family: The Taylor Mother and Son Remember the Cold War," in *Small Stories of War*, ed. Lorenzkowski, Alexander, and Burtch, exposes how the constant displacement of service families negatively affected a service child. The advocacy scholarship of American and Canadian service wives has produced excellent works for the past several decades. Laurie Wienstein and Christie C. White, eds, *Wives and Warriors: Women in the Military in the United States and Canada* (Westport, CT: Bergen and Garvey, 1997); Deborah Harrison and Lucie Laliberté, *No Life like It: Military Wives in Canada* (Toronto: Lormier, 1994). See also Jane Elliott, "Posted to Germany, Early Cold War Military Policy and its Impact on One Family's Experience," *Canadian Journal of Health History* 39, no. 1 (Spring 2022): 153–79.

41 Jean Barman, "Negotiating Aboriginality Interraciality in Three Early British Columbian Indian Residential Schools," in *Roots of Entanglement*, 203.

42 Michael S. Kimmel and Amy Aronsen, eds, *Men and Masculinities: A Social, Cultural, and Historical Encyclopedia*, vol. 1 (Santa Barbara, CA: ABC Clio, 2004), 779. We acknowledge that technology and masculinity had a contradictory relationship during this period. This work focuses more particularly on how Sinclair used technology to improve his masculine status.

43 Modern militaries divide into commissioned officers (with a minimum high school diploma), non-commissioned officers (who have risen through the other ranks), and the lowest ranks (privates).

44 John MacFarlane and John Moses, "Different Drummers: Aboriginal Culture and the Canadian Armed Forces, 1939–2002," *Canadian Military Journal* 6, no. 1 (Spring 2005): 31.

45 Campbell, "Deconstructing a Canadian Military Family," describes the strong silent fatherly role performed by the Taylor father and how his sensitive and intellectual side transformed when he served in combat during the Second World War. Robert Rutherdale, "Three Faces of Fatherhood as a Masculine Category: Tyrants, Teachers, and Workaholics as 'Responsible Family Men' During Canada's Baby Boom," in *What is Masculinity? Historical Dynamics from Antiquity to the Contemporary World*, ed. John H. Arnold and Sean Brady (New York: Palgrave Macmillan, 2011).

46 New research by Sharon Yvonne Wall, Alan English, the author's whole life oral history interviews, and other scholarship is emerging to enrich our knowledge of how diverse families coped with militarization of their lives.

47 Steven High, *Base Colonies in the Western Hemisphere, 1940–1967* (London: Palgrave MacMillan, 2009).

48 Susan Heffernan, "Moosonee, Ontario: A Model of Cold War Change" (PhD diss., Laurentian University, 2016), 56; Tillotson, "The *Canadian Historical Review* at One Hundred Years" draws our attention to the importance of reflexivity and modernization in concepts of the national state.

49 My current research on women who served in the Royal Canadian Navy from 1951 to 1968 reinforces how discriminatory measures harmed Canada's operational intelligence capacity. Isabel Campbell, "The WRENS. Contributions to Canadian and allied intelligence functions during the early Cold War," paper presented at the Cryptologic History Symposium, Washington, DC, 12 May 2022.

50 Heffernan draws upon Joy Parr, "Gender History and Historical Practice," *Canadian Historical Review* 76, no. 3 (1995): 363, for this analysis.

51 Indigenous women across North America were speaking out about their rights and the rights of their communities across North America. Heather Howard-Bobiwash, "Women's Class Strategies as Activism in Native Community Building in Toronto, 1950–1975," *American Indian Quarterly* 27, no. 3/4 (2003): 106.

52 University of Calgary, Documents on Canadian Arctic Sovereignty and Security, https://arts.ucalgary.ca/centre-military-security-strategic-studies/research/publications/documents-canadian-arctic-sovereignty-and (accessed 11 January 2021).

53 Brian Calliou, "Methodology for Recording Oral Histories in the Aboriginal Community," in *The Canadian Oral History Reader*, ed. Kristine R. Llewellyn, Alexander Freund, and Nolan Reilly (Montreal and Kingston: McGill-Queen's University Press, 2015), 29.

54 Crystal Fraser, "T'aih k'ìighe' tth'aih zhit dìidìch'ùh (By Strength, We Are Still Here): Indigenous Northerners Confronting Hierarchies of Power at Day and Residential Schools in Nanhkak Thak (the Inuvik Region, Northwest Territories), 1959 to 1982" (PhD diss., University of Alberta, 2020). Fraser offered helpful comments on Warren Sinclair's chapter. Her work offers a generational contrast to the Sinclair interpretation which focuses more closely upon the specific harms of the residential school experience.

55 Stacey A. Fritz, "DEW Line Passage: Tracing the Legacies of Arctic Militarization" (PhD diss., University of Alaska, 2010); Luby, *The Damned*; Leddy, *Serpent River Resurgence*.

56 As an example of the primacy of her lived experiences, when I suggested changing "sailed" a canoe to "paddled" a canoe, Stacey gently informed me that her canoe was fitted with sails. She had sailed more than paddled. Though I paddled a canoe throughout my childhood and kayak often, I had no idea that anyone could sail a canoe. Further her direct contact with participants in conducting oral histories provides deeper interpretative capacity than I could ever hope to achieve.

57 Samuel Lennie, interview with Stacey Fritz, Fairbanks, Alaska, 3 April 2009.

58 Gil McElroy, *Cold Comfort: Growing Up. Cold War* (Vancouver: Talon Books, 2012) and Campbell, *Unlikely Diplomats*, chapter 4; "Uncomfortable Conversations About Childhood Memories of Being 'Othered.'" "An officer looks back," paper presented at the Canadian Historical Association, Vancouver, 2019 includes how the Cold War military lifestyle sometimes led to heavy drinking, alcoholism, and family separations.

59 Steven High, Lachlan MacKinnon, and Andrew Perchard, eds, *The Deindustrialized World: Confronting Ruination in Post-Industrialized Places* (Vancouver: UBC Press, 2018).

60 Ulf Schmidt, *Secret Science: A Century of Poison Warfare and Human Experiments* (Oxford: Oxford University Press, 2015), 18.

61 Alfred McCoy, *A Question of Torture: CIA Interrogation, from the Cold War to the War on Terror* (New York: Metropolitan Books, 2006); Naomi Klein, *The Shock*

Doctrine: The Rise of Disaster Capitalism (New York: Metropolitan Books/Henry Holt, 2007); Alfred W. McCoy, "Science in Dachau's Shadow: Hebb, Beecher and the Development of CIA Psychological Torture and Modern Medical Ethics," *Journal of the History of the Behavioral Sciences* 43, no. 4 (Fall 2007), 401–17. Matthew S. Wiseman, "Canadian Scientists and Military Research in the Cold War, 1947–1960," *Canadian Historical Review* 100, no. 3 (September 2019), summarized the military research more broadly.

62 P. Whitney Lackenbauer, Matthew J. Farish, and Jennifer Arthur-Lackenbauer, *The Distant Early Warning (DEW) Line: A Bibliography and Documentary Resource List* (Calgary: Arctic Institute of North America, 2005).

63 McElroy, *Cold Comfort*. This work exposes the painful loneliness experienced by a service child and his adult attempt to come to terms with his absentee alcoholic father who often worked at isolated radar posts. McElroy's work reinforces the themes developed in this book.

64 Andrea Tone, *Age of Anxiety: A History of America's Turbulent Affair with Tranquilizers* (New York: Perseus, 2009), xvi, explores how rising Cold War anxiety in the 1950s created an American market for mass consumption of tranquilizers.

65 In this volume, we have limited the study to bipolar gender roles but acknowledge that gender fluidity undoubtedly existed.

66 Gary Kinsman and Patrizia Gentile, *The Canadian War on Queers: National Security as Sexual Regulation* (Vancouver: UBC Press, 2010); El Chenier, *Strangers in Our Midst: Sexual Deviancy in Postwar Ontario* (Toronto: University of Toronto Press, 2008).

67 Acceptable terms for "gay" and other sexual orientations have evolved. Reilly explains that "homosexuality" is a medicalized term. She uses it and the term "deviant" to refer to patients at a clinic and then studies how nomenclature changed as psychiatrists and activists increasingly questioned the medicalization of this sexual orientation. She and I will use the term "gay" as the term most accepted at this time of evolving terminology and understanding of gender and sexuality but utilize the terms "homosexuality" and "homosexuals" when referring directly to the clinic work.

68 Most of this research has been conducted at the Centre for Addiction and Mental Health Archives (CAMH, Toronto, Ontario).

69 Cynthia Enloe, *Does Khaki Become You? The Militarization of Women's Lives* (London: Pandora Press; San Francisco: HarperCollins, 1988); Cynthia Enloe, *Bananas, Beaches, and Bases: Making Feminist Sense of International Politics* (Berkeley: University of California Press, 2000).

70 Ruth Roach Pierson, *"They're Still Women After All": The Second World War and Canadian Womanhood* (Toronto: McClelland & Stewart, 1986); Tarah Brookfield

and Sarah Glassford, "Home Fronts and Front Lines: A Gendered History of War and Peace," in *Reading Canadian Women's History and Gender History*, ed. Nancy Janovicek and Carmen Nielson (Toronto: University of Toronto Press, 2019), 151–70.

71 Tarah Brookfield, "Divided by the Ballot Box: The Montreal Council of Women and the 1917 Election," *Canadian Historical Review* 89, no. 4 (December 2008): 478–501.

72 Sarah Glassford and Amy Shaw, *A Sisterhood of Suffering and Service: Women and Girls of Canada and Newfoundland During the First World War* (Vancouver: UBC Press, 2012), 317. Brookfield and Glassford, "Home Fronts and Front Lines," 151–70. See also Amy Shaw, "Expanding the Narrative: A First World War with Women, Children, and Grief," *Canadian Historical Review* 95, no. 3 (2014): 401–2.

73 Chan, Crenshaw, and McCall, "Towards a Field of Intersectionality Studies," 785–810.

74 Karen Flynn, *Moving Beyond Borders: A History of Black Canadian and Caribbean Women in the Diaspora* (Toronto: University of Toronto Press, 2011); Mary Jane McCallum, *Twice As Good – A History of Aboriginal Nurses* (Ottawa: Aboriginal Nurses Association of Canada, 2007); Kathryn MacPherson, *Bedside Manners: The Transformation of Canadian Nursing, 1900–1990* (Toronto: Oxford University Press, 1996); Cynthia Toman, *Sister Soldiers of the Great War: The Nurses of the Canadian Army Medical Corps* (Vancouver: UBC Press, 2016).

75 Joan Sangster, *Transforming Labour: Women and Work in Post-War Canada* (Toronto: University of Toronto Press, 2010). Kindle. This work focuses upon left wing activism and addresses labour as it is understood within the context of unions.

76 Ibid., 272.

77 The term "lesbian" here reflects the term used by these women at the time; some people prefer the term "gay."

78 Megan MacKenzie, *Good Soldiers Don't Rape: The Stories We Tell About Military Sexual Violence* (Cambridge: Cambridge University Press, 2023), 4–5.

79 Ibid., 8.

80 The servicewomen I interviewed in a whole life oral history project sometimes shared sexual assault stories off the record. My own experiences of harassment and stalking caused profound harm and made me determined to improve our security culture.

1

A Tale of Two Worlds – One an Open Book, the Other a Dark Secret

The Life Experiences of Elmer Sinclair in the Fort Alexander Indian Residential School and in the Canadian Army

WARREN SINCLAIR

There will always be that one memory that will haunt me –
my dad barking out the order "Warren Sinclair!!
FRONT AND CENTRE!!!!"

My father, Elmer Sinclair, served in the Canadian Army during the Second World War, the Korean Conflict, and during peacetime until the 1960s. This chapter contrasts his horrific experiences as a student in the Fort Alexander Indian Residential School from 1928 to 1931 with the positive time he spent in the Canadian Army. As one of his seven sons, I always thought of him as an open book. All his life, he proudly shared his military achievements with his family, relatives, and friends. He insisted that as "a Canadian soldier" with an Indigenous background he was treated as an equal, with no barriers regarding his military career. His sons grew up thinking of him as strong, resilient, and proud. He was not a big man. When he enlisted in 1940, he was only 129 pounds and stood five feet nine-and-a-half inches tall.[1] However, he possessed a booming voice that commanded respect among his men and brought fear among his sons.

Not one of us considered that our dad might have been a small, frightened boy, far from his parents and loved ones, mistreated by white authorities, all to eradicate his Indigenous cultural identity. Then in 2001 my father revealed his horrific experiences while incarcerated at the Catholic Indian Residential School at the Fort Alexander Reserve in Manitoba from 1928 to 1931. Between 2001 and 2007, my father revealed the sexual abuse by the priests, the physical abuse by the nuns and the older students, the separation from his parents at home and from his sisters at the school, and of the child labour he was forced to perform. This childhood nightmare had remained a dark secret until his eightieth birthday. The story was a shock to his wife and children. How were we to have known that our father had endured so much? This chapter is about how colonization affected my father's childhood and militarization affected his adult years. Both processes profoundly affected his family.

After my father's death in April 2017, I drew upon his detailed testimony about his experiences with the Indian Residential School system, placing his story and his long silence about it in the context of the historiography of the school system. My father might not have understood the colonial context or the complicated, twisted motivation behind the systematic abuses that he and others endured. It is only during the last two decades that Canadians have become aware of the severity and widespread nature of abuse. Some people ask why Indigenous survivors do not just move on with their lives, but my father did just that. He and others laboured for Canada in ways not yet adequately recognized.

My chapter details how my father's horrific childhood compared to his positive work experiences as a volunteer soldier in the Canadian Army and in post-retirement activities as a veteran. I compare his experiences to other well-known Indigenous soldiers, placing his story within the context of the historiography which celebrates the work of Indigenous people in the Canadian military. My father and other

Indigenous soldiers defended the very security state which had unsuccessfully attempted to erase their cultural identities. My father preserved his Indigenous identity, but he carefully negotiated his identity on equal terms with others serving in the Canadian forces. At times he had mixed feelings about what his cultural and racial identity meant. He rejected the shame which had been imposed upon him as a small child. His story is a triumph, but it is also the story of a man who bravely and quietly carried a heavy burden within him.

The Indian Residential School system was an extension of the Indian Act, a body of laws that for more than a century have controlled every aspect of Indigenous life. It was first introduced in 1876 as a consolidation of previous colonial ordinances that aimed to eradicate Indigenous culture in favour of assimilation into Euro-Canadian society.[2] Subsequent amendments to the Indian Act in 1894 and 1920 required mandatory institutionalization of Indigenous children at industrial or residential schools. The Indian Residential School system was a network of colonial boarding institutions funded by the Canadian government's Department of Indian Affairs and administered by Christian churches. The school system was created for the purpose of removing children from the influence of their own culture and assimilating them into the dominant Canadian culture. Over the course of the system's more than one hundred years of existence, the federal government has estimated that at least 150,000 First Nations, Metis, and Inuit students passed through these schools.[3] At least 4,100 of these students are estimated to have died and this number continues to rise as graveyards are examined.[4]

The assault on Indigenous identities began the moment the children started school. They were removed from their families. Most were in schools ten months of the year, away from everyone they had known from birth. Some stayed all year round and even for years at a time if they could not make the return trip home during the summer. Depriving them of their ancestral languages, they were forced to speak English or French. For some, these were strange tongues. If they were caught speaking their own language, they were severely punished. All correspondence from the children was written in foreign languages which many parents could not read. Parental visits were discouraged and controlled. Brothers and sisters at the same school rarely saw each other since all activities were segregated by gender. Students at residential schools were faced with a multitude of emotional and physical abuses. For most of the schools' histories, the federal government had no clear policy on punishment. Students were not only strapped and humiliated – treatments common among non-Indigenous children across Canada – but in some schools they were also handcuffed, manacled, beaten, locked in cellars and other makeshift jails, and displayed in stocks. Although the issue of sexual abuse was largely unreported during the years in which schools were in operation, this was a serious problem. Some staff sexually abused students who had no means of escape. They could not hide or return home.[5]

For the first half of the twentieth century the schools were on what was termed the "half-day system" in which students spent half the day in the classroom and the other half at work. For the boys, work largely involved farming and the crafts that a farmer might have need of. The girls were trained in the domestic sciences, meaning housework, cooking, laundry, and other chores deemed "women's work." The theory behind this was that the students would learn skills that would allow them to earn a living as adults. In the real world, this was less about training and more about child labour, undertaken to subsidize the ongoing operation of these institutions.[6] The general experience of residential school students was destructive. On return to their home communities, some children felt isolated from their families and became ashamed of their Indigenous heritage. They had lost their languages and were not provided with traditional skills or with urban working skills. These experiences mirror those described by Sammy Lennie, an Inuvialuk, in chapter 3. His father's work on the DEW Line meant that as a child Sammy Lennie never learned traditional survival skills. Indigenous children across Canada were left in a cultural and economic limbo.

The early residential school historiography reflected positive memories and indeed, some students did have those. However, in 1973 the historiography began to reveal widespread abuses and by 1990 Indigenous people participated in a national awakening about the horrific nature of these schools across Canada. Their stories included the Fort Alexander school, built on land on the Fort Alexander Reserve (now the Sagkeeng First Nation) in southeastern Manitoba. The acknowledgment of physical and sexual abuses at residential schools in the memoirs of former students has only just started. This literature allowed survivors, like my father, to finally see that they were not alone, and it reinforced the legitimacy of their constructed memoirs.[7] My father finally spoke about his three years in Fort Alexander Indian Residential School, including separation from his family, harsh punishments, child labour, sexual and physical abuse.

My father was born in 1921 near the present-day town of Selkirk. He was the son of Henry James Sinclair, a Cree carpenter and tradesman, and his second wife Catherine Simard, a Metis/Cree woman.[8] Henry James and Catherine married in 1919. By 1925 they had four children: Rose (1920); Elmer (1921); Aurillia (1923); and Henry (1925).[9] Henry James taught himself steam engineering and carpentry and worked on Lake Winnipeg as an engineer.[10] In 1927 the Sinclair family moved to the Fort Alexander Indian Reserve near the town of Pine Falls. Henry James worked at the mill, which was purchased by the Abitibi Power and Paper Company the next year.[11]

Henry James' wife, Catherine, was literate too, having attended a Catholic convent in Fort Alexander.[12] She attended the Fort Alexander Residential School for a short time in 1906.[13] After the death of her mother in 1906 she returned home to Manigotagan to help care for her father's large family.[14] As a result of her convent and residential school indoctrination against Indigenous languages, Catherine Sinclair forbade her children from speaking Saulteaux. Although everyone on the Fort Alexander Reserve spoke Saulteaux, the Sinclair children were not allowed to speak the language. Catherine Sinclair herself spoke both Saulteaux and Cree, and her husband spoke Cree. However, English was the language spoken in the Sinclair home. The one exception was when the parents talked about something they didn't want the children to know about, then they talked in Cree. Although the Sinclair children spent five years on the reserve, they never learned Saulteaux. The children they played with spoke English to them but switched back to Saulteaux when talking with each other.[15] My father explained, "Mother was determined that we should be brought up and learn the white man customs. For that I was especially grateful as I grew up."[16] Even though the family lived on a reserve, part of their Indigenous culture had already been eradicated by the early 1920s when my father

1.1 The Sinclair children, early 1930s. *Back row*: Rose and Mildred Hancock; *middle row*: Gaven Hancock, Lorna, Elmer, Charlie, and Henry; *front row*: Aurillia, Louise, and Josephine.

was born. His father, Henry James, always found work, supported his family, and carefully negotiated living in conflicting cultures.

The Fort Alexander Reserve had a residential school for Catholics on the west end and a Protestant day school near the east end. Because their home was close to the Protestant school, the parents sent my father and his sister Rose there for two years.[17] My father remembered the teacher "as a very kind person."[18] She never used a strap. Each pupil was given a little plot of ground in the school garden. They

1.2 Brothers Henry and Elmer Sinclair, late 1920s. Likely taken before they attended the residential school in 1928.

could plant what they wanted and looked after the plot each summer. Elmer commented that it "developed my love for gardening."[19] After school he played with other boys and girls. His years at the Protestant school "were very happy ones."[20] He and his siblings were fluent in English, learning useful life skills, and lived in a productive, orderly, and loving home.

Then, in 1928 a priest from the residential school visited Elmer's mother and declared that she would be excommunicated from the Catholic Church if her children were not placed in his school. Elmer explained, "Mother was very religious and when she was threatened with excommunication, she wasted no time in putting us in the Catholic school. Dad was an Anglican, he agreed the children were to be brought up in the Catholic faith."[21] By this time, Elmer's sister Aurillia was five years old and she was placed in the Catholic school with him (he was seven years old) and her sister Rose who was eight. Thus, began a three-year nightmare.

The first day of school in September 1928 for Elmer and his two sisters was traumatizing. Elmer remarked, "Going into the school was a very scary experience. We were met by the mother superior. I don't think she knew how to smile. She stood there in her habit with her hands crossed in the front of her and stuck in the large sleeves of her habit. The only visible part of her was her face and there was no sign of welcome there."[22] His sisters were taken away and that was the last time Elmer talked to them until they went home at Christmas.[23] If he turned around to smile at his sisters in class or made a sign, he risked being punished in front of the class.[24] The Sinclair children spoke English well, but in this environment, such skills counted for little. In this drastic environment, they were punished for trying to maintain normal and loving family relationships which the system sought to systematically destroy.

The children were separated from each other. The Sinclair parents were allowed to visit on Sunday afternoons. The Sinclair children were allowed to go home Christmas day after mass but had to return to school in the afternoon the following day. They had the same time off for New Year's Day and Easter Sunday. Their summer holidays lasted six weeks during July and the first two weeks of August. The remainder of the time the children stayed at the school.[25] Although the holidays provided Elmer with an opportunity to reconnect with his parents, he sadly observed, "the children who came from other parts of the province never saw their parents during the year until they went home for summer holidays. It must have been a lonely life for them. When they first arrived at the school, they must have been lonely and frightened. If anyone cried in loneliness, he got a couple of good smacks from the nuns and told to be quiet."[26]

Elmer lived on the boys' side of the school. The dormitory where they slept was a large room on the third floor of the building. In the large basement playroom, no toys were allowed. Instead, the children had to sit for "our periods of silence" on wooden benches. Elmer Sinclair remarked, "The boys were seated according to size with the smallest at one end and the tallest at the other end. The period of silence was something I never understood. We had to sit and keep absolutely quiet. It seemed as though we sat there for hours but was probably an hour at a time."[27] There was usually one nun present in a chair reading. If anyone "so much as moved an eyeball" he got a stern glare from the nun.[28]

Bullies contributed to the atmosphere of fear and violence. Former student Timothy Henderson said that the boys at the Fort Alexander school were forced to fight each other. The older students picked who was fighting that day. If you didn't fight, someone fought you and the loser was always put in a steel locker. He also remembered "staff coming in and out of there just to kind of make sure that no one was getting seriously hurt, but I knew they knew."[29] Another former student, Victoria McIntosh, said that the school reminded her of a "prison yard" and that if you didn't have older siblings to protect you, you were on your own.[30] The smaller boys were forced to fight the older boys for their bread, butter, or whatever. One of the treats the boys got occasionally at the school was a spoonful of peanut butter on a slice of bread. The only trouble was the smaller boys seldom got the chance to eat it. The older boys would take the peanut butter away, and if it wasn't handed over, the smaller boys were beaten up. Elmer recalled, "One day I decided to eat my bread and peanut butter. The older boy who was threatening me was shaking his fist and mouthing what he was going to do to me. I sure enjoyed that slice of bread and peanut butter. I sure paid for it though when that boy beat me to a pulp. I don't remember ever eating another peanut butter sandwich during the rest of my stay at the school."[31]

The discipline in the classroom was violent and often random. The students were severely punished and humiliated in front of the entire student body. A former student, Faro Fontaine, said he was not able to make his grandfather believe that the discipline at the Fort Alexander school was too strict. The grandfather said, "You guys probably deserve it." So, Fontaine quit trying to tell anybody. He stated, "If you can't tell your own family, you know, they don't believe you, who, who is gonna believe you, especially if comes to the priests and that?"[32] These children were thus twice punished. Once by the system itself and then by the disbelief of others.

Elmer remembered the lash. It had a wooden handle with a few laces. He never did know if the laces were of leather or cord, but they left a mark on the boys. He described one incident: "All the boys had to stay by their beds while the punishment took place. The priest took the boy to the front of the dormitory where everyone could see. His pants were pulled down and his shirt was pulled up so that his bare bottom and lower back were exposed. The priest held him by the scruff of his neck and made him bend over. He then swung the lash as hard as he could across the boy's buttocks and lower back."[33] When the boy didn't cry, the priest became really mad. After punishment the boys were sent to bed. Many times, a boy who had been lashed could be heard crying quietly in his bed.[34]

The students woke up at six in the morning to do chores before classes. The nuns supervised the students who performed all the tough physical farm and school labour. For example, little boys like my father worked in the laundry room before morning mass. After mass they had breakfast and then went to the classroom.[35] On laundry days, these little children went to the basement and faced three rows of washing machines. They carried pails of hot water to the machines. My father remembered that "If we didn't move fast enough the nuns were on us." It was dangerous work. Soap was added when the machines were full. The students then received an arm full of clothes to put into the machine. Then they stood there and pulled the lever back and forth until the nun decided the clothes were clean. There was a hand operated ringer attached to the machine. The clothes were wrung out in a basket and carried over to a long table.[36]

One incident remained with Elmer for many years. The lighting in the laundry room was very poor and there wasn't much room to move about. One morning Elmer suddenly stepped into a pail of boiling water. He went to the nun and told her what had happened. However, she told him to go back to his machine and that she would take care of him later. When the time came to go to mass, Elmer complained that his leg was hurting. The nun told him to go to mass and to see her after. He remembered, "When the mass was finished, I went to the nun again. She finally decided to look at my leg. When she pulled his stocking down, the skin on my leg had peeled off with the stocking. There was no doctor in the school. The nuns took care of us when we required medical treatment. I don't remember getting any medical treatment. I walked around without stockings until my leg healed."[37] Such negligence could have resulted in a serious infection leading to death.

In the spring, the school garden was planted. Unlike the children's garden at the Anglican day school, this garden was a huge farm field for feeding a hundred or more mouths a year. There was never enough food for everybody. Former student Faron Fontane said that all he could recall was "kids starving. Kids going in the kitchen to steal food."[38] These poorly fed young boys found potato planting to be another back-breaking job. Since there were no hired hands, each boy took a pail of potatoes, walked along the furrows, and planted them. The pails were often too heavy for the smaller boys to carry, so they had to drag them along the ground. Elmer recalled, "My brother Henry was six years old when he was sent out to the field with the rest of us. He started to cry because he couldn't handle the heavy pail of potatoes. When I went to help him, the nun ordered me back to my work. Henry was given a smaller pail, but he had to continue working the remainder of the day."[39] The boys worked all day, stopping only for dinner.[40]

The students provided the labour needed to keep the residential schools in operation. Andrew Speck said that at the school in Alert Bay, British Columbia, "Early in the morning you're up, like 5:30, 6:00 o'clock in the morning cause you had to do your chores before you had your breakfast. If you weren't up there, you were literally ripped out of bed and thrown in a cold shower."[41] Ula Hotonami recalled that at the school in Round Lake, Saskatchewan, she spent half the day in classes and half the day working. "We had to learn how to cook, how to do laundry, how to iron, how to do all those things, wash dishes, whatever, and clean out both dormitories, and sweep the steps, and all those things we had to do. We had to learn and that. And so it was, it was something that I never really expected, like, when I went to school."[42]

Reflecting on the work he did at the Roman Catholic school in Kamsack, Saskatchewan, Campbell Papequash noted, "I think there was a lot of slave labour in there because we had all the children, they all had to do, we all had our own jobs to do. You know all the residential school children maintained that whole building by cleaning it up and looking after the building. You know some guys worked in the boiler room and the furnace room, in the laundry room and with the dryers and the vegetables and working in the root cellar looking after the vegetables."[43]

Many Canadian children contributed to family farms by assisting their parents, increasing the time spent on chores as they grew stronger and older. Even after compulsory education came into effect across Canada, many boys and girls missed school days to perform work essential to family survival.[44] However, these children were not removed from their homes. Rather, they were part of a family team and usually given chores appropriate to their age. And so, the experiences are not comparable. Similarly, while a few Canadian children experienced sexual abuse within their homes, Indigenous children experienced widespread sexual abuse with no recourse to parents or other protectors. Most of these crimes went unreported.

In a program televised in October 1990, veteran Canadian Broadcasting Corporation reporter Barbara Frum interviewed Phil Fontaine, chief of the Assembly of Manitoba Chiefs, about his childhood experiences of sexual abuse at the Fort Alexander school. Fontaine was one of the first Indigenous political leaders to speak publicly about his residential school experiences. He described the long-term, destructive effects suffered by those who had been sexually abused at the school.[45] Others testified too. When a priest sexually abused Paul Daniel, the effects lasted Daniel's whole life. "He did a lot of damage to me. I suffered panic attacks most of my life."[46] Theodore Fontaine's life changed forever when in 1950 he entered the Fort Alexander school at the age of seven. Memories of his "childhood misfortunes" there, including sexual abuse, remained with him "at an unconscious level" throughout his life.[47] His memoir starts off with his account of sexual abuse in the opening chapter "The Menage."[48]

The menage was a weekly ritual, the washing of the boy's genitals by a man in a black robe.[49] Every evening before Theodore and the other boys went to bed, they were in classrooms for study periods. Four or five boys would be called out of the study hall and into a different room for the weekly ritual.[50] Eventually, Theodore was called. The episode in the chapter represents only a few minutes of his twelve years in the residential school system, but the scene was vividly etched in his memory. The ritual of "staying clean" happened every week or two over the years for many of the younger boys. It stopped when the boys became older and bigger, and their determination to threaten, maim, hurt, or even kill their tormentors gave them the power to refuse the treatment.[51] These rituals inflicted upon small children, too young to protest, exemplifies the church's systematic abuse of authority and its failure to adequately protect their charges. By utilizing cleanliness as an excuse to fondle children's genitals, this priest institutionalized multiple, repeated sexual assaults. The children's agency in avoiding such assaults as they grew older demonstrates how much this system preyed among the weakest and most vulnerable children. The system encouraged bullying and abuse of the youngest children, while allowing stronger, older children to escape the most dreaded rituals. No parents or relatives were present to protest or protect them. Fontaine said living in the school was a daily nightmare.[52] This nightmare did not end in adulthood; instead, those victimized carried their burdens, suffering in dark shame and silence.

Of all the horrific experiences my father suffered at the school, none was worse than the sexual abuse.[53] In 2007 he appeared before the Truth and Reconciliation Commission of Canada in Victoria, British Columbia and recalled in his testimony one particular nightmare: "There is a heavy man lying on top of me, he is holding me down and fondling my genitals with one hand. I am struggling and trying to get out from underneath. I haven't got the strength to lift him off. In my struggles I am barely able to breathe. He is covering my face so that I cannot yell."[54] Elmer said that when the man got off him and walked away, he never looked at him because he was hiding under the covers.

He added that fondling occurred on many occasions, then on two or three occasions and then it suddenly stopped.[55] Another incident took place one day when Elmer was sick. "The nun told me to stay in bed. A man approached my bed. He tried to get me to consent to allowing him to commit sodomy on me. It was a most horrifying experience as he sat on the edge of my bed and tried to make me consent. He suddenly got up and left."[56]

The adjudicator hearing Sinclair's case weighed all the evidence and decided whether the claimant (Elmer Sinclair) had proven that it was more probable than not that the alleged events happened. He remarked that although the incidents happened more than eighty years ago, it was remarkable that my father remembered anything. He wasn't concerned that my father did not know the name of the abuser. The adjudicator concluded, "There are many reasons for the Claimant's spotty memory. It is unusual that we ask someone to recall the name of someone they saw more than 80 years ago. The trauma involved in sexual abuse usually means that some memory of the abuser is preserved, but in this case the Claimant says that after the big man got off him, the child covered himself up with the blanket so that he never saw the man walk away. I think the Claimant is credible."[57]After reviewing the records and listening carefully to Elmer Sinclair's evidence, the adjudicator accepted his evidence as both credible and reliable. He believed him. He was not concerned that my father did not know the name of his abuser. Moreover, the adjudicator thought that the fact that school records did not exist should not reflect on my father's credibility or the reliability of the evidence. He found on a balance of probabilities that the key events referred to in Elmer Sinclair's testimony did occur as he had described them.[58] While the experience of testifying is often traumatic for victims, being believed is the key element in any healing process. Thus, this assessment likely made a difference to my elderly father who was still trying to come to terms with these long-ago events.

Canada's representative also thought that my father was credible and that his evidence was reliable. He remarked that Elmer Sinclair first said the sexual abuse occurred on many occasions. It was only after he questioned him repeatedly about the time intervals between the several abuses that Elmer Sinclair said it happened two or three times and then it stopped. In other words, he was not saying that he was abused two or three times and then it stopped. Rather, my father was saying that it happened on many occasions, but towards the end it happened on two or three occasions and then it stopped. The representative concluded: "The Claimant said the abuse started in the first or second year at Fort Alexander. He also reports that he was 8 or 9 years old when the abuse occurred. The Claimant left the school when he was 10 years old. The persistent part is the fact that all this abuse occurred within one school year."[59] My father testified that the nightmares had been haunting him since his time at the residential school. The last nightmare occurred one month before the hearing.[60]

One can only imagine the fear and anxiety that spread across the dormitory in the evenings. Nobody would sleep until one boy was selected. Many would be under the covers when hearing light footsteps. The priest would be sneaking in the dark and then take one of the boys. Elmer would freeze wondering if he was going to be the next victim. To the extent that they could, many boys tried to protect themselves and others from abuse. The older children tried to protect the younger ones from abuse at the hands of the priest. Sometimes they would get too tired trying to stay up at night to watch over them. Then suddenly one night Elmer Sinclair woke up and heard the screams of a boy and then realized that they were the screams of his younger brother Henry.

Yet the full details of the other Sinclair children experiences at the Fort Alexander School will never be fully known.[61] The eldest child, Rose, lived in Selkirk, became a nurse, and had five children with her first husband and four children with a second husband. She died in 1993 without ever revealing her horrific experiences to her family who were aware of her incarceration at the residential school on the reserve. Elmer's younger sister Aurilla also became a nurse. She married a soldier who served in the Second World War, the Korean Conflict, and in peacekeeping missions and had three children with him. She died in 1992 – also never confiding her terrible childhood experiences to family members.[62] Elmer's younger brother Henry served in the Second World War and was wounded in action at the age of seventeen. He worked as a miner throughout Manitoba and Ontario. Although he married and had four children, he never confided the horrific abuse he suffered to his family before he died in 1994.[63] Elmer Sinclair's three siblings were gravely marked by their traumatic childhood events, but, like so many others, they died before the silence surrounding this systematic abuse was broken. Possibly had they survived, they would have testified, though testifying was a painful process for these elderly victims.

However, there was one very important legacy that Henry unknowingly left behind. Henry was the father of Murray Sinclair, who grew up to become the chair of the Truth and Reconciliation Commission. Murray had begun his important and difficult work in 2009. One day in 2012 while visiting my father, his uncle, Murray finally learned the truth about his father Henry. My father confided that his brother Henry had been abused in the residential school. Murray had had no knowledge of the abuse until my father told him. Suddenly, everything fell into place for Murray. All his life his father was haunted by the ghosts of alcoholism, drug abuse, homelessness, mental health problems, and deep despair. As the head of a national commission probing one of the most shameful aspects of Canada's history, Murray had unexpectedly discovered a very personal and painful connection.[64] Few Indigenous people escaped this systematic abuse, many were severely impacted, but all of them contributed to their communities as well as they could. And some were able to exercise agency at key moments.

In 1932 when Elmer Sinclair was about ten years old, his mother took the children out of the school. He never knew the precise reason they were taken out,[65] but his mother had learned of the abuse and moved the entire family to St Peter's in order to get the children far away from the school. She put the children into a public school in Selkirk. Elmer remarked that the difference between a residential school and a public school was like night and day, and "to be able to talk to the other students, and to my sisters, in the class or at recess or at noon, was unbelievable."[66] He attended grade 5 (1932–33) at the Patapun School in the rural municipality of St Clement's, grade 6 (1933–34) at the Northward School in Selkirk, and grades 7 and 8 (1934–36) at the Central School in Selkirk.[67] In 1937 he completed grade 9 by correspondence through the Manitoba Provincial Department of Education.[68] He then completed grade 10 in a rural school in Peguis.[69] Like many Canadians of his generation, he was not able to continue past grade 10 due to financial difficulties. From 1937 to 1939 my father did casual work as a bush worker, farm hand, lake fisherman, teamster, ice cutter, etc. in the Selkirk and Lake Winnipeg area.[70] In the winter of 1939 and the summer of 1940 he was employed by Brown & Rutherford as a latheman in a saw mill northwest of Lake Winnipeg, an isolated area of Manitoba.[71]

On 3 September 1939 and a few days before Elmer's eighteenth birthday, France and Great Britain declared war on Germany and the Second World War began. Canada declared war on 10 September. Everyone gathered around the radio listening to the news in the early days of the war. During the next few days some of the younger men decided to head to Winnipeg to enlist. Elmer Sinclair joined them, but, not having sufficient money for the trip, he had to stay with his parents in Manitgotagan for the winter. The following spring he left for Winnipeg where on 6 June 1940 he enlisted with the Princess Patricia's Canadian Light Infantry (PPCLI).[72] He was not yet nineteen years old. Elmer Sinclair was one of an unknown number of non-status Indigenous and Metis, and approximately 3,000 status Indigenous living on the reserves who served in the Canadian Army.[73]

Despite the militarization of their lives, their allotted space in Canadian military history remains limited. Little military history was produced through the 1950s and 1960s, apart from official and regimental histories. In both cases Indigenous servicemen and women were not subjects of particular interest. Overall, the colonization and militarization of Indigenous Peoples in the post Confederation era were neglected until the 1970s.[74] During the 1970s and 1980s Indigenous veterans began publicizing their experiences in a host of Indigenous newspapers and magazines.[75]

Fred Gaffen's *Forgotten Soldiers* (1985)[76] drew upon the experiences of prominent Indigenous soldiers, including anecdotal stories from sailors, soldiers, and airmen.[77] Janice Summerby's *Native Soldiers, Foreign Battlefields* (1993)[78] chronicled the sacrifices and achievements of Canada's Indigenous Peoples in the First and Second World Wars and the Korean War, highlighting notable individuals.[79] By the late 1980s and early 1990s, graduate students began to study this topic. L. James Dempsey's master's thesis "Indians of the Prairie Provinces in World War I" (1987),[80] later published as *Warriors of the King* in 1999,[81] remains the starting point for students looking to learn about Indigenous soldiers in the First World War. Dempsey's articles and book chapters

1.3 Pte Elmer Sinclair and his mother at their home in St Peter's, 1941.

on both world wars, alongside Gaffen's work, laid the groundwork for much of the literature regarding Indigenous soldiers.[82] Janet Davison's master's thesis "We Shall Remember Them: Canadian Indians and World War II" (1992),[83] used archival sources and interviews with several First Nations veterans from Ontario.[84]

In 1997 the Gabriel Dumont Institute in Saskatoon produced *Remembrances: Metis Veterans*,[85] an important collection of transcribed interviews with thirty-three Metis veterans, signalled a change in methodology. The interviews provided valuable insights into why individuals enlisted: some were motivated by poverty and alienation from their communities and others by patriotism or a need for adventure. The storytellers spoke for themselves, sharing battlefield experiences and personal struggles after the war. Many painted a portrait of regrettable neglect at the hands of Canadian society after they returned home.[86] At last, lived experiences were coming to the fore.

However, because of the silences surrounding the residential school experiences, historians did not make a connection between these service people's horrific childhood traumas and their adult difficulties. Bruce Sealey and Peter Van De Vyer's biography of Thomas George Prince published in 1981 is an example of this issue.[87] As an army cadet at the age of sixteen, Prince learned that there was one thing in which the "White men" made no distinction and that was the colour of the skin on the trigger of a Lee-Enfield rifle.[88] He was awarded eleven medals, including the Military medal and the US Silver Star. Although the biography traces his tragic life from the Brokenhead Reserve to his exploits with the First Special Service Force in Italy and France in the Second World War, to his tours in Korea and his return to a life of alcoholism and poverty on the streets of Winnipeg, it does not connect Prince's difficulties with the childhood trauma in residential schools.[89]

After the Korean war, Prince became frustrated, realizing that the equality he experienced in the army did not carry over to civilian life. Prince's life descended into bitterness and alcoholism and he died on 25 November 1977. Prince's problems were typical of a certain type of returned soldier. After being in a low socio-economic position, they became respected men with a uniform that commanded attention. Promoted to the rank of non-commissioned officers, they had authority over others. Then they were demobilized from the army and all the power and respect which their uniforms commanded suddenly disappeared. Many went back to doing menial and unsatisfying tasks. Prince was one such man. His position was even worse for his skills as a hunter, trapper, woodsman, and army patrol leader were of no marketable value in an urban centre like Winnipeg. Further, his childhood experiences in a residential school traumatized him and so many others, leading directly to addictions and, most likely, untreated PTSD.

Among the crowd of five hundred who attended Prince's funeral on 30 November 1977 at the Brookside Cemetery in Winnipeg was my father who was related to Prince. Their grandmothers were first cousins,[90] and both men enlisted together on 6 June 1940 during the Second World War. Prince joined the Royal Canadian Engineers and Elmer Sinclair had joined the PPCLI. They didn't meet again until 1950 when they served in Korea. They both eventually settled in Winnipeg after the Korean war and had met "quite a few times."[91] Elmer praised Thomas Prince's skill as a soldier, "Tommy was very good on camouflage, and what they call, going to ground. He could lay on the ground, and take off, and you'd never see him again. And he'd appear somewhere else. And he was expert at that."[92] On the other hand, Elmer Sinclair remarked on the tragic part of Prince's life, "But he had a lot of trouble with his legs ... It was thought he could have a good job. He had a fair education but he chose to stay in a hostel downtown and do odd jobs. He'd stayed at the Salvation Army hostel. He was quite happy there."[93] The two men last met in 1977 before Prince died.[94] Even my father, a relative, a residential school survivor himself, and a soldier, did not connect the trauma of Prince's childhood residential school incarceration with his later difficulties in life. And it is only now, that with knowledge derived from the Truth and Reconciliation process that Canadians are relating residential school incarceration with adult poverty, addiction, and homelessness.

Like Prince, the military offered Elmer Sinclair a path to equality. In his case, the military provided a long-term career and pride in himself which helped him overcome his horrific residential school experiences. It is the contrasting, healing and educational aspect of my father's military career which forms the focal point for the second half of this chapter about his life. His experiences were not typical or representative; rather his path was unusual from the first moment. He qualified as

1.4 Pte Elmer Sinclair and Pte Roy Leclair at Camp Debert, NS, 1942.

a sharpshooter but with an unorthodox shooting style. Elmer related that as a young boy his father taught him how to shoot a rifle. His instructions were to more or less look along the barrel, get his sights lined upon the target and pull the trigger. He explained further: "so when I joined the army, they were very strict on rules, everything was done according to rules. And shooting, one of the rules was close that vision one eye. I couldn't do it. I got on the rifle range and I had both eyes open. The instructor said I will never be able to shoot that rifle and hit the target. You must close the other eye. I didn't do it. Bang. Bull's-eye. Bang, another bull's-eye. Bang, another bull's-eye. I qualified as a sharpshooter ... I kept both eyes open and I always have. I never learned to close one eye."[95]

In the fall of 1941 Elmer transferred to the Canadian Corps of Signals and became a radio operator. He excelled at complex technical tasks as well as combat infantry skills. His expertise in transcribing and transmitting Morse code kept him off the front lines. He monitored army allied radio transmissions ensuring secure broadcasts stayed on proper frequencies and sensitive information was not leaked over the airwaves. His detachment was attached to the 50th British Division, landing at Gold Beach about a week after D-Day. He stayed with them until the end of July 1944 when he was posted back to the Canadian Army, serving in Northwest Europe until the end of the war.[96]

When the war in Europe ended, my father worked with the Red Cross as a signaller and wireless operator. He sent messages and reported on the condition of soldiers and their whereabouts to their next of kin in Canada.[97] After returning to Canada and leaving the army, he got a job as an attendant at a psychiatric hospital in Selkirk where he met my mother, Phyllis Hay.[98]

Phyllis Hay was born 8 December 1925 in the Ochre River Hospital in Ochre River, Manitoba, the daughter of a settler family, Andrew Hay and Dorothy Drummond.[99] My mother, spent her childhood years in the Gilbert Plains and Grandview areas of Manitoba. She attended a day school in the Tamarisk Township of Grandview and then the Grandview high school.[100] Her father, Andrew Hay, was a labourer in Gilbert Plains. In 1929 he moved to Grandview where he leased a farm. In January 1938 he died in a hunting accident.[101] After his death, the family left the farm and moved into town. In August 1944 the family moved to Charleswood, a neighbourhood in Winnipeg, where her uncle, Richard Hay, lived.[102] Although facing poverty and the loss of her father, as a settler child, she never faced forcible residential school incarceration and separations from her mother. While neither of my parents was privileged, they had very different childhoods based solely upon the systematic discriminations of race.

In 1945 Phyllis trained as a nurse at the Selkirk Mental Hospital in Selkirk, Manitoba.[103] She left the nursing program to marry my father, Elmer Sinclair in December 1946.[104] In 1947 they moved to Bissett, Manitoba where my father took a job as a diamond driller and underground miner with San Antonio Gold Mines.[105] Over the next three years they had three sons: Elmer (10 May 1947); Robert (26 March 1948); and Douglas Sinclair (20 November 1949).[106]

When the Korean War broke out in 1950, my father quit his job and left my mother and three brothers with his parents in St Peter's and went to Winnipeg to enlist again.[107] My mother stayed with her in-laws and then moved with my brothers to the nearby town of Selkirk where she rented a small house. My father's army allowances gave my mother the option to move to town and be independent, but she remained

1.5 Wedding picture of Phyllis Hay and Elmer Sinclair, 1946.

1.6 Sgt Elmer Sinclair, his wife Phyllis, and three sons – Elmer, Robert, and Douglas – in Selkirk before his departure to Korea, 1950.

less than a mile away from her in-laws.[108] My father, Elmer Sinclair, joined the Special Service Force for an eighteen-month period of service, serving as the signal sergeant for the Second Battalion, PPCLI. He maintained the radio set and all communications from the battalion command post to the brigade headquarters.[109] For two days over 24–25 April 1951 on the hills of Kapyong, the battalion fought off repeated attacks by the Chinese. The unit was awarded the United States Presidential Unit Citation for holding the line while being attacked by the Chinese Army.[110]

Upon his return to Canada in October 1951 Elmer transferred back to the Signal Corps. He was soon posted as an instructor to the School of Signals in Kingston, Ontario, staying at the school until 1957.[111] His transition to peacetime was very different from Prince's unhappy experience. Instead of losing status and being treated as a second-class citizen simply because of his Indigenous background, my father gained status and prestige. He also had a loving family and security. During 1957–58 Elmer was posted on a peacekeeping mission to Egypt with the United Nations Emergency Force. He explained his exciting role with understandable pride: "It was quite an experience with the UN … we

1.7 Mike Iham and Sgt Elmer Sinclair in Korea, 1951.

1.8 Sgt Elmer Sinclair in uniform wearing his medals at CFB Kingston, 1959.

1.9 The Sinclair boys. *Back row*: Elmer, Douglas, Robert, and Gregory; *front row*: Warren and Bruce in Kingston, Ontario, 1959.

were responsible for all communications between the different units of the UNEF. And also we set up a detachment in the UNEF headquarters in Gaza, where our men worked with the UN operators to get traffic back to New York. And our traffic was sent back to New York and then to Ottawa."[112] Elmer Sinclair spent a year in the Middle East, returning to Canada in 1958.[113] He enjoyed being one of the very first group of Canadian peacekeepers to serve in the Middle East and to provide key technical skills for which the Canadians became celebrated.

My mother stayed in Kingston during my father's postings and gave birth to three more sons: Gregory (8 August 1953); Warren (7 February 1956); and Bruce (29 March 1958). Looking after six boys might have been a daunting task, but the wives of other Canadian soldiers serving in the Middle East supported my mother. They babysat the boys and helped out with the housekeeping chores, while the sons of the other soldiers kept the yard and the house in good order. My mom's mother from Winnipeg stayed with us for a few months and helped out when she could. My older brothers, particularly Elmer and Bob, also looked after the younger brothers and helped out with chores. My mother, as usual, looked after the finances, kept the books, did all the shopping and prepared all the meals.[114] The family fit into the military community well.

My father, Elmer Sinclair returned to Canada in October 1958 and was posted back to the signals school in Kingston where he took a radio technician course. After completing the course in May 1959, he was posted to the 2nd Regiment, Royal Canadian Horse Artillery in Winnipeg as a sergeant in the signals group.[115] In 1960 he was promoted to staff sergeant and went to I [Instructional] Staff Manitoba Area Headquarters. Then on 19 October 1962 he passed the "Radio and Training Operators Group 3 Conversion Course."[116] From those who knew and had worked with Elmer Sinclair, he was said to be a good and dependable non-commissioned officer (NCO). However, like many other soldiers, he chafed at the rigid army discipline. Perhaps, because of a new commander determined to rectify minor misdemeanours, Elmer received a cluster of three minor service offences during an eleven-month period of 1956–57. He returned to his usual high standards until December 1963 when he was reduced in rank for striking a superior officer. This unusual behaviour arose after he had been tried and convicted of a service offence which later was quashed. However, before exonerating evidence arose in the trial of another NCO, Elmer was marched out in the hall to be punished. Deeply upset by this unusual and unfair procedure and perhaps reminded of his humiliating experiences at the Fort Alexander residential school, he lashed out and struck a warrant officer 1st class (WO 1). Although he was innocent of the first 1963 misdemeanour, he was tried by a Disciplinary Court Martial for striking the officer and was reduced to the rank of sergeant.[117]

Elmer Sinclair's demotion had a profound demoralizing effect on him, contributing to his decision to request a voluntary release from the regular (full-time) army. He requested a posting to trade employment without success. During the twelve years he had served with the Royal Canadian Corps of Signals, he had only been employed in his trade of radio and telegraph operator for one year and in the trade of radio technician for eighteen months. The remainder of the time he had been on instructional duties, and he believed that he had been deliberately by-passed in posting preferences. In short, his morale "deteriorated seriously and he has lost his desire to continue serving."[118]

A personnel officer tried to keep my father in the forces, criticizing my father's plans to take up a civilian apprenticeship. The officer stressed my father's age, the low apprentice pay, and the length of time it would take to complete this training. He also mentioned how my father had a wife and seven sons to support with the birth of Shawn on 8 February 1964. Finally, the officer noted that with less than eight years to retirement, my father would collect $75,000 or more over his remaining lifetime. However, Elmer Sinclair was determined to throw even this security aside rather than suffer in what had become an untenable situation. The personnel officer, therefore, concluded that with Elmer's stubbornness and pride and his determination to seek release, the only logical course was to grant him the release he requested.[119] My father, therefore, was "honourably released" on 26 July 1964.[120]

Six months later on 14 December 1964, my father enlisted in Winnipeg with the Canadian Militia (part-time), and was posted to the 10 Independent Signals. He was promoted to acting warrant officer 2nd class and was awarded a fifth service chevron with the maple leaf, indicating ten years of service. One year later he was promoted to warrant officer 2nd class.[121] During his service with the militia, he worked at Canadian Aviation Electronics (CAE) (1964–66) as a technical clerk and at the Winnipeg Post Office as a postal clerk (1966–67).[122] When he was hired in 1967 by Manitoba Hydro as a first aid attendant in northern Manitoba hydro camps, Elmer could no longer serve part-time with the militia.[123] He received his release from it on 31 October 1967.[124]

Throughout his military career Elmer denied racial discrimination in the Canadian Army. It was the opposite of his residential school experience. In a 2001 interview, he declared "And there's one thing I want to bring out now, is that in all the time I served in the army, and all the men I met who were Aboriginals, I don't recall ever hearing or seeing one of them being treated as other than a soldier. We served in units overseas and we were treated as equals. When I came back, and got out of the army, and attended memorial services on November 11, we all marched shoulder to shoulder as veterans. Nobody was called an Aboriginal, nobody was called an Indian. We were veterans, and I want to make that very clear."[125] In another interview in 2001 Elmer remarked that he did not see the need for special recognition for his Indigenous background or other ethnic backgrounds. He also said that he and his brothers never experienced any racial discrimination in the army: "No such thing. It never happened. There were English Canadians, French Canadians, Irish Canadians and Japanese Canadians. There were no distinctions. When we were overseas, we were just Canadian soldiers."[126]

Most Indigenous veterans who have spoken about their time in the Canadian military have spoken of the equality and camaraderie with white people that they experienced for the first time in their lives. For my father and some other Indigenous soldiers, this contrast produced great pride which helped them achieve more stable and happy adult lives, despite the terrible secrets they hid deep inside. Metis veteran Euclide Boyer explained, "In the army, I found no discrimination. It was the only time the Natives were equal to the whites."[127] Indigenous veteran Willis Johnson remembered that there was "no difference between Indians and whites – all brothers ... racial quality."[128] Finally, the words of Wilfred Westeste in 2001 of the Birdtail First Nation, captured the heart of many Indigenous veterans' experiences: "when we're in our own units, I said we got to know one another, we started to realize that we have to work together, in order to stay alive. We went up to the front, I said, in the fighting zone ... We were all equals. The only time in my life I was equal to the white society or anybody else."[129] This testimony is reinforced in the next chapter.

While the Second World War taught Indigenous soldiers about equality, the army also taught them about Euro-Canadian masculine ideals of leadership and good discipline. Many non-commissioned officers during the war were for the first time in positions of authority over white men.[130] They were subject to a militarized, disciplined regime and also enforced that regime on others. Only a few became commissioned officers, perhaps because most lacked the higher education required for commissions. A few Indigenous officers, including Lieutenant David Grey-Eyes of Saskatchewan and Brigadier-General O.M. Martin of Ontario, support the argument that Indigenous soldiers were able to rise up through the ranks in the Canadian military if they conformed to military standards of conduct which were rigidly enforced. Indigenous veteran Adam Cutham explained that in the army "You are Canadian. You were promoted on merit, no matter who you were. If you happened to be black or white or yellow. You were promoted on merit, not because you happened to be Anglo-Saxon."[131]

1.10 The Sinclair family in Gillam, Manitoba, in 1968. *Back row*: Elmer, Robert, Douglas; *front row*: Bruce, Shawn, Mrs Phyllis Sinclair, Gregory, and Warren.

My father believed the same principles of merit applied to his career, though he had defied and then left the system when it was unfair: "Yeah, course, promotions, were available to everyone, whether you were an Indian ... Or whatever. If you had the qualifications, you were given a course. If you were good enough, you were given a promotion, and I know a lot of men, Aboriginals, who became NCOs [non-commissioned officers] ... Others got their promotions, and they also got their trades training. If the course was available, nobody was turned down. And nobody asked if you were attending because of your race."[132]

At the end of his military career, my father studied the St John's Ambulance course in the fundamentals of first aid[133] to prepare for his new career. In 1967 he started working for Manitoba Hydro as a First Aid Man on their northern hydro projects on the Nelson River. He stayed there until 1974 when he went to work in the health and safety department of Versatile Manufacturing, a Winnipeg-based farm equipment manufacturer. Then, in 1986 at age sixty-five he retired and moved with my mother to Vancouver Island.[134] The leadership experience and confidence he gained in the military helped him transition successfully to his civilian career which he also enjoyed a great deal. Importantly, he returned to an area of Manitoba where his extended kin lived and he was able to reunite with family members and to work in the northern regions where his ancestors had lived for generations. In some ways, his life had come full circle.

In retirement, my father promoted commemoration of the Indigenous community and its relationship with the Canadian military. He was especially proud of his work initiating the naming of the first Indigenous National Memorial (Silver) Cross Mother in 1971, forming the Vancouver Island chapter of the National Aboriginal Veterans Association in 1999, and finally taking part in the Aboriginal Spiritual Journey to Europe in 2005. At the annual national Rememberence Day ceremony in Ottawa on 11 November, the National Memorial (Silver) Cross Mother is chosen by the Royal Canadian Legion to represent the mothers of Canadian soldiers who lost their lives. The Silver Cross Mother lays a wreath at the base of the National War Memorial on behalf of all mothers who lost children in the military service to their nation and then continues to perform other ceremonial duties over the course of the following year.[135] Before 1971 no Indigenous mother had ever been named the Silver Cross Mother. In 1970 Sinclair began corresponding with the Canadian Legion and was successful in having Mrs Mary Anderson, a Metis with a Cree background and a resident of Selkirk, Manitoba, named as the Silver Cross Mother for 1971. She lost two sons during the Second World War.[136] My father stated that he was especially proud of this achievement and spoke of it for years.

Another of my father's proudest achievements was his involvement in the formation in 1999 of the Vancouver Island chapter of the National Aboriginal Veterans Association (NAVA). NAVA was formed in 1986 to represent the interests of Indigenous veterans and heighten public awareness of the outstanding contributions that Indigenous veterans made to preserve the freedom of all Canadians.[137] Elmer Sinclair assisted in getting the chapter incorporated and became its first

1.11 1971 National Memorial (Silver) Cross Mother, Mary Anderson. Manitoba Métis Federation.

president. He remarked, "It's a lot of work, getting that organized. None of us knew what to do, where to go ... So, I went down to the government offices where they form a group, companies and so on. And I talked with one of the people in the offices there. Told him I what I wanted to do. Wanted to form a chapter on the island, for Aboriginal veterans. He said, no problem. He got me all the papers. First thing I knew, we were organized. And that's how it started. And it's going good now. We hope it will get bigger."[138] When Elmer Sinclair moved to Nanaimo at age eighty in 2001, he stepped down as president and remained a regular member. He continued to attend meetings and parades.[139] In 2002 there were about thirty members, men and women, in the chapter representing different Indigenous groups across Canada.[140]

In 2005 Elmer Sinclair was one of twenty Indigenous veterans who participated in the Aboriginal Spiritual Journey to Europe from 25 October to 4 November. The journey included spiritual elders, Indigenous veterans, caregivers, fourteen members of the Indigenous youth delegation, departmental staff, and dignitaries such as the Governor General Michaëlle Jean. Many of the fifty-two cultural groups within Canada's Indigenous population, including Inuit and Metis, were represented.[141] The purpose of the journey was to recognize the contributions of Canada's Indigenous community in times of war. The year 2005 was also designated as the "Year of the Veteran" and marked the sixtieth anniversary of the end of the Second World War.[142] My father attended ceremonies at the First World War sites Hill 62 and Vimy, and then the Second World War sites at Juno Beach and Beny-sur-Mer. He mourned the tragic losses, declaring "To see all the young men's names on the crosses, so many of them in their teens and ... early 20s. It's a shame that all those men had to go."[143]

My father spent two hours visiting with "his fallen comrades buried" at the Beny-sur-Mer cemetery who had died on D-Day sixty-one years before. It was a special day and my father was able to share a rare moment at a military function with me. At the time I served as the chief archivist of National Defence's Directorate of History and Heritage (DHH) and was part of the journey as a historian for DHH. It was awkward and difficult to see my elderly father in tears as he walked from grave to grave. At times he stopped, said a few words, and then continued on to the next grave. There were a few brief visits to fallen comrades and friends. After two hours my father left the cemetery and met me at the entrance. There were tears in our eyes but no hugs. That was not my father's way. He remained the proud soldier. He turned around, offered one final salute and then marched out of the cemetery.[144]

1.12 Two former students of the Fort Alexander Indian Residential School meet; Elmer Sinclair talking to Phil Fontaine at the reception dinner at Rideau Hall in Ottawa, October 2005.

1.13 Elmer Sinclair and his son Warren at the Juno Beach Centre in France, October 2005.

1.14 Elmer Sinclair's medals, 2010.

Another rare father and son moment happened on the last day of the Spiritual Journey. On the afternoon of 4 November, we visited the war memorials in Ottawa. We saw the Tomb of the Unknown Soldier and the National War Memorial, the Monument to Fallen (Korean War Memorial), and the National Aboriginal Veterans Monument. Photographs were taken, including one of us together in front of the First World War portion of the National War Memorial. My dad was very pleased with the Korean War Memorial. However, although he was happy to see a memorial to Indigenous veterans, he remained firm in his conviction that no special group be recognized for their service and sacrifice to their country. My dad's only comment to me was "We were all Canadian soldiers!!" We looked at each other, smiled, had a good laugh, and returned to the hotel.[145]

The visits to the war memorials in Ottawa, to the Beny-sur-Mer cemetery, and to other military ceremonies and functions during the Spiritual Journey were both important and memorable for my dad. On those occasions he held his head high and proudly wore his "pride and joy" – his medals – on his chest. He wore his medals at all parades on Remembrance Day, at all PPCLI and Signals Corps functions and reunions, military funerals of fellow veterans, and various other military functions. He also built a special wooden case for his medals and proudly showcased them in the living rooms of his homes in Victoria and Nanaimo. He received the following medals:

Second World War (1939–45)
1 1939–1945 Star[146]
2 France and Germany Star[147]
3 Defence Medal[148]
4 Canadian Volunteer Service Medal[149]

Korean War (1950–53)
1 Canada Korea Medal[150]
2 United Nations Service Medal (Korea)[151]
3 Canadian Volunteer Service Medal for Korea[152]

United Nations Emergency Force (1957–58)
1 United Nations Emergency Force Medal[153]
2 Canadian Peacekeeping Service Medal[154]

Other Medals
1 Queen Elizabeth II Golden Jubilee Medal[155]
2 Queen Elizabeth II's Diamond Jubilee Medal[156]
3 1943–2010 Thank You Canada and Allied Forces Medal[157]
4 Canadian Aboriginal War Veterans Medal[158]
5 South Korea Veterans Ambassador for Peace Medal[159]

My youngest brother, Shawn, presented our father with the Canadian Peacekeeping Service Medal, forty-four years late, before a large gathering of Legion members and Korean veterans. This special event took place on 23 August 2001 at Branch 257 Legion in Victoria. The Canadian Legion had asked Shawn if he would do the honour of presenting the medal. My father gave a short speech just before receiving his medal and Shawn remarked, "Handing him that medal was really special. The best part though? When dad made his speech, he said it was even more special because his son gave him the medal. As you know well enough, dad never expressed himself, so when he said that, in a room full of people, it almost brought a tear from me."[160]

1.15 Elmer Sinclair wearing his Peacekeeper's Medal (*middle*) with his wife, Phyllis (*right*), and his son Shawn (*left*) in Nanaimo, BC, 2001.

My father's pride in his military achievements helped him heal from the trauma of his childhood residential school experience. He felt like an equal, wearing his uniform and medals with great pride. He considered himself a Canadian, even as he kept close bonds with his kin in Manitoba and began to acknowledge and promote recognition of Indigenous military contributions. In 2001 my father opened up to one of the historians with the Department of National Defence's Directorate of History and Heritage. Elmer Sinclair was one of more than sixty Canadian Indigenous and Metis veterans interviewed who served in the Canadian Forces during the Second World War, the Korean War, or in a UN or NATO peacekeeping mission. The interviews were to be used in the writing of "The History of Aboriginal Peoples in the Canadian Military."[161]

The question arises as to why my father spoke of his experiences at the residential school to a historian and not to his family. First, the context of the interviews was important. The interview took place in a Legion Hall and, in addition to the historian and my father, there were two other former Indigenous veterans discussing their past experiences. The atmosphere was friendly. Second, the reference of his experiences came unprompted, suggesting that he had thought it was important and had planned to use it in his account. Finally, he was probably uncomfortable discussing it with his family. Because his military career was being recorded, he may have considered it a professional duty to put the events on record. He may have also wanted to illuminate the account of his personal journey to help future generations understand how many Indigenous people of his time lived.[162]

Elmer Sinclair's remarks in the interview were limited to general statements with little detail regarding any physical or sexual abuse. At about the same time he began writing his autobiography. Unfortunately, it was never completed. He got as far as his days following his stay at the school. There were rumours of its existence in the family. It was found among his personal papers shortly after his death in April 2017. In the memoir my father recorded in detail his first day at the school, the separation from his sisters and parents, the harsh discipline exhibited by the priests, the bullying of the older students, and the child labour. In 2007 he gave his testimony before the Truth and Reconciliation Commission. In it he gave his first and only reference to sexual abuse. The nightmares of the sexual abuse haunted him for the rest of his life, but he was one of the lucky ones because his experience in the military gave him pride and stability and, most of all, a feeling of equality with others.

In conclusion, the "dark secret" in my dad's life is no more. The nightmares that haunted him all his life have ended. His life experiences during his time at the school are now part of his "open book."[163] His story is an important one, partly because his happy years with the Canadian Army and during his retirement helped him heal from the trauma of his horrific incarceration. His war medals are on display in the Medals and Awards Gallery of the museum of the PPCLI in Calgary, Alberta. His military memorabilia, photograph albums, and personal papers are also on display and showcased in the homes of

1.16 The final resting place for Elmer and Phyllis Sinclair in Victoria, BC.

his sons. The family distributed photographs of my father, Elmer Sinclair, in his uniform and wearing his medals, to his grandchildren and great-grandchildren. Finally, his complete story documenting both the "dark secret" and "open book" periods has been researched and will be made available to all four surviving generations of the Sinclair family. We will never forget my father, and we will celebrate his difficult but impressive life journey.

NOTES

1 Interviews BC-4, BC-5, BC-6, Robert Ducharme, Robert Rogers, Elmer Sinclair, Directorate of History and Heritage Archives (hereafter DHH), 2003/29, file BC-4, BC-5, BC-6, 5 July 2001, part 1, 6.

2 William B. Henderson, "Indian Act," last edited 23 October 2018, https://www.thecanadianencyclopedia.ca/en/article/indian-act (accessed 17 May 2021).

3 Truth and Reconciliation Commission of Canada, *The Survivors Speak: A Report of the Truth and Reconciliation Commission of Canada* (Winnipeg: Truth and Reconciliation Commission of Canada, 2013), vi.

4 Stephanie Scott, "215 Innocent Children," NTCR, 1 June 2021, https://nctr.ca/215-innocent-children/#:~:text=215%20families%20were%20never%20given,leaders%2C%20all%20stolen%20from%20us (accessed 29 November 2021).

5 Truth and Reconciliation Commission of Canada, *The Survivors Speak*, viii–ix.

6 Ibid., vii.

7 Scott Trevithick, "Native Residential Schooling in Canada: A Review of Literature," *The Canadian Journal of Native Studies* 18, no. 1 (1998): 56.

8 "My Life," 1. Warren Sinclair Archives, Warren Sinclair fonds, Elmer Sinclair Records series, Textual Records subseries, Personal Narratives (1) file, box 1 file 28.

9 Ibid.

10 Ibid.

11 Rose (Sinclair) Shrupka, interview by Nicole St Onge, 12 June 1985, 2. Archives of Manitoba, Metis Oral History Project 1984, C375 and "Historic Sites of Manitoba: Pine Falls Paper Mills (Powerview–Pine Falls)." Manitoba Historical Society, modified 6 August 2017.

12 Shrupka, interview, 2, Archives of Manitoba.

13 Mark Kennedy, "Truth Seeker: Murray Sinclair's Relentless Quest for the Facts About Residential Schools," *Ottawa Citizen*, 23 May 2015, https://ottawacitizen.com/news/politics/truth-seeker-murray-sinclairs-relentless-quest-for-the-truth-about-residential-schools (accessed 17 May 2021); *Dominion of Canada Annual Report of the Department of Indian Affairs for the Year Ended March 31, 1906* (Ottawa: Printed by S.E. Dawson, Printer to the King's Most Excellent Majesty, 1907), 77. The school was founded in 1906.

14 Letter from Roman Catholic Rectory to Warren Sinclair, 1 May 1974. Warren Sinclair Archives, Family History Records, Family History Reference Files subseries, Simard, Louis (1855–1920) file, box 4 file 134.

15 "My Life," 1, Warren Sinclair Archives.

16 Ibid., 6.

17 Ibid., 1–2.

18 Ibid., 2.

19 Ibid.

20 Ibid.

21 Ibid., 3.

22 Ibid.

23 Ibid.

24 Truth and Reconciliation Commission of Canada, *The Survivors Speak*, 91.
25 "My Life," 6, Warren Sinclair Archives.
26 Ibid.
27 Ibid., 3.
28 Ibid.
29 Presumably the nuns and staff were aware of the bullying by the older boys and would either ignore it or let it go unpunished. Truth and Reconciliation Commission of Canada, *The Survivors Speak*, 165–6.
30 Ibid., 167.
31 "My Life," 5, Warren Sinclair Archives.
32 Truth and Reconciliation Commission of Canada, *The Survivors Speak*, 149.
33 "My Life," 5, Warren Sinclair Archives.
34 Ibid., 5–6.
35 Ibid., 4.
36 Ibid.
37 Ibid.
38 Truth and Reconciliation Commission of Canada, *The Survivors Speak*, 71.
39 "My Life." 5. Warren Sinclair Archives.
40 Ibid.
41 Truth and Reconciliation Commission of Canada, *The Survivors Speak*, 79.
42 Ibid.
43 Ibid.
44 Isabel Campbell, "Exemplary Canadians? How Two Canadian Women Remember Their Roles in a Cold War Military Family," *Journal of the Canadian Historical Association*, 18 July 2017, https://www.erudit.org/en/journals/jcha/2016-v27-n1-jcha03132/1040525ar/ (accessed 23 August 2023).
45 Krista Maxwell, "Settler-Humanitarianism: Healing the Indigenous Child-Victim," *Comparative Studies in Society and History* 59, no. 4 (2017): 974–5.
46 Shari Narine, "Survivors Gather in Winnipeg to Share Experiences at TRC event," AMMSA.com, 2010, https://ammsa.com/publications/windspeaker/survivors-gather-winnipeg-share-experiences-trc-event (accessed 23 August 2023).
47 Theodore Fontaine, *Broken Circle: The Dark Legacy of Indian Residential Schools, A Memoire* (Surrey, BC: Heritage House, 2010), 188.
48 Ibid., 13–20.
49 Ibid., 14.
50 Ibid., 13.
51 Ibid., 18–19.
52 Holly Alexandruk, "Winnipeg Residential School Survivor Shares His Story," *Global News*, 20 June 2015, https://globalnews.ca/news/2031692/winnipeg-residential-school-survivor-shares-his-story/ (accessed 23 August 2023).

53 Natalia Iiymak, "'To Rob the World of a People': An Instance of Colonial Genocide in the Fort Alexander Residential School" (master's thesis, University of Manitoba, 2015), 19.

54 "Fort Alexander School Recollections," 2007, Warren Sinclair Archives, Elmer Sinclair Records series, Textual Records subseries, Indian Residential Schools – Claim file, box 1 file 11.

55 "Notice of Decision Re: Application by Elmer James Sinclair," 21 December 2009. Warren Sinclair Archives, Indian Residential Schools – Claim file.

56 Ibid.

57 Ibid.

58 Ibid.

59 Ibid.

60 Ibid.

61 More details on the family histories of Rose, Aurillia, and Henry can be found in Warren Sinclair's family history archives.

62 Facebook message from Jim Sinclair to the author, 22 June 2018, Warren Sinclair Archives, Personal Narratives (1) file.

63 Kennedy, "Truth Seeker."

64 Ibid.

65 Interviews BC-4, BC-5, BC-6, part 1, 7. DHH, 2003/29.

66 Ibid.

67 "Indian Residential Schools Independent Assessment Process, Application Form," 2009, 15. Warren Sinclair Archives, Indian Residential Schools – Claim file.

68 Personnel File, box 1 file 20, Department of Veterans Affairs W.D. 12, 10 October 1945, Warren Sinclair Archives, Elmer Sinclair Records series, Textual Records subseries, folio 7. Elmer Sinclair's military personnel file is stored at Library and Archives Canada. The file in the Warren Sinclair Archives consists of copies of documents from Elmer Sinclair's military records that could be released. Some personal information had been removed from these documents.

69 Personnel Selection Record, 16 August 1950, folio 48. Warren Sinclair Archives, Department of National Defence (Army).

70 Ibid.

71 Personnel File, Warren Sinclair Archives, Personnel File, Department of Veterans Affairs, W.D. 12, folio 7.

72 "Nine Months to Enlist," Warren Sinclair Archives, Elmer Sinclair Records series, Textual Records subseries, Personal Narratives (2) file, box 1 file 29, 1994.

73 MacFarlane and Moses, "Different Drummers," 26.

74 P. Whitney Lackenbauer and R. Scott Sheffield, "Moving Beyond 'Forgotten': The Historiography on Canadian Native Peoples and the World Wars," in

Aboriginal Peoples and the Canadian Military: Historical Perspectives, ed. P. Whitney Lackenbauer and Craig Leslie Mantle (Winnipeg: Canadian Defence Academy Press, 2007), 211–12.

75 Some of the articles were anonymous and general in nature and included: "Canadian Indians in the Wars" in *Indian News* (1979); "Canada's Indians in the Wars: A Tribute" in *Tekawennake* (1980); "The Dreavers of Metawus: A Saga of Service" in *The Saskatchewan Indian* (1982); and Diane Parenteau, "Battles, Friendships from War Remembered by Métis Vet," *Windspeaker* 7, no. 36 (10 November 1989); Lackenbauer and Sheffield, "Moving Beyond," 212.

76 Fred Gaffen, *Forgotten Soldiers* (Penticton: Theytus Books, 1985).

77 Lackenbauer and Sheffield, "Moving Beyond," 214–15.

78 Janice Summersby, *Native Soldiers, Foreign Battlefields* (Ottawa: Veterans Affairs Canada, 1993).

79 "Native soldiers, Foreign battlefields," Government of Canada, 3 April 2013, http://www.publications.gc.ca/site/fra/9.687733/publication.html.

80 L. James Dempsey, "Indians of the Prairie Provinces in World War I" (master's thesis, University of Calgary, 1987).

81 L. James Dempsey, *Warriors of the King: Prairie Indians in World War I* (Regina: Canadian Plains Research Centre, 1999).

82 Lackenbauer and Sheffield, "Moving Beyond," 215.

83 Janet Davison, "We Shall Remember Them: Canadian Indians and World War II" (master's thesis, Trent University, 1992).

84 Lackenbauer and Sheffield, "Moving Beyond," 215.

85 Anne Dorion, ed., *Remembrances: Metis Veterans* (Saskatoon: Gabriel Dumont Institute, 1997).

86 Lackenbauer and Sheffield, "Moving Beyond," 223–4.

87 B. Bruce Sealey and Peter Van De Vyvere, *Manitobans in Profile: Thomas George Prince* (Winnipeg: Peguis Publishers, 1981).

88 Sealey and Van De Vyvere, *Thomas George Prince*, 15, 17.

89 Lackenbauer and Sheffield, "Moving Beyond," 213.

90 Interviews BC-4, BC-5, BC-6, part 2, 12, DHH, 2003/29.

91 Ibid.

92 Ibid.

93 Ibid.

94 Ibid.

95 Interviews BC-4, BC-5, BC-6, part 1, 6, DHH, 2003/29.

96 "Veteran Rejoined Army After Start of Korean War," *Globe and Mail*, 24 October 2005, and "Lest We Forget Remembrance Day Reflections," *Nanaimo News Bulletin*, 8 November 2001. Warren Sinclair Archives, Elmer Sinclair Records

Series, Textual Records subseries. Newspaper Clippings 2001–12 file, box 1 file 21.

97 "Untitled Narrative," 2001, Warren Sinclair Archives, Personal Narratives (2) file, "Untitled Narrative," 2001.

98 Personnel Selection Report, 7 April 1952, Warren Sinclair Archives, Personnel file, Department of National Defence (Army), folio 51.

99 Certificate of baptism, 12 September 1926. Warren Sinclair Archives, Elmer Sinclair Records series, Phyllis Sinclair subseries, Certificates file, box 1 file 38.

100 Summary of interview with Phyllis Sinclair by Warren Sinclair, Warren Sinclair Archives, Family History series, Family History Reference subseries, Elmer Sinclair (1921–2017) file.

101 *Grandview Exponent*, 27 January 1938, 1.

102 Summary of interview with Phyllis Sinclair by Warren Sinclair. Warren Sinclair Archives.

103 Ibid.

104 Certificate of marriage, 26 December 1946, WSA, Warren Sinclair Archives, Elmer Sinclair series, Textual Records subseries, Certificates: Civilian file, box 1 file 1.

105 Personnel Selection Report, 7 April 1952, Warren Sinclair Archives.

106 Summary of interview with Phyllis Sinclair by Warren Sinclair. Warren Sinclair Archives.

107 Interviews BC-4, BC-5, BC-6, part 1, 22, DHH, 2003/29.

108 Summary of interview with Phyllis Sinclair by Warren Sinclair. Warren Sinclair Archives.

109 Interviews BC-4, BC-5, BC-6, part 1, 23, DHH, 2003/29.

110 Interviews BC-4, BC-5, BC-6, part 1, 24, DHH, 2003/29.

111 Interviews BC-4, BC-5, BC-6, part 2, 5, DHH, 2003/29.

112 Ibid.

113 Interviews BC-4, BC-5, BC-6, part 2, 9, DHH, 2003/29.

114 Summary of interview with Phyllis Sinclair by Warren Sinclair. Warren Sinclair Archives.

115 Transcript of proceedings of a disciplinary court martial of S/Sgt EJ Sinclair, 10 December 1963, Warren Sinclair Archives, Elmer Sinclair Records series, Textual Records subseries, Disciplinary Court Martial file, box 1 file 7.

116 "Record of Service," Warren Sinclair Archives, Personnel file, folio 42.

117 Personnel Selection Report, 22 May 1964, Warren Sinclair Archives, Personnel file, Department of National Defence (Army), folio 54.

118 Ibid.

119 Ibid.

120 "Record of Service," Warren Sinclair Archives, Personnel file, folio 44.
121 "Record of Service," Warren Sinclair Archives, Personnel file, folio 55.
122 "Indian Residential Schools Independent Assessment Process, Application Form," Warren Sinclair Archives, Indian Residential School – Claims file, folio 15.
123 "Indian Residential Schools Independent Assessment Process, Application Form." Warren Sinclair Archives; Interviews BC-4, BC-5, BC-6, part 2, 10, DHH, 2003/29.
124 Canadian Army Certificate of Service, 31 October 1967, Warren Sinclair Archives, Personnel file, folio 55.
125 Interviews BC-4, BC-5, BC-6, part 1, 8, DHH, 2003/29.
126 *Nanaimo News Bulletin*, 8 November 2001.
127 Roy P. Toomey, "Canadian Indians and the Second World War: The Pivotal Event of the 20th Century for Canadian Indians and Canadian Indian Policy?" (master's thesis, University of Northern British Columbia, 2007), 32.
128 Ibid.
129 R. Scott Sheffield, *A Search for Equity: A Study of Treatment Accorded to First Nations Veterans and Dependents of the Second World War and the Korean Conflict* (Ottawa: National Round Table on First Nations Veterans Issues, April 2001), 49.
130 Toomey, "Canadian Indians and the Second World War," 34.
131 Ibid., 35.
132 Interviews BC-4, BC-5, BC-6, part 1, 9, DHH, 2003/29.
133 Fundamentals of First Aid [Certificate], 23 January 1961, Warren Sinclair Archives, Elmer Sinclair Records series, Textual Records subseries, Certificates: First Aid file, box 1 file 2.
134 Interviews BC-4, BC-5, BC-6, part 2, 17, DHH, 2003/29.
135 "National Memorial (Silver) Cross Mothers," Veterans Affairs Canada, 30 March 2017, https://www.veterans.gc.ca/eng/remembrance/memorials/books/silver (accessed 23 August 2023).
136 "1971 National Memorial (Silver) Cross Mother – Mary Anderson," Veterans Affairs Canada, 30 March 2017, https://www.veterans.gc.ca/eng/remembrance/memorials/books/silver/1971 (accessed 23 August 2023).
137 "National Aboriginal Veterans Association," Aboriginal Veterans Society of Alberta, 2013, https://www.aboriginalveterans.com/national (accessed 23 August 2023).
138 Interviews BC-4, BC-5, BC-6, part 2, 18, DHH, 2003/29.
139 Interviews BC-4, BC-5, BC-6, part 2, 17, DHH, 2003/29.
140 Interviews BC-4, BC-5, BC-6, part 2, 18. DHH, 2003/29.
141 "A Spiritual Homecoming," *Legion Canadian Military History Magazine*, 1 January 2006, https://legionmagazine.com/en/2006/01/a-spiritual-homecoming/ (accessed 23 August 2023).

142 Aboriginal Spiritual Journey Interdepartmental Working Group, 10 August 2005. Warren Sinclair Archives, Personal Papers series, Employment: Dept. of National Defence, Directorate of History and Heritage subseries, Aboriginal Spiritual Journey: Aboriginal Spiritual Journey 2005 (1) file, box 5 file.

143 Phil Hahn, "Aboriginal Veterans Recall Journey of Healing," *CTV News*, 7 November 2005, http://www.ctv.ca/servlet/ArticleNews/story/CTVNews/20051107/aboriginal_veterans_feature_051107/20051108/ (accessed 23 August 2023).

144 Personal recollections of Warren Sinclair and his Dad regarding the 2005 Aboriginal Spiritual Journey, 2018, Warren Sinclair Archives, Elmer Sinclair Records series, Textual Records subseries, Miscellaneous (1) file, box 1 file 1.

145 Personal recollection of Warren Sinclair and his Dad regarding the 2005 Aboriginal Spiritual Journey. Warren Sinclair Archives.

146 The medal was a Second World War medal and was awarded for six months service on active operations for Army and Navy, and two months for active air drew. "1939–1945 Star," Veterans Affairs Canada, 17 October 2017, https://www.veterans.gc.ca/eng/remembrance/medals-decorations/details/11 (accessed 23 August 2023).

147 The medal was a Second World War medal and was awarded for one day or more of service in France, Belgium, Holland, or Germany between 6 June 1944 (D-Day) and 8 May 1945. "France and Germany Star," Veterans Affairs Canada," 17 October 2017, https://www.veterans.gc.ca/eng/remembrance/medals-decorations/details/19 (accessed 23 August 2023).

148 The medal was a Second World War medal and was awarded to Canadians for six months service in Britain between 3 September 1939 and 8 May 1945. "Defence Medal," Veterans Affairs Canada, 17 October 2017, https://www.veterans.gc.ca/eng/remembrance/medals-decorations/details/20 (accessed 23 August 2023).

149 The medal was a Second World War medal and was granted to all persons of any rank in the Naval, Military, or Air Forces of Canada who voluntarily served on active service and honourably completed eighteen months total voluntary service from 3 September 1939 to 1 March 1945. "Canadian Volunteer Service Medal," Veterans Affairs Canada, 17 October 2017.

150 The medal is a Korean War medal and awarded to Canadian military personnel for one day on the strength of an army unit in Korea between 7 July 1950 and 27 July 1953. "Canada Korea Medal," Veterans Affairs Canada, 17 October 2017, https://www.veterans.gc.ca/eng/remembrance/medals-decorations/details/24 (accessed 23 August 2023).

151 The medal was instituted 12 December 1950 for service from 27 June 1950 to 27 July 1954 and was earned for serving one day under United Nations command in Korea. "United Nations Service Canada Medal (Korea)," Veterans Affairs

Canada, 17 October 2017, https://www.veterans.gc.ca/eng/remembrance/medals-decorations/details/26 (accessed 23 August 2023).

152 The medal was established in 1991 for service between 27 June 1950 and 27 July 1954. "Canadian Volunteer Service Medal for Korea," Veterans Affairs Canada, 17 October 2017, https://www.veterans.gc.ca/eng/remembrance/medals-decorations/details/25 (accessed 23 August 2023).

153 "UN Emergency Force (UNEF)," Veterans Affairs Canada, 17 October 2017, https://www.veterans.gc.ca/eng/remembrance/medals-decorations/details/130 (accessed 23 August 2023).

154 The prestigious Nobel Peace Prize was awarded to all United Nations Peacekeepers in 1988 in recognition of their collective efforts in the cause of peace. This inspired the creation of the medal to acknowledge the contribution to peace that Canadian peacekeepers have made since 1947. It was awarded for a minimum of thirty days cumulative service in a UN or international peacekeeping mission, National Defence and Canadian Armed Forces. "Canadian Peacekeeping Service Medal (CPSM)," Veterans Affairs Canada, 25 March 2018, https://www.veterans.gc.ca/eng/remembrance/medals-decorations/details/129 (accessed 23 August 2023).

155 The medal commemorates the fiftieth anniversary of the accession of Her Majesty Queen Elizabeth the Second to the throne. Canadian Forces members must be recommended by the chief of Defence Staff to the Government of Canada. "Queen Elizabeth II Golden Jubilee Medal," Veterans Affairs Canada, 17 October 2017, https://www.veterans.gc.ca/eng/remembrance/medals-decorations/details/196 (accessed 23 August 2023).

156 The medal commemorates the sixtieth anniversary of the accession of Her Majesty Queen Elizabeth the Second to the throne as Queen of Canada. Eligible candidates had to be alive on 6 February 2012 and have made significant contributions to Canada or for an outstanding achievement abroad that has brought great credit to Canada. "Queen Elizabeth II's Diamond Jubilee Medal," Veterans Affairs Canada, 17 October 2017, https://www.veterans.gc.ca/eng/remembrance/medals-decorations/details/197 (accessed 23 August 2023).

157 The medal commemorates the sixty-fifth anniversary of the liberation of The Netherlands and Victory in Europe day. "Princess Margaret of the Netherlands Awards the First 1945–2010 Medal to a Canadian Veteran," Veterans Affairs Canada, 23 October 2014, https://www.veterans.gc.ca/eng/about-vac/news-media/image-gallery/view/80 (accessed 23 August 2023).

158 Interviews BC-4, BC-5, BC-6, part 2, 18–19, DH, 2003/29.

159 The commemorative medal was an expression of appreciation from the Korean government to American service men and women who served in the Korean War. It was also made available for the veterans who had participated in UN

peacekeeping operations until the end of 1955. "Korean Ambassador for Peace Medal," *Legion*, 16 February 2016, https://www.legion.ca/news/2014/04/09/korean-ambassador-for-peace-medal (accessed 23 August 2023).

160 Facebook message from Shawn Sinclair to the author, 8 October 2018, Warren Sinclair Archives, Personal Narrative (1) file.

161 Email message from John MacFarlane to Warren Sinclair, 8 September 2017, Warren Sinclair Archives, Elmer Sinclair Records series, Textual Records sub-series, Interview file, box 1 file 14.

162 Email message from John MacFarlane to Warren Sinclair. Warren Sinclair Archives, Interview file.

163 It will be deposited at the National Centre for Truth and Reconciliation Archives at the University of Manitoba in Winnipeg.

2

"We Are Willing to Stand on our Own Two Feet," Cold War Moosonee

Adaptation to Change and to Closure of a Radar Station

SUE HEFFERNAN

In the early 1950s, residents of Moosonee could dip a water pail in the Moose River or in nearby Store Creek and drink this water without fear of illness. Almost overnight, that changed. The RCAF used Moosonee to ship supplies to the Mid-Canada radar line after 1955 and then opened a Pinetree radar station there in 1961. By 1963 one of the health inspectors, C.H. Kretch, a sanitary engineer, declared that the local waterways, used for drinking water, were being polluted by sewage and posed a danger of epidemics.[1] This chapter will explore how Cold War labour transformed the lives of the residents of Moosonee and the surrounding area. Military employment offered them new skills, better pay, and other attractive benefits but also degraded the environment and threatened their traditional ways. Many, like Elmer Sinclair whose story is told in chapter 1 of this volume, welcomed new economic opportunities and technologies. Yet, others saw the harms and actively promoted improvements to their community as is evident in this chapter and the next.

2.1 Map of Moosonee and James Bay communities.

Moosonee is a small, northern Ontario Cree community located south of James Bay, directly across the Moose River from Moose Factory Island (see figure 2.1). In the early years of the Cold War, Moosonee was targeted by military planners. The community was not singled out for bombs or planes. Instead, it was mapped and studied as a potential radar station as part of the Pinetree radar line. Initially, in the mid-1950s, Moosonee was designated as a shipping centre to supply northerly Mid-Canada Line radar stations such as Fort Albany and Winisk.[2] Construction materials and radar equipment were shipped to Moosonee by train and plane, especially after a winter airstrip was built in 1955. Additionally, a huge construction camp was built on the main street of the town. From 1961 to 1975, Moosonee had its own Royal Canadian Air Force (RCAF) radar station.[3]

The people of Moosonee adapted to two types of Cold War development: population growth due to the influx of labourers and military members and environmental degradation generated by military construction and activity, followed by redevelopment initiated by the closure of the RCAF station. Community adaptation to growth required major changes to local infrastructure and services. The slow pace of these improvements spurred community demands for local governance. Once the radar station closed in 1975, the residents seized the opportunity to use the housing and infrastructure on the RCAF station to fill local needs.

Research on Cold War radar stations focuses on the Distant Early Warning Line (DEW), the most northerly radar line with few works about the Mid-Canada Line and the Pinetree Line, the more southerly radar lines located closer to municipalities than the DEW Line. Locations for DEW Line stations were mandated by the United States which paid for all its construction and operating costs. The Mid-Canada Line radar sites were chosen by Canada which wholly financed that line. Finally, the Pinetree Line radar stations were funded two-thirds by the Americans and one-third by Canada. The majority of the Pinetree sites were chosen by the United States, although Canada was involved in siting of the final seven Pinetree sites, including Moosonee.[4]

Very little research on radar lines examines the influences military development had on small municipalities. There were more than forty Pinetree Line stations across Canada between the mid-1950s and late 1980s, and yet we know almost nothing about how these communities were transformed by these stations in their midst. This case study of Moosonee takes a different approach than traditional military history. It exposes how residents, labourers, and their families reacted to the radar station, to population growth and infrastructure limitations, and lobbied for local governance particularly related to water and sewage problems.[5]

POPULATION GROWTH AND ENVIRONMENTAL DEGRADATION

In the early 1950s, residents of Moosonee could dip a water pail in the Moose River or in nearby Store Creek and drink this water without fear of illness. Furthermore, in 1959, just before the RCAF set up a radar station beside the town, they had the river water tested and it was considered "Satisfactory," that is, free of coliform bacteria.[6] One woman said that during this time, "we used to haul our water from the Moose River, carrying pails with a yoke."[7] Residents never thought about treating their water or their sewage. Rather, they simply relied upon local waterways for their needs without chemical interventions.

However, even before construction of the station was completed in 1961, provincial health officials documented environmental deterioration and warned of potential water-borne epidemics. Health and other provincial officials reported internally that drainage of sewage was "just less than dangerous" (1960) and that "a hazard to health exists" due to lack of proper sewage disposal (1961).[8] Suddenly, life changed. No one could count on safe water from the sources they had relied on. Moosonee's waterways could handle sewage generated by the small number of the original residents, but the rivers became polluted as the population of labourers and their families grew. Moosonee had been a small settlement prior to Cold War military development; its population was only 124 in 1951. This number doubled during shipping operations to northerly Mid-Canada sites in 1955 and it quadrupled to almost 1,000 people in early 1961, just before the radar station was completed. The Cree people from northern James Bay communities such as Attawapiskat and Fort Albany (see figure 2.1) came to Moosonee looking for Cold War construction work and employment at the RCAF station. As they looked for work, most of the northern Cree settled just south of Moosonee's original town site in an area that became known as the "Indian Village" or simply the village (see figure 2.2.). This area contrasted with the original town site which was regarded by some provincial government staff as primarily "white" or non-Indigenous.[9]

Interviewees stated, however, that many of Moosonee's residents had a rich heritage and that their mixed ancestry could be traced back to the fur trading days. The English, French, Scottish, and even Norwegian employees of the Revillon Frères Company (Moosonee) and Hudson Bay Company (Moose Factory) operations often married local Cree people.[10] What this meant for the radar station period (1961–75), is that sixty years after Revillon Frères set up shop in Moosonee, local Indigenous and non-Indigenous people were already quite accustomed to

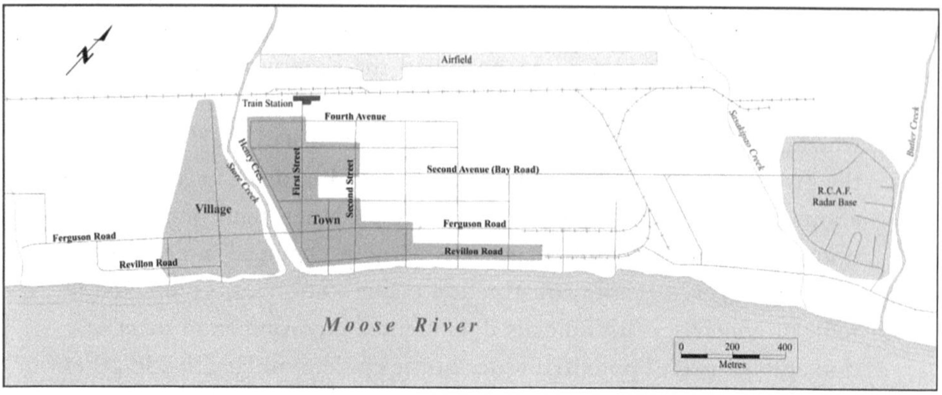

2.2 Map of Moosonee settlement areas circa 1962.

socializing and doing commerce with migrants to the community. The non-Indigenous people who arrived to live and work on the RCAF base were a different kind of migrant – military rather than economic – but the situation for Cree, mixed ancestry, and white residents was something they had experienced before. Local people were not averse to newcomers; they were used to diversity and to working together across racial boundaries.

Figure 2.3 below shows the spike that occurred in Moosonee's population between 1951 and 1961 due to the influx of labourers.[11] This spike was directly connected with environmental degradation. Since 1932 the Ontario Northland Railway (ONR) had provided a couple of streets in town with piped water, but it did not build a sewage treatment plant. In addition, private methods of sewage disposal – septic tanks and beds – did not work in the muskeg landscape.[12] Sewage collected in ditches and flowed into local water supply sources, including the Moose River, formerly the source of safe water.

By 1963 one of the health inspectors, C.H. Kretch, a sanitary engineer, declared that the local waterways, used for drinking water, were being polluted by sewage and posed a danger of epidemics. Kretch warned "Septic tank effluent, which is tantamount to raw sewage, is either lying or flowing in the ditches of almost all the main streets in the Townsite ... eleven [town] drains are found to be discharging wastes directly to the Moose River. Some drains also discharge to Store Creek ... The presence of [e-coli] bacteria in large numbers indicates

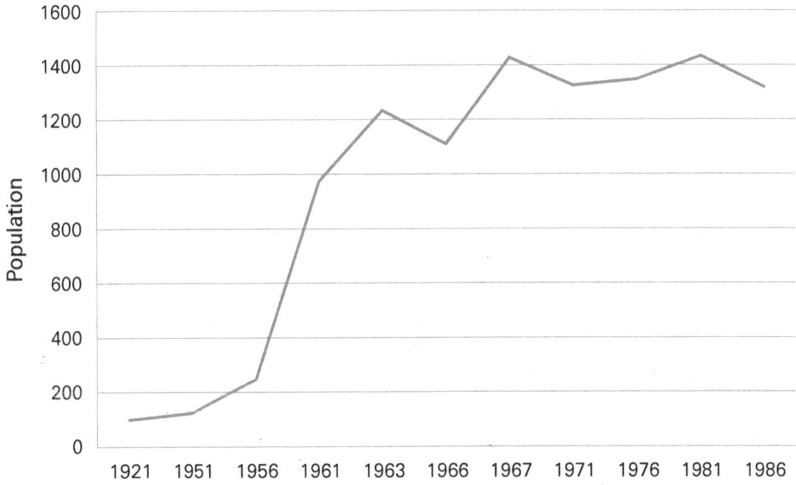

2.3 Moosonee's population, 1921–86.

that ... diseases such as typhoid fever and poliomyelitis could be present."[13] Lianne Leddy's research and writing on Serpent River First Nation (SRFN) echoes what was reported in Moosonee in the '60s.[14] Leddy examined uranium mining at Elliot Lake (a critical Cold War mineral site) and the associated Cutler Acid Plant which was adjacent to the Serpent River reserve. Leddy describes some of the health reports, produced by provincial scientists in the '60s in her analysis of the effects of the mine and plant on local people. One such report, from 1964, indicated that nuclear wastes had contaminated the Serpent River and that levels of radioactivity in certain (upstream) lakes were "ten times what is considered tolerable for a life-time exposure."[15] The key similarity with the Moosonee and Serpent River situations is that pollution experts provided confidential reports to the provincial and federal governments of the times, but no one informed the residents of Moosonee or of Serpent River reserve of the dangers they faced due to contamination of local water sources. The situation was especially dire for the Serpent River First Nation, which was not advised until 1974 that residents should not drink water or eat fish from the Serpent River.[16]

In Moosonee's case, local employees of the radar station became aware of the potential for proper sewage treatment and production of clean drinking water because of their role as civilian workers. The Moosonee radar station was typical of Pinetree sites with its own water, sewer, and power plants, recreational facilities (pool, bowling alley, and gym), public school, chapel, barracks, and housing subdivision. The base, with its population of 440 people (145 military personnel and their families), was located within walking distance of the town site of Moosonee.

The RCAF employed an average of sixty-eight civilians, mostly drawn from the town of Moosonee. Interviewees indicated that they learned their lifelong employment skills at the radar station and that they benefitted from the recreational facilities and sports activities at the station. Local civilian employees also observed the running water, flush toilets, and sewage and water treatment facilities at the station. Some of them managed the water, sewer, and power plants. After maintaining the RCAF's plants during the day, civilian employees returned by bus to the town and village, places without sewage treatment and with limited clean drinking water. They saw daily what could be, and should be, made available to all. Moosonee employees knew that adequate services were achievable, and they insisted over time that such services be made available to them, whether they lived in the town itself or in the village.

The RCAF had its own sewage treatment and therefore it was not directly responsible for the water pollution, but the very existence of the station and its requirement for labour triggered migration from other northern communities. This population growth resulted in polluted waterways. It took almost ten years for water and sewage facilities to be completed in Moosonee (from 1961 to 1968), and during that time environmental issues became the impetus for local activism.[17] In contrast, as described by Leddy in *Serpent River Resurgence*, the environmental issues that affected community members were not resolved until almost three decades of demanding action. Leddy aptly describes the lengthy process of questioning, documenting, hiring experts, engaging the press, and finally dumping, and later burning, hazardous wastes along the edge of the provincial highway. Clearly the people in Serpent River First Nation had a firm "community memory of betrayal" in regard to the way they had been treated by all levels of government.[18] The people of Moosonee also remember their fight for clean water and for sewage treatment facilities, but at least some felt empowered by the expertise they had gained in their work at the radar station.

LOCAL INVOLVEMENT AND LOCAL GOVERNANCE

Moosonee was not a formal municipality during the early Cold War years (1945–65). In fact, it had, since 1932, been loosely managed as a railway town under the control of the ONR. Because of the environmental degradation noted above, residents from both the town site and the village began, in the early 1960s, to lobby for specific measures to improve water and sewage treatment and other quality of life issues. They also lobbied, at the same time, for local involvement in governance, hoping to gain some control over their own community and its infrastructure. Residents started by gathering at public meetings to discuss how to get safe drinking water and public sewer systems. They also demanded better roads and fire protection services.

In June 1961 residents had a public meeting to discuss the deplorable roads and the fact that septic systems were draining into the ditches beside downtown streets. A Department of Health employee who attended this public meeting later wrote that "it was unanimously agreed that a type of municipal organization, probably an Improvement District, was the only effective means of affecting a permanent improvement [in local services]."[19] One year later, in June 1962, with no apparent action by the ONR or the provincial government to improve the town, residents filed an application to become an Improvement District, the first step toward municipal incorporation. Sewage treatment was the prime motivator for their application, which stated, "we find raw sewage running down our open ditches [which could] cause an outbreak of typhoid or other diseases of epidemic proportions ... In fact, warnings have been issued from the health department regarding our present conditions. That we are willing to stand on our own two feet and do something for ourselves is best expressed in our petition to the Municipal Board to have this area made an Improvement District."[20]

Unfortunately, after another year of government inaction on local issues, it became apparent that the Improvement District application had been indefinitely stalled when the provincial government indicated it could not proceed until extensive studies had been done on the issue. This *defacto* rejection was a decisive step before citizens decided to forge their own future. In August 1963, town residents formed the Moosonee Townsite Development Board (MTDB). They demanded local improvements, especially in water and sewer systems. This new group reflected Moosonee's diverse population as Wendy Thomas, a welfare development worker, who attended the formative meeting for the MTDB observed in the unselfconscious racial terminology of the day. She wrote, "There followed the creation of the Moosonee Townsite Development Board. A Treaty Indian was elected chairman [*sic*] by the gathered representation of the community. One Indian and one non-Indian were elected to head each of six committees to deal with the specific problems of Moosonee: Employment, Housing, Law enforcement, Health and Sanitation, Education and Recreation ... These elected representatives would appear to have the potential necessary to get action."[21]

The formation and composition of the MTDB demonstrated that local people, whether Indigenous or non-Indigenous, male or female, intended to work together to improve their community. A few months after the initial meeting, a Department of Health inspector, H.C. Raiche, provided more details on this diverse group and its connection to the Improvement District application. Eight of the fifteen members of the MTDB had signed the Improvement District application.[22] The chairman of the board, Thomas Archibald, was an employee of the RCAF, was a treaty Indian, and a member of the New Post band.[23] As for the other members of this citizens group, Raiche described them as "business owners, housewives, and ONR [railway] employees." Then he noted that "There are 8 white status Indians, two of which are women, 6 whites [and] 1 Indian."[24] Ironically, white status Indians were Indigenous people who had lost their official status and yet the very use of the term indicated a subtle distinction between their "white status" and that of the local whites. The most significant part of the categorization of local people was not simply what various terms meant but the fact that the provincial government staff utilized a profoundly colonial "sorting" of Indigenous and non-Indigenous people.

It took until 1966 for the provincial government to pass legislation creating the Moosonee Development Area Board (MDAB), a provincially supervised body, which would act in a quasi-municipal manner to help manage and/or provide input into the town's sewer and water construction projects. This legislation was not formally enacted until August 1968. Apparently, the province did not consult any local people or groups like the MTDB during the preparation of the legislation or its enactment. In fact, a member of the local Chamber of Commerce, Dick Knowles, who was also on the MTDB, had to write to the province, in November 1967, just to get a copy of the legislation.[25] At this point more than five years had passed since the Improvement District application had been sent to the province and more than four since the local MTDB had been formed. Despite the evident health risk, consultations with residents were put on the "backburner."

However, one more group of residents tried to change governance structures while the province was studying how to implement the MDAB Act. In August 1967, a small group of local people from the village filed a petition with the federal government to become a reserve.[26] The petitioners referred to themselves as "the Indians of the West Coast of James Bay" who were now residing in Moosonee. Eight of the nine people who signed the petition were members of the Attawapiskat and Fort Albany bands.[27] The petitioners wrote that "We, the Indians of Moosonee, want to draw the attention of the Canadians on the miserable condition of our community, our urgent need for public utilities such as housing, electricity, water, sewage and telephone. These things we need to develop a model reserve ... adjacent to the present town of Moosonee."[28] Like the earlier request by town residents for an Improvement District, the reserve application was rejected. Federal representatives suggested that the real issue was provision of better services and housing by the province, rather than the establishment of a new reserve.[29] The residents of Moosonee were thus caught between two bureaucracies and their various rules and regulations.

Likely, the reserve application and earlier requests for an Improvement District pressured the provincial government to finally enact the Moosonee legislation which had been passed in 1966 but not yet implemented on the ground. Local efforts thus led to the eventual formation in 1968 of the Moosonee Development Area Board (MDAB).[30] The local MPP Rene Brunelle had prepared a confidential list of potential appointees to the MDAB back in 1966. This list was supplemented by nominations from a February 1968 public meeting organized by the Chamber of Commerce.[31] Nine of the 14 people nominated by the public had an RCAF connection. They were either employees and/or members of the RCAF messes. In effect, the community had a strong connection to the radar station.[32] The chairman of the board Ed Butcher was the only person who had been recommended by Brunelle and also nominated by the public. Butcher was a local non-Indigenous businessman who was also a member of the Sergeant's Mess at the RCAF station. Two other new board members who had been recommended by Brunelle were Pat Gray, a retired RCAF officer and Archie Michel a local businessman. The government apparently discriminated against women because the five board members were all men, even though two local Indigenous women, Maude Tyrer and Dorothy Wynne, had been nominated at the chamber's public meeting. It took another five years before one of these women, Maude Tyrer, was appointed to the MDAB.[33] Only two of the five male appointees – David Wynne and Xavier Wesley – were Indigenous, but at least they represented the town site and the village.[34]

At the same time as the MDAB legislation was enacted, major infrastructure projects, related to water, sewer, and roads were initiated in the town.[35] Infrastructure development served two purposes. Firstly, it provided clean water and sewage treatment – services that were vital to the health and safety of town residents. Secondly, the planning and construction of infrastructure fostered a climate of public participation or at least public demand for ongoing and expanded improvements in other community services, like fire protection and recreation. The development of a local voice and local government placed Moosonee citizens in an ideal position to demand control of the RCAF station when it closed in 1975. The community's adaptation to the station closure was almost a welcome challenge to the residents of Moosonee, who were, by 1975, savvy participants in local government processes.[36]

CLOSURE OF THE RADAR STATION AND LOCAL ACTION

The closure of the radar station affected local people personally and the community physically. This closure influenced local employment, activities, and infrastructure, but Moosonee's future was also determined by how local people took control of their own future.

On 16 January 1975 Canada's minister of National Defence James Richardson formally announced the closure of Moosonee's radar station.[37] Excerpts from the announcement included the following: "Several Government departments such as Regional Economic Expansion and Manpower and Immigration, will be working with the Department of National Defence and local authorities to minimize the disruptive effect on the communities concerned and to assist civilian employees to find other employment. Armed Forces personnel at the stations will be posted to vacant positions at other units."[38] The full announcement consisted of six paragraphs, three of which dealt with the effects upon civilian labour. The loss of local work was a powerful consideration for the community. The Moosonee closure was not an isolated situation. Three other Pinetree stations (Ramore, Foymount, and Armstrong) had closed in 1974. Radar operations had become automated and fewer stations were required.[39] In addition, the minister of Defence told the press that he was "determined to cut costs in his ministry" and that station closures were necessary as part of personnel and facility reductions across the Canadian Forces.[40]

Press coverage started immediately after the closure announcement and for the first half of the year concerns about closure were highlighted in newspaper articles with headings such as: "Defence Budget Cuts Killing CFS Moosonee,"[41] "Moosonee Base Closing Opposed by Civilians,"[42] "Moosonee Troubles Spotlighted,"[43] "Moosonee 'Coming to a Stop' with Loss of Radar Base Jobs,"[44] and "Moosonee Military Base Winds Down to a Ghostly Stillness."[45] In the first newspaper article on the station's closure, dated 18 January 1975, Major R.C. Conn confirmed that armed forces personnel would be transferred to other stations and that the DND was working to "relocate as many of the civilian employees as possible."[46] Conn stated that there were currently 141 armed forces personnel and 60 civilians employed at the Moosonee site.

Two days after the first news article appeared, the union representing civilian employees rallied and started to voice objections. Ken Sweigard, the president of Local 628 of the Union of National Defence Employees and an electrician on the Moosonee station, told the *Timmins Daily Press* that the civilian employees would be pushing to reverse the federal government's decision.[47] Sweigard stated that "closing the base would be a 'slap in the face' to the Indian and Metis who learned a trade to work at the base."[48] He also said that forty of the sixty civilians employed on the station were Cree and they, like all of the employees, "were really shocked and pretty perturbed by the whole thing."[49] It is worth noting that interviewees tended to describe their training as "on the job, at the base" rather than prior to being hired as Sweigard suggested in the news article. However, Sweigard's key point was correct, which was that the radar station jobs were significant for civilians. Sweigard sounded "union tough" at the beginning of the news article, but by the end, he was proposing that the radar station be given to the Moosonee Development Area Board if the federal government did not back down.[50]

The MDAB sprang into action as quickly as the union. The board held two special meetings within hours of the announcement, and they sent telegrams to their MP Ralph Stewart and to Defence Minister Richardson.[51] The Secretary Treasurer of the MDAB, John Pringle, told the press that the telegrams were intended to highlight Moosonee's concerns and to establish Moosonee as a priority bidder on the sale of station assets. He said, "We're asking that we be given the opportunity to participate at all levels in the disposition of the base and that we be given some priority in it [in sales]." Pringle also indicated that it would be "madness" to sell the assets to outside parties.[52] Finally, he noted that the board was concerned there might be temporary power failures when the station's power plant was shut down because the town was not expecting to hook up to the new Ontario Hydro transmission line until November 1975.[53]

After the initial flurry of special board meetings, the MDAB called a public meeting for 28 January 1975, to discuss the closure and, as Secretary Treasurer Pringle told the press, to "gather ideas and receive local input."[54] Despite what Pringle indicated, the real purpose of the public meeting appears to have been the board's wish to assess its public support; the board wanted to hear from local people to ensure that they regarded it as a truly representative body for local residents. Perhaps the board entertained some doubts because the MDAB had been structured by the province and its members, although informally elected by local people, were still appointed by the province.[55]

While there is no indication how many people attended the public meeting or if there was a vote taken on the board's role, the board heard enough from local people to feel comfortable moving forward; it felt it had been given a community mandate to proceed. The public meeting also likely ensured that the MDAB had half the seats on a closure committee that was formed a few days later by the provincial government.[56] The chairman and secretary of the Joint Closure Committee for the radar station became Velko Novakovich, who was also chairman of the MDAB, and John Pringle, secretary of the MDAB. The Closure Committee also included five more members of the MDAB, three members of the Moose Factory Fire Prevention and Roads Committee, and three members of Moose Band Council.[57] At its second meeting the Closure Committee invited Grand Council Treaty Number Nine to participate thereby ensuring that all First Nations communities on the western side of James Bay were represented in discussions.[58] Although the committee's report does not discuss if members were Indigenous or non-Indigenous, an Ontario cabinet submission on the Joint Closure Committee's report indicates that the members of the committee were "Treaty and Non-Treaty Indians, Metis and whites."[59] The fourteen members of the Closure Committee included three women. These were Jane Moore and Nina Hunter who were members of the MDAB and Nellie Faries who was a member of Moose Band Council.[60]

One of the first activities of the Closure Committee was to seek further public input. The committee instructed its secretary "to write each business and social group in both communities [Moosonee and Moose Factory] to this end."[61] The Closure Committee considered a wide variety of ideas for how the radar station and its assets could be used. Two ideas generated at the 28 January public meeting included a high school and an industrial park.[62] Interviewees indicated that the high school concept was a top priority for both Indigenous and non-Indigenous residents. All high school age children in Moosonee and Moose Factory, and indeed the entire James Bay area, had to travel south to complete grades 9 to 13. Everyone agreed that using some of the buildings on the closed station for a high school would be a wonderful outcome for the region. The *Timmins Daily Press* had also supported the high school concept, indicating that "The entire James Bay area could be facilitated by the station [high school]."[63] By March, even the *Toronto Star* was recording support for a high school: "Although residents have numerous ideas about what they'd like to see replace the base – ranging from a minimum-security prison to a technical school – officials say most people agree that part of the facilities should be used as a high school ... Currently the 300 or so high school age children from the area have to live in North Bay, Timmins or other cities to go to school."[64]

The high school became the top priority in *The Report of [the] Joint Committee re: Closure of Canadian Forces Station – Moosonee* (hereafter referred to as the *Closure Report*), which was submitted to the provincial government in March 1975.[65] The goal of the *Closure Report* was clearly laid out by the committee: "To set forth the ideas coming from the people of Moosonee, Moose Factory and surrounding area regarding the utilization of the Canadian Forces Station Moosonee such that the people living in these communities might reap the maximum benefit from them both from the standpoint of employment of the residents, the economic welfare of the area, and improvement of social amenities."[66]

It is significant that the Closure Committee referred to "ideas coming from the people." While local community leaders had made their views known earlier, the province had not generally acknowledged their input. At least by 1975, the province seemed more responsive to their input and the Closure Committee stressed local input as a means of justifying and strengthening its case.[67] The true intent of the *Closure Report*, however, was an even more powerful statement, which was labelled as "Miscellaneous" and subtly placed in a section at the end of the report's preamble: "Throughout the [closure] period there has been much communication with the Provincial Government and to a more limited degree with the Federal Government. It appears clear that this committee must take the initiative in the project by exploring the best way to handle things [and] then use its influence with both Provincial and Federal bodies to give assistance in attaining these goals."[68]

Clearly, the Closure Committee was a team; that is, it was "taking the initiative" and working together to benefit everyone in the area. Furthermore, it was exercising agency together by assuming that it had charge of the future use of the station. Finally, the committee was prepared to stand either with or against governments to achieve what was needed. The Closure Committee's report laid out eight recommended uses for the base. These were, in order of priority: secondary school complex, utilization of housing from the base, use of the base recreation complex, local Native craft industries, community and social facilities (e.g., nursing home), tourist facilities, facilities for government (e.g., air sea rescue station), and "Other" (e.g., garage and storage facilities for Ontario Hydro). This discussion will focus on the leading two suggestions: a high school and housing, primarily because those seemed the most urgent to the committee. A secondary reason for focusing on these two items is that they were the changes that were eventually implemented and that influenced the lives of local people.

The creation of a regional high school had been highlighted by the press as an appropriate use of the base facilities. The Closure Committee emphasized that the area needed not only a local high school but also accommodation for students from outside Moosonee and access to the station recreation facilities to be fully effective. The committee wrote that "the pleas for local high school facilities are very strong particularly from the Indian population in Moosonee and Moose Factory."[69] They also stated, "This is by far the most definite and substantial proposal and its implementation would go a long way towards meeting the objectives of this committee."[70] At the end of its report, it reiterated, "The Committee recommends first and foremost the establishment of grades 9 and 10 High School classes ... The strong bid for a High School by the Indian population of Moosonee and Moose Factory was impressive. The authorities should perhaps look upon the base closure as the 'incident' that brought the need for a high school to the fore rather than simply a suggestion for the use of the base."[71]

Although the *Closure Report* emphasized the support of local Indigenous people, interviewees said that the high school concept was strongly supported by both Indigenous and non-Indigenous people, all of whom were tired of sending their children away for high school. Even those persons whose children were quite young at the time of the base closure said they were dreading the day that they would need to put their teenagers on the train south, to board with strangers in North Bay or Sudbury.[72] The Ministry of Education also supported the regional high school concept, which it stated would serve "Moosonee and Moose Factory, as well as [students] from Fort Albany, Kashechewan, Attiwapiskat, Fort Severn and Winisk, on a boarding school basis."[73] It indicated that a high school would need most of the facilities on the radar station, including "the [primary] school, the recreation centre, the church and social hall, the combined officers' mess, the single barracks block, the administrative building, the skating rink and ice arena, the mechanical and civil engineering workshops and twenty of the houses [for teachers]."[74] The assumption by the Ministry of Education seemed to be that students would be housed in the RCAF's former single barracks and that all other structures would be needed for high school programs.[75]

While the high school request was the community's top priority, the use of houses from the station was a close second in the *Closure Report*. The report's authors described the base subdivision and its housing as follows:

> Permanent married quarters (P.M.Q.s) – it seems generally agreed that the housing at the base is too crowded and that thinning to perhaps 50% would still leave 57 houses at the base. People from Moosonee, Moose Factory both on the Reserve and elsewhere – have expressed an interest. Some see a demand for them from places like Albany and Kashechewan. These buildings are movable having come in on wheels and fastened together to make a 20' wide building ... Thirty-eight applications for houses either to be occupied at the base or to be moved to sites elsewhere have currently been received by the committee.[76]
>
> ...
>
> As this study progresses the feasibility of using the base as [a] subdivision of Moosonee becomes more and more practical. The lack of serviced lots [in town] and the high cost of servicing them contributes greatly to this position.[77]

As the *Closure Report* was being deliberated by the Ontario Cabinet, Commanding Officer Major Conn provided more closure details in a guest editorial printed in *Moosetalk* in April 1975. Conn used the opportunity to both describe the dismantling of the station and to say farewell to local people:

> During the last couple of weeks there has been a considerable amount of activity occurring at the base; helicopters flying over, many strangers arriving and leaving and perhaps most

> significantly, the change in the skyline with the dismantling of the radomes ... On 1 April 1975, as planned the radar stopped functioning and the air navigation beacon (TACAN) ceased, ending the operational role of this station ... On 10 April 1975 a crew of technicians arrived from USAF to dismantle the radomes ... which will be returned to the U.S. ... [This] is an immense task, especially when combined with the one hundred and twenty families which are leaving at the same time. As people depart, buildings must be closed and prepared for whatever future the station may have.
>
> As plans stand now, the station will be closed by 1 Aug. 75 ... Although many rumours are circulating, concerning the future, we at the station have had no news and we are just as concerned as the townspeople.
>
> Since the opening of the station in 1961, several hundred people have been posted here and many more have visited the area on business. All these people will regret the closing of CFS Moosonee; since we have enjoyed the area and particularly the hospitality the townspeople have shown the station. The present members, all wish the Moosonee area well, in the future.[78]

Major Conn was not required to give this update to local people; he simply spoke on his own, providing a heartfelt parting message. Many who served on Pinetree Line stations across Canada felt the same genuine regret when other stations closed over the next decades, expressing appreciation for the close community connection. Even now, years after the 1988 closure of the last Pinetree station, websites and even Facebook posts, echo the warm message from Major Conn.[79] In addition, books like Peter Kvas' *Lobster, Lighthouse and Long-Range Radar*, hold the stories and fond memories of local labourers, their families, and service people.[80]

By June 1975 provincial government staff had reviewed the *Closure Report*, circulated it to twelve government ministries, and prepared a cabinet submission. Generally, provincial ministries were supportive of the recommendations by the Joint Closure Committee. The focus of the province shifted to implementation issues and to collaboration with the federal government to transfer the radar base to either the province or the town. Part of ensuring a good future for Moosonee was taking care of the radar station's structures so that they would not deteriorate while the provincial and federal government deliberated on options for the station's assets. In this regard, the Department of National Defence (DND) prepared a thorough report by April 1975 on "the requirements for the continued preservation of all useable buildings at CFS Moosonee after the 1 Aug 75 closure date."[81] The report stated that it would be necessary to operate the heating and power plant, the water and sewage plants, and the MQ [likely PMQ] furnaces in order to avoid freezing the infrastructure. It also indicated that approximately twenty personnel, either civilians or military, would be needed to manage utilities, maintenance, and security on the former station. The estimated monthly cost of preserving the condition of the station was $45,250, but the more pressing issue was that the DND expected there would be no military personnel and "few qualified civilians" available once the station closed.[82] In addition, the DND report stated that "the present fuel contract terminates 1 Aug 75 [and] a new contract would have to be negotiated prior to that date."[83] The time for decisions was very tight but, other than the DND, the provincial and federal governments did not seem to realize the need to protect the station's assets before they were divested.

By June 1975 more facilities were closing on the station and people were moving away. The *North Bay Nugget* provided a description of the situation:

> The first of the regular facilities to close was the base Chapel … The next to close were mess facilities for the Officers and Junior Ranks. These were moved to a combined operation with the sergeants and became an All-Ranks Mess … on June 1st. The next major closure of facilities came when the Canex (the base shopping centre), the Post Office and the Snack Bars closed.
>
> Personnel started leaving the Base at the end of March and the exodus continued. Each evening now the lighted windows of the married quarters get fewer and fewer. Personnel board the train daily with their families and head for new postings …
>
> As of August 1, the Canadian Forces Station that was built in 1960 will be patrolled by two or three Commissionaires, a couple of Military Police and a whole bunch of blackflies and

> mosquitoes. They won't be fogging the grounds anymore to keep the bugs down.[84]

This *North Bay Nugget* article is one of the few archival records to give any indication of the status of buildings as the station neared its closure date.

By early 1976, Moosonee's residents must have been getting concerned about the slow pace of asset transition at the station. The CBC picked up on this subject and broadcast a show on *The Fifth Estate* on 24 February 1976, which showed empty housing on the station, while some residents of Moosonee were living in shacks.[85] The show generated a flurry of letters to Premier Bill Davis.[86] The names and addresses of writers have been redacted (blacked out) as part of Freedom of Information and Protection of Privacy procedures, but writers generally explained where they were writing from. Most of the writers in this case were from southern Ontario and most of the letters were written the same night as the *Fifth Estate* program. All the writers were adamant that the province immediately deal with housing and other issues in Moosonee, as the following excerpts show:

> Yesterday I saw the program "The Fifth Estate" and I was appalled to hear about the closed base at Moosonee. The base is being heated without anyone benefitting, while the native population is spending huge sums of money to heat their primitive huts.[87]

> After watching ... Fifth Estate ... and their report on the living conditions of the people of Moosonee and Moose Factory area, the government red tape in trying to decide to sell them empty, government housing that my tax dollars are paying for, I am as a citizen of this province asking for your resignation. You are not man enough for the position you hold.[88]

> Do what you can to see that the "Liberal" red tape and the "Conservative" indecision in Ontario is circumvented so that the native people of the Moosonee district of Ontario are enabled to use NOW the abandoned C.F.B. Moosonee which is their right and our responsibility.[89]

> The 114 houses, the school and the recreational facilities that are standing idle in this community while the residents are living in very substandard dwellings is a national disgrace.[90]

> Tonight, I learned about what goes on at Moosonee and I'm appalled ... How your government can allow those poor Indian and Metis to live in such squalor with all that housing standing there vacant is past all understanding. It is a provincial and national disgrace.[91]

> LET THE TOWN IN NOW – work out your usual RED TAPE LATER.[92]

> Is this [Moosonee] an example of how democracy works? ... Taxpayers are keeping 114 empty houses heated while children grow up resentful and bitter toward their country. Old people suffer and deteriorate in mind and body ... If Democracy can't work ... then let's have Castro come up and straighten us out and teach us how to share our blessings.[93]

These excerpts from letters written to Premier Davis are representative of the complaints to the Ontario government. Some letters were also sent to Prime Minister Pierre Elliott Trudeau. This correspondence may have been the impetus needed to get the province and federal governments to transfer the station to the MDAB.

In the wake of this criticism Premier Davis responded. He agreed with some of the accusations, but he also clarified that the province had been building infrastructure for some years and housing more recently. Specifically, Davis responded in his form letter:

> I admit that it has taken considerable time to make arrangements for the use of the housing and other components of the abandoned armed forces base. The determination of the best solution has involved complex discussions between several provincial agencies, the municipality, the Treaty Nine organization, several Indian bands, the Metis Association, the Indian community on Moose Factory Island and several federal agencies ... The Ontario Government has now authorized the Moosonee Area

Development Board to negotiate with the Federal Government as to the disposition of the [housing] units.[94]

One month after the premier's reply, the provincial secretary confirmed that all federal and provincial documents had been finalized, "clearing the way for the final transfer of the assets of the former CFS Moosonee to the MDAB."[95] That same week, negotiations were underway with "the Indian Band [Moose Band] and the Métis and Non-Status Indian Association to purchase fifty houses from the D.N.D. Radar Base – 25 each."[96] Interviewees indicated that the sale of these houses benefitted everyone. People who purchased homes on the former station knew they would have more yard space since every second home had been removed, while people who purchased homes from the Métis and Non-Status Association could either live in those homes on the station or could move their new homes onto a site in the town. Homes sold to Moose Factory Island's residents were moved "over the ice" during the winter of 1976–77 helping fill the demand for housing on the island.[97]

Progress also occurred on the fledgling high school. By June 1976 a principal had been appointed for the James Bay Lowlands District Secondary School, and plans had been made to hire ten teachers, "three of which are native."[98] James Auld, the chair of the Management Board of Cabinet, had visited with the new principal and had observed "extensive repainting and refurbishing ... to the gymnasium/swimming pool complex and the school buildings."[99] The principal anticipated that 100 to 150 students would start at the school in September 1976, and Auld mentioned that students from Moose Factory Island would need to be transported to and from the high school by helicopter during freeze-up and thaw periods.[100]

Although a cursory sketch was attached to Auld's memos, information from interviewees provides a much clearer picture of the amount of transformation that was occurring for the high school. One interviewee described the changes as follows:

> Twenty-one homes on the base were kept for teachers' houses. These houses were scattered throughout the former base property.
>
> The barracks were kept for student housing. Students from Moose Factory came over on Monday morning and returned

> home on Friday. They travelled by boat or helicopter depending on the season.
>
> The Junior Ranks Mess became the high school library and the Sergeants' Mess became the Home Economics room. The Officers' Mess became the Art room, and the combined mess cafeteria was retained as a high school cafeteria.
>
> The Henry Hudson School [now called H-block apartments] was used for high school classrooms.
>
> The ME building (Mobile Equipment & Supply building) was used for Automotive Shop, the Carpentry Shop, Drafting room and Electrical Shop.
>
> The Administration/Base Headquarters building was used for School Board offices. This was a brand-new School Board since there had never been a high school in the James Bay area.
>
> The Recreation Centre on the base originally included a ninety-four-seat theatre and a bowling alley. The students were still able to use the bowling alley. The seats were removed from the theatre, and it was turned into a music room. The snack bar room was turned into offices. The base pool was maintained and is still the same pool that is in the current high school, although the pool closed about four years ago [2009] due to lack of funds for major upgrades. The gym in the current high school is the original gym that was constructed on the base and that formed part of the Recreation Centre. This was the gym where the RCAF held its dances and balls.[101]

The comprehensive transformation of the radar station's buildings into a high school campus was impressive. The exercise of agency by the town and regional representatives resulted in a full-service high school and in new housing for Moosonee and Moose Factory. Both initiatives demonstrated how people from the town and the entire region seized the opportunity that the station closure represented. The Closure Committee was unique. It was one of the few groups created by local people during this era in this region, and it represented both Indigenous and non-Indigenous people. That is, the committee was locally empowered, and it was representative. The appointees were not government selected and approved individuals. Rather, the communities that chose to be involved in the station's transformation selected the appointees. Such representation clearly impacted the committee's momentum, enthusiasm, and determination.

Researchers who study community initiatives suggest that one of the components for community development is "finding a group that is passionate about the initiative."[102] Wayne Caldwell et al. suggest that a passionate "community-based group is able to provide motivation, credibility, people power, and the resources to make change in a community."[103] Moosonee demonstrated all the criteria for a successful community-based group. The MDAB ensured that it had the support of the community before it acted; it ensured that it had a mandate to proceed. Next, it sought the opinions of residents and presented them to the Closure Committee. The Closure Committee itself prepared a comprehensive report on options for the radar station and then it ensured that the report was implemented. The Closure Committee represents a valuable example of change that reached both within and beyond the community of Moosonee, bringing together Indigenous and non-Indigenous people.

DIVERSE EXPERIENCES, LOCAL VOICES, AND WORKING TOGETHER FOR THE COMMUNITY

Interviewees believed that the station produced many positive results for the community. Their constructed memories describe the employment and training opportunities provided at the radar station, the ability to participate in social and recreational activities, and the opportunity to utilize the infrastructure and buildings left in the community after the station closed. On the latter point, as discussed above, the radar station's facilities provided a huge benefit both to housing stock and to the ability to form a local high school complex. The high school complex did not just mean that classrooms and workshops were available. Rather it meant that high-school-aged children no longer had to move away for five years to complete their education.[104]

Although interviewees stressed the Cold War's positive impacts, change in Moosonee was experienced differently depending on the social status of residents. Effects varied depending on where people lived, in the town site or in the village, and their social status. The term social relationships or social status broadly relates to a combination of gender, race, and class.[105] The first element of social status that demonstrates differing impacts is gender. Joy Parr explains that, when historians examine gender along with race and class, they assume that "in important ways, the experience of women was not like the experience of men, the experience of First Nations was not like the experience of colonizers [and] the experience of workers was not like that of bosses."[106] Parr has specifically examined how men and women experience local government differently. In her study of two Ontario factory towns, Parr observed that, when it came to local decision making, for men "their assent was required if a community consensus was to be formed."[107] However, she found, that in comparison, women were "neither functionally nor ideologically ... fully citizens of the town. They were more considered than consulted in the public affairs of the municipality."[108]

Parr's research on gender and local government is applicable to the situation in Moosonee. During the period studied here (1955–75) women were, to borrow Parr's words, barely "considered" by outside agencies. Furthermore, women were merely "noted," and they were not consulted regarding infrastructure, local government, and development issues. Provincial reports on public meetings show women as having been present but dismissed them as "only housewives." While some of the women who pushed to have their voices heard were employees of local businesses, surely, they and the "housewives" had a right to be heard and to have their opinions count. The dismissal of women's roles inside and outside of the home was commonplace during the 1950s and 1960s as documented by Ruth Roach Pierson and Doug Owram.[109] These authors illustrate how women were encouraged to leave the workplace after the Second World War and to devote themselves to marriage and family.[110] As Owram states, "Women remained in the home. Men worked. At mid-century this ideal was pervasive."[111] Women were certainly not encouraged, during the postwar era, to become involved in the public sphere, particularly not in politics.[112]

However, Moosonee's women refused to conform to the prevailing gender norms. Instead, they actively participated in citizen's committees such as the Moosonee Townsite Development Board and the Moosonee Community Council Steering Committee. Some served as leaders of community groups such as the Homemakers' Club and gained experience in organizational roles.[113] Despite these engagements and women's expertise, the province never considered women for the initial appointments to the MDAB in 1968. This discrimination occurred even though women such as Ellen Morrison and Dorothy Wynne had lobbied for services for local people and particularly for those who lived south of Store Creek.[114] Moosonee women worked outside the home in paid jobs in the town and on the radar station and they spoke out when issues arose.[115] The lack of recognition of their work and their value to the community, which would have been remedied by appointment to the MDAB, must have irked women and the community at large. After all, the community had nominated women for those initial positions. In effect, local female leaders were elected by the community but rejected by a patriarchal provincial bureaucracy. Leddy also describes politically active women in the Serpent River First Nation who pushed for recognition by government and mining company representatives when dealing with the horrifying levels of pollution in their area. The best example of this was when the Environmental Assessment Board attempted to exclude women from tours of the ten tailings ponds at the uranium mine sites. Fortunately, a union representative said, "No, let the women go." As Leddy notes, "the women were [then] able to participate, ask questions, and report back to their community about the extent of the damage they witnessed."[116]

Moreover, the radar station itself did not encourage or enable women's voices. Military documents recorded women when they gave birth or were involved in sports teams but did not regard them as equal participants in radar station life. Instead, most women simply fell into the category of "dependents," lumped into the same group as their children, and treated as passive recipients of policies, rather than active adult members of the community. Women were referred to as "the distaff side," or the "other."[117] Nonetheless, several years after the station opened, women formed active sports teams, which often included the local women who were spouses of civilian employees. These women participated in a range of sports, including curling, bowling, and baseball. Single women who were civilian employees also joined teams and enjoyed the social and physical aspects of sport. These were important community activities that benefited the local women and not just the wives of service people. Unfortunately, there is no information on the very few servicewomen who worked out of the Moosonee station. All that the archival reports tell us is that the unnamed women were "Nursing Sisters."[118] Chapter six of this work reveals more about the constraints placed upon these servicewomen, who challenged the idea that their place was solely within the home.

The second element of social status that demonstrates variation in impacts is race. Provincial government reports from departments such as Welfare and Social and Family Services tended to categorize Moosonee's residents as "White," "Status Indian," "Non-Status Indian," "Metis," and "White-Status Indian."[119] These reports also indicated that almost all the residents who lived south of Store Creek were Indigenous people.[120] This is the area that had to wait longer than the town for water, sewer, and fire services. It would be simplistic to attribute the lack of services solely to race. The most expensive properties in Moosonee, the industrial lots, were also denied water and sewer services despite lobbying by their owners to the provincial government. Provincial planners indicated that both the village (south of Store Creek) and the industrial area were outside Moosonee's main downtown area, and that the focus of stage one of water and sewer construction was the original built-up area of Moosonee (i.e., the original town site). Despite the planning rationale, the delay in services for the village was dangerous for Indigenous people. It was Indigenous people who returned to inadequate shacks, or even tents after receiving health services, and it was Indigenous people who were more likely to experience house fires.[121] In effect, the consequences of lack of services were dire in the village compared to other areas of town. It was these dreadful impacts that inspired Indigenous residents like Tom Archibald, Ellen Morrison, and Dorothy Wynne to constantly lobby for improvements.[122]

In contrast to the provincial records, race does not appear in archival materials about military or civilian positions relating to the radar station. The RCAF used only two categories – military and civilian – in their annual historical reports. While these categories overlook the heritage of Indigenous service people and employees, further reading of the RCAF's records determined that, to the military, there were only two distinctions deemed important. The RCAF's purpose was to defend Canada from nuclear attack. Station commanders and other officers only cared whether personnel had completed military training and could handle radar or other equipment, or whether the person could handle the essential civilian employee functions. Interviewees did note, however, one digression from the RCAF's records. They indicated that the distasteful, and potentially dangerous, job of applying creosote for walkways fell to the Indigenous civilian employees.[123] Further research, and particularly interviews, might provide an enhanced picture of racial aspects of employment on the station.

Race and class are closely entwined and that is why it is imperative to examine class as a third element of social status that demonstrates different impacts. Class can be a difficult aspect to measure or categorize, especially without any detailed evidence about income. However, in Moosonee as in other communities, the type of housing that people lived in was an indicator of class. The following description of housing demonstrates the class distinctions that existed in Moosonee. Wendy Thomas, a Department of Welfare worker, assessed housing in Moosonee during 1963.[124] She indicated that the town's homes tended to be "well-built and spacious" but that two-thirds of the village's homes, which were occupied by Indigenous people, were either "inadequate" or "unfit for human habitation."[125] A few years after the Thomas report, another provincial employee, J.K. McAully, provided housing excerpts from a land use planning report on Moosonee, which described the town's housing as "average" and the village's housing as "sub-minimal."[126] The combination of the Thomas and McAully reports provide a use beyond structural assessments. That is, the reports provide a picture of a divided community – Moosonee's town site versus the village. Residents of the town were perceived as primarily white and of a class that could afford reasonable housing while residents of the village were described primarily as Indigenous people who did not have decent housing.

Despite housing conditions, employment at the radar station crossed the boundary between the town site and the village and acted as an impetus for change. For example, Tom Archibald the first chairman of the Moosonee Townsite Development Board told the press in 1965 that he was a full-time employee at the radar station but that he lived in a "shack" in the village.[127] For civilian employees of the station, seeing a modern community at the station every day on the job meant that they knew change was possible, and they were not going to be content with living a substandard life. Most of the civilian employees hired at the radar station lived in town, but there were at least seven people employed from the village area.[128] Interviewees emphasized that civilian employees, from both the village and the town, wanted more of what they saw daily at the station, especially clean water, better roads, and adequate housing.

Although Moosonee's residents experienced change in diverse ways, they collaborated and spoke with "one voice" when it came to demanding improvements. First, the Moosonee Townsite Development Board has already been mentioned as one example of the shared purposes of people who were from distinct cultural and racial backgrounds. A second example of demanding change was the action sought by the first members of the MDAB in 1968. This new board was made up solely of provincial appointees who were male and primarily white (three out of five members were non-Indigenous). Three days after their first meeting, the MDAB told their provincial advisor that their top priority was to get clean water for people living south of Store Creek.[129] The members understood that people living south of the creek had not benefitted as much as town residents from employment and recreation at the radar station and from sewer and water construction. Thirdly, the formation of the Joint Closure Committee, which formulated the recommendations for transforming the radar station, bridged social differences to effect change. This committee was made up of both men and women who lived not only in various areas of Moosonee but also in other neighbouring communities, and who were "Treaty and Non-Treaty Indians, Metis and whites."[130] Not only did Moosonee's citizens bridge gender, race, and class differences but they also crossed geographic boundaries. Thus, the radar station initiated the creation of a powerful model of inclusive community change.

As we will see in the next chapter, the DEW Line radar development continued the processes of militarization and transformation of Indigenous lives. It also created environmental harms which in turn resulted in community activism.

NOTES

1 Memo by C.H. Kretch titled "Survey of Sanitary Conditions," in Moosonee: Original Sanitary Engineering Report. Division of Sanitary Engineering, Ontario Water Resources Commission. (OWRC), 18–19 June 1963, 6–7, Archives of Ontario (AO), RG 84-12, B355820.

2 As part of an air defence system to detect potential Soviet bombers, three radar lines were built in the Canadian north. The Pinetree Line was the most southerly one, the Mid-Canada line was north of it, and the DEW line was the farthest north.

3 This chapter refers to the Royal Canadian Air Force (RCAF) throughout as the themes cross back and forth over 1968 when Canada's Air Force, Army, and Navy were unified and became the Canadian Forces (CF). The RCAF station is therefore also referred to in later quotes as Canadian Forces Station (CFS) Moosonee.

4 Roy Fletcher, "Military Radar Defence Lines of Northern North America: An Historical Geography," *Polar Record* 26, no. 159 (1990): 265–76. Also see P. Whitney Lackenbauer, Matthew J. Farish, and Jennifer Arthur-Lackenbauer, *The Distant Early Warning (DEW) Line: A Bibliography and Documentary Resource List* (Calgary: Arctic Institute of North America, 2005); and P. Whitney Lackenbauer and Matthew Farish, "The Cold War on Canadian Soil: Militarizing a Northern Environment," *Environmental History* 12 (October 2007): 920–50. Also see P. Whitney Lackenbauer, "The Cold War at Cold Lake: The Primrose Lake Air Weapons Range, 1951–1965," in his *Battlegrounds: Canadian Military and Aboriginal Lands* (Vancouver: UBC Press, 2007), 144–75. Lackenbauer describes in detail how Indigenous groups and their traditional hunting and fishing territories were influenced by the creation of an immense Cold War air range in northern Alberta/Saskatchewan.

5 For an introduction to community planning see Jill Grant, "Planning Canadian Communities," in *A Reader in Canadian Planning: Linking Theory and Practice*, ed. Jill Grant (Toronto: Nelson Publishing, 2008); and Gerald Hodge and David Gordon, *Planning Canadian Communities: An Introduction to the Principles, Practice, and Participants* (Toronto: Thomson Nelson, 2008).

6 Test results for 27 January 1959 to 21 July 1959, OWRC, AO, RG 84-22, B120655, file Federal Government RCAF Station–Moosonee, 1958–65.

7 This research is based on archival materials and on interviews conducted primarily in 2013. Susan Heffernan, "Moosonee, Ontario: A Model of Cold War Change" (PhD diss., Laurentian University, 2016).

8 Memo from A.L.S. Nash, director Community Planning to Deputy Minister Cumming, Department of Municipal Affairs, 28 September 1960, AO, RG 19-77,

B388332, file 117.8 Moosonee 1960–63. Also see report by K.H. Sharpe, "Sanitary Conditions in Moosonee and Moose Factory," Sanitary Engineering Division, OWRC, 16 October 1961, AO, RG 19-77, B388332, file 117.8 Moosonee 1960–63. Note that references to "sanitation" throughout this chapter generally refer to sewage disposal.

9 Provincial government staff suggested that the townsite's population was between 330 and 400 people. For example, one health inspector wrote that there were 355 whites and 43 Indians in the town and about 700 Indians in the village in 1961. Memo from W.H. Oerton to W.G. Cooke, 23 June 1961, re Sanitary Survey Moosonee, AO, file: Townsite Committee Studies–Moosonee, RG-19-1, B113127. In her PhD diss., Dr Sheila Coté-Meek indicated that she used terms such as "Indian" where that term was used in quotations from archival literature. However, she used "mixed ancestry" rather than terms like Metis wherever possible. Coté-Meek also wrote that "despite the fact that some terms are considered dated I use them because they are used in the literature that I draw from." Sheila Coté-Meek, "Exploring the Impact of Ongoing Colonial Violence on Aboriginal Students in the Postsecondary Classroom" (PhD diss., University of Toronto, 2010).

10 Gwen Reimer and Jean-Phillippe Chartrand, *A Historical Profile of the James Bay Area's Mixed European-Indian or Mixed European-Inuit Community*, report prepared for Department of Justice Canada, 2005, http://www.metisnation.org/media/141039/dojreport (accessed 20 June 2013). See Heffernan, "Moosonee," chapter 4 for further discussion on the 1903 opening of the Revillon Frères trading post in Moosonee.

11 It is important to note that the 1961 Census Canada population of Moosonee included solely the townsite and the area just south of town known as the village. The census did not include any military personnel or families. Most RCAF personnel moved to Moosonee in 1962 and thus were missed by the previous year's census.

12 Heffernan, "Moosonee," chapter 7 includes a full discussion and documentation of provincial water and sewer reports retrieved from the Archives of Ontario.

13 Kretch, "Survey of Sanitary Conditions."

14 Lianne C. Leddy, *Serpent River Resurgence: Confronting Uranium Mining at Elliot Lake* (Toronto: University of Toronto Press, 2022).

15 Ibid., 96–7.

16 Ibid., 101–2. It took another decade for the effects of radioactive wastes to be confirmed for the SRFN. Serpent River First Nation had been forced to reach out to independent researchers and academics to confirm the health impacts of

the pollution of its lands and waters because government reports were either vague or ineffective.

17 Heffernan, "Moosonee," chapter 7.

18 Leddy, *Serpent River Resurgence*, 126–9. Chapter 6 describes how "community members grew weary of endless meetings and promises of studies."

19 Memo from W.H. Oerton to W.G. Cooke, 23 June 1961, re: Sanitary Survey Moosonee, in Townsite Committee Studies-Moosonee, AO, RG-19-1, B113127. Improvement districts had been used in Ontario between 1943 and the early 1990s to aid with a limited number of municipal services where resource towns had sprung up around resource activities such as mines. See Heffernan, "Moosonee," chapter 8.

20 Memo from L.K.W. Dorland, president, Cochrane Board of Trade to J.A. Kennedy, chairman, Ontario Municipal Board, 19 June 1962, AO, RG 19-43, B232755, Moosonee – Improvement District, 1962–63. The cover letter was prepared by the Cochrane Board of Trade, but the application was clearly from local residents. For example, the thirty-six petitioners who signed the application were from the community of Moosonee.

21 Report by Wendy Thomas, welfare development officer, 23 August 1963, AO, RG 29-01-1480, B334469, Department of Public Welfare (DPW), Deputy Minister's Files, File Indians–Moosonee, 1963–66. Although this labelling of individuals would be unacceptable today it is recorded here to indicate how provincial staff at the time identified the diversity of citizens demanding change in Moosonee.

22 Memo from H.C. Raiche, provincial health inspector to W.G. Cooke, chief health inspector, Department of Health, 7 October 1963, AO, file 117.9 Moosonee 1963–64.

23 The New Post band is now called Taykwa Tagamou First Nation. The two reserves for this First Nation are located southeast of the Town of Cochrane, Ontario.

24 The term "white status Indian" was not defined in any of the documents that used this term, but it appears to mean non-treaty Indian. This term was used in Moosonee's archival documents, but it was only clarified in one item. A list showing housing conditions was indexed as "T=Treaty Indian" and "N/T=White Status Indian" and appended to a report by Wendy Thomas, welfare development officer, 23 August 1963, AO, RG 29-01-1480, B334469, Department of Public Welfare (DPW), deputy minister's files, File Indians–Moosonee, 1963–66. The term "white status" could also have meant Indian women who had married non-Indigenous men and had lost Indian status, and it could mean the children from such marriages. This is suggested by the fact that the term "white status Indian" is applied in Raiche (above) to both men and women. An examination of Bill C-31, changes to the Indian Act, is beyond the scope of

this research. For an overview of women and Indian status, see Olive Dickason, *A Concise History of Canada's First Nations* (Toronto: Oxford University Press, 2006), 303–5.

25 Memo from Dick Knowles to the minister of Municipal Affairs, 2 November 1967, AO, RG 19-6-1, file 19-47-1, B269789, Cochrane District, Moosonee Townsite Gen (KF).

26 Memo from J.M. Dufour, Department of Public Welfare (DPW) to J.S. Band, deputy minister, Department of Social and Family Services, 18 December 1967, AO, RG 29-01-1481, B430939, file Indians–Moosonee, 1967–70. The 3 August 1967 petition for a reserve is attached to this correspondence.

27 Departmental memorandum from R. Rivard, Department of Social and Family Services (DSFS) to C.J. Williams, DSFS, 24 November 1967, AO, RG 19-F-7, file General Administration: Moosonee Development Board. Attawapiskat and Fort Albany are now referred to as First Nations.

28 Memo from J.M. Dufour, Department of Public Welfare (DPW) to J.S. Band, deputy minister, Department of Social and Family Services, 18 December 1967. AO, RG 29-01-1481, B430939, file Indians–Moosonee, 1967–70. The petitioners also indicated that their home reserves (Attawapiskat and Fort Albany) had not been adequately compensated by Treaty Number 9. However, their main concern was inadequate services.

29 Memo from Minister Rene Brunelle to Minister John Yaremko, minister of Social and Family Services, 22 December 1967, AO, RG 29-01-1481, B430939, file Indians–Moosonee 1967–70.

30 The MDAB became a municipality in 2001 and is now known as the Town of Moosonee.

31 Handwritten notes labelled "Moosonee Municipal Board" provided by MPP Rene Brunelle to Minister Spooner, without a cover letter, stamped as received 23 November 1966 by Department of Municipal Affairs, AO, RG 19-77, B388332, file 118.3, Moosonee 1966. Also see memo from Dick Knowles to Minister Darcy McKeough, 21 February 1968 (Dick Knowles was the president of the Chamber of Commerce who provided the list of nominations from a public meeting held in Moosonee), AO, RG-6-1, B269790, file Cochrane District–Moosonee Townsite.

32 Heffernan, "Moosonee," chapter 8.

33 Maude Tyrer and Dorothy Wynne were nominated in 1968 for the first Moosonee Development Area Board. Both women were eventually appointed to the MDAB, starting with Maude as the first woman on the board in 1973. These women have served on numerous public boards and have been models of local involvement.

34 Briefing note for Darcy McKeough, 18 August 1968. David Wynne was shown in the archival documents as a store owner and resident of the townsite and Xavier Wesley was shown as employed in town but residing in the village. Both men were shown as treaty Indians in the minister's briefing material used for the MDAB's inaugural meeting. David Wynne had been nominated by the local MPP Rene Brunelle and Xavier Wesley had been nominated by the public at a February 1968 public meeting. AO, RG 19-6-1, B269789, file 19-47-1 Cochrane District–Moosonee Townsite General KF.

35 Heffernan, "Moosonee," chapter 7.

36 Ibid., chapter 8.

37 Statement by the minister of National Defence, 16 January 1975. Directorate of History and Heritage (DHH), Permanent Reference File (PRF) Moosonee CFS.

38 Telex from the minister of Defence, Ottawa to CFS Val D'or and CFS Moosonee, 16 January 1975. The telex was marked "Priority, Confidential, and Exclusive." It included parts of the minister's closure announcement. Library and Archives Canada (LAC), RG24, Series G-16-1, Vol 23534, file 1901–1, part 1. Moosonee: Organization–General, 1965/02–1975/01.

39 Paul Ozorak, "Remembering Pinetree," http://67.69.104.76:84/Pinetreeline/articles (accessed 9 September 2013). Also see Fletcher, "Military Radar Defence Lines of Northern North America: An Historical Geography."

40 Len Gillis, "Defence Budget Cuts Killing CFS Moosonee," *Timmins Daily Press*, 18 January 1975. AO, RG 68-9, B503347, Northern Affairs Branch, Director's Files, *Moosonee Vol. 3*. Although the material is from the *Timmins Daily Press*, it was located in Ministry of Northern Affairs' files.

41 Gillis, "Defence Budget Cuts Killing CFS Moosonee," Northern Affairs Branch, *Moosonee Vol. 3*.

42 "Moosonee Base Closing Opposed by Civilians," *Timmins Daily Press*, 21 January 1975. AO, RG 68-9, B503347, Northern Affairs Branch, Director's Files, *Moosonee Vol. 2*. (Note: Newspaper articles were not found in chronological order in the files, hence the later date – 21 January in an earlier volume – volume 2).

43 "Moosonee Troubles Spotlighted," *Timmins Daily Press*, 28 January 1975. Northern Affairs Branch, *Moosonee Vol. 3*.

44 Stef Donev, "Moosonee 'Coming to a Stop' with Loss of Radar Base Jobs," *Toronto Star*, 13 March 1975. AO, RG 64-8, B217371, Provincial Secretariat for Justice files, file The North: Moosonee Base Closure.

45 Don Gauthier, "Moosonee Military Base Winds Down to a Ghostly Stillness," *North Bay Nugget*, 20 June 1975, AO, Northern Affairs Branch, *Moosonee Vol. 3*.

46 Gillis, "Defence Budget Cuts Killing CFS Moosonee," Northern Affairs Branch, *Moosonee Vol. 3*.

47 "Moosonee Base Closing Opposed by Civilians," Northern Affairs Branch, *Moosonee Vol. 2*. The press described Ken Sweigard as both the union president and the Pentecostal minister for Moosonee. Claudia Milne notes that Sweigard was a member of the MDAB from March 1973 to the end of 1974. See Claudia Milne, "Access and Services in Local Government: A Case Study of Moosonee, Ontario" (master's thesis, University of Waterloo, 1974), 111.

48 "Moosonee Base Closing Opposed by Civilians," Northern Affairs Branch, *Moosonee Vol. 2*.

49 Ibid.

50 Ibid. Also see Letter from Ken Sweigard to the editor of *Moosetalk*, the local Moosonee newspaper, January 1975. (Note: *Moosetalk* editions were dated solely by month, not by specific dates as the paper was only published every month or two.) AO, Northern Affairs Branch files, *Moosonee Vol. 2*.

51 "MDAB To Discuss Effects," *Timmins Daily Press*, 21 January 1975. Northern Affairs Branch, *Moosonee Vol. 2*.

52 Ibid.

53 Ibid. In the 21 January 1975 news article, Pringle indicated that the radar station supplied one-fifth of the total hydro-electric supply to Moosonee (ONR supplied the remainder).

54 "Moosonee Troubles Spotlighted," Northern Affairs Branch, *Moosonee Vol. 3*.

55 "M.D.A.B. Report," *Moosetalk,* February, 1975, AO, Northern Affairs Branch, *Moosonee Vol. 3*. The local newspaper *Moosetalk* indicated that the MDAB "recognized that it had a responsibility to assume a leadership role in looking after the Community's best interests ... It called a public meeting on January 28th at which the Board was, in effect, given a mandate to represent the people in Moosonee."

56 Ibid. The Joint Closure Committee (hereafter the Closure Committee) was formed on 3 February 1975.

57 Moose Band Council, now called Moose Cree First Nation, operates out of Moose Factory Island (see figure 2.1).

58 "Base Committee Takes Proposals to Queen's Park," *Moosetalk*, March, 1975. Northern Affairs Branch, *Moosonee Vol. 3*.

59 Cabinet Submission on Moosonee Area, 25 June 1975, 5. AO, RG 1-121, B207227, Ministry of Natural Resources, file: "Lands-Status Report to the Cabinet Committee on Resources Development (CCRD) on the Moosonee Area, 1975."

60 Moose Band Council is now called Moose Cree First Nation and is situated on Moose Factory Island. Other members of the MDAB who sat on the closure committee were Andrew Wesley, Bert Trapper, and Homer Brooks.

61 Memo from G.H.U. Bayly, secretariat for Resources Development, to all Ontario deputy ministers re: Canadian Forces Station–Moosonee, 9 April 1975.

The Report of [the] Joint Committee re: Closure of Canadian Forces Station – Moosonee (hereafter the *Closure Report*) was included as an attachment to Bayly's letter and dated March 1975. The reference above to "instructing their secretary, etc" is on page 2 of the *Closure Report*. The *Closure Report* was located in an MOE file because the deputy minister of MOE was a recipient of the report, not because it was circulated by that ministry. AO, RG 12-45, 762-2, B126157, correspondence of the Minister and Deputy Minister of Environment, file: Moosonee 1975.

62 "Moosonee Station: School is Perfect Idea," *Timmins Daily Press*, 1 February 1975. Northern Affairs Branch, *Moosonee Vol. 2*.

63 Ibid.

64 Donev, "Moosonee 'Coming to a Stop' with Loss of Radar Base Jobs," Provincial Secretariat for Justice files, file The North: Moosonee Base Closure.

65 *Closure Report*, correspondence of the Minister and Deputy Minister of Environment, AO, RG 12-45, 762-2, B126157, file: Moosonee 1975.

66 *Closure Rep*ort, 1. Emphasis mine.

67 See also the lack of public input to infrastructure projects and to formation of the MDAB in Heffernan, "Moosonee," chapters 7 and 8.

68 *Closure Report*, 2.

69 *Closure Report*, 3.

70 Ibid., 4.

71 Ibid., 8.

72 *Moosetalk* articles, "A High School Now!" and "Let's Give It Some Thought," and *Moosetalk* editorial, "Dribs and Drabs." In AO, RG 68-9, B503347, Northern Affairs Branch, Director's Files, *Moosonee Vol. 1*, April 1975.

73 Lands-Status Report to the Cabinet Committee on Resources Development (CCRD) on the Moosonee Area, 1975, 7.

74 Ibid.

75 *Closure Report*, 4.

76 Ibid.

77 Ibid., 9. The reference to high servicing costs would have referred primarily to water and sewer service costs in the townsite of Moosonee and in the area south of Store Creek.

78 Editorial, "Dribs and Drabs," *Moosetalk*, April 1975. Northern Affairs Branch, *Moosonee Vol. 1*.

79 See the Facebook group site: "Canadian Aircraft Control and Warning (AC&W), Pinetree, MCL (Mid-Canada line), DEW and Radar Sites, RCAF." This site has daily to weekly posts from former service people and from others who were civilian employees and/or residents of radar stations. The Facebook posts on this site consistently note fond memories of postings at radar stations.

80 P.C. Kvas, *Lobster, Lighthouse and Long-Range Radar* (Barrington: Canadian Forces Station Barrington, 1987).

81 CFS Moosonee Contingency Plan, 1 April 1975. LAC, Department of National Defence, Air Defence Command Headquarters, Hornell Heights, Ontario [North Bay], "Moosonee: Organization–General, 1965/02-1975/01," RG 24, Series G-16-1, Vol. 23534, file 1901-1. part 1.

82 Ibid.

83 Ibid.

84 Don Gauthier, "Moosonee Military Base Winds Down to a Ghostly Stillness," *North Bay Nugget*, 20 June 1975. AO, Northern Affairs Branch, M*oosonee Vol. 3*. Note that the reporter's reference to the Canex as the base shopping centre was somewhat exaggerated. Interviewees indicated that the Canex was a grocery store. The reporter also noted that the chapel had closed. It was dismantled and moved to Kashetchewan during the winter of 1975–76. Information on the chapel was supplied by retired Archbishop John R. Clarke in response to my blog post on Moosonee (see http://niche-canada.org/2013/11/03/the-cold-war-in-the-near-north-moosonee-and-the-pinetree-radar-line).

85 Memo from D.F. Taylor, executive director, Local Government Services Division, Ministry of Treasury, Economics and Intergovernmental Affairs to Rose O'Regan, executive officer, Office of the premier, re: Fifth Estate–CBC–Moosonee, 15 March 1976. AO, Premier W. Davis Correspondence, RG 3-57, B239657, file: Moosonee Base Closing, 1976.

86 Premier W. Davis Correspondence, file: Moosonee Base Closing, 1976. This file contains seventeen letters written to the premier, mainly by residents living outside of Moosonee and in southern Ontario. Most of the letters were written on the same day as the *Fifth Estate* program (24 February 1976). Some dates had been redacted.

87 Ibid.

88 Ibid.

89 Ibid.

90 Ibid.

91 Ibid.

92 Ibid.

93 Ibid.

94 Form letter from Premier Davis responding to individuals re: "The Fifth Estate" program, 31 March 1976. The premier also indicated that the Ontario Housing Corporation had built sixty-eight homes "for Indians and Metis in Moosonee over the past few years." Premier Davis Correspondence, Moosonee Base Closing, 1976.

95 Memo from D.R. Irving, provincial secretary to W. Darcy McKeough, treasurer of Ontario, 29 April 1976. Premier Davis Correspondence, Moosonee Base Closing, 1976.

96 Memo from K.J. Scully, supervisor, Northern Affairs Branch, Northern Regional Office, Ministry of Natural Resources to R.V. Scott, director, Northern Affairs Branch, 27 April 1976. AO, RG 68-9, B503347, Northern Affairs Branch, Director's Files, *Moosonee Vol. 4*.

97 Ibid.

98 Memo from James Auld, Management Board of Cabinet to Tom Wells, minister of Education, 19 July 1976. AO, RG 2-152, B202730, minister of Education Correspondence. file: minister's meeting re: Moosonee Education Facilities, 1976.

99 Ibid.

100 Ibid.

101 Interviews, 2013. This information is quoted from an interview so the term "base" is used rather than "station" since this was the term used by the interviewee.

102 Wayne Caldwell, Paul Kraehling, and Suzanna Kaptur, "A Healthy Rural Community Tool Kit," *Municipal World* 125, no. 9 (2015), 30.

103 Ibid.

104 A few interviewees wondered what had happened to diesel fuel drums and to generators, which would have contained PCBs. This study did not yield any files indicating if burial of hazardous wastes occurred when the Moosonee station closed. The federal government did, however, clean up the diesel fuel site at the station in the early 1990s. I toured the diesel fuel site with federal government staff in the 1990s and they showed me the observation points that remained at the diesel fuel site for monitoring the cleanup that had occurred.

105 Joan Wallach Scott, "Gender: A Useful Category of Historical Analysis," *American Historical Review* 91, no. 5 (1986): 1069.

106 Joy Parr, "Gender History and Historical Practice," *Canadian Historical Review* 76, no. 3 (1995): 363. Also see Beverly Leipert and Linda Reutter, "Women's Health in Northern British Columbia: The Role of Geography and Gender," *Canadian Journal of Rural Medicine* 10 (2005): 241–53 on the role of women in northern resource towns.

107 Joy Parr, *The Gender of Breadwinners: Women, Men, and Change in Two Industrial Towns, 1880–1930* (Toronto: University of Toronto Press, 1990), 230.

108 Ibid. Although Parr's work on Paris and Hanover examined the period prior to the Cold War, her comments about women being "considered" rather than being "consulted" are applicable to Moosonee during the Cold War.

109 Ruth Roach Pierson, *"They're Still Women After All": The Second World War and Canadian Womanhood* (Toronto: McClelland & Stewart, 1986); Doug Owram, *Born at the Right Time: A History of the Baby Boom Generation* (Toronto: University of Toronto Press, 1996).

110 Pierson, *"They're Still Women After All,"* 215–20.

111 Owram, *Born at the Right Time*, 22.

112 Pierson, *"They're Still Women After All,"* 215. Pierson indicates that postwar Canada was an era of "male primacy" both in the economic sphere and in decision making roles.

113 Heffernan, "Moosonee," chapter 8 reviews the Moosonee Community Council Steering Committee, a ratepayers group formed shortly after the MDAB began. This chapter also describes the role of the homemaker's clubs in Ontario and in Moosonee.

114 Memo from Mrs Kenneth Wynne and Mrs Ellen Morrison, to Don Taylor, Community Planning Branch, Department of Municipal Affairs, 17 January 1968. OA, RG 19-77, B354517, file 118.5 Moosonee 1967–68.

115 Heffernan, "Moosonee," chapter 6 discusses that it is difficult to tell how many women benefitted from civilian jobs or what type of work they did at the radar station. Also see Jennifer Blythe and Peggy Martin-McGuire, "Changing Employment of Cree Women in Moosonee and Moose Factory," in *Women of the First Nations: Power, Wisdom and Strength*, ed. Christine Miller and Patricia Chuchryk (Winnipeg: University of Manitoba Press, 1996), 134. The authors interviewed 246 women as part of a research project on women and work in 1984 in Moosonee and Moose Factory. The only reference to employment on Moosonee radar station was "In the 1950's, work associated with a Canadian Forces base and the DEW Line early-warning radar system became available for Cree men in Moosonee. A few of their wives also found employment as the town grew." Also see Jennifer M. Blythe, Peggy Martin Brizinski, and Sarah Preston, *"I was Never Idle": Women and Work in Moosonee and Moose Factory*, TASO Report No. 21 (Hamilton: McMaster University, 1985).

116 Leddy, *Serpent River Resurgence*, 119.

117 Heffernan, "Moosonee," see chapter 6 for a further description of family life on the radar station.

118 The annual historical reports (AHRs) for the Moosonee Station had sections for men and women with four categories for each gender: Officers, Warrant Officers, Non-Commissioned Officers, and Airmen/Airwomen. On average there were 145 service personnel at the station. For the years 1964–69 the AHRs show one woman per year in the airwomen category. Canadian Forces Museum of Aerospace Defence (CFMAD), North Bay, Ontario. *Annual Historical Reports* (hereafter AHRs) *for Moosonee RCAF Airbase*, 1961–75. It is important to note that

the years 1970–72 are missing from these reports. Directorate of History and Heritage (DHH) files also included the AHRs, and they were helpful in filling in missing pages but did not yield the 1970–72 reports.

119 AO, RG 29-01-1480, B334469, Department of Public Welfare (DPW), Deputy Minister's files, file: "Indians–Moosonee, 1963–66," report by Wendy Thomas, welfare development officer, 23 August 1963. AO, "General Admin., Moosonee Development Board," RG19-F-7, B350920, R.A. Rivard, regional administrator, DSF to C.J. Williams, executive officer, DSFS, 24 November 1967.

120 Claudia Milne, "Access and Services in Local Government: A Case Study of Moosonee, Ontario" (master's thesis, University of Waterloo, 1974), 109.

121 Memo from Peter Szego, director, Indian Community Development Services Branch to Deputy Minister Borczak "Re-Tents in Moosonee," 11 February 1970. AO, RG 29-01-1481, B430939, Department of Social and Family Services, Deputy Minister's Files, file: "Indians–Moosonee, 1967–70." This file also contained the following news clip: Anne Moon, "'Keep Moosonee Clean' but Nobody Collects the Indians' Garbage," *Toronto Star*, 16 June 1969. See also: Nigel Dunn, "Place of Hidden Beauty: Moosonee's Worth Impresses Those with the Right Eyes," *Toronto Daily Star*, 11 August 1960, and "2 Children Die in Shack Fire at Moosonee," *Globe and Mail*, 12 December 1963. AO, RG9-1, B113127, Townsite Committee Studies–Moosonee.

122 Heffernan, "Moosonee," chapter 8 provides further information on the role of Tom Archibald as chairman of the Moosonee Townsite Development Board and Ellen Morrison and Dorothy Wynne as members of the homemakers club. See in particular: Memo from Mrs Ellen Morrison, Homemakers Club to Minister J. Yaremko, Department of Social and Family Services, 19 June 1969, AO, RG 19-77, B354517, file 119.5, Moosonee 1969 and memo from A.J. Elie, Senior Planner, Community Planning Branch, Department of Municipal Affairs to Don Taylor, Director and Supervisor, Official Plans Section, Community Planning Branch, 6 June 1969, AO, RG 19-77, B354517, file 119.4, Moosonee 1969. Elie stated that the "homemaker club" was "composed of many vocal Indian women in the community." Chapter 8 also includes a discussion on Maude Tyrer, an Indigenous resident, who was the first woman appointed to the MDAB. For a broader perspective on Indigenous lobbying during the 1960s, see Bryan Palmer, "The 'Discovery' of the 'Indian'" in his *Canada's 1960's: The Ironies of Identity in a Rebellious Era* (Toronto: University of Toronto Press, 2009).

123 Interviews, 2013.

124 Report by Wendy Thomas, welfare development officer, 23 August 1963. file: "Indians–Moosonee, 1963–66."

125 Ibid. Thomas indicated that "inadequate" meant that houses were too small or had "unstable construction." The "unfit for human habitation" structures were

shacks with tarpaper or canvas roofing and they were uninsulated. Another report, issued in 1967 by the Department of Social and Family Services (DSFS), indicated that eleven homes south of Store Creek were "tent shacks, having wood frame walls and a canvas roof." See R.A. Rivard, regional administrator, DSFS, to C. Williams, executive officer, DSFS, AO, RG19-F-7, B350920, file General Admin., Moosonee Development Board, 24 November 1967.

126 Memo from J.K. McAully, senior accounting advisor, Department of Municipal Affairs to R.J. Watson, director, Municipal Accounting Branch, re: Townsite of Moosonee Proposed Water and Sewage Program, 30 May 1966, AO, RG19-F-7, file General Admin., Moosonee Development Board. McAully's housing material was extracted from *Moosonee, A Community Development Plan*, April 1964, by Project Planning Associates, a Toronto planning firm. The original 1964 planning report could not be accessed from the Ontario Archives, despite repeated searches.

127 Bob Pennington, "Why Indians Smash So Many Windows," *The Telegram*, 15 February 1965, 8. AO, file 118.3, Moosonee 1966.

128 R.A. Rivard to C. Williams, file General Admin., Moosonee Development Board, 24 November 1967. The RCAF employment number for south of Store Creek was derived from charts and a map attached to this correspondence. There was no map for the area north of Store Creek; that is, for the main townsite.

129 Heffernan, "Moosonee," chapter 7. Also see memo from F.A. Braybrook to Deputy Minister Palmer, re: "Report on the Organization of the Moosonee Development Area Board – Current Administrative and Other Matters Affecting the Board," 9 September 1968, AO, RG19-77, B354517. file 119.2, Moosonee 1968. Although the report was dated 9 September, Braybrook wrote that he toured the village with the new MDAB members 30 August, two days after their inaugural meeting. Board members told Braybrook they wanted immediate action on services for the village.

130 Cabinet submission on Moosonee Area, 25 June 1975, 5. AO, RG 1-121, B207227, Ministry of Natural Resources, file: "Lands-Status Report to the Cabinet Committee on Resources Development (CCRD) on the Moosonee Area."

3

Voices from the DEW Line

STACEY FRITZ AND ISABEL CAMPBELL

Mary Ann Warden, an elder, who experienced DEW Line construction as a child on Barter Island, Alaska, said, "Wow. DEW Lines! There were that many? Wow. That is so amazing. Well, I knew there were some along the coast, but I never saw them this way," when interviewed years later. Another elder, Nora Jane Burns, reacted to a map of all sixty-three sites as follows: "Holy cow! They went all over. That's a lot. And that was for their radar, huh? It's surprising because when you are growing up you think that that was the only site and then later you hear there's some to the east and some to the west and when you go to Barrow you find out they have one too."[1]

As the quotes above reveal, the DEW Line crossed the American and Canadian north, continuing the processes of colonization and militarization begun centuries before. Work on the DEW Line stations transformed the lives of many Inuit, First Nations, and other workers and their families. As this chapter will show, while some, like Elmer Sinclair in chapter 1, or the Cree workers in Moosonee in chapter 2, welcomed better paying jobs and opportunities to learn new skills, many also mourned the losses of traditional lifestyles and practices.

3.1 AVGAS station bar, 1956.

3.2 POW-1, undated.

This chapter explores how the construction of Distant Early Warning (DEW) Line radar stations and Cold War ideologies affected labourers, their families, and their communities in the western Arctic. During the 1950s, the American military and its contractors built sixty-three radar sites, while the Canadian government encouraged Indigenous Peoples of the area to adopt southern concepts of citizenship.[2] This new policy marked the gradual acceptance of Canadian responsibility for the welfare of northern Indigenous residents after a long period of non-interference. Ideological conflicts within the government and with the American military contractors complicated these efforts. Indigenous residents were glad for the jobs and other amenities the DEW Line brought, but the environmental damage left by the radar sites on their homelands left many feeling they were not, in fact, considered full citizens.

The DEW Line was a unified system with standardized structures, spaced at roughly fifty-mile intervals, spanning the entire northern coast of North America. Although the DEW Line's infrastructure was homogenous, the unique historical context of each region, a radar facility's specific location relative to a community, and the different personalities of station chiefs resulted in diverse effects for people living near different stations. Individual attitudes towards the new industrial military developments were also shaped by people's age, gender, life experiences, personality, and worldview. An Indigenous Second World War veteran who had travelled the world and experienced combat, for example, would have different perspectives on a radar station built in his home village than would a young woman who had lived there her whole life.

To learn about DEW Line legacies, Stacey Fritz, the primary author of this chapter, interviewed people in numerous communities near stations over the course of several years and spent two summers sailing and paddling a canoe through the western Arctic to numerous remote sites. She listened to people's life experiences with the radar stations, the DEW Line's influences on economic systems, gender and race relations, effects from the importation of alcohol, and how land use and contamination gave rise to a regional consciousness of environmental justice. She explored how American and Canadian leaders during the

Cold War used authority, fear, and patriotism to gain the cooperation of northern citizens.[3]

Most people in the western Arctic became familiar with the radar sites in their own regions, but at the beginning of these interviews, few seemed aware of the monolithic nature of the early warning line or its exact purpose, which was to detect incoming Soviet airplanes that could be armed with nuclear weapons early enough for the joint US/Canadian North American Air Defense Command (NORAD) to scramble jets and defense missiles to defend the continent.[4] As participants heard more about the DEW Line during the interviews, they expressed their surprise.

When the Arctic emerged as a frontline for continental defence after the Second World War, military activity transformed large areas of people's homelands and had serious economic and environmental consequences which were not immediately evident. The Cold War boom and the concurrent secularization of social services dismantled the balance of power in the region among traders, missionaries, and the government. Socioeconomic connections among Indigenous Peoples and southern missionaries and traders eroded while new relationships with the national government emerged. At the height of this transformative period with the rapid construction of the DEW Line, federal officials grappled with their plans and visions about what kind of Canadian citizen an Arctic Indigenous people should be. Some feared that the DEW Line would destroy the Indigenous way of life, while others *hoped* the new development would transform the Indigenous way of life into something that resembled a more southern and financially self-reliant Canadian lifestyle.

Boom and bust economic cycles had buffeted the western Arctic since Yankee whalers came north in the 1880s. When ships ventured into the Beaufort Sea, they transformed Herschel Island into a major over-wintering whaling station. Whalers employed Inuit crews on a seasonal basis and traded for fresh meat during winter, cementing trade for modern goods as a fundamental part of the local economy. Whalers also brought alcohol, disease, and diversity, spurring local missionaries to send sensationalized reports of depravity to the government which then established a small Royal Canadian Mounted Police detachment on Herschel Island.[5] Petroleum eventually reduced demand for whale oil and the ships were largely gone by 1920 but not before commercial whaling depleted the populations of bowhead whales and walrus in the region and led to widespread starvation.

As whaling waned, the Hudson Bay Company (HBC) and its competitors pushed into the Mackenzie River Delta and established the trapping/trading system in the region. HBC dominated the western Arctic economy for the next three decades as more people began to settle around trading posts. There, success in the fur trade created new social mobility and the best hunters often became the best trappers and were able to purchase more and better equipment. The HBC began grubstaking trappers before the season began, introducing a credit and debt system that pumped up furs and profit. Then, Indigenous residents, traders, missionaries, and the government wrestled with the problems of dependence and relief.[6]

Roman Catholic and Anglican missions competed over Indigenous souls and established their own supply depots, competing with the HBC by underselling them. Missions also extended into areas rich with potential converts and often became the sole source for goods and other services. While churches were coaxing people to settle around missions so as to attend church and school and fur traders were coercing people to move towards game and trading posts, the RCMP and northern administrators were trying to persuade people to return to the land and subsist independently.

A 1939 Supreme Court decision (*Re: Eskimos*) established that the Canadian federal government was responsible for Inuit, but the government maintained a policy of laissez-faire economics and a "hands-off" strategy in the north until the mid-1940s. When several trading posts and missions failed, officials were forced to establish rudimentary relief distribution systems. While some authorities believed that welfare was shameful and should only be administered when starvation was imminent, others argued that delivering aid to Inuit would be evidence of legitimate sovereignty[7] in the increasingly geopolitically strategic Arctic. The government began portraying its northerly holdings as a key to prosperity and a dominant force in the Canadian psyche just as a crash in fur prices left the region ready for the next economic boom, which came with fast-paced, wage-based industrial construction jobs on the DEW Line.

Most people living around Canada's Mackenzie Delta region (predominantly Inuvialuit [Inuit] and Gwich'in Athabaskan) were familiar with traditional regional Indigenous conflicts and the Second World War military presence, but Richard Gordon of Inuvik said modern warfare was a foreign concept to them: "We knew nothing about what w-a-r meant ... Somebody tells you a bushman is coming for you ... We didn't know we had a part in this whole thing." Gordon wondered how his grandfather had felt when strangers came to the door to hand off a rifle and warn him to put his seal oil light out at night. "Spy!" he whispered. "Watch out for the bushman, like the boogie man, going to get you!"[8]

Over the border in Alaska Territory during the Second World War, people were ready to travel east into Canada at a moment's notice in case the Japanese should invade. Dog sleds were kept packed and ready on Barter Island, less than one hundred miles from the border where the village of Kaktovik is located, and several families relocated to Herschel Island where their relatives may have lived during the height of whaling. The war caused upheavals in many regions of the territory as new military facilities restricted people's movements and activities, including commandeering reindeer herds from their owners. War created almost unlimited opportunities for wage employment and booming markets for carvings and fur clothing. Whereas local ecological conditions had restricted the size of settlements around missions, schools, and trading posts,[9] the military created urban hub communities and outlying smaller villages shrank when waves of people migrated. Reports noted that locals made good labourers, faced hardships cheerfully, and often acquired plumbing, carpentry, engine repair, and machinery operation skills when working at military stations. Regular work and good pay raised people's economic status vis-à-vis southerners, their health often improved with the abundant diet, and medical care helped check the spread of tuberculosis and other diseases.[10]

The wartime collapse of the fur industry was particularly difficult for people in the western Arctic who were habituated to a mixed-cash economy. Liberal government ideologies, infused with post-war humanitarian intent and espousing "compassionate interference," proposed to help Inuit readjust and regain independence. In 1953, the Department of Northern Affairs and Natural Resources (hereafter: Northern Affairs) was established to study and regulate all aspects of the north. Northern Affairs official J.W. Burton expressed the department's main goals: "The Department of Resources and Development is by no means satisfied that this group of Canadian peoples should remain at their present standard of economy. An active and continuing study of ways and means of improving the Eskimo's welfare and economy is well in hand and all practices and projects which are considered to be of value in raising the standard of the Eskimo economy are given a high priority."[11] Burton exemplified the post-war, reform-minded thinking that advocated that Inuit were full Canadian citizens due the same opportunities and rewards as every citizen and that ushered in a wide-ranging, ambitious plan for the "civilization" of the Arctic.

Northern Affairs created a new category of civil servant, Northern Service Officers (NSOs), to facilitate communications among construction crews, government agencies, and Indigenous people. NSOs were to protect Indigenous interests, encourage Inuit participation in local government, and prevent difficulties that could slow the pace of construction.

Northern Affairs, sensitive to criticism after international media relayed a sensationalized story about Inuit starving to death, published images of happy, healthy Inuit who prospered under fair governmental policies. The department established an Eskimo Research Section to investigate means of educating Inuit and helping them adapt to changing economic conditions by improving hunting and fishing techniques, encouraging greater use of local food resources, and promoting handicraft manufacturing, whaling, cod fishing, eiderdown gathering, and boat building.[12] The Eskimo Research Section also planned relocations of Inuit from overpopulated and depleted areas to regions where game was more plentiful or where employment could be found. Relocation projects were also used as strategic sovereignty movements to cement Canadian ownership of the High Arctic.[13]

As Northern Affairs officials considered which aspects of Indigenous culture to preserve, what changes industrialization might bring, and whether they should relocate people to subsist off the land or to find jobs, American crews were surveying the western Arctic for DEW Line locations. The United States Air Force contracted Bell Systems for the project, which gave responsibility for design and construction to its subsidiary Western Electric Corporation.[14]

In 1954, Deputy Minister of Northern Affairs Gordon Robertson hoped northern construction projects would employ as many locals as possible. The population was steadily increasing, the fur market had crashed, and using local labour cut relief payments. Yet Northern Affairs preferred a more northern route for the DEW Line because "a more southern route would pass through an area where there were many Eskimo who were not adjusted to contact with modern civilization."[15] Northern administrators insisted that

> Where primitive Eskimos in remote areas are relatively free from contact with white civilization, it is planned to leave their present economy as undisturbed as possible. In those areas where there is already permanent contact, integration with the white economy will be encouraged. Between these two extremes employment of Eskimo will be encouraged provided it does not interfere unduly with their normal life. It is also planned to diversify the Eskimo economy and to transfer families from unproductive areas to regions where game is more abundant, or employment is available.[16]

Instead, surveyors and defence planners chose locations based on geography, logistics, and defence strategy and built the first, five-station prototypical sector of the line at fifty-mile intervals running from Barter Island in Alaska Territory to Atkinson Point in the Northwest Territories. Officially, Inuit were not to be troubled by the military or construction companies, and a DEW Line agreement signed by Canada and the United States in 1955 was explicit: "The Eskimos of Canada are in a primitive state of social development. It is important that these people be not subjected unduly to disruption of their hunting economy ... or other effects of the presence of white men which might be injurious to them."[17] The treaty established six comprehensive conditions to govern contact with Inuit under which the government accepted responsibility for managing all aspects of relations between Indigenous residents and the DEW Line. To succeed in building the entire DEW Line within the ambitious time frame, construction firms across the entire Arctic coast hired virtually any Inuit who asked for work and, according to one long-time Arctic contractor, they never could have built it without them.[18]

The five-station prototype system in the western Arctic was built and tested before the treaty was written, but in that region, officials preferred new employment opportunities for those already integrated into the cash economy and hardest hit by the collapse of the fur trade. The DEW Line's path through the region missed the settlements of Herschel Island and Aklavik, but the development was still disruptive to those communities. Instead of jobs coming to people where they lived, people left their families and followed the work. In other cases, especially towards the eastern side of the delta, men brought their families to the radar sites, set up camp, and found themselves in inhospitable areas that were often characterized by inclement weather and scarce wildlife, firewood, and other resources.[19]

Once construction began, prospects for wage employment at DEW Line sites made news throughout the region. Only two months after the arrival of the work crew at Komakuk Beach, Yukon, the air was full of rumours 250 kilometres away in Aklavik. Robert Alexie, a Gwich'in Athabaskan of Aklavik and Fort McPherson, remembered it was "[B]ig news! Lotsa money!" After the spring muskrat trapping season, numerous Aklavik residents headed to the coast to see what was available and the sites absorbed almost all who wanted to work. "Sixteen dollars a day!" Alexie exclaimed. "Ten hours! Good money!" He recalled that electricians made $2.85 per hour and, as a carpenter's helper, he made $2.50. In 2008, Alexie still had the gun he bought with his DEW Line wages back in 1957. Despite the good money, Robert Alexie did not envy the few local people who stayed to work permanently on the DEW Line. "They just stuck at that job. That's what they say: once people start working there they are not a hunter anymore." Alexie laughed when he recalled a headline that appeared in the local paper: "Eskimos are joining the DEW Line, throwing their harpoons away."[20]

In 1956, Northern Affairs accepted anthropology graduate student Jack Ferguson's proposal to investigate how the DEW Line sites were influencing the Inuvialuit. Ferguson spent the summer of 1956 in the western Arctic and returned to Tuktoyaktuk in 1957 to observe how the community was adapting. Administrators were keenly interested in Ferguson's letters and reports, which relayed valuable details and non-governmental perspectives. Other archival material, primarily reports from game wardens stationed in the region at the time and correspondence among government officials in Ottawa, further illustrate the challenges they had in shaping new Arctic citizens.

Some hoped that DEW Line wages would be a panacea that would save Inuit from desperate subsistence lifestyles. Canadian game warden Rees reported from the delta region in March 1955: "[T]he fact the natives at Tuk are showing more interest in the prospect of working on the Dew [*sic*] Line demonstrates they are well into the transitional stage between being straight hunters and casual labourers. It has always been difficult to get these people to work in the settlement, but the DEW Line may prove the turning point."[21]

At the other extreme, some saw the influx of money and employment leading to significant social disruption that would bring about the death of Indigenous culture. What Game Warden Rees hoped would be the "turning point," Ferguson, the anthropologist, called "the last nail in the coffin." Ferguson warned the government that Inuit living near DEW Line sites were "on the threshold of a radical change in both their means of livelihood and their basic culture." Ignoring the dynamic nature of culture, Ferguson wrote that except for Tuktoyaktuk, "indeed it could not be said that there are any true Eskimo communities located in the ... area."[22]

Counter to both totalizing ideologies, Indigenous residents interviewed for this research did not recognize any widespread economic impact from the DEW Line. They certainly did not believe it was a nail in the coffin of their culture nor did they see it as a turning point that convinced them that steady wage labour was better than hunting and trapping. Instead, the DEW Line brought about short-term economic benefits for many individuals during construction and long-term benefits for a few individuals and their families during subsequent decades of operation.[23]

The short-term boom was impressive: suddenly, around one quarter of the population in the western Arctic experienced steady wages and a fundamentally different living pattern. Even people used to a cash-based economy had usually worked outdoors and set their own schedules. Steady, wage-based industrial labour made "severe demands" upon people, Ferguson reported, characterizing the work as different and baffling, requiring none of the traditional skills of the hunter-trapper. A man's time, Ferguson observed, was no longer his own, and he could no longer travel when and where he pleased. Whether men left settlements to work at nearby sites or brought their families and set up new camps adjacent to stations, the communities were "split in two; the men working at the DEW Line site, the women and children trying to maintain a traditional life in an economy in which they ha[d] no part."[24] Especially for Inuvialuit employees at remote sites in the western sector, the obligation to support families in another place required a significant portion of their earnings. Absenteeism and high turnover among Inuit employees were chronic issues at the sites, but it was difficult to differentiate between real absenteeism and what was merely casual employment. "The Eskimos did not stay away from their jobs; they simply quit them, moved on to another site, or returned to their homes."[25]

Warden Rees, clearly disappointed that Tuktoyaktuk residents' interest in unskilled wage labour appeared to be short-lived, reported they were "too keen on dancing all night and playing poker. At the time of our visit only two Eskimos were left on the payroll at this site. The others had quit or been fired."[26] DEW Line construction jobs had not become the "turning point" Rees had hoped for in Letty Harbour either: "The DEW Line project appears to be having no effect on these people," he reported, explaining that some men worked for a week or so but did not like it and quit to return to their families. He recognized that forbidding Inuit to take their families with them to DEW Line sites left residents in a difficult situation: "On the bleak and inhospitable coast where even fuel wood is scarce a family without a man is in sore strait indeed," and he sympathized that the men "cannot be blamed too much for wanting to quit and return to their families." He understood that southerners at the radar sites didn't want to live in the same camps as Inuit, but he felt that officially establishing Indigenous camps a few miles away would encourage the Inuit to work on a more permanent basis.[27]

Reporting from Tuktoyaktuk in November 1955, Rees said people there were "perhaps better off now than ever before in their history.

About twenty of the Eskimos are now working on the DEW Line site and they have just completed building seven new log homes for themselves. They are also spending their money more wisely than in former years. This is something they have learned through bitter experience, not one but many times."[28]

By Christmas, Rees reported that, thanks to the DEW Line, Inuvialuit in Tuktoyaktuk were particularly happy and danced every night until seven in the morning for two weeks – a longer period than their finances would normally allow. He also reported that it looked like another poor season for white fox, but "generally speaking this should not bother the Eskimos too much this year as they can make infinitely more money on the Dew Line than on the Trapline."[29]

By March of 1956, Rees concluded that the basic economy of the Inuvialuit had been transformed. That winter, the Hudson Bay Company at Tuktoyaktuk had only one man doing serious trapping. "All the other Eskimos are employed on the Dewline [*sic*] and getting along quite well. The Eskimos seem to have settled down to the idea of steady employment now."[30] Absenteeism was declining rapidly and the "Northern Construction Co. seems to be more satisfied now with the Eskimo labour than hitherto." News that nine coastal vessels would be operating out of Tuktoyaktuk to supply all the DEW Line sites in the western sector promoted Rees to conclude it "would have a profound effect on the way of life of the natives, many of whom have already lost all interest in trapping for a living."[31]

The anthropologist Ferguson found less evidence that Inuvialuit were accepting steady employment, and he was particularly pleased with the views of one DEW Line station chief who had good success with Indigenous employees. That chief said his Inuit employees were getting tired of employment, and he expected them to vanish onto the ice any day, but he couldn't see why they should bother to work anyway since it seemed to him that money was of no real importance to them. "I was rather surprised at [his] attitude of disillusionment towards Eskimo employment since the official one both on the part of [Northern Affairs and the Northern Construction Company] is that employment and money-making is 'a good thing,'" Ferguson wrote. "In fact, that is just about the only justification that anyone can bring forward ... the sum total of all this employment ... is that some good hunters and trappers will be turned into indifferent wage-earners."[32]

That spring, Warden Rees began reporting side effects of the new economy: "The widows and aged people, who customarily get someone to assist them on their trapping areas are finding it very difficult to get help this year. There have been many young men hanging around town but they are not interested in trapping and when approached on the subject, a far away, dreamy look comes their eyes and they speak of getting jobs on the Dewline [*sic*] … someday."[33]

More likely, working at radar sites was the only real economic choice. By February 1958, the chief game warden of Aklavik, R.C. Timmins, reported wasting time and having great difficulty contacting trappers to renew their licences because many were employed on DEW Line sites away from town.[34] Those trappers he did see reported that they had not abandoned trapping in favour of steady employment and higher wages but that, due to extremely low prices for fur, trapping was simply no longer any kind of option. Visiting the new DEW Line site in Cambridge Bay, Ferguson asked every Inuit employee whether he liked his new job. Almost all replied that they did, but when the older men were asked whether they would prefer to remain at wage employment or go back to their old lifestyle, "doubt was immediately apparent and most of them finally said that they would prefer to return to hunting and trapping."[35]

DEW Line wages were usually not equal for southerners and Inuit. Varying degrees of corporate greed, condescension, and racism caused the disparity. When anthropologist Norman Chance interviewed DEW Line managers on Barter Island (Kaktovik), Alaska during fieldwork in the early 1960s, he asked them why their Iñupiat employees were paid less than Whites for the same work. He received a response grounded in what militarism scholars call the "gift economy": "Do you know what Eskimos get in Canada for working on the DEW Line? Two hundred a month. We give them three times that amount. By comparison, the people here are making out really well. Sometimes I think we do too much for the Eskimos. Eventually, they become unappreciative."[36] People in Kaktovik corroborated that locals were not paid at the same rate as imported southern workers, but they needed the money at the time and were in no position to demand equal pay.

Northern officials wanted only full-time jobs for Inuit at DEW Line stations to prevent contractors exploiting them as a floating labour pool.[37] Conveniently, Federal Electric usually selected single young men and sent them to distant sites where abandoning the job would be difficult. Even working for lower wages than southerners, many young men made enough money to set themselves up as homeowners, earning more they could have made trapping – even when trapping was lucrative. Working at remote sites was better suited for single young men who, without an accompanying family, were much easier to accommodate in bunkhouses just like, and sometimes alongside, southerners. Because young men lived on site, they learned their jobs and picked up English more quickly and tended to adopt the clothing and other habits of their co-workers. They were less prone to miss work or quit entirely to be with families, and construction superintendents tended to prefer them and train them for more heavy equipment operating and other skilled labour jobs. Working continuously without families to support or trapping equipment to purchase let young men rise to an income bracket above most established, mature men.

DEW Line wages also levelled incomes between different types of trappers: men who had simply gotten by or had been patently ineffective trappers and untalented hunters worked as equals alongside the most highly skilled and respected trappers. Skilled trappers with plenty of assets and high status had been rare, perhaps one in ten, but at least 50 per cent of DEW Line employees, including lower-ranked trappers who didn't take time off to hunt and trap, were able to obtain similar levels of wealth or more.[38] Conflicts arose, Ferguson wrote, when "leaders of the community no longer had their status conferred through their superior performance of occupation."[39] Growing up as the son of a long-time DEW Line employee, Sammy Lennie recognized the economic benefits of his dad's profession. "Yea, in a way I could say he was lucky to have that job because it was either that or go trapping. At that time anyway when we moved to Tuk – no roads, no housing, everybody was trappers, everybody lived strictly off the land. [There were a] few seasonal jobs at NTCL, barging company, transportation company. Sometime I felt like we had the advantage, we had all this other stuff, you know, more better fresher groceries."[40]

Sammy and his brother also had fewer chores than most kids "['c]ause we didn't have to go and get firewood because we had an oil stove." Even when tasked with feeding the dog team while their parents were gone, Sammy had opportunities. Instead of thawing out and cooking fish for the team, he and his brother grabbed can openers and filled the food bucket with tuna fish "['c]ause we used to get them by the cases."[41]

Ferguson noted that the nature of an occupation determined one's material needs: trapping required very few luxury items or European goods and thus did not displace Indigenous culture to any great degree, he argued. Wage employment intensified the need for goods that reflected European values to such a degree that, he argued, it affected the very fabric of Inuvialuit culture. Ferguson observed that young men saved about half of their earnings and spent the rest on clothing, watches, guitars, and violins. "None of them bought anything which might be regarded as hunting equipment and there is no intention among any of them to return to traditional life," Ferguson lamented.[42] The anthropologist asserted that moving to a wage economy and the dominance of southern culture "would be quite satisfactory if the new filled the gap left by the disappearance of the old, but the plain fact is that the Eskimos are offered only a fraction of the incredible volume of European civilization." He thought that although the abundance of comic books, cowboy music, and junk jewelry was a sign of a healthy economy, the basic culture was impoverished. "This is the way that 'hill billies' are created," Ferguson complained.[43]

Again, Robert Alexie and other interviewees did not corroborate Ferguson's notions about a widespread permanent departure from traditional life due to DEW Line money. The ability to shop from catalogs, donate to charities, and in particular to incorporate musical instruments into village life was particularly celebrated in several communities. Alexie did remember that some people were duped into paying exorbitant prices for cheap watches or buying electric devices that were of no use once they got home (where they had no electricity). Conducting his study during the height of DEW Line construction, Ferguson, like government officials, seemed to believe the steady wage labour opportunities would last forever. In fact, very few Indigenous men became permanent employees. More importantly, the decision to hunt was usually a matter of individual preference and, if anything, DEW Line employees could buy more boats and build more hunting cabins.

Indeed, the adoption of southern goods in the Mackenzie Delta region rose. The HBC store in Tuktoyaktuk normally cleared about

$55,000 annually. In 1955, the manager expected $150,000, and the store made $24,000 in the first three weeks of August alone. Meanwhile, mail-order business increased from virtually nothing in the late 1940s to more than $10,000 by the latter half of the 1950s. Most purchases were for boats, outboard motors, and related capital goods. For example, Alexie said the DEW Line was big money, but that it was also the arrival of oil companies in the delta that led to such widespread wealth that many people bought boats and motors. This equipment became necessary to support traditional activities: working a full-time job means people only have the weekends to travel the long distances required to harvest fish and game.

Northern Affairs officials, having accepted that traditional lifestyles were not viable near most DEW Line stations, turned to the welfare of employed and unemployed Inuit, their families, and the mixed cash/subsistence economy. Government policy shifted toward principles of "guided self-determination" under Inuit-led community councils and related initiatives that gave Inuit more say in decisions. Officials saw the DEW Line as critical because long-term employment could create a secure middle class, especially if people learned western money management concepts. Northern Affairs Deputy Minister Gordon Robertson wrote that once people were trained for wage labour, "we can expect that their adjustment and integration into our industrial society will follow progressively."[44] Northern Affairs studied Inuit labour policies on the north slope of Alaska Territory, where the US Navy had employed them in large oil exploration projects for several years. Officials circulated American military reports that described how, with time and patience, policies promoting "maximum utilization of Eskimos" could provide a "potential source of man-power that will be invaluable to our future military efforts ... which, if utilized to the full extent, will result in material savings to the Government."[45]

Canadian officials did not approve of all of the American labour policies. The American Federal Electric Corporation posed one challenge when its vice president told Northern Affairs at their first meeting that he was a strong segregationist.[46] Reporting to Northern Affairs Deputy Director Robertson on the meeting, Northern Affairs administrator Cunningham said that "we hold equally strong views against segregation and that what we said represented government policy ... We made it quite clear ... that ... we would not supply Eskimos unless they were treated in exactly the same fashion as the single white men."[47] Deputy Director Robertson wrote to Federal Electric that "the Government of Canada is determined that Eskimo people should have full opportunity in common with all other Canadian citizens to develop their talents."[48] Robertson also established that Inuit would have the same holidays as other Federal Electric employees (two weeks per year) and that Federal Electric would provide dependents of Inuit employees lateral transportation when switching sites, for annual leave, or to visit the nursing station. He stressed that "there is in this country a wide and keen public interest in DEW Line activities as they affect Canadians and a similar interest in Eskimo affairs ... From previous experience we know this project for Eskimo wage employment can be successful. The consequences of it turning out otherwise would be catastrophic for the Eskimo people concerned and I wish to leave nothing to chance in arranging what is necessary."[49]

Little confirms status in mainstream society more than one's home, and Northern Affairs officials struggled with ideological and logistical quandaries in their efforts to house Indigenous DEW Line employees. At some stations, traditional homes were destroyed to make room for stations. Originally from Tuktoyaktuk, Sammy Lennie's parents travelled to Banks Island in 1954, but when they returned the following year to the site near Tuk where they and other families had lived, the Lennies found the houses were gone and their family had moved to the main village site. Construction of BAR-3, the Tuktoyaktuk Auxiliary DEW Line, had subsumed the traditional village site at Tuk just as BAR-Main had subsumed Kaktovik, Alaska Territory, 200 miles west. "They just bulldozed their house and everything that they owned," Sammy explained. "Get out of the way." [50]

Some residents believed Barter Island, where the village of Kaktovik is located, was under attack when the Air Force first came in 1947 to build an airstrip. In addition to their semi-subterranean homes which could not be moved, the residents' food was stored in valuable ice cellars that can take over a year to construct, require annual maintenance, and hold as much meat as a family can catch. Cellars could not be moved and there was nowhere to put the food that was preserved in them. The Kaktovikmiut (Qaaqtuvigmiut) took all their moveable possessions and moved into tents up on the bluff where the military directed them, eventually building wooden frame homes on the new site out of military dunnage, packing crates, and other material. These homes were cold and presented fire hazards: many families converted fifty-five-gallon drums into oil drip stoves to burn waste oil for heat. Within a few years, the military erected a large hangar directly over the original village site. Residents were relocated two more times to accommodate the DEW Line site.[51]

Disagreements between Northern Affairs and the American Federal Electric Company over corporate responsibilities complicated employee housing decisions. The construction companies did not want Indigenous employees to live with white employees, but they did want the Indigenous workforce to camp nearby – in part because the companies wanted Indigenous workers available during off hours to unload planes but did not want to take an extra hour to transport them back and forth if they lived miles away. Government officials like Arctic Division Chief Ben Sivertz worried that children's school attendance would fail if they had to commute and that Inuit families living away from town would lose their social lives. Sivertz tried to persuade construction officials that housing families near radar stations would invite trouble and require restrictions, and that worse problems could result if young, single women lived close to stations.[52]

Growing up in "Eskimo Housing" next to the DEW Line station next to Tuk, Sammy Lennie confirmed that the experience disrupted his family. At times, he and his brother were sent away to residential schools, and he believes his father lost a close connection with his children during these periods. Even when the family lived together and the children walked to a local school, they were harassed for being DEW Line kids. "'Cause we were different – we stayed out of town. DEW Line kids get in lots of fights, I know I used to get into a few scraps here and there. 'You are a DEW Line kid! Why don't you go back to the DEW Line where you belong?' ... 'Stay on your side!' Because, you see, it kind of is on that side. Miles away." One good thing about the distance was that Sammy and his brother always held first and second place in foot races for their age because they ran all four miles when they wanted to go to town.[53] The fights the Lennie children endured mirror some of the bullying that Elmer Sinclair recounted in chapter 1, yet Sammy Lennie's memories do not delve into the darkness of the emotional, physical, and sexual abuse endured by Sinclair.

After serious debates over quality and long-term implications for Inuit identity, Northern Affairs eventually ordered several hundred "Structofoam" and similar prefabricated units for Inuit DEW Line employees.[54] Arctic Division head Sivertz embraced the reform agenda and objected strongly to incrementally raising overall standards of living by building more numerous but less expensive homes.

> Would we be wise to house Eskimos and their families in such sharply inferior accommodations ...? What would be the effect on (a) the Eskimos (b) other Dew-line [*sic*] employees? We have always gone on the assumption that it is essential to provide housing that accords with livelihood, – and not based on what the Eskimos might be willing to accept in light of his background ... The most serious and inimical effects on the whole concept of Eskimo development, acculturation, protection and emancipation could flow from this ready acceptance of the idea that Eskimos can be made to accept any standard however low ... never mind putting the wage-earner onto a plane where he can hold his head as high as the white man ... Pulling down the standards of housing for wage-employed Eskimos is dangerous to our most important objectives.[55]

Via frequent visits to DEW Line stations, NSOs were to stay informed of local concerns and maintain tight control over Indigenous/non-Indigenous relations. This was practicable at more remote DEW Line stations but unmanageable at larger stations near communities. Nevertheless, NSOs attempted to minimize disruptions of Inuit life, protect the old way of life for those able and interested in pursuing it, and provide alternative work for not able to make a subsistence living. NSOs monitored threats to game and promoted Inuit awareness of the need to protect game. Non-Indigenous DEW Line employees were not permitted to hunt. Government officials also tried to establish a patronizing financial management program out of concern that people couldn't handle their money. Inuit wages were deposited directly into NSO-managed trust funds until the job was done, then NSOs deposited the money into bank accounts available by mail or with the local trading post with a semi-compulsory saving component. This system, not surprisingly, proved unsatisfactory when Inuit wanted to spend the money they had earned and demanded post managers give it to them.

Northern Affairs organized educational courses for Inuit so they could serve as a valuable labour source for the DEW Line and future industry. Originally held outside of Edmonton, Alberta, courses were designed to integrate Inuit into standard white society and mold an Arctic citizen. Classes emphasized widely applicable practical skills rather than abstract thinking in order to render the student immediately and generally "useful."[56] Objectives included "foster[ing] an understanding of the need for, and hence an appreciation of good workmanship" and "promot[ing] as much as possible a feeling of satisfaction and achievement that comes from the ability to perform jobs to recognized standards of efficiency and workmanship." In patronizing terms, Northern Affairs officials explained the courses were "the means for assisting Eskimos and others in the NWT to make the transition from their own relatively primitive cultures to a more complex one."[57]

Northern Affairs Vocational Coordinator T.M. Taylor helped plan field trips to acquaint trainees with a modern southern community and claimed that any Canadian citizen should appreciate the fire department, the flour mill, the laundry, the frozen food lockers, the brewery, and the police station. The government allotted trainees money to buy clothes but only at the Hudson Bay Store under the direction of their NSO. The government also promoted TV and radio interviews of English-speaking Inuit but only when accompanied by an NSO and outlined beforehand. Paternalistic instructions extended to communication between trainees and their families: "Someone should be responsible for seeing that all Eskimo trainees write their families at specified regular intervals" and checking on families who did not write back to encourage them to do so weekly. Taylor determined that Inuit trainees should never be left alone: they needed instructions on basic aspects of southern civilization (e.g., operation of traffic lights) if the administration was to avoid "embarrassing or even unpleasant situations."[58]

Taylor believed it was critical to accommodate students in boarding houses where they could "associate with whites in their normal way of life"[59] and made special efforts to teach trainees English "which will have far-reaching effects of the gradual integration of the Eskimo ... [and] into the wage earning economy of the Northwest Territories."[60] This vocational training, Northern Affairs hoped, would provide a source of "lead hands" and foremen for future northern industrial and defence development. Training costs were high, but the government argued it would be "self liquidating as the high earning power of equipment operators will result in substantial recovery through income tax payments."[61]

Delta resident Sammy Lennie's father attended one of these training courses and was evidence of their long-term financial benefits – at least for industry and the government. In the mid-1950s, Sammy's father went to Leduc outside of Edmonton with approximately fifty other Inuvialuit to train for DEW Line work. He returned to work at Tununuk (BAR-C I-site), Shingle Point (BAR-2), and Tuktoyaktuk (BAR-3). Sammy reviewed his father's records, which showed he had missed only two days of work without arranging it during twenty years of work on the DEW Line. In retirement, however, he was never able to collect a pension. Officials informed Sammy that local people hadn't been interested in pensions at the time they worked. If his father had officially opted out of a pension plan, he was not aware of it. Bureaucrats also told him that fiscal responsibility for these plans was unclear because of the joint Canadian/US ownership and management of the Line.[62]

Issues of Inuit/Canadian identity dominated the Arctic Division's first Arctic Conference in 1957. Northern administrators and NSOs discussed "how Eskimos can be made to feel that they are really a part of the modern communities in which many of them now live" and how they could be made to feel a part of the *national* community. The revealing agenda questions included:

- What can be done to encourage the Eskimo to take part in managing his own affairs?
- What does the Eskimo want out of life and is he being helped to achieve his aims?
- Is Eskimo culture being undermined?

- What is the future of the Eskimos and of the land in which they live?
- What do they think of us, the invaders from the south?

The remote and vast field of operations made it difficult to ensure that every newcomer to the north made the correct impressions on the Inuit, so Northern Affairs developed guidelines for proper Canadian values to be exemplified, including a type of progressive industrialism. To mitigate negative impressions southerners coming north might have about Inuit, Northern Affairs published *This is the Arctic*, a booklet with a cover depicting smiling cartoon Inuit wearing parkas and mukluks, chasing wolves with pistols, sporting sunglasses, and holding fashion magazines with Quonset huts in the background, while taking pictures of a confused white man debarking from an airplane. It had a positive "creating initiative" motto: "None of this means that the Eskimos are being pampered. Spoon-feeding is definitely out; they are simply being helped to help themselves. The Eskimos are not wards of the state and they are not being treated as wards. They are full Canadian citizens, and as citizens the day may come when Eskimo administrators will direct Arctic affairs and when an Eskimo will sit in Parliament at Ottawa."[63]

Effects of Cold War industrial military activities, however, differed in key ways from earlier military activity in the Arctic. During the Second World War, coastal residents had been justifiably fearful of further attacks, many from the Alaska Territory moved to Canada, and almost every single man and several women there enlisted in the Alaska Territorial Guard (ATG, also known as Eskimo Scouts, and roughly equivalent to Canadian Rangers). Hundreds of Inupiaq and Yupik men served in the war and many more built airfields and pipelines. Military leaders valued ATG members' vigilance, sharp-shooting abilities, and knowledge of the land and sea. ATG leaders credited the ATG with challenging institutionalized racism in Alaska Territory and helping secure the 1945 Non-discrimination Act, Alaskan statehood, and the formation of the Alaska Federation of Natives.

Cold War military activities, by contrast, replaced Indigenous guards with machines as defenders of the coastline and otherwise disenfranchised people[64] by commandeering Indigenous land and removing residents from it. The Cold War military needed wage labourers and help with fresh water sources, not sharpshooters. Alaskan interviewee George Agnasagga said the DEW Line made him a leader but not because it was empowering. Rather, he said it made him angry and he felt forced to fight for the rights of his people.[65]

People were also disenfranchised by the Cold War secrecy. When construction had begun, many people did not know the purpose of the DEW Line buildings and towers and, according to several informants, did not particularly care. Although they served a military purpose, according to Sammy Lennie, DEW Line labourers were not particularly conscious of this particular purpose. "People didn't even really notice. It was just a, it was there. Nothing you could do about it ... [M]y dad used to tell me stories when, during the way, back in '41, in that war, about how he remembers travelling around and passing camps and people would wave from the beach, 'Hi! Any word on the war?' And stuff like that. And DEW Line, nobody even thought anything of it ... We just thought they were working. Like anybody else."[66] Gwich'in elder Robert Alexie, who worked on construction, said, "Well they didn't know! They didn't know what it was about ... No, they didn't know, people didn't know, nobody cared nothing about it." He knew they were preparing for war, but otherwise just that they were building industrial outposts called DEW Lines. He discovered later, after construction, that it was for defense. Susie Avery of Shingle Point and Aklavik said she knew that her dad worked there, but it never occurred to her and the other children to ask him what they were building. Richard Gordon of Inuvik and Herschel Island said that people didn't understand the premise of the Cold War or the DEW Line's purpose in the beginning, but "as time went on and they became more involved they began to understand, from the Aboriginal standpoint, where they stood in the scheme of things."[67]

The DEW Line industry magazine *Polar Echoes* reminded readers to be always aware that the radar stations were "natural, logical targets for enemy agents"[68] who aimed to subvert the public and infiltrate classified defense projects.[69] Readers were warned to trust no one, to avoid indiscriminately helping those less fortunate, and not to speak to their family and friends. "Saboteurs of the Atomic Age" were a far cry from previous traitors, and the survival of the planet and mankind was at stake.[70]

Gordon believed that these pervasive Cold War ideologies and security measures worked: commanding people to watch for spies and warning them against talking to strangers instilled fear. "They were always on the alert," he said. Once people got jobs at the radar stations, they protected those jobs and enforced the highly secretive DEW Line culture. "So, it was something that was put upon you – again, we did not understand what kind of a war we were or what W-A-R meant but if you leaked it out we were going to hurt everybody so we were hush hush." Gordon said there were secrecy stories from DEW Line workers "that you wouldn't believe." Sammy Lennie described "Unauthorized Personnel Prohibited" signs everywhere and military planes quickly hiding in hangars upon arrival.[71] In particular, the scenario of Soviet and US submarines plying the depths of the ocean or right off the coast of the Beaufort Sea scared residents.[72] "That's the thing, *we don't know* what's out there," Gordon said.

Watching thrilling Cold War movies from the security of the radar stations, on the other hand, was a popular activity. "It was a radar system and to us, a radar system was like, top secret, James Bond. And we used to watch all those movies, James Bond and *A Man Called Flint* [*sic*]." Several people said their perception of the military was formed more by those movies, and later, TV, than it was by the military outpost in their town.

While Indigenous men learned skills and became wage earners, the DEW Line had myriad different implications for women. Traditional military histories tend to underestimate or ignore the effects of militarization on women's lives despite substantial evidence of far-reaching impacts, and this research tried explicitly to address this aspect.[73] Women were not permitted to work at male-dominated DEW Line sites until the 1970s and few ever did, but interviews indicated that the DEW Line provided dance partners, boyfriends, and husbands for young women in communities. This dismayed some male residents, one of whom said it seemed like an official policy to dilute the gene pool.[74]

When husbands left to work, live, eat, and drink at remote stations, married women often had to care for families without a hunter or firewood gatherer, childcare provider, and emotional support network. Yet married women who lived with their husbands and families near remote stations could also be very isolated. While Sammy Lennie's family lived in the "Eskimo Housing" next to the Shingle Point DEW Line station, strict rules kept them from going to the Shingle Point settlement or leaving the station much at all and forbid southern DEW Liners from visiting them at home. Sammy's mother had no sisters or aunties around to share chores and time with. "That's why she sewed a lot," Sammy said. "I used to ask her, 'Did you ever get lonely? Did you ever want to go?' and she said 'No.' My mother is the person that 'I chose that life, so I live that life.'" He also recalled the wild beauty of this location and how his mother picked "yellow berries by the millions."[75]

Not surprisingly, strict rules did not prevent widespread fraternization between DEW Liners and residents. During the heyday of construction, Jack Ferguson reported that the RCMP charged two employees with contributing to the "juvenile delinquency" of a fourteen-year-old girl and sleeping with other young women. The magistrate in Yellowknife found them guilty, and Ferguson wrote, "I believe that every effort was made by all parties to keep the thing quiet."[76] Sammy said girls in Tuk liked to party with DEW Liners, who would head to town with a stash of booze to go curling or partying at the RCMP and to try to pick them up. Late night parties in Tuk with alcohol got "pretty rowdy – *really* rowdy," he said. "It got pretty scary for DEW Liner, being the only white guy and everybody else is Native, it got time for them to go home."

"I could say they did leave a few DEW Line babies behind ... I have a few DEW Line relatives.'" The girl's parents usually raised the children born of these unions. Sammy remembered one couple in Tuk who did marry: the husband still lived at the site and would visit his wife in town. According to his account, the DEW Line did not really impact other people's lives much – except for the babies. There were "a lot" of DEW Line babies and he considered this to be the main effect for families who did not work at the sites. [77]

The Canadian anthropologist Diamond Jenness, free from US military censors in his reporting on wartime bases in Alaska Territory, reported that alcohol was the most destructive factor in the welfare of the

Indigenous people.[78] Although liquor been available before the war, it was rare and only available in small amounts. At the bases, however, it "flowed like water," and hard-earned wages disappeared while resistance to tuberculosis weakened.[79] The DEW Line created a veritable cult of alcohol in the Arctic during the decades of the Cold War because the radar network created a sanctioned drinking atmosphere and an efficient system in which alcohol flowed up to and throughout the stations in enormous quantities. Each station had a bar and DEW Liners celebrated constant consumption of booze and relayed stories about Indigenous drinking that were funny, friendly, cute, brotherly, patronizing, and devoid of reference to the repercussions of alcohol in Indigenous communities. Loneliness, boredom, camaraderie, the lack of social deterrents, and the sheer availability of alcohol exacerbated the problem.[80] A teacher on Baffin Island described the legacies:

> In the late 1980s when I arrived the people were still struggling with the challenges of acculturation ... The DEW Line never did manage to employ more than a small handful of local Inuit on a full-time basis. The few positions that Inuit held were usually at the lowest level and often took men away from their families for several months at a time, which created strain on the family unit. As well, the DEW Line had negative effects on the hamlet by making alcohol available to the community. DEW Line employees, most often single men, fraternized with women, especially younger women from the village, and often permanently disrupted family units in Anurapaktuq. Many men fathered children there, yet never stayed long enough to provide support for those children.[81]

Most Indigenous interviewees also saw the influx of alcohol as the DEW Line's worst influence on labour and family life. Sammy Lennie, for one, grew up believing that all men had strong whiskey breath. He described the DEW Liner life, including his father's, as "drink, drink, drink, drink, drink" and said that the bar at the station in Tuk seemed to have undergone a great number of renovations and was the most looked-after place. "Yeah, I mean, like, the only thing I thought about DEW Line is there was a lot of alcohol. Lot of drinking on the DEW

Line. All, like my dad, all of them that lived on the DEW Line, my uncles, they were all heavy drinkers. And they drank a lot. I mean, it did affect my family life, the family structure ... White guys, natives, all drank a lot. Yes, it was a culture of drinking."[82] Robert Alexie said the DEW Line changed the social order in the community due to the availability of alcohol and money to buy it. "That was big mistake, nobody asked, nobody knew about it ... Alcohol is the biggest problem in this part of the country. The whole damn North."[83]

At the BAR-Main station adjacent to Kaktovik, Alaska, it was the luxurious Barter Island Social Club that centred in everyone's stories. White DEW Line employee Harry Merriman said he made more money bartending than he did at his regular DEW "radician" job. An Alaskan Iñupiat described travelling the Arctic coast after construction of the DEW Line as "bar hopping." Another worked for decades expediting cargo for the line, and in describing the amount of alcohol that moved through this system "John" rolled his eyes, shook his head, and asserted that it was an unimaginable amount. He joked that it was "their main business" and that certain people made an extremely rich profit on the alcohol delivery system.[84]

Inuit also suffered from environmental pollution of their communities. While some employees eventually got prefab homes, people opportunistically incorporated DEW Line infrastructure and debris into every level of their ecosystem across the Arctic. Residents built homes, schools, and hunting and fishing cabins with leftover industrial material and used drums and petroleum to heat those buildings in new ways. Connections to DEW Line society and Cold War ideology may have affected Arctic people's perspectives and life experiences, but the stations – with waste material and dumps, gravel roads and pads, massive white geodesic radomes, tall towers, and other infrastructure – physically transformed their environment.[85]

"For the most part we had a ball because year 'round, the DEW Line was our playground," said Sammy Lennie of the advantages of growing up a DEW Line kid.[86] Every part of the radar stations and their adjacent dumps provided endless entertainment and opportunities for adventure. "We used to climb in and around all those towers and dishes and around ... They didn't see us. We were like the little foxes; we just came out when no one was around. We just didn't dare get caught by the

3.3 Fox 2, 1991.

old man too. We knew we weren't supposed to be climbing around so we were sneaking." When their father worked at BAR-3 next to Tuktoyaktuk, Sammy and his brother hauled their bikes through nearby sand dunes to an enormous radar dish that had been knocked over and partly buried. It was a fifteen foot climb up into it, but the boys hauled their bikes up with them. Once there, they could ride around and around having great fun – until the time Sammy's brother was seriously injured, and the game was over. The DEW Line got rid of that playground by completely burying it in the sand.

Richard Gordon stopped by DEW Line stations to camp while travelling the western Arctic coastline with his parents. "We as kids didn't know anything about 'DEW Line site,' we just knew there was a camping site and there was a couple of buildings that we stayed in as a family and I remember during the day when we came out there was garbage and metal and stuff all over the place and there was ground squirrels at that time in those areas and we as kids were hunting the ground squirrels and running around all these things like a playground."[87]

While perspectives vary on the value of industrial buildings and radomes, there is broad agreement that people of the western Arctic

3.4 D Doppler Antenna, 1961.

loved their local 240-foot-tall Doppler towers and put them to skilful use for generations. In a place where any vantage point provides incredible vistas, the towers were generally irresistible and extremely useful for scoping game. "Like, I wonder what is up there, I wonder how far I can see. But we did climb. I climbed all the towers,"[88] remembered Sammy Lennie. One Alaskan interviewee confessed she cried when the tower at her hunting camp was torn down.[89] Another said, "Yeah, we climb them all the time. Like, all the time. I'd throw my parka down. Every chance I'd get, I'd climb them. I don't care how long it took. It was 205 steps. I can never forget that number, yup. My legs were like Jello after."[90]

Sammy confirmed that people still climb the remaining towers, but it is strange now that the stations are automated and monitored remotely by video camera from the other side of Canada. He told of a man who, having lost track of his hunting group near Running River/Shingle Point, went up to the station and climbed the tower to scout for them. A loud official voice came over a microphone: "Please get off the tower. I am watching you from Gander, Newfoundland."

Not all DEW Line infrastructure was so popular. Sammy Lennie could not believe the irony when a radome from Tuk was reconstructed in Inuvik to house a local wireless telephone and internet business. "I grew up looking at that big ball and somebody bought it and took it all the way to Inuvik and now I have to grow old looking at that big ball."[91]

DEW Line infrastructure landmarks and outposts significantly impacted Arctic logistics and Richard Gordon confirmed that everybody uses the DEW Line stations when they travel: in the wintertime people could see the light and, in the summer, the white radome would contrast with the green landscape. "[I]t's used as a safe haven – you know there was humans there. Nowadays it is unmanned but you are still going to have contact with the outside world."[92] Gordon said the DEW Line was "there for those things – it is one of those things you adapt to it and you use it for some way as part of survival ... We still use them as part of our travel, we'll use them as reference, they are even in our GPS at least by people who are travelling along the coast."[93]

When military sites are normalized, over time they blend into the background and are easily accepted. Many interviewees reported knowing every square inch of the radar station near their town. Militarism scholars understand military-themed toys as evidence of social militarization, thus that adults found DEW Line infrastructure useful and children found it an irresistible playground certainly helped normalize it. Whether and to what degree it militarized people is more complex and complicated by the toxic and legal legacies of the infrastructure.

Both the useful infrastructure and the toxic waste of the DEW Line have shaped land and lives along the Arctic coast. Decades after the DEW Line construction boom, many children and grandchildren of Indigenous DEW Liners got jobs cleaning up the radar stations and the staggering numbers of fifty-five-gallon drums associated with them.

From identifying known hotspots to monitoring cleanup projects, the people who worked at the stations and live on the land have had to fight to remediate the environment. Many DEW Line materials, particularly transformers and other electrical equipment, contained PCBs and other persistent chemical contaminants. Environmental contractor Defense Canada characterized the DEW Line as the largest environmental problem in Canada,[94] and another study estimated that DEW Line pollution constituted 5 per cent of the total Arctic contamination burden.[95] Because most Arctic coastal communities overlap with contaminated DEW Line stations, anyone familiar with the DEW Line might suspect that that percentage of total contaminant burden has a disproportionate effect on residents because it is concentrated in areas where people are more likely to live and hunt.

For example, Richard Gordon would hear stories about the spring cleanup ritual of the DEW Line's early years when boats hit the submerged hazard off Seagull Island (near Shingle Point, Yukon). Crews would pile garbage, drums, dead equipment, and debris onto old cat trains. Then they would turn the tractor on, point it north, and let it go across the ice to the open ocean. Sometimes, as is suspected with Seagull Island, the garbage train fell off the ice edge in a bad spot and created a navigational hazard for subsequent generations. Environmental consultants in Canada refined DEW Line risk assessments by including Inuit traditional environmental knowledge and learned that similar methods of waste disposal (including the dumping of trucks and radio towers) were commonplace at other stations even up to the time of deactivation in the early 1990s.[96]

The garbage, equipment, and debris that were not dumped off the ice edge were pushed into massive dumps, often directly off beach bluffs or into lakes and lagoons. Sammy Lennie had a wealth of experience with DEW Line dumps after growing up at three different stations in the Mackenzie River Delta area (Tununuk [BAR-C]; Shingle [BAR-2]; and Tuktoyaktuk [BAR-3]) and he never understood why the first DEW Line dump near Tuktoyaktuk was never cleaned up or why the second dump was very close to the community's drinking water source. That dump was then moved back to the lagoon near Tuk, which runs off into the ocean – right where people used to fish for bottom feeders. Indicating on a map where the dump is, Sammy said "[I]t is *atrocious*

... There's a lot of garbage there and a lot of run off, and it just runs off into the ocean."[97]

Sammy recalled that people used the dumps quite a bit, even taking dog teams there to set them loose and let them feed – an efficient and opportunistic, if industrial, form of pastoralism. "We used to go there all the time. Me and my younger brother spent the whole day there, especially on the weekends with friends. Especially when they were burning the garbage, we'd find old paint cans and pound the lids on, throw them into the fire and watch them explode. We loved blowing up things."[98]

The *taigruaq* (drum or tank, usually: fifty-five-gallon drum) is the legacy of Cold War activities most thoroughly integrated into people's lives and labour. Richard Gordon worked a long time to secure funds for a shoreline drum cleanup, "because there was so much ... bureaucracy, politics mixed into it, because they knew it was American DEW Line sites but anything out of their jurisdiction was Canadian – whatever, some big money talkers as to who was going to pay for that clean up."[99] Eventually the project was funded and people travelling along the coast collected drums.

A ship that Bruce Inglangasak worked on hauled out only drums for two years. Bruce Inglangasak's grandfather, Old Irish, worked on the DEW Line stations in Canada's western Arctic for several years and built a house out of DEW Line material at Stokes Point. An example of the cyclical nature of DEW Line employment, Bruce worked decades later demolishing many of those same stations. "We didn't take any housing materials; those were all buried. No, we didn't take much out of the site. Mostly the drums, just the drums were taken out of the DEW Line sites and shipped south. Not sure why. Maybe because they couldn't cover it all up, I guess. But there were lots of drums." Inglangasak described Canadian sealift barges 150 feet wide and 340 feet long with drums "ten high stacked" from bow to stern, "[j]ust from one DEW Line site."[100] At Barter Island, Alaska, a smaller island within the lagoon was known for decades as Drum Island due to the enormous mountain of barrels covering it and residents there pick rusty pieces of drums out of their fishing nets.

Military contractors had produced and moved prodigious amounts of gravel to construct the stations in the 1950s. Roads and airstrips had to be topped with six feet of gravel while pads underneath heated buildings had to be topped with twelve feet to keep the permafrost from thawing.[101] In terraforming the landscape, they often dredged gravel from beaches, exposing them and leaving critical locations more vulnerable to erosion. The erosion now threatens communities themselves and, in many places, DEW Line dumps and infrastructure eroded for decades, releasing garbage and contaminants into rivers, lagoons, and the ocean. With climate change, longer periods when no shore-fast ice is present to protect the coastline from storm surges and crashing waves can lead to sudden and dramatic erosion events.

"Over the years now that the world is changing with this global warming and the erosions that's happening along the shoreline, all the contaminants that were buried over when the DEW Line sites were started – we're starting to see all those things come up again and it worries us because now we are educated about what these things held that were unknown in the past," said Richard Gordon.[102] "Never was told it was dangerous, we were touching this and touching that and I guess our parents at the time were uneducated, didn't have the reading abilities if there were warning signs." Sammy Lennie corroborated this: "I wasn't aware of it, didn't know what contamination was. I remember seeing 'Caution: Radiation,' but I didn't know what it was. Especially around the big radar dishes they were used to have signs on them: 'Caution, radiation, radioactive material.' But you see, that was our playground."[103]

Sammy Lennie also remembered DEW Liners pouring half barrels of very dark black sticky sludge over the bank at the edge of the station in Tuk. "They done it for years," he said, and recalled that a friend who was working as cleanup project foreman asked Sammy whether he had ever been tested. The cleanup crew had found extensive arsenic and PCB contamination over the entire beach. Sammy Lennie remembered that the cleanup crews, after removing the buildings, removed the entire top of the mountain and stored the contaminated dirt in large containers on the site for years.[104]

Bruce Inglanasak said they never actually removed most trash, just moved it to other sites and buried it. They tore down the buildings at Tuk, cut them up into big slabs and loaded them on barges – then pushed the barges to Cape Perry (PIN-Main) and buried everything there. Bruce had no idea why they decided to bury material from Tuk at Cape Perry but guessed it was just to get it out of Tuk.[105] At Cape Perry, the crews dug a huge hole right on top of the mountain and put a heavy liner in it. "I guess when they were filling it, they punctured the lining and the following year after the project was over some people went and checked it out. They thought they did something good there, but it got worse."[106] "We've taken quite a bit of PCB out of the sites. *Lots*."

Susie Avery pushed for cleanup at Stokes Point Intermediate station after she was dismayed by the widespread debris and contamination there. Her family had cabins near Stokes before the DEW Line was built and her family cabin at Running River near Shingle Point is built from DEW Line material. Susie said it wasn't just the dump at Stokes that was dirty but that garbage was all over and unbelievably "gross"; visiting with her children she found the ground around the site was soaked with oil. When they built fires, the wood produced thick black smoke. "I didn't like my little ones to go out that way 'cause when you walk you could just see bubbles coming up – on the ground!"[107]

Bruce Inglangasak said that "Shingle Point was another one – I don't know why they find that they can bury trash in a river or a gorge. They just dug a hole on the side of the river, dug a pit, and then they bulldozed everything into it and buried it. Right in the river. Right alongside the river. And that area there is full of wildlife during the spring and summer seasons, all these swans, cranes, all kinds of ducks, geese. We've even got eagles nesting in that area, a lot of eagles along the rivers. Two of them rivers. The trash just drains out into the Beaufort ... A lot of herring use that bay. Belugas, seals, they are all contaminated."[108]

"Pierce Point Harbour is going to be a hard one, 'cause it's right on top of another mountain, and they just dumped the garbage over the cliff on the south side of the site. If you look over the cliff, you can see rust, metal, batteries, equipment, drums, etc. And there is a river that runs right along, comes out by that mountain. And a lot of fish use that river. That site, I remember taking eight fifty-five-gallon drums of PCBs. This was taken just from the top, right from the site, the exact site where the houses were. I know they gotta work on that one."[109]

Residents worked on the jobs, but Bruce was not aware of any local, Indigenous oversight of the cleanup and thought employees were not professionally trained. "I guess they weren't told how it should have been done to begin with. They just said, 'Here's a pick and shovel and go bury this for us,' and pay you this. Pretty much the way it went ... I don't know how these people think to bury PCBs right smack damn in the middle of all this wildlife that happens. They're not very bright. Maybe they don't value life, or anything."[110]

Like many interviewees, Bruce had no confidence that the cleanup is adequate. "You can take a picture of a cleaned area, but you can't see what is under the soil or the water, or what's draining out into it. If they were going to clean it, they should have dug it right out. Shipped the whole thing, dirt and all. Out of the Arctic." He thought that contractors got away with this kind of cleanup because it was on Indigenous land, and he believed that DEW Line contamination has caused cancer. "All our elders – they all got cancer, and they are dying at an early age. All our kids, all their kids are, everybody's contaminated now." [111]

After two years on a job, the contractor transferred Bruce Inglangasak to a different boat for, as he put it, "saying things ... against some other people about the way things were done." Once he had his own eco-guide business in Kaktovik some years later, he did not have to worry about getting hired again for cleanup work.

Most informants agreed that remaining infrastructure should be removed completely. Even Sammy Lennie, who might have been nostalgic after a fabulous time as a kid with the exciting industrial playgrounds he grew up on, wanted the sites gone. "They should tear them down and clean them up and get everything out of there," he said. "'Cause I know what's in them now."[112]

Cleanup of the DEW Line stations in Canada was not, according to the 1955 Canadian/US agreement on the radar system, supposed to be left up to Canada.[113] Cleanup eventually cost Canada $575 million and was the largest engineering project in the world at the time.[114] The Canadian government asserted that the US was legally obliged under international law to pay for the environmental cleanup of these former US military installations, but the US determined there was no legal obligation and decided that the US would make an *ex gratia* settlement in the sum of $100 million, subject to obtaining specific legislative authority from the United States Congress, for twenty-one DEW Line stations and three other military sites on Canadian property.[115]

CONCLUSION

Despite rebounding fur prices and increasing oil activity, the end of the DEW Line construction boom had real effects. Canadian filmmaker and author Kevin McMahon claimed the DEW Line bust led to the first ideological dispute in Tuktoyaktuk: some people advocated a return to pure subsistence while others demanded government jobs and subsidies to maintain the standard of living that wage labour had enabled. McMahon lamented that the quandary has intensified over the years but that the choice supposedly given to Inuit to work or subsist is not real because traditional life gets no support while industry gets immense incentive.[116] This sentiment over-generalizes a complex reality and diverse situations. Many successful Indigenous leaders connected to the oil industry on the north slope of Alaska, for example, are also whaling captains and, with their wives and families, run "super subsistence" households (harvesting and sharing Native food among the community at high levels).

Several militarization scholars analyze how military activity shapes small communities, dominating their economy and influencing residents' notions about security and the military itself in myriad ways.[117] Compared to most military sites, DEW Line outposts were very small and a type that is normally far less socially impactful: they were purely defensive and manned mostly by civilians. Relative to the size of communities they affected, however, the DEW Line stations were dominant features in terms of infrastructure and sometimes population. Research findings did not indicate that living in this militarized landscape necessarily resulted in much societal militarization, though the stations clearly damaged the environment and influenced people's lives.

Militarization's strength over a society is complicated when its geographic footprint is as dramatic and troublesome as it was on the Arctic coast. Perhaps its power over people's perspectives on threats and how society should be organized to address them is inversely proportional to the amount of damage a local military site does.[118] The military's impact on the physical environment in several Arctic communities is so significant that it is a regular reminder of environmental injustice – reminders that seem stronger than those of the economic benefits a few families enjoyed. Distrust, feelings of powerlessness, and anger over contamination and frustrating bureaucratic processes are a core legacy. Some people appeared to have actively resisted attributing any significance at all to the strange radomes and towers looming over their town. They ignored it or derided it as much as possible – and the sites were, in the larger context, little more than a blip. The old DEW Line stations were only one aspect of colonialism. Richard Gordon characterized the compounding cumulative effects of militarization, climate change, pollution, and battles over sovereignty as a different kind of war, one which pitted his people against those who brought destructive elements to the north. "As Aboriginal people, it is a war ... I mean, our definition of war is going to be totally different from country [*sic*] – where we fight to survive in our own land."[119]

NOTES

1 Mary Ann Warden, interview with Stacey Fritz, Kaktovik, Alaska, 28 May 2009, and Nora Jane Burns, interview with Stacey Fritz, Kaktovik, Alaska, 20 August 2005.

2 In this chapter, the term "Indigenous" refers to Inuit or Iñuit (Caribou, Central, and Copper) and other First Nations peoples residing in Alaska and northern Canada, who had experienced historical conflicts and who did not necessarily share cultural practices. The term Eskimo is used when it appears in quotes. For a general overview of the DEW Line, see Adam Lajeunesse, "The Distant Early Warning Line and the Canadian Battle for Public Perception," *Canadian Military Journal* (Summer 2007): 51–9.

3 Cynthia Enloe, *The Curious Feminist: Searching for Women in the New Age of Empire* (Berkeley and Los Angeles: University of California Press, 2004); Catherine Lutz, *Homefront: A Military City and the American 20th Century* (Boston: Beacon Press, 2002).

4 Since 1981, NORAD has stood for North American Aerospace Defense Command. For a general overview, see Lajeunesse, "The Distant Early Warning Line," 51–9.

5 John Bockstoce, *Whales, Ice, and Men: The History of Whaling in the Western Arctic* (Seattle: University of Washington Press, 1986).

6 Royal Canadian Mounted Police report entitled "Eskimo Relief," Library and Archives Canada (LAC), RG 85, Vol. 101, file 253-2/119 pt. 1 and pt. 2: Reports on Inuit of Western Arctic 1939–51. All Canadian archival documents cited here were generously provided by the late David Neufeld, Yukon and Western Arctic historian for Parks Canada. Neufeld researched and published widely on the DEW Line in the Inuvialuit area (e.g., "Trigger for Atomic Holocaust: Aircraft Detection on the DEW Line," *Cultural Resource Management* 14 (1997): 10–11; "BAR-1 DEW Line Report," *Parks Canada* (1997); "The Distant Early Warning (DEW) Line: A Preliminary Assessment of its Role and Effects upon Northern Canada," *Parks Canada* (2002)). In all cases where original archival citations are available, they are cited. Where the original citation was unclear, the citation will read: DEW-line documents collection, courtesy of David Neufeld. This photocopied collection is held by Stacey Fritz, Fairbanks, Alaska.

7 Frank J. Tester, and Peter Kulchyski, *Tammarniit (Mistakes): Inuit Relocation in the Eastern Arctic 1939–63* (Vancouver: UBC Press, 1994).

8 Richard Gordon, interview with Stacey Fritz, Herschel Island, Yukon Territory, July 2008.

9 Diamond Jenness, *Eskimo Administration, Alaska.* Technical Paper No 12 (Calgary: Arctic Institute of North America, 1962), 39–41. For a brilliant and relevant criticism of Jenness, see Diane Newell and Arthur J. Ray, "An Appealing Anthropology, Frozen in Time: Diamond Jenness's *The Indians of Canada*" in *Roots of Entanglement*, 373–99. Nonetheless, his work is of comparative value here. In his words: "In 1931 the mean population of all villages north of the Bering Strait was 165, and south of the Bering Strait just half that number: and in 1940, out of more than 200 Eskimo communities in northern Alaska, only twenty contained more than 200 inhabitants, and not a single one as many as 500."

10 Ibid.

11 Report entitled "Wildlife in Relation to the Eskimos" by J.W. Burton for the Department of Resources and Development, Northern Affairs and National Resources, and Canadian Conservation Association, 1955. LAC, RG 85, Vol. 59, file 160-5-3, pt. 5: Wildlife & Eskimo Economy.

12 Department of Resources and Development document establishing the "Responsibilities of Northern Administration and Lands Branch" (NALB), including the Eskimo Research Section, 1953. The guidance called for "measures by which the economy of the Eskimo people can be placed on a solid footing and the Eskimos successfully adapted to civilization" and "research into the best means of educating and adapting the Eskimos to changing economic conditions through improvement of hunting and fishing techniques, greater use of local

food resources, handicrafts, whaling, cod fishing, eiderdown, boat-building. Plans transfers of Eskimos from overpopulated, depleted areas to areas where game is more plentiful, or where employment may be found. Recommends loans to Eskimos or investments in their projects. Studies Eskimo–trader relations." DEW-line documents collection, courtesy of David Neufeld.

13 Shelaigh Grant, *Errors Exposed: Inuit Relocations to the High Arctic, 1953–1961*, Documents of Arctic Sovereignty and Security, No. 6 (Calgary: University of Calgary, 2016). https://Arctic.ucalgary.ca/dcass-documents-canadian-Arctic-sovereignty-and-security (accessed 8 January 2021). Whitney Lackenbauer disputes whether sovereignty was a primary government motivation in his work, P. Whitney Lackenbauer, Introduction, *Human Flagpoles or Humanitarian Action? Discerning Government Motives behind the Inuit Relocations to the High Arctic, 1953–1960*, Documents on Arctic Sovereignty and Security, No. 16 (Calgary: University of Calgary, 2020), https://Arctic.ucalgary.ca/dcass-documents-canadian-Arctic-sovereignty-and-security (accessed 20 January 2021).

14 Western Electric Corporation, "The DEW Line Story in Brief" (corporate publication circa 1960). "The key roles were played by Bell System people. Western Electric, Bell Telephone Laboratories, nineteen Bell telephone companies and the Long Lines Department of A.T. & T. in the U.S. and the Bell Telephone Company of Canada contributed some of their best men to make up a Bell System team 2,000 strong." Bell System, also known as Ma Bell, was a system of companies headed by American Telephone and Telegraph (AT&T).

15 Memorandum entitled "Construction Projects in the North" from R.G. Robertson, Deputy Minister of the Department of Northern Affairs and Natural Resources for the Advisory Council on Northern Development, 1954, LAC, RG 85, Vol. 376, file 1009-3 pt. 6.

16 "Long-term Plans, Review of 1953 Operations," Canada Department of Northern Affairs and National Resources Northern Administration and Lands Branch, 1954. DEW-line documents collection, courtesy of David Neufeld.

17 "Exchange of Notes Between Canada and the United States of America Governing the Establishment of a Distant Early Warning System in Canadian Territory," Canada, Treaty Series 1955, No. 8.

18 Robert Pittenger, "Arctic Tales and Arctic Trails," unpublished manuscript from the Robert Pittenger Papers covering years 1946–64. Rasmuson Library Archives, University of Alaska Fairbanks.

19 Jack D. Ferguson correspondence with the Department of Northern Affairs and Natural Resources Northern Research Co-ordination Centre, 1956, LAC, RG 85, Vol. 1654, file NR 2/3-3 pt. 1: Effects of DEW Line.

20 Robert Alexie, interview with Stacey Fritz, Fort McPherson, NWT, July 2008.

21 Report by Game Warden H.J. Rees, 1955, LAC, RG 85, Vol. 456, file 420-2/119 pt. 2 Monthly Reports Aklavik Game Warden District A. "Tuk" was a nickname for Tuktoyaktuk.

22 Jack D. Ferguson correspondence with the Department of Northern Affairs and Natural Resources Northern Research Co-ordination Centre, 1957, LAC, RG 85, Vol. 1 1654, file NR 2/3-3 pt. 1 Effects of DEW Line.

23 Stacey Fritz, "DEW Line Passage: Tracing the Legacies of Arctic Militarization" (PhD diss., University of Alaska, 2010). The infrastructure associated with DEW Line sites, particularly airstrips, may have directly supported the viability or re-establishment of two Alaskan Arctic communities (Kaktovik and Point Lay). However, a primary informant from Kaktovik insisted that the DEW Line had not changed her town at all, and a primary informant from Point Lay described, convincingly, how the DEW Line had temporarily killed his town.

24 Ferguson, Effects of DEW Line correspondence, 1957.

25 Ibid.

26 Report by Game Warden H.J. Rees, 1955, LAC, RG 85, Vol. 456, file 420-2/119 pt. 2 Monthly Reports Aklavik Game Warden District A.

27 Ibid.

28 Ibid.

29 Ibid.

30 Ibid.

31 Ibid.

32 Jack D. Ferguson correspondence with the Department of Northern Affairs and Natural Resources Northern Research Co-ordination Centre, 1956, LAC, RG 85, Vol. 1654, file NR 2/3-3 pt. 1: Effects of DEW Line.

33 Report by Game Warden H.J. Rees, 1956, LAC, RG 85, Vol. 456, file 420-2/119 pt. 2. Monthly Reports Aklavik Game Warden District A.

34 Report by Game Warden R.C. Timmins, 1958, LAC, RG 85, Vol. 456, file 420-2/119 pt. 2. Monthly Reports Aklavik Game Warden District A.

35 Ferguson, Effects of DEW Line correspondence, 1957.

36 Norman A. Chance, *The Iñupiat and Arctic Alaska: An Ethnography of Development* (Fort Worth, TX: Holt, Rinehart and Winston, 1990).

37 Ferguson, Effects of DEW Line correspondence, 1956.

38 Ibid.

39 Ferguson, Effects of DEW Line correspondence, 1957.

40 Samuel Lennie, interview with Stacey Fritz, Fairbanks, Alaska, 3 April 2009.

41 Ibid.

42 Ferguson, Effects of DEW Line correspondence, 1957. Ferguson and other anthropologists used the term "European" rather than "southern." The authors

substituted "southern" as nearly all the goods and dominant white cultural influences came from southern Canada or the United States by this period.

43 Ferguson, Effects of DEW Line correspondence, 1956.

44 Memo from Department of Northern Affairs and Natural Resources Deputy Minister Robertson to Herb Donaldson, the General Superintendent of Northern Construction Co. 23 January 1957, LAC, RG 85, Vol. 233, file 680-4 NANR 1956–57 Eskimo Vocational Training.

45 Paper by Palmer W. Roberts entitled "Employment of Eskimos by the Navy at Point Barrow, Alaska," in proceedings of the Third Alaskan Science Conference (Mt McKinley National Park [now Denali National Park] and Fairbanks, Alaska: American Association for the Advancement of Science, Alaska Division, 22–7 September 1952). The paper was prepared by Roberts and read by R.C. Jensen (Civil Engineer Corps, US Navy). G.W. Rowley of the Arctic Research branch of the Canadian Defence Research Board attended the conference and sent the paper to J.G. Wright, Esq, of Canada's Northern Administration Department of Resources and Development, LAC, RG 85, Vol. 233, file 680-4 Eskimo Vocational Training.

46 After F.J.G. Cunningham and other Northern Affairs and Natural Resources (NANR) officials had their first meeting with Admiral Cruzen, vice president of the Federal Electric Company, in 1956, Cunningham reported to NANR Deputy Minister Robertson: "[W]e had an interesting general talk on segregation ... Admiral Cruzen told us frankly he is from the Southern United States and holds quite strong views for segregation," 21 December 1956, LAC, RG 85, Vol. 233, file 680-4 NANR 1956–57 Eskimo Vocational Training.

47 F.J.G. Cunningham, report on meeting with Federal Electric, 1956.

48 NANR Deputy Minister Robertson letter to Admiral Cruzen of the Federal Electric Corporation regarding "FEC employment of Eskimos," 24 March 1958, LAC, RG 85, Vol. 478, file 207-3 pt. 1 DEW – Housing for Eskimo.

49 Robertson, letter to Admiral Cruzen of the Federal Electric Corporation, 1958.

50 Fritz, DEW Line Passage, 2010, 163–5.

51 Ibid.

52 Letter entitled "Eskimo housing at DEW site" from Ben Sivertz, director of the Northern Administration and Lands Branch Arctic Division, to Royal Canadian Air Force Commander Wing Commander Wiseman, March 1958, LAC, RG 85, Vol. 478, file 207-3 pt. 1 DEW – Housing for Eskimos.

53 Samuel Lennie, interview, 2009. All DEW Line stations were time synchronized with Winnipeg. The sites Sammy Lennie lived at in the Mackenzie Delta area were two hours different than local time. Lennie recalled that in Tuktoyaktuk he would get up very early in the morning to catch the school bus, but four

hours after his father had started work. When fathers worked at remote sites (for the Lennies, these were Tununuk and Shingle Point), school-age children were sent away to residential boarding schools from fall to spring every year.

54 Ferguson, Effects of DEW Line correspondence, 1957; Susie Avery (pseudonym), interview, 2008. Before this policy was in place, Ferguson noted that Iñuit camps cobbled together around DEW Line sites contrasted sharply with those constructed for the non-Native workers, who were snugly housed in heated and specially insulated modular buildings. Many of the earliest stick-frame houses in the Arctic were built from DEW Line packing crates, dunnage, and other leftover material. Susie Avery (pseudonym), whose father worked at the Shingle Point site, recalled that the DEW Liners asked the people at the Shingle Point camp if they needed left over materials. Her family's cabin at Running River camp near Shingle Point was built out of DEW Line material, but Susie clarified that just the outside of the house had DEW material, not the inside. Almost everyone along the coast is aware that much of the material recycled from the DEW Sites was produced before there were any regulations on lead paint, PCBs, asbestos, and other hazardous material.

55 Sivertz, letter on DEW housing, 1958. Emphasis in original. The same debate arises again over homelessness in Alaska and new home design to replace substandard housing in villages threatened by climate change. "At Home in the North," Cold Climate Housing Research Center, http://cchrc.org (accessed 11 January 2021).

56 Northern Affairs document entitled "Mechanics Course East 3 Aklavik," January 1957, LAC, RG 85, Vol 406, file 680-3-21-1 pt. 1 Vocational Training – Mechanics. The implication is hard to ignore: without proper education and industrial skills, a person was useless. Pushing their assumptions even further, course designers explained that "this general usefulness may earn them ready recognition and acceptance. Should this be the case, many of the trainees will gain a measure of pride and satisfaction impelling them to seek and get further training of a more specific nature."

57 Ibid.

58 Memo entitled "Accommodation for Eskimo Trainees" by T.M. Taylor, Vocational Coordinator, for the director, August 1967, LAC, RG 85, Vol. 411, file 680-4 pt. 1 & 2 DEW Training for Eskimos.

59 Taylor, memo on DEW training, 1957.

60 Ibid.

61 Ibid.

62 Samuel Lennie, interview, 2009.

63 R.A.J. Phillips, G.F.T. Parsons, and W. Rudnicki (illustrations), *This is the Arctic* (Ottawa: Queen's Printer, 1958).

64 Samuel Lennie, interview, 2009. Asked if people thought they were playing a role in defending North America, Lennie said, "Nooooo."

65 George Agnasagga, interview with Stacey Fritz, Wainwright, 13 September 2009.

66 Samuel Lennie, interview, 2009.

67 Richard Gordon, interview with Stacey Fritz, Herschel Island, Yukon Territory, 24 July 2008. Susie Avery (pseudonym), interview with Stacey Fritz, Running River, Yukon Territory, 18 July 2008.

68 Federal Electric Company, Dewline Department, *Dewline Polar Echoes*, Vol. IV, No 5, 1959: 3. (Several issues of this corporate periodical are available at the University of Alaska Fairbanks Rasmuson Library.)

69 Ibid.

70 Ibid.

71 Samuel Lennie, interview, 2009.

72 Fritz, DEW Line Passage, 2010, 203. Many interviewees had stories about and serious fear of submarines.

73 Cynthia Enloe, *Maneuvers: The International Politics of Militarizing Women's Lives* (Berkeley, Los Angeles, London: University of California Press, 2000), 235–6.

74 James Tazruk, interview by Stacey Fritz, Point Lay, Alaska, September 2009.

75 Samuel Lennie, interview, 2009. Sadly no one will pick these lovely cloudberries now because they may be contaminated.

76 Ferguson, effects of DEW Line correspondence, 1956.

77 Samuel Lennie, interview, 2009.

78 Jenness, *Eskimo Administration, Alaska*, 39–41.

79 Ibid., 40.

80 Various policies and restrictions on alcohol were in place at different times and in different sectors. Sometimes strict quotas were established (e.g., one six-pack per week).

81 Joanne Tompkins, *Teaching in a Cold and Windy Place: Change in an Inuit School* (Toronto: University of Toronto Press, 1998).

82 Samuel Lennie, interview, 2009.

83 Robert Alexie, interview, 2008.

84 Harry Merriman, interview with Stacey Fritz, Fairbanks, Alaska, 3 March 2009; John (pseudonym), interview with Stacey Fritz, Kaktovik, Alaska, 30 May 2009.

85 John Griffin, *Icy Cape* (Sterling, MA: Quail Roost Press, 1980), 8–9. Radomes are the large, white, geodesic domes that housed DEW Line radars. Griffin wrote, "The most distinctive feature of the station was the bulbous geodesic dome which squatted above the long, low module train. The same housed search radar antennas. Their slowly rotating back-to-back snowplow antennas sent out a million-watt ray of focused radar energy hundreds of miles into the

Arctic skies. These giant plastic protuberances hunkering on four stilts gave the station an air of ominous unreality. The buildings and other antennas could be accepted by the landscape, but not this ugly bulb. These electronic warts were positioned every hundred miles across the pate of the earth."

86 Samuel Lennie, interview, 2009.

87 Richard Gordon, interview, 2008.

88 Samuel Lennie, interview, 2009.

89 Ida Olemaun, interview with Stacey Fritz at Peard Bay (Tachim Isua), Alaska, September 2009.

90 James Tazruk, interview with Stacey Fritz, Point Lay, Alaska, 24 September 2009.

91 Sammie Lennie, interview, 2009.

92 Richard Gordon, interview, 2008.

93 Ibid.

94 Indian and Northern Affairs, Northern Contaminants Program, "Canadian Arctic Contaminants Assessment Report (CACAR II)" (Ottawa: Ministry of Public Works and Government Canada, 2003).

95 Heather Ducharme, "Here We Fight the Coldest War: Environmental Science and Feminist Autobiography on the DEW Line," Outstanding Graduate Papers series, York University, 2003. https://yorkspace.library.yorku.ca/xmlui/handle/10315/18093.

96 Inutiq Karl, Geronimo Cote, Philippe Simon (Qikiqtaaluk Environmental), and Sheila Street (Independent Consultant), "Collection and Use of Inuit Traditional Environmental Knowledge in DEW Line Site Investigations" (Edmonton: paper presented at the Assessment and Remediation of Contaminated Sites in Arctic and Cold Climates conference, 2005).

97 Samuel Lennie, interview, 2009.

98 Ibid.

99 Richard Gordon, interview, 2008.

100 Bruce Inglangasak, interview with Stacey Fritz, Kaktovik, Alaska, 24 May 2009.

101 Western Electric Corporation, DEW Line Story, circa 1960.

102 Richard Gordon, interview, 2008.

103 Samuel Lennie, interview, 2009.

104 Ibid.

105 Bruce Inglangasak, interview, 2009.

106 Ibid.

107 Susie Avery (pseudonym), interview with Stacey Fritz, Running River camp near the Shingle Point DEW Line station, Yukon Territory, 18 July 2008.

108 Bruce Inglangasak, interview, 2009.

109 Ibid.

110 Ibid.

111 Ibid.

112 Samuel Lennie, interview, 2009.

113 "U.S.–Canadian Agreement on Distant Early Warning System," (Department of State Bulletin 33.836, 1955).

114 National Defence. The Distant Early Warning Line. https://www.canada.ca/en/department-national-defence/corporate/video/other/distant-early-warning-line-an-environmental-legacy-project.html (accessed 21 January 2021).

115 US–Canadian Agreement on environmental cleanup of defense sites effected by exchange of notes, signed at Washington 7 and 9 October 1996; Entered into force 9 October 1996, https://www.state.gov/wp-content/uploads/2019/02/12806-Canada-Defense-Misc-Agreement-10.7.1996-and-10.9.1996.pdf (accessed 18 January 2021).

116 Kevin McMahon, *Arctic Twilight: Reflections on the Destiny of Canada's Northern Land and People* (Toronto: James Lorimer & Company, 1988).

117 Lutz, *Homefront*; Catherine Lutz, "Making War at Home in the United States: Militarization and the Current Crisis," *American Anthropologist* 104, no. 3 (2002): 723–35; Andrew J. Bacevich, *The New American Militarism: How Americans are Seduced by War* (New York, NY: Oxford University Press, 2005).

118 In contrast, Whitney Lackenbauer's work on Canadian rangers suggests it has had a more profound and lasting influence on the Canadian Inuit population. Whitney Lackenbauer, *The Canadian Rangers: A Living History* (Vancouver: UBC Press, 2013).

119 Richard Gordon, interview, 2008.

4

Overcoming Monotony

Sensory Deprivation and Psychological Research in the Cold War

MATTHEW S. WISEMAN

In May 1954, *Maclean's Magazine* printed a five-page article about a series of psychological research experiments initiated three years earlier at McGill University. Author Frank Croft reported that Professor Donald O. Hebb had paid a group of student volunteers $20 per day to lie isolated in a soundproofed room, wearing opaque goggles and arms cuffs while listening to propaganda.[1] Instructed to remain silent except when completing minor cognitive tests, the research subjects remained isolated for as long as individually possible. While in this state of perceptual isolation and confinement, Hebb and his research assistants studied the physical and emotional responses of each person subjected to the experiment. Of a reported 200 volunteers, sixty-three students participated, most ending the experiment after a few hours.[2] The experience of isolation produced a strong reaction. One person visualized a field of floating eyeglasses while another saw a troop of squirrels marching on snowshoes, and both experiences were illustrated for Croft's article by artist Bruce Johnson.[3] Others recalled feeling vibrations and hearing sounds or aural sensations. None of the volunteers knew that they were the first subjects in a series of related experiments that would occur for the next twenty years, research firmly grounded in the evolving security context of the early Cold War.

The *Maclean's* article is one of the few remaining sources with first-hand accounts of Hebb's sensory deprivation research. Touted as an experiment into the dangers of boredom, neither Croft nor his readers questioned the motivations or funding behind the research. Subject responses produced amusement rather than concern and there was little realization of any potential long-term effects. At the same time, not a single participant expressed concern publicly over their individual safety. Perceived as purely scientific research, there was also no suggestion linking the experiment with military research involving psychological warfare. The article stated clearly that Canada's Defence Research Board (DRB) covered "the $20-a-day fee for volunteers," but Croft did not inquire as to why the federal government funded the experimentation. His description of Hebb's research focused on the scientific importance of the study, urging readers to understand and appreciate the health implications of sensory stimulation.

Concerned that communist forces in Korea had used mind control techniques to induce false confessions from captured soldiers, military and defence officials from Canada, Britain, and the United States funded sensory deprivation research to investigate a possible scientific method for manipulating human behaviour. In theory, psychological experimentation provided information considered useful for training soldiers to recognize and withstand brainwashing if captured by the enemy. Hebb's sponsors funded his research accordingly, an important detail unbeknownst to Croft and his readers at the time of publication. Two years later in April 1956, press reports out of New York and Montreal claimed that the Canadian government had financed Hebb's work for military purposes.[4] The media was unaware of the full extent of the research, but the press reports led to a parliamentary debate and criticism of the federal officials who had approved the research funding. Little came of the debate and psychological research involving sensory deprivation continued, only becoming publicly controversial more than a decade later when international events brought a heightened awareness to the experimental work.

This chapter examines the controversial history of sensory deprivation research in Canada, drawing a discernable link between Hebb's work and later isolation research involving radar technicians in the Canadian north. In addition to investigating behavioural control, government officials sponsored Hebb's research to learn about human responses to monotonous work environments. Worried that an operator might fall asleep while watching a radar screen in an isolated booth, military authorities supported sensory deprivation research as a plausible solution for an issue of increasing significance during the atomic age: effective early warning against the long-range bomber threat. The existing secondary literature on the history of sensory deprivation research in Canada has dismissed the scientific investigation of monotony as a legitimate cause for the experimental studies, opting instead for sensationalist accounts linking Hebb's work with techniques developed for brainwashing and torture.[5] While the fear associated with communist brainwashing motivated sensory deprivation research, Canadian officials also funded isolation research to overcome the practical problems associated with operating a functioning radar network in northern Canada. Radar technicians and military personnel often performed mundane but crucial work in remote and unusual surroundings, labouring on the frontlines as part of Canada's wide-ranging efforts to wage the Cold War. The work they performed factored into decisions about sensory deprivation research and military-funded experimentation involving human subjects, thus signalling the need to consider the role and implications of monotonous labour within the context of the Cold War Canadian state.

DONALD HEBB, EWEN CAMERON, AND MK-ULTRA

Canada's role in sensory deprivation research and Cold War-era psychology is a complex and controversial subject, largely because of the disturbing history involving psychiatrist Ewen Cameron. In the 1980s, former patients of the Allan Memorial Institute (AMI) in Montreal sued the US Central Intelligence Agency (CIA) for financing a series of medically unethical research experiments linked to mind control and brainwashing. Cameron was a former chair of McGill University's Department of Psychiatry, which was founded in 1943 and based at the

AMI. As department chair and director of the AMI, he had received funding from a CIA front during the 1950s to conduct psychiatric experiments on unknowing medical patients. A small but important body of scholarship has documented the Cameron experiments, including Anne Collins's *In the Sleep Room*, winner of the Governor General's Award for English-language non-fiction and the inspiration for Anne Wheeler's 1998 film, *The Sleep Room*.[6] The CIA code word for the research was MK-ULTRA subproject 68, but the exact details of Cameron's involvement remain unclear. Because the CIA funded his research through a front organization, Cameron may not have known the true source of the funds or the intentions of the CIA to use the results of his research for psychological warfare purposes. Nevertheless, the testimony of Cameron's former patients revealed a startling connection between the American national security state and the Canadian medical profession.

Information implicating the Canadian government became public during the CIA court proceedings when documents revealed that Cameron had also received research funding from the DRB. Established in April 1947 as the research branch of the Canadian armed services, the DRB funded and carried out scientific research projects of value to security and national defence.[7] During a deposition recorded in August 1988, Omond Solandt, who chaired the DRB between 1947 and 1956, denied knowledge of Cameron's alleged brainwashing work for the CIA. When asked about the allegations concerning the involvement of the CIA in Cameron's psychiatric research at the AMI, Solandt referenced Hebb's research and the CIA but claimed that neither he nor the DRB had any connection with Cameron's work under MK-ULTRA. "I had no contact with the CIA in relation to their work with the Allen [*sic*] Memorial or with Dr Cameron," said Solandt. "I knew nothing about it – well, I guess the first time I knew about it was when there was some publicity in the papers about the suits in Canada by Orlikow and Merrill. But I was not involved at all. I had no communication with anybody about it."[8] Solandt took his comments further, condemning Cameron outright in a statement supporting the victims of the experimental psychiatric treatment. "It was my view at the time and continues to be that Cameron was not possessed of the necessary humanity to be regarded as a good doctor," continued Solandt, seemingly contradicting his earlier statement that he knew nothing of Cameron's research.[9] In the end, the CIA settled the lawsuit and the Canadian government ordered a judicial report into Cameron's experiments.[10]

Canada's Justice Department assigned former federal parliamentarian George Cooper the responsibility of determining whether the federal government had any legal or moral obligation to the victims. Cooper ultimately decided that Ottawa was not responsible.[11] Eight years later, in 1994, the Government of Canada awarded $100,000 to seventy-seven former patients who suffered "total depatterning," meaning Cameron's experimental psychiatric treatment had rendered each patient to a childlike state.[12] More than 250 others had their compensation denied at the time of the court ruling. Recently, the CBC's Elizabeth Thompson reported that the federal government quietly reached an out-of-court settlement with Alison Steel, the daughter of Jean Steel, a former patient and one of Cameron's experimental test subjects.[13] According to Thompson's report, Steel received $100,000 in exchange for dropping a legal action that she launched in September 2015. "She was never able to really function as a healthy human being because of what they did to her," Steel said referring to her mother.[14]

The parallels between Cameron's psychiatric experimentation and sensory deprivation research have led to accusations against Hebb.[15] As faculty colleagues at McGill, Cameron and Hebb crossed paths as professional academics and the two certainly discussed research in medical science. They also received research funding from government and military sources, including the DRB, and there is some evidence to suggest that Cameron's research was a continuation of Hebb's initial study. In fact, Washington lawyer James Turner, who represented the Canadian plaintiffs in their lawsuit against the CIA, obtained documents about a CIA project called Operation Bluebeard that showed the US spy agency had secretly infiltrated and monitored Hebb's entire study.[16] The documents reportedly showed that the CIA had financed Cameron to carry on Hebb's work using hallucinogens like LSD. When interviewed about the revelations from his Nova Scotia home in February 1984, Hebb retrospectively linked his work to interrogation: "I had no suspicion when we began that it would turn out to be what it did ... It was clear when we wrote our report to the Defence Research

Board that we were describing formidable interrogation techniques."[17] Whether Hebb understood the CIA's role or connection with Cameron at the time of the research is unclear, however, and the surviving information is murky at best.

Regardless of the finer details, both Cameron and Hebb exposed human subjects to experimental research that caused immediate harm. This does not suggest that Hebb's research subjects experienced harm comparable with the short- and long-term psychological damages inflicted upon Cameron's experimental patients. Both experiments produced different results and any shared association with mind control research should not reduce the subjects to one harmful experience. Sensationalist accounts about the history of human experimentation can blur the lines between fact and fiction, obscuring the past at the detriment of context and the development of fulsome historical understanding. This chapter takes a step back, intervening in the existing literature, to investigate the wider history of sensory deprivation research and monotonous work in Cold War Canada. As Isabel Campbell explains in the introductory chapter, developing a complete picture of the Cold War state requires acknowledging the accomplishments of diverse labourers while unearthing silences in the historical record. In Canada, science bridged the divide between labour and security, and monotony offers a unique window into the interconnected experience of government authorities, military personnel, research subjects, and civilians who worked to ensure and protect Canadian interests.

THE FORMATIVE YEARS OF SENSORY DEPRIVATION RESEARCH

During the first year of the Korean conflict in 1950–51, senior military officials in Canada, Britain, and the United States became concerned about the development and use of so-called mind control techniques by communist forces. Authorities cited public denouncements of the conflict made by captured American soldiers as evidence that the Chinese had developed a method for brainwashing.[18] With little or no evidence of physical coercion, the Western authorities believed that communist forces had found a successful method for controlling the mind and inducing voluntary or genuine confessions.[19] Long periods of isolation, followed by repetitive indoctrination to new beliefs, seemed to be key to mind control and confessional extraction. In response, all three countries committed to research in the hope that science might yield a solution for training soldiers to recognize, resist, and overcome brainwashing if captured.

Canadian authorities took a leading role in promoting science as a solution to the mind control problem. In May 1951, senior DRB representatives organized a high-level meeting for military representatives and scientists to discuss psychological coercion.[20] The meeting occurred on 1 June at the Ritz-Carleton Hotel in Montreal, mere blocks from McGill University, Canada's premier institution in the field of medical psychology. As chair of the DRB, Omond Solandt served as Canada's leading representative. Sir Henry Tizard, chief scientific adviser to the British defence ministry, represented the UK government. Tizard had visited the United States and Canada during the Second World War to facilitate scientific co-operation in military research and development.[21] The British shared technical information to secure assistance in maintaining the war effort. Technical information shared during the Tizard Mission advanced the development of such wartime innovations as radar, the proximity fuse, submarine-detection equipment, gyroscopic gunsights, and rockets. Tizard and Solandt developed a professional working relationship during the war and fostered a strong postwar connection between the federal defence agencies of Canada and the United Kingdom. Representatives of the CIA also attended the meeting, including Commander R.J. Williams and researcher Caryl Haskins.[22]

The Montreal meeting had an immediate and lasting impact on psychological research in Canada. Of the many scientific theories discussed, a suggestion by McGill psychologist and Solandt invitee, Donald Hebb, piqued the interest of the group. Hebb proposed experiments in "sensory isolation" for inducing opinion changes or attitudinal conversion in individuals: "[Hebb] suggested a situation whereby an individual might be placed in a situation (translucent suit) in which, by means of the cutting off of all sensory stimulation save some minor proprioceptive sensations and by the use of 'white noise,' the individual could be led into a situation whereby ideas, etc. might be implanted."[23] Hebb's proposed study of experimental isolation for inducing psychological manipulation gained traction, edging out other such suggestions as the use of depressing drugs to elicit behavioural changes chemically.

Hebb's idea for a sensory isolation research study had developed over the course of fifteen years. He earned his doctorate from Harvard University in 1936, where he examined the learning processes of rats raised in complete darkness. He expanded his research in 1942 after accepting a research position at the Yerkes Primate Lab in Florida.[24] He studied the cognitive functioning of chimpanzees alongside experimental psychologist Austin Riesen, who became a leading expert in deprivation research involving animals.[25] Appointed a professor of psychology at McGill University in 1947, Hebb moved to Montreal and continued his research. He published *The Organization of Behavior* two years later, a formative book that introduced his theory about the neural basis of learning.[26] Hebb expanded his research on animals at McGill by raising rats and dogs in various environments, work that provided the theoretical basis for his sensory deprivation research.

In September 1951, three months after the Montreal meeting, DRB officials contracted Hebb to conduct a series of fundamental research projects concerning the experimental manipulation of attitude in individuals subjected to sensory isolation. At the time, the operant conditioning work of notable behaviourist B.F. Skinner attracted numerous psychologists to research involving the modification of human behaviour. The anxiety-laden context of the early Cold War period created an appetite for this field of research. Security concerns about espionage and the spread of communism, inflamed by the prisoner of war confessions in Korea, fed a growing intrigue in mind control among Western officials and the public. Physicians and researchers did not sit idle. Psychiatrist Robert Jay Lifton deconstructed the mechanisms of "thought reform" in communist China, while cardiologist Lawrence Hinkle and neurologist Harold Wolff wrote about interrogation and indoctrination in China and the Soviet Union.[27] As for Hebb, he commenced his sensory isolation experiments on human subjects during this peak period for psychological research into behavioural modification.

The key to Hebb's proposal was the idea of a psychological research study not involving any physical punishment, because scientists did not consider isolation to be a form of torture when he began his experiments at McGill.[28] Hebb's previous research on animals indicated the effectiveness of isolation for influencing changes in attitude. The non-violent nature of the research appealed to Solandt, who expressed concern at the Montreal meeting about the possibility of a press leak and any public reaction to an experimental study. Whether the DRB's chair was unwilling to engage the public in debate about experimental science is unclear, but Solandt's reluctance to discuss psychological research into sensory isolation suggests an awareness of treading on morally questionable grounds.

Solandt's correspondence indicates that he alone made the decision to contract Hebb. Solandt was a member of the Chiefs of Staff Committee, equal in status to the head of the army, navy, and air force. He was also the senior most scientist in the Department of National Defence and held considerable power and authority over research funds distributed by the DRB. "It was thought," Solandt explained in a January 1954 letter to Minister of National Defence Brooke Claxton, "that if we knew more about what was possible, any remedy or safeguard which we should use would suggest itself more readily."[29] Given the large quantity of research projects financed by the DRB, it is likely that Claxton had simply forgotten that he had approved Hebb's research three years earlier. Under the amended National Defence Act of April 1947, appointed members of the DRB had the authority to distribute funds from the federal defence budget to support military research projects.[30] The approval process was clear and efficient. Solandt and his senior staff reviewed grant applications, recommended projects considered valuable for the armed services, and the defence minister forwarded the recommendations to the governor in council for final authorization.[31] Approval was a mere formality, however. Officers in the federal finance department maintained a trust fund for the DRB and there is little evidence to suggest that senior ministers ever rejected a research project submitted for budgetary approval. Solandt's recommendations held considerable weight and no one in the federal government disagreed with his decision to support Hebb's research.

ISOLATION RESEARCH AT MCGILL UNIVERSITY

Donald Hebb's confidential study for the DRB aimed to develop a technique for influencing attitude through isolation and propaganda.[32] Subjects recruited from the McGill student body received $20 per twenty-four hours spent in isolation.[33] Each student wore light-defusing goggles and arm cuffs while resting backside-down on a bed. The cuffs extended from the elbow joint beyond the fingertips to reduce tactile perception.[34] Instructed to remain silent except when asking to hear the recorded propaganda or when completing minor cognitive tests as assigned by Hebb and his research assistants, test subjects remained isolated until they chose to end the experiment.

Aware of the potential short-term risks involved with the research, Hebb implemented minor safeguards to minimize any emotional or cognitive danger. Students participated out of their own volition and could terminate the experiment at any time. The only inducement to be a subject was monetary and the researchers never urged the participants to stay in isolation. Rather than use propaganda related to politics or religion, the experiment tested the subjects for responses to "such relatively innocuous topics as ghosts, poltergeists, extra-sensory perception and the Lamarckian theory versus the Darwinian theory of evolution."[35] The subject matter of the propaganda and circumstances of sensory isolation evoked strong responses, nonetheless. "The human being kept for prolonged periods without the normal variability of sensory input is not only very restless and unhappy ('bored')," Hebb wrote in a letter describing the experiment.[36] "Intellectual capacity is significantly affected, and very elaborate visual and somesthetic hallucinatory activity is apt to occur." Despite Hebb's clear awareness of the intense psychological response produced in subjects, he showed little realization of any long-term dangers associated with exposing humans to sensory isolation.

Surprisingly, neither the Canadian press nor Parliament reacted to the research experiment when *Maclean's* published Frank Croft's article in May 1954. Croft linked the DRB with Hebb's work, but his article produced intrigue rather than concern. "From the experiments at McGill," wrote Croft, "there is now firm ground for the belief that boredom is not a harmless condition, having no physical effect on the brain. It upsets the proper functioning of the brain and can upset it to such a degree that one's job or even one's life is endangered."[37] The experiment had allegedly indicated the dangers of monotony, a point that overshadowed any concern for the safety of the test subjects.

The potential military applications of sensory isolation research surfaced eight months later when a group of veterans in Montreal asked Hebb to speak about brainwashing. Indicating a deep interest in reports that communist forces had broken the "will and resistance" of captured soldiers, the group wanted to learn about the psychological science of mind control.[38] Hebb turned down the request, to the surprise of the veterans, who learned from McGill's leading psychology professor that Ottawa had funded classified research on the subject. Hebb reportedly told the veterans that the federal government had funded research linked with brainwashing. He openly stated that his work was classified and informed the group that any subsequent talk required official clearance, which he did not expect to receive.

Hebb had tried unsuccessfully to declassify his DRB-funded research. In November 1953, fourteen months before he met the veterans, he sent a letter to the DRB requesting permission to speak publicly about his research at a psychology conference. "While I regret it very much if I appear to be unreasonable," replied the DRB's Nelson Morton, "I still feel that as a matter of policy it would not be desirable for us to give any publicity whatever to that part of the contract which relates to the use of isolation as a condition under which to attempt to influence subjects' attitudes."[39] Morton subsequently denied the request, stating his concern that the press might misinterpret or distort the reason for the experimental research. Hebb respected the security restrictions, which precluded him from discussing his research and divulging information when approached by the veterans. Local press in Montreal did not follow up the story and Hebb continued his research under the security restrictions established by the DRB authorities.

Another fifteen months passed before the experiments became publicly controversial. On 17 April 1956, Liberal defence minister Ralph Campney came under criticism in the House of Commons when Progressive Conservative MP Davie Fulton questioned the financial involvement of the federal government in the alleged brainwashing research conducted at McGill.[40] Referring to press reports from *The New York Times* and *The Gazette* (Montreal), Fulton said he found it difficult to believe that the Canadian government had reportedly financed and encouraged brainwashing research involving human test subjects. In response, Campney conceded that federal research funding had supported a series of experiments conducted at McGill between 1951 and 1953. "Certain experiments were made which demonstrated pretty conclusively," said the defence minister, "that purely by mental suggestion people could be reduced to a certain state of mind and that while in that state of mind you could get them to accept any suggestion and assert it as the truth."[41] Interestingly, Campney claimed that the experiments had ended before he had assumed his post as defence minister in July 1954. That was untrue. According to a later statement by Hebb, the experiments at McGill ended in 1955 and the research funds for the study originated from the Canadian defence budget.[42] Campney either misinformed Parliament or was merely unaware that the defence department had continued funding the McGill research after he had assumed his post.[43]

Judging by the banter of the House debate, Parliament did not appreciate the gravity and severity of the experiments under question. While making his remarks, Campney inappropriately compared the isolated subjects of the research to "some members of the opposition; they accepted anything and even believed it to be true." Fulton followed Campney's response by asking if the Liberal's had access to the research results and questioned why Parliament had only learned of the experiments through external press reports. Liberal MP Lorne MacDougall then asked Fulton if he wanted "to be a guinea pig" in future experiments.[44] Fulton replied, "No; there are enough of them of your side, so I do not need to volunteer."[45]

Unsatisfied and surely sensing an opportunity for political blood, Fulton raised the issue again one week later. "In light of the minister's earlier answer to a question on this subject on April 17," he said in the House, "I wonder if the minister's brains have been washed so that he has forgotten he was minister in the years 1954 and 1955."[46] Campney responded by reiterating his initial statement, again claiming that the experimentation occurred between late 1951 and early 1953. "This was all before my time as minister," Campney declared. "There were other experiments carried on at McGill following that date, but they had nothing to do with changing the mental attitude of [the] persons to which I referred."[47] Campney based his statement on information provided by his officials, suggesting that he was unaware of the research prior to the press leak. The minister provided a detailed financial breakdown two weeks later, in response to a final round of questions from Fulton. Campney verbally listed research grants for 1951–53, claiming that the Department of National Defence paid approximately $17,000 over three years.[48]

Despite reports linking the experiments with brainwashing, the public response showed little concern for the safety of the research subjects. Amid escalating Cold War tensions, local press in Montreal took pride in the fact that McGill had made a newsworthy contribution to Canadian security and national defence. One report referred to the experimental study as a "fantastic secret, closely guarded by students, professors, faculty and even the janitors of the building where the experiments took place ... One of McGill's 'progressive' professors [Donald Hebb] has studied Russian tactics for many years. He is now considered one of the world's leading authorities on methods of torture, brainwashing and indoctrination."[49] Even considering this red flag, there were no reports of coercion, or any other form of subject mistreatment having occurred during the experimentation. The students subjected to isolation participated willingly, although the term volunteer is a slightly misleading label. Local and national media knew of the DRB's involvement, but no subsequent investigation followed, and the experiment faded from the public eye.

PSYCHOLOGICAL WARFARE AND RESEARCH PRIORITIES

Sensory isolation research had wide applicability, or so was the belief of the authorities who championed the work. In his correspondence with other branches of the federal government, Solandt argued that Hebb's research was valuable for assessing enemy capabilities and developing countermeasures to train military and government personnel. Consider Solandt's written explanation to D.M. Watters of the Department of Finance:

> For example, if an individual realizes that under conditions of close confinement he is likely to lose some of his ordinary perspective and sense of normal values and probably be susceptible to suggestion, he may by virtue of this realization be able to keep his guard raised more consciously and deliberately than he would otherwise tend to do. Similarly, if he appreciates that under such conditions there may be some loss of normal intellectual efficiency and he may suffer hallucination-like experiences he is less likely to believe that he is actually "losing his mind" or his normal control over himself.[50]

While Solandt's description implies that authorities in the DRB financed Hebb's research solely for defensive purposes, archival records indicate an institutional interest in the offensive possibilities of psychological manipulation. In February 1952, senior DRB representatives devised a priority system for military research projects undertaken or supported by the defence department.[51] The system stipulated two essential criteria: (1) operational research and analysis; and (2) the development of new and improved weapons, equipment, and *techniques* for warfare.[52] Canadian authorities prioritized both research areas for potential military applications.

For senior DRB officials, the potential military applications of sensory isolation research fit an institutional interest in psychological warfare and Cold War operations. Defined as "the employment of any non-lethal or clandestine means to affect morale and behaviour for a specific military purpose," authorities in the DRB supported research in this area to determine the feasibility and potential uses of psychological warfare techniques, for both defensive and offensive purposes.[53] Possible research subjects included not only military and government personnel but also civilians, with the aim of developing methods to protect Canadians from "enemy propaganda, sabotage, and the psychological threat of material warfare."[54] DRB authorities also emphasized the value of psychological warfare for the reconstitution of government and military personnel of defeated enemy nations.[55] Although described as an area of only "very slight" interest to Canada, the forethought of funding psychological warfare research highlights the extent to which Cold War security anxieties permeated military research planning inside the Canadian defence department.[56]

Canada's top military and defence officials also believed that sensory isolation research was valuable for understanding and counteracting the effects of monotonous military tasks, especially radar booth operation. In fact, records concerning Hebb's sensory isolation research often cited the difficult and mundane work involved with watching a radar screen for long periods.[57] According to a confidential memorandum prepared for the DRB's panel of psychiatry experts, researchers designed the study to cast light on "the problem of the intellectual functioning of individuals on isolated outpost duty," including the gradual inattention of a technician performing monotonous tasks.[58] From the perspective of senior leaders in the Canadian armed services, the implications of research concerning radar operation were both scientific and practical. Nuclear bombers posed the primary threat to North American safety during the early 1950s, and scientists and engineers in the DRB played a pivotal role in facilitating the strategic placement of early-warning radar sites in northern Canada.[59]

Hebb undertook his research at a time when human error in a radar booth meant the possible failure to detect and defend against a major nuclear strike, potentially resulting in a devastating attack against North America. Continental air defence against nuclear bombers depended on the construction and operation of an effective early warning network. As early as 1946, the Canada–US Permanent Joint Board on Defence had initiated plans to construct a series of radar stations near the border along the fiftieth parallel.[60] Funding prevented the project until 1949 when Congress agreed to co-finance radar construction with the Royal Canadian Air Force. Officials in Ottawa and Washington agreed on a construction plan for thirty-three radar stations known as the Pinetree Line, located across the mid-north from Vancouver Island to Labrador.[61] Before construction finished, the Soviet Union had upgraded its bomber force and the North American representatives agreed to co-fund radar stations farther north.[62] Circumstances worsened again in August 1953 when the Soviet Union first tested a hydrogen bomb, leading to a series of successful detonations that began in November 1955 and ended in October 1961. In response to the escalating nuclear threat, strategic analysts in Ottawa and Washington planned the construction of the Mid-Canada Line (MCL), along the fifty-fifth parallel, paid for entirely by Canada. The number of northern radar stations increased for a third time by joint agreement in May 1955 when both countries agreed in principle to construct and operate a Distant Early Warning Line in the far north.[63] Construction was only one issue, however. Effective operation of the North American radar network required advanced technology and capable operators.

Anticipating the active requirements of a functioning radar network meant learning about the human and technical issues of constant operation and surveillance. Concerned that an operator might lose focus in the sensory-deprived environment of an isolated radar station, the supporters of sensory isolation research believed in the dual-use applicability of the potential results. "With this new understanding," wrote A. Hartley Zimmerman, Solandt's successor as DRB chair, "we believe that practical application in relieving monotony in isolated posts (such as radar operators on the DEW line) by introducing sound, colour and other external stimuli may be developed."[64] In short, authorities in the defence department tied isolation research to multiple aspects of security in the nuclear age. They supported Hebb's research not only in response to the fear of communist mind control but also to avoid having bored and exhausted radar operators miss a major attack, thus negating the entire air defence effort.

ISOLATION RESEARCH AT THE UNIVERSITY OF MANITOBA

The launch of Sputnik in October 1957 reaffirmed the practical value of sensory deprivation research, or so scientists funded by the federal government contended. Canada did not train or produce astronauts at the time, but DRB-funded scientists made significant contributions in telecommunications and space research. The International Geophysical Year of 1957–58 saw hundreds of Canadian scientists participate in national projects carried out at several research establishments across the country, including work on atmospheric physics and the aurora borealis conducted at the Churchill Research Range in northern Manitoba.[65] Government scientists at Churchill developed and tested the Black Brant series of sounding rockets, for instance. Scientists in the DRB also initiated the Alouette satellite program, a technology designed to study the effects of the ionosphere on long distance communications.[66] The launch of Alouette-I in September 1962 marked Canada's first satellite and the only successful satellite constructed by a country other than the Soviet Union or the United States.[67] As the Cold War space race captivated public observers, scientists and engineers in Canada contributed new research with the goal of advancing Western superiority. Anticipating the challenges of space travel for astronauts, DRB scientists in Toronto constructed a human centrifuge and carried out experiments to study the effects of gravitational force on pilots.[68] Sensory deprivation research conformed to this pattern, since Canadian scientists theorized the practical value of psychological testing for astronaut training.

John Zubek, a psychologist at the University of Manitoba, began his research into sensory deprivation two years after the launch of Sputnik. Zubek was a close colleague of Donald Hebb. The two had worked together at McGill University before Zubek relocated to Winnipeg in 1953. "It is unfortunate from the point of view of this laboratory that we lost Dr. John Zubek to the University of Manitoba," Hebb wrote in a research report for the National Research Council, "but he contributed a great deal of lasting value before leaving here, and we now have a group of senior graduate students and young members of the full-time staff who are fully capable of independent work."[69] Canada had few research centres undertaking work in experimental psychology during the mid-1950s, but a growing body of qualified scientists expressed interest in the field. Curiosity about the human mind was one motivator, as was the increased government funding available for specific research projects undertaken at Canadian universities. Security interests shaped the medical research community, producing a cohort of individuals who supported and encouraged work in this area.

Hebb's research clearly influenced Zubek, who also subjected people to isolation and confinement for psychological research purposes. Zubek created an isolation laboratory at the University of Manitoba and initiated a series of sensory deprivation experiments in 1959.[70] During the first year of tests, twenty-two people ranging in age from nineteen to thirty-four spent multiple days isolated in a darkened, soundproofed chamber, approximately seven feet tall and nine feet in diameter.[71] The test subjects included graduate students in the biological sciences and aircrew personnel from RCAF Station, Winnipeg. Lying flat on their back and wearing noise-cancelling earmuffs, each person endured isolation until they decided to end the experiment. Six requested their release from isolation within the first three days. The other sixteen subjects experienced at least seven days in isolation, one remaining in the chamber for ten days. Research assistants passed food through a small lock device and occasionally tested the cognitive and perceptual abilities of each isolated individual, but subjects otherwise had no visual or aural contact and used rudimentary lavatories located under the floor.

Authorities in the DRB approved Zubek's isolation research under the assumption that the experiment would not cause long-term negative health effects. In March 1960, the DRB's Morley Whillans contacted Professor George Sisler, head of the Faculty of Medicine at the University of Manitoba, while reviewing Zubek's research grant for renewal. Whillans asked Sisler to provide information about the safety procedures for selecting student research subjects. "Since experience thus far indicates no undesirable continuing psychological effects on the subjects, and the present screening consists of utilizing persons considered by their supervisors to be well adjusted and stable, and subjecting them to preliminary psychological tests," Sisler replied, "I do not believe that a psychiatric interview would add anything of value to this."[72] Whillans accepted Sisler's explanation and the DRB subsequently renewed Zubek's research grant.

Four months later, Zubek submitted a report that gave Whillans cause for concern. In a paper vetted for publication, Zubek described a nurse who had experienced trouble adjusting to regular professional duties after leaving the isolation chamber. The paper caused Whillans to question Zubek's safety procedures and visit Winnipeg, where he personally inspected the isolation laboratory on campus. "There is no check of each subject's condition beyond one day after the completion of tests," Whillans documented in his report. "Dr. Zubek is confident that the 7-day period of isolation (the maximum period now planned is 7 days for each test) will result in no undesirable after-effects beyond 24 hours following the test period. The only undesirable effect he had noted has been loss of recent recall, leading to annoyance and frustration."[73] Convinced that Zubek had taken the necessary precautions to protect the safety and wellbeing of his research subjects, Whillans returned to Ottawa and filed his report approving the experimental procedures.

Despite Whillans' report, senior military officials expressed concern for the safety of Zubek's test subjects. On 10 August, Lieutenant General S.F. Clark, chief of the General Staff, wrote a letter seeking clarification about the experiment. Zubek had argued that monetary incentives were necessary for motivating service volunteers, but Clark hesitated to sign a submission to the Governor General requesting authority to pay military personnel a special remuneration for volunteering as test subjects. "Because civilians at a particular university have to be paid a rapidly increasing wage scale to participate in unpleasant exercises or experiments, and if for this reason we attempt to get authority to pay servicemen for similar experiments, I believe we may set a bad precedent," Clark explained.[74] In a follow-up memorandum, Major General Desmond Smith indicated that Surgeon General T.B. McLean thought Zubek's experiment could "impose [a] severe physiological and psychological reaction on the participants" involved.[75] McLean wanted all participating service personnel to receive medical monitoring. As an added safeguard, Zubek recommended no flying by aircrew test subjects for two days after isolation. RCAF medical officers accepted the recommendations and examined volunteer participants before return to regular service duties. Although Whillans had expressed concern for the safety of non-military research subjects, the civilians who participated did not receive the medical attention given to the RCAF volunteers.

The long duration represented a significant difference between Zubek's research, and any prior isolation experiment conducted by Canadian scientists. Subjects received $100 for spending a minimum of one week in the isolation chamber, with bonus payments if their confinement meant absenteeism from work. "The purpose of the research project is to answer three main questions," Zubek wrote in a 1961 research report prepared for the DRB. "First, what are the effects of various adverse environmental conditions (e.g., darkness and silence, constant light and noise), operating in restricted quarters, on intellectual and perceptual functioning? Second, what methods or procedures might be employed to counteract or minimize any impairment that may occur under the previously mentioned conditions? Third, what type of personality structure might be most conducive to adequate psychological functioning under various adverse environmental conditions?"[76] Despite the intensity of the experimental research, participation did not guarantee payment. Like Hebb's research at McGill, subjects who decided to leave Zubek's isolation chamber within twenty-four hours received no pay. "We would like to have them stay in longer [than one week] but we are running risks," Zubek said when interviewed about the experiments.[77] "We are pushing into unexplored territory. These are very drastic conditions." Despite this clear recognition of the dangers associated with prolonged isolation, the experiment continued. Much like his mentor, Hebb, Zubek willingly accepted the risks associated with the research to make scientific gains.

Zubek's concern for the safety of his test subjects derived from his own personal experience. Before he conducted research on willing participants, Zubek himself spent ten days isolated in the chamber. He lived in confinement, with minimal contact, for nearly one week longer than any previously recorded experimental period. His experience and the reactions of the people isolated for one week or more produced surprising results, because long periods of confinement allegedly produced no discernable impairment of individual cognitive abilities. "The complex reasoning processes do not seem to be impaired," Zubek explained.[78] "There is a very strong suggestion that for the first two or three days the processes are better than normal." It is difficult to say whether Zubek consciously underplayed the human problems of his research, but he knowingly and deliberately reiterated the value of his research when speaking with the media. He understood isolation affected his test subjects, but firmly convinced in the value of sensory deprivation research, he conducted the experiment, nonetheless.

While Zubek stressed the most positive outcomes, some of his volunteers recalled harmful experiences. The volunteer nurse who concerned Whillans was distraught after her first day back to work because she experienced short-term memory loss and forgetfulness.[79] Others vividly described the uneasy experience of isolation. Ernest Enns, a third-year arts student described his six and a half days in isolation as "comfortably boring." He exited the chamber feeling "very groggy" and recalled having had suffered a headache for the first two days followed by hallucination-like visualizations on the third, fifth, and sixth days.[80] Eleven participants reported visual and aural sensations ranging from amorphous flickering or pulsating lights, lines, and shadows to wind and water noises. Some recalled eerie whistling sounds while others endured the noise of a repetitive alarm clock or the constant howling of dogs.

The experiment kickstarted Canada's longest running study of human isolation. For fifteen years, Zubek subjected more than five hundred volunteers to his isolation laboratory at the University of Manitoba.[81] Some participants experienced darkness and silence for up to two weeks, while others endured constant light and white noise in a translucent Plexiglas dome (see figure 4.1). Throughout the various experiments, Zubek tested the effects of sensory deprivation by monitoring his subjects for behavioural, cognitive, and psychological responses. "It was horrible, really uncomfortable," psychology major Gordon Winocur told investigative journalist Cecil Rosner.[82] "If you have any latent claustrophobia, it's going to come out." Winocur was not alone. Others recalled experiencing physical and mental discomfort during the experiment, as evidenced by Zubek's closely related research into physical stillness.

Zubek's isolation chamber doubled as an experimental laboratory for subjecting volunteers to physical confinement. In a related study, the psychology professor immobilized people by securing the hands, arms, legs, and head of each test subject while they laid flat on their back with their eyes toward the ceiling (see figure 4.2). Zubek confined his subjects and restricted movement because he theorized a connection between immobility and mental degeneration. He suggested that the experiment could prove beneficial in the treatment of patients confined to iron lungs or in training astronauts for space travel. Zubek conducted his research as the competition in space research escalated between the superpowers. The Canadian public watched with anticipation and alarm in April 1961 when Yuri Gargarin became the first human to enter space and orbit the Earth. As the Soviets appeared to gain an edge on their American rivals, reassurances from scientists like Zubek reiterated Canada's commitment to the West.

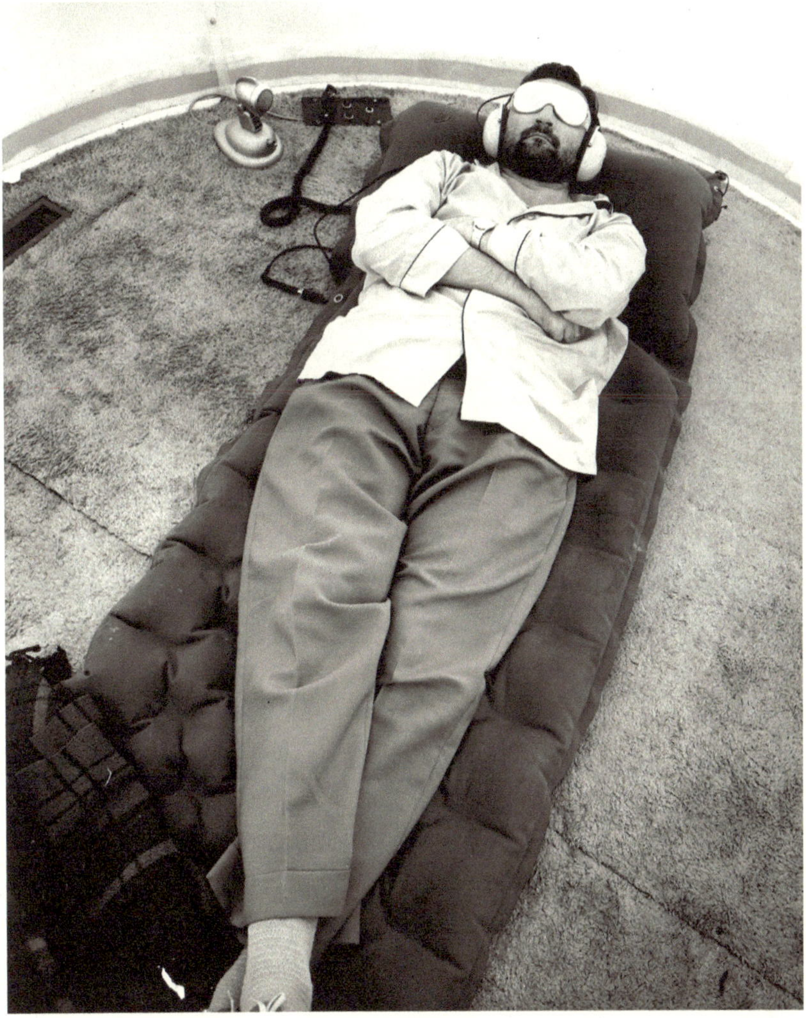

4.1 Zubek in sensory deprivation test.

Zubek used the human challenges of space travel to justify subjecting his volunteers to much longer periods of isolation and confinement. Extended discomfort, he thought, produced the physiological and psychological conditions necessary to understand the limits of the human body. "Our work of the past month has indicated that merely restricting the degree of bodily movements for a week, with

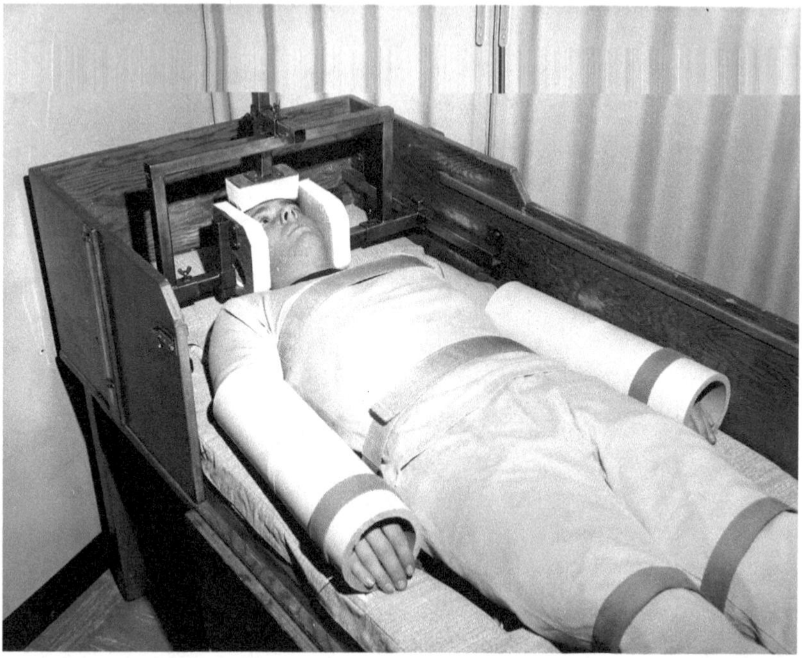

4.2 Subject lying strapped in position.

no interference of vision or hearing, can produce intellectual and perceptual impairments as severe as those occurring in the isolation chamber," Zubek wrote in an October 1962 letter requesting additional research funds from the DRB. "These preliminary results ... [will] have important Defence [*sic*] applications since there are numerous military situations in which the human operator is required to work in cramped quarters involving restrictions of body movements, e.g., tanks, aircraft, space capsules, etc."[83] Of a reported forty test subjects, only a small number endured the experiment for an extended period. Most experienced short-term cognitive deficiencies, regardless of time spent confined. "There is a definite impairment of intellectual ability as well as in their ability to observe the world around them," Zubek explained in an interview. "The entire experiment suggests that stimulation of muscles in a human being is very important. Without it there could be intellectual damage."[84] Several subjects thought that their heads and limbs had swelled or shrunk to abnormal sizes, while others recalled hallucinatory experiences and the feeling of floating above the test apparatus.

Although Zubek admitted physical confinement caused his subjects cognitive harm, he put a positive spin on the experiment. "We've never thought about the importance of movement before," he told one reporter. "It is a subject that has never been thoroughly investigated. A patient could well be deteriorating mentally, and we wouldn't know about it. In long cases of immobilization it is possible there would be no recovery."[85] Zubek also suggested women reacted differently than men. Wilma Sansom, one of four research assistants, allegedly reported no visualizations or ill effects during a confinement of six hours and thirty minutes. Sansom's experience led Zubek to speculate that women might be physiologically capable of longer space flight. This theory convinced Zubek to pursue experimental confinement as a method for investigating human responses to isolated work environments, including space travel, which loomed large as satellite and rocket technology took off in the 1960s.

Zubek continued his research until the early 1970s when international scrutiny of interrogation and torture cast a negative spotlight on his work. In 1969, he edited a comprehensive collection titled *Sensory Deprivation: Fifteen Years of Research*.[86] Along with a lengthy list of related publications in top scientific journals, the book cemented Zubek's reputation as a leading authority in the field. Two years later in August 1971, in a seemingly unrelated event, police arrested 342 people in Northern Ireland after the British government passed legislation allowing for interment without trial. Twelve of the detainees endured in-depth interrogation, leading to accusations of torture and two official inquiries. In the report of the second inquiry, a minority opinion about the moral justification of interrogation referenced experimental work published in Canada. The reference ignited a media storm among Canadian journalists, with Zubek's isolation research in the crosshairs. "There have been statements that we are involved in brainwashing techniques, and that is not the case at all," Zubek told the press when approached for his opinion.[87] He thought the media had misrepresented his research and responded by reiterating the positive outcomes of experimental science involving isolation and confinement.

To underscore the potential value of his research, Zubek cited military and civilian problems associated with confined work. In addition to northern radar stations, he mentioned bomb shelters, aircraft, submarines, spacecraft, and prisons – each human situation a potential beneficiary of isolation and confinement research. Unconvinced by this explanation, student activists denounced military research at the University of Manitoba. More than one hundred students attended a meeting in November 1972 to discuss the university's connection with the interrogation techniques used in Northern Ireland.[88] Zubek refused an invitation to attend, avoiding direct confrontation. He maintained his position when communicating with the media, defending his research, and refuting any suggestion directly linking his experiments with techniques developed for interrogation and torture.

As for the sinister uses of his research, Zubek never explicitly denied the possible connection between sensory isolation and interrogation. He told reporters that his focus was basic research but conceded that scientists have little or no control over the wrongful uses of their work. When asked about the application of his research for developing techniques related to mind control or brainwashing, Zubek responded, "I can say that in certain circumstances, for example during the war, that it would be extremely important to get certain types of information down there. There's a time and place. What bothers me about the cases in Northern Ireland is that these are non-convicted individuals on whom these techniques have been employed."[89] This convoluted explanation backfired, adding to the growing tide of scepticism that fuelled the controversy about Zubek's experimental work.

Facing constant criticism and mounting pressure to explain his research, Zubek's health began to diminish. His research funding from the Defence Research Board ended in March 1974. Although under the age of fifty and still near the height of his career, the following month, amid the continuing controversy over his research, Zubek resigned from the board of the Canadian Psychological Association. He disappeared unexpectedly on 17 August.[90] His body appeared three days later, found floating in Winnipeg's Red River. Initially, the exact cause of death was unclear. Some of Zubek's colleagues suggested disorientation led to his accidental death, while others thought he had committed suicide. The coroner's report confirmed the latter.[91]

The circumstances of Zubek's death shaped the opinion of his colleague and friend Alexander Pressey, who also worked in the Department of Psychology at the University of Manitoba during the 1960s.

"He was born in 1925 and we tend to forget that great public adoration was heaped upon those who opened up the frontiers of the Arctic, the Antarctic, and the open skies," Pressey wrote upon reflection in May 2012.[92] "Names like Amundsen, Lindberg and Earhart were venerated for their selfless commitment to gain knowledge ... So it is not surprising that he chose a high profile project such as sensory isolation to define his scientific career." Zubek's rise to prominence in his field made his fall more dramatic. He was a top scientist who lost research funding and gained an association with torture because of events on the other side of the Atlantic over which he had no control. For Pressey, Zubek's story demonstrated how involvement in experimental research could result in tragic and unintended consequences for a scientist.

Although widely discussed during the 1960s, brainwashing, Pressey claimed, was not the goal of Zubek's isolation research. He conceded that Zubek viewed science as a heroic enterprise but remained adamant that caution and pragmatism guided the work of his former colleague. In Pressey's opinion, Zubek conducted isolation experiments "to determine how well individuals could tolerate a prolonged monotonous environment."[93] Where some saw space research as an excuse or cover-up for a hidden agenda, Pressey remained convinced about the honesty and integrity of his colleague, claiming Zubek was the victim of "loutish radicals and juvenile journalists" who wrongly connected his research with torture techniques such as brainwashing.

The media scrutiny Pressey referenced continued well after Zubek's death. In March 1982, the CBC's *Fifth Estate* televised a report called "The Hooded Men" that investigated the reports of torture in Ireland. Documented by reporters Brian McKenna and Eric Malling, the investigation involved interviews with members of the Irish Republican Army who claimed to have had experienced internment and torture at the hands of the British Army. "Use of isolation techniques, a torture more effective than old-fashioned beatings, was refined by a Canadian psychiatrist, John Zubek, at the University of Manitoba," wrote journalist Jim Bawden in a column applauding McKenna and Malling for their reporting. "Zubek was not using his experiments for torture but to explore the mind. But they were misused by a wide variety of agencies from British forces in Northern Ireland to military officers in Argentina and Nicaragua."[94] Recorded footage of Zubek added to the controversy. In a CBC interview filmed before his death, Zubek explained that the brainwashing of prisoners by communist forces in Korea provided the original impetus for sensory deprivation research.[95] He maintained that mind control was not the goal of his work, but the documentary implied the purpose of his research was obvious.

For Gordon Winocur, the former psychology student who described his claustrophobic experience in isolation as horrible and uncomfortable, Zubek's motives remain suspect. In fact, Winocur doubted the scientific basis of the research while studying at the University of Manitoba. "As a young, impressionable graduate student, I didn't question it in the early stages," Winocur recalled during an interview. "We were encouraged to think this was groundbreaking research. As I became more sophisticated and talked to more people, I realized there was little of theoretical interest attached to it." Now a senior scientist at the Rotman Research Institute and professor of psychology at both Trent University and the University of Toronto, Winocur's unfortunate experience as a student subject raises stark questions about the intent and purpose of Zubek's research. "The major question was how well people reacted to this kind of treatment and what kinds of changes there were in perceptual and cognitive functions, things that might be useful in developing interrogation techniques," said Winocur. "I began to realize there was a different agenda."[96] Whether Zubek's research contributed to a hidden agenda involving torture remains unclear, but his experiments resulted in short- and long-term health effects for Winocour and other documented subjects.

RADAR OPERATORS AND ISOLATION RESEARCH ON THE MID-CANADA LINE

Simultaneous research involving radar technicians in northern Canada suggests that concerns about monotonous military work inspired other scientific investigations into the human effects of isolation. While Zubek conducted laboratory experiments during the early 1960s, other Canadian scientists studied isolation on radar stations to develop selection criteria for northern military posting. Theoretically, military officials wanted to identify personnel with characteristics suitable to living and working in isolated circumstances. Morgan W. Wright, a fellow psychologist at the University of Manitoba, devised and carried out a study to investigate personality characteristics associated with isolation and confinement in a northern setting. Wright's research never received notoriety, partly because he did not subject people to laboratory isolation or confinement. He studied observational data about radar technicians compiled by station supervisors. Nonetheless, there are discernable connections between his work and Zubek's sensory deprivation research. Both investigations occurred in the same period, received funding from the DRB, and contributed to a distinct military research agenda.

Born in Winnipeg in 1921, Wright served as a navigator in the RCAF during the Second World War.[97] He earned his doctorate in clinical psychology at the University of Toronto and began his professional career in Regina, where he became the founding president of the provincial psychological association. Following his tenure in Regina, the University of Manitoba recruited Wright to teach in its newly formed psychiatry department. He successfully persuaded the university management to establish courses in clinical psychology, and later helped to establish and direct a Winnipeg clinic for the treatment of children and adults known as the Psychological Services Centre.[98]

Wright was the lead scientist for two studies conducted to investigate personality characteristics associated with work and social adaptation in the Canadian north. He and his co-investigators sought to produce a screening procedure for identifying people capable of living and working in relative isolation. Published in 1963, the first study examined 197 electronic technicians from the Bell Telephone Company who had volunteered for a one-year "tour of isolation duty" to staff radar stations on the Mid-Canada Line.[99] A follow-up study appeared in 1967, which investigated "a larger, more heterogeneous and unscreened sample" of 614 employees from the federal Department of Transport.[100] Each study indicated a correlation between antisocial behaviour and inefficient functioning in conditions of isolation, but neither achieved the initial goal of producing an effective screening procedure for identifying candidates for northern posting.

During the mid-1950s, the problems associated with radar target detection received increasing attention at the DRB's Defence Research Medical Laboratories (DRML) in Toronto. In a series of related

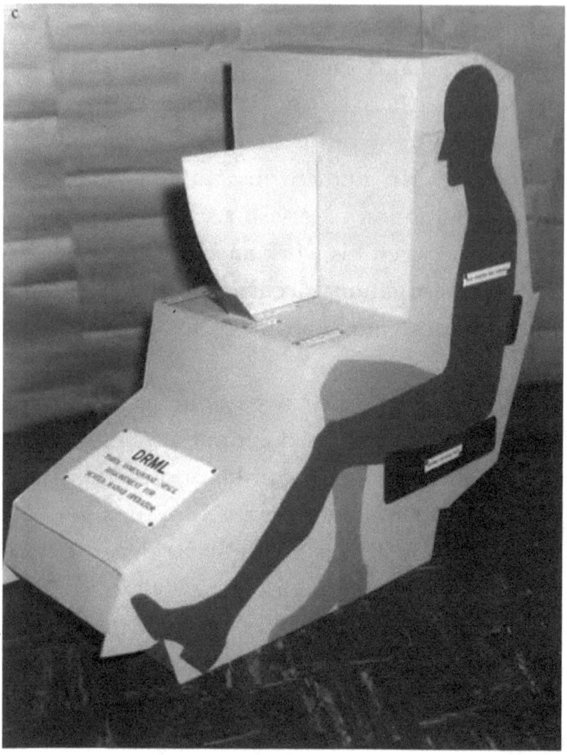

4.3 The three-dimensional space requirement for seated radar operators developed by Walter de la Riviere.

experiments, scientists at DRML simulated the work environment of a northern radar station. They studied the relative efficiency of two radar operators versus one and how advanced knowledge about monotony affected operator performance, using scientific data and prototypes to optimize the radar booth as a crucial military work environment (see figure 4.3). "Failure to take full advantage of the maximum range of radar sets and an unduly high percentage of errors in reading the radars often occur due to faulty operator techniques," wrote DRB chair A. Hartley Zimmerman in 1958. "Laboratory studies have demonstrated important increases in accuracy of detection and in effective range, with improved methods of watching the position indicators, certain changes in room lighting and instrument illumination and minor alterations in equipment design."[101] According to a DRML report from 1959, experiments using a mirror-image type radar display demonstrated a marked improvement in operational alertness and

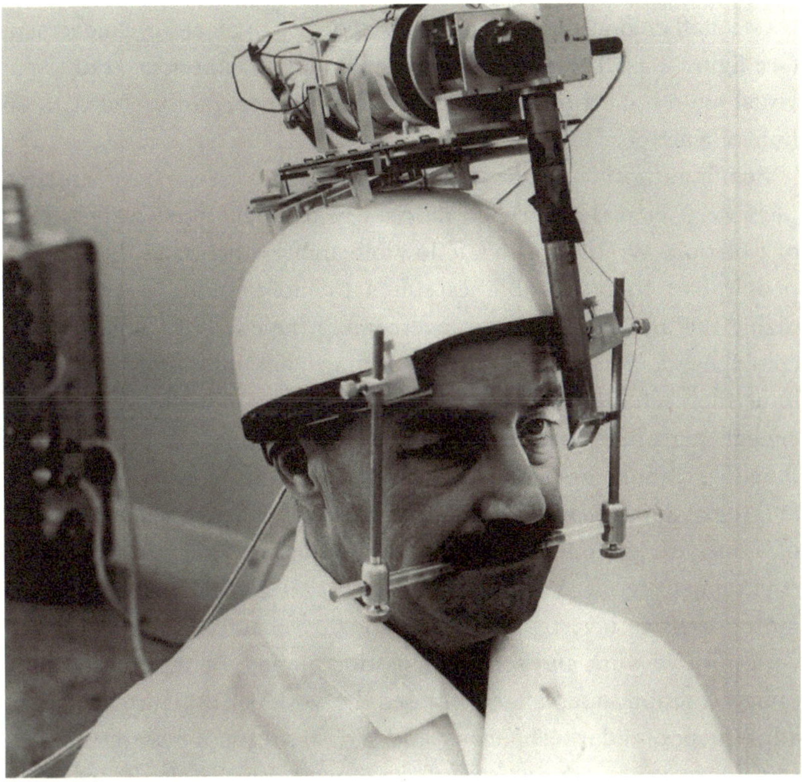

4.4 A head-mounted eye movement recording device worn by Doug Scott in 1962.

efficiency.[102] This type of information inspired further research into the physical environment and technology of a radar booth, but also hinted at psychological approaches for improving the operator's effectiveness.

Scientific research at DRML concentrated on problems encountered by military personnel relative to their operational environment and service duties. To understand and improve upon soldier functionality, DRML scientists studied human tolerance and efficiency under conditions of heat and cold, motion and gravitational absence, mental fatigue, and noise. They also studied the creation and transportation of foods and rations, individual diet, and protecting personnel from the natural elements. Under the umbrella of applied experimental psychology, scientists at DRML carried out research related to the human factors involved with monotonous work and vigilance.[103] For instance,

DRML staff engineered a head-mounted device to record eye movement (see figure 4.4). The subject wearing the device experienced different visual stimuli, and the experiment aimed to generate useful data on human reactions.

Senior authorities in the DRB funded Wright's research for a related purpose. Whereas controlled laboratory research showed the effects of isolation, Wright and his fellow researchers theorized that certain people had cognitive abilities suited to monotonous work. Recognizing the human inability of overcoming the effects of isolation and confinement, Wright's team proposed an elaborate study to "determine the usefulness of certain psychological tests in the selection of civilian personnel for northern posting."[104] During the first study in 1962–63, station supervisors on the Mid-Canada Line rated the work and social adjustment of individual radar technicians after completion of a one-year period. Technicians who adjusted poorly to their work environment received low ratings. The first study led to a second and more extensive investigation of personality characteristics associated with positive work and social adaptation among a larger, unscreened sample. Station supervisors appraised the work performance and social adjustment of radar technicians, and Wright's team of researchers used this information to assess the effects of isolation and confinement on individual performance in the north.

Unlike the experiments conducted by Donald Hebb and John Zubek, we know little about the experiences of the individuals monitored for the effects of isolation in northern Canada. The experimental reports did not contain quotes from radar technicians. Supervisors merely recorded numeric performance ratings without commenting on the actual nature of the difficulties experienced by those who did not adapt well, leaving an incomplete record of the human toll of isolation testing in the north. Whereas Hebb and Zubek studied the effects of isolation and confinement in a controlled laboratory, the monitoring of civilian radar technicians on the MCL served to assess real-life circumstances in a so-called natural isolated work environment. Military and defence officials expressed concern about an individual's focus and concentration in a northern station, but the researchers who monitored the radar technicians obtained no evidence that isolation resulted in hallucination-like experiences or other extreme effects.

To be certain, the circumstances of confinement in a northern radar station differed vastly from the experiences of persons subjected to sensory isolation at McGill University and the University of Manitoba. There was a clear difference between the responses recorded on radar postings and the university research conducted in isolation laboratories, which clearly had a harmful impact on some of the participants. Researchers did not attempt to alter the opinions of the radar technicians who participated, though some individuals had trouble adapting to isolated postings. Moreover, life on a radar line differed immensely for each operator. Isolation is a fluid term, imbued with different meanings based on the context of a specific radar site. As Sue Heffernan demonstrates in her chapter about Moosonee, understanding the contrasting levels of isolation is important for reconstructing the experiences of military personnel and civilians who lived and worked in the north. While workers posted to the Pinetree Line experienced some degree of isolation, military families often served on location and mixed with the small rural communities near each radar site. Nonetheless, even at the relatively southern location of Moosonee, life was much more isolated than in most Canadian urban environments.

Canadian officials funded the construction of domestic living quarters near radar sites and encouraged family cohesion to maintain morale and productivity. Radar technicians emphasized the importance and positive effect of living with family while working at northern radar sites. "The isolation, irregular hours and hardships imposed by a military life were made tolerable by the cohesion of the family unit," wrote historian Gordon Wilson, who interviewed former radar operators while researching the history of North American air defence.[105] Unfortunately, the community concept was not possible at all locations. Only the basic amenities sustained work life at northern stations, adding to the relative isolation experienced on site.

Despite the fluid circumstances encountered by military personnel and civilians who lived and worked at northern stations, gender perceptions of virile manliness shaped popular attitudes about radar technicians. "The men who man Canada's radar stations are tough," proclaimed a 1959 photo story produced by the National Film Board. "[E]ach day they pit their strength, their wits, their intelligence, and their endurance against savage weather conditions, where the temperature drops mercilessly to 60 degrees below zero, and against the inevitable loneliness which accompanies the desolate isolation of these vital outposts. Only a few crack, the majority grow tall."[106] In actuality, radar operators worked long and tiresome shifts because their job and national security depended on early threat detection. "The poor Fighter Control Operators watched boards with moving pins like a seismograph, for hours," commented RCAF Captain Dan Farrel when asked about the Mid-Canada Line.[107] In one documented case from 1961, a technician operating a radar booth on the DEW Line fell asleep and immediately lost his job. "The distraught console watchman, conscious he was in deep trouble for missing the bogie, vehemently denied having dozed off," recalled Frances Dickson, the daughter of a former radar line worker. "The man on watch continued to wring his hands claiming something had gone temporarily wrong with the radar, but before his shift had ended, he was told to gather his belongings and await pick-up on the next flight south."[108] Effective operators remained alert despite the arduous conditions and there was simply no acceptable excuse for missing a target.

Morgan Wright's research conformed to contemporary ideas of masculinity. His theory about isolated radar technicians suggested that certain workers outperformed others because of innate psychological characteristics. He postulated that "strong-minded" men had the psychological traits required for overcoming monotony. He studied radar technicians with data compiled by supervisors on the Mid-Canada Line because, unlike the Pinetree and DEW Lines, the Canadian government constructed and operated radar sites on the MCL independently.[109] That his research failed to produce criteria for selecting personnel for northern posting demonstrates the flawed assumptions that underpinned popular attitudes about male performance and isolated radar work in the north.

Importantly, Wright's isolation study conformed to a distinct military research agenda to understand and overcome the practical difficulties associated with servicing an active radar network. While laboratory simulations conducted in Toronto produced useful knowledge for DRB scientists, examining real-life conditions of isolated and monotonous work at northern radar stations provided information derived from actual human experiences. It is unclear whether Wright's research influenced decisions about radar or military service in the north because the MCL closed in 1965.[110] Two years later, the publication of Wright's 1967 follow-up study marked a culmination for government-funded research involving human participants who worked under isolated conditions in the north.[111] The Pinetree Line stayed operational until 1974, however, meaning the results of Wright's study remained applicable for nearly one decade after the closure of the MCL.

Scientists funded or employed by the DRB conducted further research into sensory environments, human psychology, and behavioural functionality, though. As student activists increasingly denounced military research on university campuses, laboratory work at DRML continued into the 1970s and a small group of DRB scientists tested research subjects under conditions meant to simulate a northern environment.[112] Wright's work had ended, but defence funding sustained military research concerning the effects of adverse conditions on human psychology and performance.

CONCLUSION

In a Canadian context, the controversial Cold War-era history of brainwashing and covert medical science has overshadowed research linking psychological experimentation with the practical issue of operating an effective radar network. Although sensory isolation research funded by the Defence Research Board produced some very troubling side effects, including hallucination-like experiences, the development of brainwashing techniques for interrogation and torture was not the sole purpose of the experimental research. While Donald Hebb and John Zubek considered the possibility of altering opinions and the possible harmful effects of isolation, the psychological experimentation that occurred at McGill University and the University of Manitoba had a direct connection with investigations into monotonous military labour. This does not mitigate any of the harmful effects of the research. Hebb and Zubek were genuinely troubled when their research became associated with brainwashing and interrogation techniques, but the underlying importance of their work to military preparedness and national defence are essential for understanding the scientific motivations behind the experimentation.

Moreover, although the history of sensory deprivation research and Cold War psychology provides a potent reminder of the dangers of experimental medical research involving human subjects, any judgment bearing on the past must consider and appreciate context. The research experiments described in this chapter conformed to contemporary ethical standards in a way that Ewen Cameron's psychiatric experiments never did. To condemn Hebb and Zubek would be to ignore the confluence of ideas and events that created and perpetuated the circumstances for their research in experimental psychology. They held university posts and voluntary positions with academic associations, and trained student psychologists who later practiced or taught elsewhere in Canada. Although a small group of scientists stand out in the historical record, it is important to remember the larger cohort associated with the individuals discussed here and to distinguish their work from Cameron's experimental treatments.

Isolation research was a product of the early Cold War. Intense anxiety and concern about the psychological warfare capability of China and the Soviet Union influenced a deepening relationship between the Canadian state and medical science community. Military officials, scientists, and government representatives supported experimental psychology involving human research subjects because they perceived difficult and perilous circumstances. As the top Canadian scientist in the defence department, Omond Solandt promoted psychological research in response to concerns about communist brainwashing and monotonous military labour. He recruited Hebb, who then conducted the first in a series of experiments that inspired the controversial isolation research of Zubek. "The first experimental work on this topic began in 1951 at McGill University under the direction of D.O. Hebb," Zubek wrote in a draft paper prepared for the *International Encyclopedia of the Social Sciences*. "Its purpose was to further our understanding of the mechanisms underlying 'brainwashing' and of the lapses of attention noted under monotonous environmental conditions e.g., watching a radar screen."[113]

The response of these Canadian scientists and the military officials who supported their ideas typified attitudes of the period. The Cold

War produced secrecy at the political level, and Canadian officials, like their American and British counterparts, avoided public discussion of security-related research. Although select scientists challenged government secrecy, most accepted the practice as a condition of performing federally funded research. Indeed, access to government capital allowed scientists to advance their professional careers while satisfying a deep curiosity for psychological research. As the values of the medical research profession evolved through the mid-Cold War period, new standards and ideas arose that challenged the practices and procedures of the 1950s and 1960s.

Available records demonstrate that Canada's top military and defence officials also funded and supported experimental psychology to investigate the challenges associated with operating an effective radar network during the early Cold War. Effective military service in the north provided numerous challenges. Whether monitoring a radar screen alone in a metal booth encrusted with snow and ice or piloting a long and tiring reconnaissance flight, Canada's northern geography posed several practical issues for the Canadian armed services. Given that military personnel served these roles in the north, authorities in the DRB considered the study of isolation and monotonous labour as essential for ensuring Canada's northern security.

Experimental isolation research served a distinct military purpose and fit a wider pattern of government-funded research conducted in Canada during the early Cold War. In response to the security circumstances of the period, DRB authorities encouraged and sponsored medical research to find solutions to the specific problems associated with the fear of communist brainwashing and the challenges of monotonous military work. At the same time, the Canadian experiments originated out of a wider agenda to support and contribute to Western military research. Accordingly, the history of isolation research serves as a warning against definitive statements about the impact of the Cold War in Canada. That northern Canada became an important space for Cold War science resulted only in part because of its geography and perceptions of its harsh, barren, isolated and challenging environment. Indeed, the consequences of the military science examined in this chapter resulted from multiple and complex factors that resist general and simple explanations.

While the Cold War demanded a concerted scientific response, it also generated the circumstances for unprecedented research opportunities. If not for modern advancements in engineering and construction, the scientists who monitored the labour and personality traits of radar technicians on the Mid-Canada Line would not have had access to a real-life laboratory space or military work environment in northern Canada. To recognize the depth and perceived value of sensory isolation research and experimental psychiatric treatment is to acknowledge the presence and power of Cold War anxieties over defence, security, and military preparedness. Government officials and civilian scientists worked toward a common cause, which affected Canadians directly and indirectly linked to military research.

Ultimately, isolation research advanced the professional careers of participating scientists while meeting the perceived security needs of the Canadian defence and military establishment. Researchers received financial support, published findings, and took up both academic and government positions. In return, authorities in the federal government learned about human psychology and the impact of isolation on service and military labour in the Canadian north. While difficult to discern, the history of isolation research in Canada demonstrates that state, military, and academic institutions developed a deep connection during the early Cold War. Medical science was not immune to the heightened security politics of the period – a reality that had immediate and lasting consequences for both researcher and subject.

NOTES

1 Frank Croft, "Look What Utter Boredom Can Do," *Maclean's Magazine*, 15 May 1954, 18–19, 88–90.

2 [A.H. Zimmerman,] Chairman, [Defence Research Board] to The Minister re: "Isolation Tests at McGill," 17 April 1956, Appendix 23, DRB file materials, correspondence and news clippings, *Appendices to the Opinion of George Cooper*. Zimmerman succeeded Solandt as chairman of the DRB in April 1956. The exact number of experimental research subjects is unclear. One news article stated that soldiers and military officers also participated as test subjects: "MCGILL STUDENTS BRAIN-WASHED!" 5 May 1956, McGill University Archives (MUA),

Donald Olding Hebb fonds (MG 1045), file 0000-2364.01.78, box C.9 1341C. I was unable to find official records of DRB Contract X-38 that corroborate the involvement of military personnel as test subjects. In an interview conducted decades later, Hebb said that ninety undergraduate students participated in the DRB-funded experiment but made no mention of military personnel: "Cameron's LSD Study Followed: Research Aided Interrogators," *Medicine Hat News*, 18 February 1984.

3 Croft, "Look What Utter Boredom Can Do," 18–19.

4 Canada, House of Commons, *Debates*, 22nd Parliament, 3rd Session: Vol. 3, "National Defence: Inquiry as to Reported Research in Brain-Washing," 17 April 1956, 2990-1. For the referenced news articles, see "Tank Test Linked to Brainwashing: U.S. and Canadian Scientists Report to Congress on Their Experiments," *New York Times*, 15 April 1956, 18; "'Brainwashing' Defence Found: McGill Explains Experiments, Findings Give Answer to Many Problems," *The Gazette* (Montreal), 26 April 1956, 1.

5 Alfred McCoy, *A Question of Torture: CIA Interrogation, from the Cold War to the War on Terror* (New York: Metropolitan Books, 2006); Naomi Klein, *The Shock Doctrine: The Rise of Disaster Capitalism* (New York: Metropolitan Books/Henry Holt, 2007); Alfred W. McCoy, "Science in Dachau's Shadow: Hebb, Beecher and the Development of CIA Psychological Torture and Modern Medical Ethics," *Journal of the History of the Behavioral Sciences* 43, no. 4 (Fall 2007): 401–17.

6 Anne Collins, *In the Sleep Room: The Story of the CIA Brainwashing Experiments in Canada* (Toronto: Lester and Orpen Dennys, 1988); Anne Wheeler, Director, *The Sleep Room*, DVD (Montreal: CINAR, 1998); Don Gillmor, *I Swear by Apollo: Dr Ewen Cameron and the CIA-Brainwashing Experiments* (Montreal: Eden Press, 1987); Harvey Weinstein, *A Father, a Son and the CIA* (Toronto: J. Lorimer, 1988); and Christopher Hyde, *Abuse of Trust: The Career of Dr James Tyhurst* (Vancouver: Douglas & McIntyre, 1991).

7 D.J. Goodspeed, *A History of the Defence Research Board of Canada* (Ottawa: Queen's Printer, 1958); Jonathan Turner, "The Defence Research Board of Canada, 1947 to 1977" (PhD diss., University of Toronto, 2012).

8 United States District Court for the District of Columbia, David Orlikow, et al., Plaintiffs v. United States of America Defendant, Civil Action No. AD-3163, deposition of Omond Solandt, 11 August 1988, 9, University of Toronto Archives and Records Management Services. Omond McKillop Solandt fonds, vol. B93-0041-004, file B93-0041.

9 Omond Solandt, quoted in "The Legacy of Dr Cameron," University of Toronto Archives and Records Management Services, Omond McKillop Solandt fonds, vol. B93-0041-004, file B93-0041.

10 "Montreal Woman Seeks Compensation in '50s Brainwashing Case," 8 January 2007, *CBC News*, http://www.cbc.ca/news/canada/montreal/montreal-woman-seeks-compensation-in-50s-brainwashing-case-1.670151 (accessed 18 September 2017).

11 George T.H. Cooper, *Opinion of George Cooper, Q.C., Regarding Canadian Government Funding of the Allan Memorial Institute in the 1950's and 1960's* (Ottawa: Department of Justice, 1986).

12 Dene Moore, "Brainwashed 'Guinea Pig' Seeks More Damages," *Canadian Press*, 8 January 2007, https://www.thestar.com/news/2007/01/08/brainwashed_guinea_pig_seeks_more_damages.html (accessed 18 September 2017).

13 Elizabeth Thompson, "Federal Government Quietly Compensates Daughter of Brainwashing Experiments Victim," *CBC News*, 26 October 2017, http://www.cbc.ca/news/politics/cia-brainwashing-allanmemorial-mentalhealth-1.4373590 (accessed 27 October 2017).

14 Alison Steel, quoted in Thompson, "Federal Government Quietly Compensates."

15 Psychologist Richard Brown contends that some scholars have incorrectly implicated Hebb in CIA-funded research on brainwashing; see Richard E. Brown, "Alfred McCoy, Hebb, the CIA and Torture," *Journal of the History of the Behavioral Sciences* 43, no. 2 (Spring 2007): 205–13.

16 "Cameron's LSD Study Followed."

17 Donald Hebb, quoted in ibid.

18 Mark Moran, "When Ethical Lines Were Crossed in Service to the Nation," *Psychiatric News* (American Psychiatric Society), 17 June 2011, http://psychnews.psychiatryonline.org/doi/10.1176/pn.46.12.psychnews_46_12_16_2 (accessed 25 September 2017).

19 Cooper, *Opinion of George Cooper*, 31.

20 Canada/US/UK meeting re: communist "brainwashing" techniques during the Korean War, Appendix 21, Minutes of June 1, 1951, *Appendices to the Opinion of George Cooper, Q.C., Regarding Canadian Government Funding of the Allan Memorial Institute in the 1950's and 1960's: Volume 1.*

21 Ronald W. Clark, *Tizard* (London: Methuen, 1965), 259–62; C.P. Stacey, *Arms, Men and Governments: The War Policies of Canada 1939–1945* (Ottawa: Queen's Printer, 1970), 507–14; Donald Avery, *The Science of War: Canadian Scientists and Allied Military Technology During the Second World War* (Toronto: University of Toronto Press, 1998), 52–9.

22 Solandt to The Minister, 25 January 1954, Appendix 23, DRB file materials, correspondence and news clippings, *Appendices to the Opinion of George Cooper*; Cecil Rosner, "Isolation: A Canadian Professor's Research into Sensory Deprivation

and its Connection to Disturbing New Methods of Interrogation," *Canada's History* (August–September 2010), 29–37.

23 Cooper, *Opinion of George Cooper*, 31.

24 D. Hebb, "Donald O. Hebb," in vol. 7. *A History of Psychology in Autobiography*, ed. G. Lindzey (San Francisco, CA: W.H. Freeman, 1980), 273–303; P.M. Milner and B. Milner, "Donald Olding Hebb, 22 July 1904–20 August 1985," *Biographical Memoirs of Fellows of the Royal Society* 42 (1996): 192–204.

25 Duane M. Rumbaugh, "Austin H. Riesen (1913–1996): Obituary," *American Psychologist* 53, no. 1 (1998): 60–1; Mical Raz, "Alone Again: John Zubek and the Troubled History of Sensory Deprivation Research," *Journal of the History of the Behavioral Sciences* 49, no. 4 (Fall 2013): 379–95.

26 D.O. Hebb, *The Organization of Behavior: A Neuropsychological Theory* (New York: Wiley, 1949).

27 Robert J. Lifton, "Home by Ship: Reaction Patterns of American Prisoners of War Repatriated from North Korea," *American Journal of Psychiatry* 110, no. 10 (April 1954): 732–9; Lifton, *Thought Reform and the Psychology of Totalism: A Study of "Brainwashing" in China* (Chapel Hill: The University of North Carolina Press, 1989) first published in 1961; Lawrence E. Hinkle Jr and Harold G. Wolff, "Communist Interrogation and Indoctrination of 'Enemies of the States': Analysis of Methods Used by the Communist State Police (A Special Report)," *AMA Archives of Neurology and Psychology* 76, no. 2 (August 1956): 115–74.

28 Although closely related to isolation, the well-established practice of shunning did not figure into the equation as a viable option for altering opinions. Theoretically, the controlled environment of an isolation room provided a higher degree of scientific certainty.

29 O.M. Solandt, Chairman, Defence Research Board to The Minister, 25 January 1954, Appendix 23, DRB file materials, correspondence and news clippings, *Appendices to the Opinion of George Cooper.*

30 Minister of National Defence, *Canada's Defence: Information on Canada's Defence Achievements and Organization* (Ottawa: Department of National Defence, 1947), 47–8.

31 Brooke Claxton, Minister of National Defence to His Excellency, The Governor General in Council, 12 April 1949, LAC, RG 24, vol. 4230, file DRBS 2-1-87 pt. 1.

32 Omond Solandt, Chairman, Defence Research Board to D.M. Watters, Assistant Secretary of the Treasury Board, Department of Finance re: DRB Contract X-38 with McGill University covering "Experimental Studies of Attitude Changes in Individuals," 3 August 1954, Appendix 24, DRB report to Treasury Board, *Appendices to the Opinion of George Cooper.*

33 Ibid.

34 Croft, "Look What Utter Boredom Can Do," 88; John Scott, "See, Hear, Feel Nothing Research Shows Bored Brain Acts Queerly: Isolation Tests at McGill Paid Human Guinea Pigs $20 a Day – But Few Can Take It," *The Gazette* (Montreal). MUA, Donald Olding Hebb fonds, MG 1045, box C.9 1341C, file 0000-2364.01.78.

35 Solandt to Watters, 3 August 1954.

36 D.O. Hebb, Department of Psychology, McGill University to Dr Andrew J. Warren, Director, Division of Medicine and Public Health, The Rockefeller Foundation re: Annual Report to the Rockefeller Foundation, 30 September 1953, Rockefeller Archive Center (RAC), RG 1.2, Rockefeller Foundation records, projects, subseries 427.A: Canada – Medical Sciences, series 427, box 4, folder 33.

37 Croft, "Look What Utter Boredom Can Do," 90.

38 "On and Off the Record: Ottawa Studies Brain-Washing," *The Gazette* (Montreal), 17 January 1955, MUA, Donald Olding Hebb fonds (MG 1045), box C.9 1341C, file 0000-2364.01.78.

39 N.W. Morton, Chief of Division D [Defence Research Board], to D.O. Hebb, Department of Psychology, McGill University, 16 November 1953, Appendix 23, DRB file materials, correspondence and news clippings, *Appendices to the Opinion of George Cooper*.

40 Canada, House of Commons, *Debates*, 22nd Parliament, 3rd Session: Vol. 3, "National Defence: Inquiry as to Reported Research in Brain-Washing," 17 April 1956, 2990–1.

41 R.O. Campney (Minister of National Defence), Canada, House of Commons, *Debates*, 22nd Parliament, 3rd Session: Vol. 3, "National Defence: Inquiry as to Reported Research in Brain-Washing," 17 April 1956, 2990.

42 D.O. Hebb, cited in "McGill Explains Experiments: Finds Give Answer to Many Problems," *The Gazette* (Montreal), 26 April 1956, MUA, Donald Olding Hebb fonds (MG 1045), box C.9 1341C, file 0000-2364.01.78.

43 It is possible that Campney misinformed the House of Commons or that, as MND, he was unaware that the department under his direction had funded the experiments at McGill through the Defence Research Board.

44 J.L. MacDougall (Vancouver–Burrard), Canada, House of Commons, *Debates*, 22nd Parliament, 3rd Session: Vol. 3, "National Defence: Inquiry as to Reported Research in Brain-Washing," 17 April 1956, 2991.

45 E.D. Fulton (Kamloops), Canada, House of Commons, *Debates*, 22nd Parliament, 3rd Session: Vol. 3, "National Defence: Inquiry as to Reported Research in Brain-Washing," 17 April 1956, 2991. For press coverage of the Campney–

Fulton debate, see "Brainwashing Simple, McGill Research Finds," *Globe and Mail*, 18 April 1956, 1.

46 E.D. Fulton (Kamloops), Canada, House of Commons, *Debates*, 22nd Parliament, 3rd Session: Vol. 4, "National Defence: Inquiry as to Reported Research in Brain-Washing," 26 April 1956, 3287.

47 R.O. Campney (Minister of National Defence), Canada, House of Commons, *Debates*, 22nd Parliament, 3rd Session: Vol. 4, "National Defence: Inquiry as to Reported Research in Brain-Washing," 26 April 1956, 3287.

48 Campney claimed the exact amounts as $4,178 for 1951, $8,502 for 1952, and $4,320 for 1953. See Canada, House of Commons, *Debates*, 22nd Parliament, 3rd Session: Vol. 4, "Starred Questions: Brain-Washing Research, McGill University, Question No. 52," 16 May 1956, 3988. Financial records suggest Campney underreported the amount paid to Hebb. According to Hebb's records, he received $20,000 from the Defence Research Board for the first two years of the study. See McGill University – Psychology, D.O. Hebb, Department of Psychology, McGill University to Dr Robert S. Morison, Director, Division of Medicine and Public Health, The Rockefeller Foundation, 27 August 1952, RAC, Canada, RG 1.2, Rockefeller Foundation records, projects, box 4, folder 33.

49 "MCGILL STUDENTS BRAIN-WASHED!" 5 May 1956, MUA, Donald Olding Hebb fonds (MG 1045), box C.9 1341C, file 0000-2364.01.78.

50 Solandt to Watters, 3 August 1954.

51 The Defence Research Board originally produced a draft of the priority system in May 1951. "Defence Research Board, Ottawa: Standard Priority System DND Research and Development," 9 May 1951, Memorandum by Omond Solandt, "Defence Research Board, Ottawa: Priority System for Research and Development Projects," 4 March 1952. LAC, RG 24, vol. 4243, file DRBS 5260-0-267-1, DRBS-5001-0-240.

52 Ibid.

53 "Defence Research Board, Ottawa: Priority System for Research and Development Projects," 29 February 1952, 20, LAC, RG 24, vol. 4243, file DRBS 5260-0-267-1.

54 Ibid.

55 In this context, the term reconstitution closely resembled the goals of "denazification," an ongoing process in Germany intended to re-educate Germans in political democratic practices.

56 "USA Master Plan System," document attached to "Defence Research Board, Ottawa: Standard Priority System DND Research and Development," 9 May 1951, LAC, RG 24, vol. 4243, file DRBS 5260-0-267-1, DRBS-5001-0-240.

57 *Appendices to the Opinion of George Cooper*, particularly appendix 21–4.

58 "Prepared for Meeting of Psychiatry Panel and Human Resources Research Advisory Committee," 4, Appendix 22, DRB file materials on research by Dr Donald O. Hebb on sensory deprivation experiments, *Appendices to the Opinion of George Cooper.*

59 "The Canadian–United States Scientific Advisory Team, 1953–1959 (CUSSAT)," DHH, George Lindsey fonds 87/253-II-24.3, box 5, file 8, 87/253-II-24.3; Joseph Jockel, *No Boundaries Upstairs: Canada, the United States, and the Origins of North American Air Defence, 1945–1958* (Vancouver: UBC Press, 1987), 64–79.

60 The Canada–United States Permanent Joint Board on Defence (PJBD) emerged at Ogdensburg, New York, in August 1940. By September 1945, the PJBD became the principal forum for bilateral negotiations among senior defence officials from Ottawa and Washington. Joel J. Sokolsky and Joseph T. Jockel, eds, *Fifty Years of Canada–United States Defense Cooperation: The Road from Ogdensburg* (New York: Edwin Mellen Press, 1992).

61 Daniel Heidt and P. Whitney Lackenbauer, "Sovereignty for Hire: Civilian Airlift Contractors and the Distant Early Warning (DEW) Line, 1954–1961," in *De-icing Required! The Historical Dimension of the Canadian Air Force's Experience in the Arctic*, ed. P. Whitney Lackenbauer (Ottawa: National Defence and the Canadian Forces, 2012), 95–112.

62 Goose Bay, Labrador served as a location from which the US air force could potentially bomb the Soviet Union and see its aircraft return. Under the direction of Prime Minister Louis St Laurent, Canada approved an expansion of American strategic bombing forces stationed at Goose Bay in the autumn of 1950. Isabel Campbell, "A Tale of Submarine Sightings and a Golden Goose: American–British–Canadian Intelligence Sharing in the Early Cold War," *Journal of Military History* 85, no. 4 (October 2021): 1001.

63 Heidt and Lackenbauer, "Sovereignty for Hire," in *De-icing Required!*, 95–112.

64 [A.H. Zimmerman,] Chairman, [Defence Research Board] to The Minister re: "Isolation Tests at McGill," 17 April 1956, Appendix 23, DRB file materials, correspondence and news clippings, *Appendices to the Opinion of George Cooper.*

65 T. Harwood, "The International Geophysical Year," in *The Unbelievable Land: 29 Experts Bring us Closer to the Arctic*, ed. Norman Smith (Ottawa: Queen's Printer, 1964), 114–18. Richard C. Powell, "Science, Sovereignty and Nation: Canada and the Legacy of the International Geophysical Year, 1957–1958," *Journal of Historical Geography* 34 (2008): 618–38.

66 Edward Jones-Imhotep, *The Unreliable Nation: Hostile Nature and Technological Failure in the Cold War* (Cambridge, MA: MIT Press, 2017).

67 Andrew B. Godefroy, *Defence and Discovery: Canada's Military Space Program, 1945–74* (Vancouver: UBC Press, 2011).

68 E.A. Sellers, "Defence Research Medical Laboratories," *Medical Services Journal Canada* 14, no. 2 (1958): 119–29.

69 D.O. Hebb, Department of Psychology, McGill University, Annual Report to the National Research Council of Canada, 4 January 1954, RAC, RG 1.2, Rockefeller Foundation records, Canada – Medical Sciences, series 427: Canada, Projects, subseries 427, box 4, folder 33.

70 DRB engineers originally constructed the isolation chamber in Toronto. Zubek and his staff reconstructed the chamber after it had been shipped to Winnipeg.

71 J.P. Zubek, Annual Progress Report, Grant No.: 9425-08, Title: Effects of Adverse Environmental Conditions in Restricted Quarters on Intellectual and Perceptual Processes, 16 September 1960, LAC, RG 24, vol. 7574, file DRB 9425-08 pt. 1. Other reports suggest that twenty-five people may have served as test subjects during the first year. See "Forget in Isolation Test: Phantom Dogs Heard, Space Pioneers May Age Quickly," *Globe and Mail*, 9 June 1960.

72 George C. Sisler, M.D., Professor and Head, Faculty of Medicine, University of Manitoba to M.G. Whillans, Defence Research Board, 21 March 1960, LAC, RG 24, acc. 1983-84/167, file DRB 9425-08 pt. 1.

73 M.G. Whillans, DRB, Interview with Dr John P. Zubek, Dept. Psychology, U. of Manitoba – 8 July 1960, Respecting his project "Effects of Adverse Environmental Conditions on Intellectual and Perceptual Processes," 13 July 1960, LAC, RG 24, vol. 7564, file DRB 9425-08 pt. 1.

74 Lieutenant-General S.F. Clark, Chief of the General Staff to Chairman, PMC, 10 August 1960, LAC, RG 24, vol. 7564, file DRB 9425-08 pt. 1.

75 Surgeon General [Rear-Admiral T.B. McLean] quoted in Major General J.D.B. Smith, Chairman, Personnel Members Committee to Secretary, Chiefs of Staff Committee, 14 September 1960, LAC, RG 24, vol. 7564, file DRB 9425-08 pt. 1.

76 Defence Research Board, Annual Progress Report – 1961, Grant No. 942-08, Title: Effects of Adverse Environmental Conditions on Intellectual and Perceptual Processes, Grantee: Dr J.P. Zubek, October 1961, LAC, RG 24, vol. 7564, file DRB 9425-08 pt. 2.

77 J.P. Zubek, quoted in "Forget in Isolation Test," 9 June 1960.

78 Ibid.

79 Raz, "Alone Again: John Zubek and the Troubled History of Sensory Deprivation Research."

80 "6 1/2 Days in Capsule 'Comfortably Boring,'" *Toronto Daily Star*, 17 December 1959, 65.

81 Rosner, "Isolation," 29–37.

82 Gordon Winocur, quoted in ibid, 33.

83 J.P. Zubek, Research Professor to Mr H.R. Lowe, Executive Secretary, Grants and Contracts, Defence Research Board, Ottawa, 4 October 1962, LAC, RG 24, vol. 7564, file DRB 9425-08 pt. 2.

84 John Zubek, quoted in "Tough on Men: Study Effects of Stillness," *Globe and Mail*, 9 November 1962, 10.

85 Ibid.
86 J.P. Zubek, ed., *Sensory Deprivation: Fifteen Years of Research* (New York: Appleton-Century-Crofts, 1969).
87 John Zubek, quoted in Rosner, "Isolation," 35.
88 Ibid.
89 John Zubek, quoted in ibid.
90 Ibid.
91 Liam Lacey, "Torturers and the Tortured Go on Record in TV Special," *Globe and Mail*, 20 March 1982.
92 Alexander Pressey, "John Zubek: Mentor, Friend, Victim," *Pressey's Pieces*, May 2012, http://www.awpressey.com/uploads/1/1/5/5/11553586/mentor.pdf (accessed 15 September 2017).
93 Ibid.
94 Jim Bawden, "Nightmare World of Torture Exposed in Tough CBC Show," *Toronto Star*, 22 March 1982.
95 Lacey, "Torturers and the Tortured Go on Record in TV Special."
96 Gordon Winocur, quoted in Rosner, "Isolation," 33.
97 "Morgan Wilkes Wright" (obituary), *Winnipeg Free Press*, 3 September 2008, https://newspaperarchive.com/winnipeg-free-press-sep-03-2008-p-31/ (accessed 12 March 2017).
98 Ibid.
99 Morgan W. Wright, George C. Sisler, and Joanne Chylinski (University of Manitoba), "Personality Factors in the Selection of Civilians for Isolated Northern Stations," *Journal of Applied Psychology* 47, no. 1 (1963): 24–9.
100 Morgan W. Wright, George C. Sisler, and Joanne Chylinski (University of Manitoba), and Bruce Quarrington (University of Toronto), "Personality Factors in the Selection of Civilians for Isolated Northern Stations: A Follow-Up Study," *The Canadian Psychologist* 8a, no. 1 (January 1967): 23–31.
101 Defence Research, Chairman's Office, Ottawa, 2 December 1958, University of Saskatchewan, University Archives and Special Collections (USASC), JWT Spinks fonds (MG 74), series 10, box 67, file DRB 51-53.
102 Defence Research Medical Laboratories, Annual Report 1958 to the Chairman, Defence Research Board, USASC, JWT Spinks fonds (MG 74), series 10, box 73, file DRB 59-61.
103 Ibid.
104 According to the original published article, this study received financial support from the Defence Research Board (Grant No. 9425-07) of Canada's Department of National Defence.
105 Gordon Wilson, *NORAD and the Soviet Nuclear Threat: Canada's Secret Electronic Air War* (Toronto: Dundurn, 2011), 116.

106 NFB Photo Story: Men Who Man Mid-Canada Line, 1959, LAC, National Film Board fonds, R1196-0-7-E, box 81, item no. 91127.

107 Captain Dan Farrel, 414 Electronic Warfare Squadron, RCAF quoted in Wilson, *NORAD and the Soviet Nuclear Threat*, 110.

108 Frances Jewel Dickson, *The DEW Line Years: Voices from the Coldest Cold War* (Lawrencetown Beach, NS: Pottersfield Press, 2007), 75.

109 "Memorandum from Minister of National Defence [George Pearkes] to Cabinet," 22 July 1957, *Documents on Canadian External Relations Volume 25, 1957–1958, Part II*, ed. Michael D. Stevenson (Ottawa: Dept. of Foreign Affairs and International Trade, 2004), 28–39.

110 Wilson, *NORAD and the Soviet Nuclear Threat*, 117.

111 It is unclear whether Wright and his co-authors used data recorded before 1965 to publish the 1967 study.

112 "Ice cold in Downsview," *Toronto Sun*, 3 December 1973, 18, 31.

113 J.P. Zubek, University of Manitoba, "Perceptual Deprivation," LAC, RG 24, vol. 7564, file DRB 9425-08 pt. 2; J.P. Zubek, "Perceptual Deprivation," in *International Encyclopedia of the Social Sciences: Volume 11*, ed. D.L. Sells (New York: Macmillan and Free Press, 1968), 551–6; J.P. Zubek, "Behavioral and Physiological Effects of Prolonged Sensory and Perceptual Deprivation: A Review," in *Man in Isolation and Confinement*, ed. John E. Rasmussen (Chicago, IL: Adline Publishing Company, 1973), 9–83.

5

"The Most Common Deviation"

The Problem of Pathologizing "Homosexuality" and the Fear of Masculine Weakness at the Toronto Forensic Clinic

FRANCES REILLY

INTRODUCTION

In 1961, journalist Joan Holloban wrote about the Toronto Psychiatric Hospital's Forensic Clinic and its cutting-edge study of sexual deviancy. By way of introduction, she wrote, "Sex has been a major subject of academic study ever since Freud and unscientific conversation since men developed language, but remarkably few scientific facts are known about it once the emotions and theories are dispersed."[1] In reality, the study of sex – even at the clinical level – was dominated by emotion and subjectivity. This was evident in clinician's attitudes towards perceived deviancies and in critical statements found within the studies themselves.[2]

A few years earlier in 1956, forensic psychiatrist Dr Kenneth Gray confidently declared that the Toronto clinic (running from 1956 to 1967) was a place where psychiatrists worked to dispel the myths and anxiety surrounding sexual deviancy and crime.[3] The Toronto Forensic Clinic focused on a variety of so-called sexual deviancies over the years, but the pathologization of homosexuality, which remained criminalized in Canada until 1969, was especially complicated. Sexual deviation, as it was known, did not smoothly shift between categories of morality, criminality, and pathology. Rather, these classifications overlapped, and the clinic often categorized homosexuality by all three. Despite a faith in science and technology to provide clarity in the unknown, clinicians and researchers struggled to classify the condition of homosexuality as deviancy. Apparent in this episode of Canadian psychiatry is the linguistic control over the precarious elements of masculinity, normalcy, and threat.

The Toronto Forensic Clinic holds a particular space within the history of sexual pathologization's shifting psychiatric etiology (cause) and nomenclature (classification) in a Cold War context.[4] Wrapped up in this clinic, its research, and its treatment programs is the contemporary anxiety among clinicians in defining and identifying sexual normalcy or healthy sexuality. Moreover, fears of masculine weakness, male sexual abnormality, and a covert Otherness – that could easily masquerade as something safe in men passing as sexually "normal" – carried extra weight during the Cold War. This chapter examines the pathologization of male homosexuality at the Toronto clinic during the early Cold War as a search for truth in a period of anxiety.[5] By looking at the clinician's work within the institution, this chapter approaches the history of pathologization as one of ideas. Binaries of safety and danger, normalcy and abnormality permeated clinicians' understanding of psychological health and wellness, and of masculinity.

Divided into three parts, this chapter starts with the clinic's beginnings and its relatively humane research and treatment. Arguably it is difficult to categorize any treatment of homosexuality as a psychiatric condition as humane, but in a field renowned for its cruel management of homosexuality during the 1950s, the Toronto clinic was notable for avoiding invasive chemical, surgical, and psychiatric treatments.[6] The second section focuses on psychiatrist Dr Robert Edward (Ed) Turner (1926–2006). As director of the Toronto Forensic Clinic, he promoted forensic psychiatry across Canada throughout the 1950s and 1960s. Turner led the clinic's benevolent attitude, taking a balanced approach to sexual criminality. Increasingly, he became aware that the current codes of normalcy were fallible. His embrace of uncertainty and his empathy for patients stood in direct contrast to the Cold War desire for unequivocal truth. Finally, this chapter's third section examines how Turner and his colleagues, in particular Dr Johann W. (Hans) Mohr (1928–2008), defined and categorized patients at the forensic clinic through a case study of sexual deviation and recidivism. These psychiatrists – examples of white, male, heterosexual, middle-class Toronto privilege – struggled to define sexual normalcy.[7] Their goal was to establish a guide to help them better understand and classify sexual deviancy in an era of changing gender roles and anxiety about masculine weakness but establishing objective truths in forensic psychiatry proved difficult.

This chapter is a study of psychiatric nomenclature from the psychiatrist's perspective. It draws on psychiatrists' published reports from the 1950s and 1960s, which being cognizant of privacy, expose few patient details. Indeed, patients are central to these documents, but their voices are muted, and the hierarchy is clear: the patient was someone to observe not consult. In using these clinical sources and by focusing on clinical nomenclature, terminology is central to this chapter. "Homosexuality," for instance, is a medical term that I use specifically in reference to patients at the clinic. Beyond the psychiatric gaze, I refer to men and women as "gay" or "lesbian."[8] The term "deviancy" was central to the clinical purpose of identifying and treating so-called abnormal sexual behaviour. This chapter explores how this term, which privileges heterosexual objective norms, is problematic – particularly how it linked homosexuality with crimes such as pedophilia and exhibitionism.

This brings us to the place of homosexuality at the Toronto Forensic Clinic and how it came to be known as the "most common deviation." The forensic clinic was an out-patient facility, meaning that patients were neither residents nor confined to the facility. The clinic treated patients who had committed "minor" crimes – such as theft, alcohol-related violations, and physical assaults – along with sexual conditions that were seen as pathological in nature – which included pedophilia, exhibitionism, homosexuality, voyeurism, fetishism, transvestism, incest, sadomasochism, and bestiality.[9] The clinic's goal was to reduce patients' chances of recidivism (reoffending) and return them to society. The Toronto psychiatrists therefore emphasized treatment over punishment. The clinic did not treat criminals guilty of violent sexual assault or murder. These crimes and the pathology that drove them, however, greatly interested the Toronto psychiatrists.

Evident in the earliest clinic reports, many clinicians recognized that homosexuality did not fit with the other conditions treated at the clinic. They referred to homosexuality as "the most common deviation" because gay men made up the largest patient group.[10] Dissatisfied with the current codes of classification, clinicians like Ed Turner and Hans Mohr worked to categorize homosexuality separately from the clinic's other two most common sexual deviations: exhibitionism and pedophilia. They wrote that as the "most common deviation" homosexuality was "prone to over generalization," and its etiology was "unclear mainly because a number of different phenomena are grouped under the term."[11] They viewed homosexuality as a mystery and a condition to be studied and treated, if not cured.

Psychiatrists puzzled over where homosexuality fit in a rapidly evolving spectrum of sexual normalcy. Some of the era's most influential studies were those conducted by American biologist Alfred Kinsey and his team.[12] While sex was, unsurprisingly, a consistent subject of interest among humans, the 1950s obsession with science and technology led to a belief that sexuality could be fully understood through scientific methodology. Unlike previous studies, the "Kinsey reports" focused not on "abnormality" but on general human sexual behaviour.[13] Kinsey placed all sexual behaviour on a continuum, showing how homosexuality, or same-sex activity at least, was more pervasive and common within American society than previously thought. This conclusion ignited fears about homosexual infiltration and the destruction of society through masculine weakness. Such anxieties mirrored the concurrent "red scare" of communist infiltration expedited by weak citizens easily seduced by leftist politics.[14]

Homosexuality was often referred to as a "character weakness" – a vague but pervasive term implying that better self-control might eliminate abnormal behaviours.[15] Amid fears of communist infiltration, the red scare purges of the civil service were often surpassed by the "lavender" purges in both Canada and the United States.[16] Gay civil servants were considered susceptible to Soviet blackmail, although not a single one was ever found guilty of treason.[17] Male communists were often described as physically weak, emotional, and effeminate.[18] More importantly, homosexuality threatened to subvert the sexual and domestic order of post-war society, namely the nuclear family. Within this context, homosexuality was associated with a crisis of masculinity.

Patients classified as "sexual deviates" were exclusively men.[19] Men were understood to be perpetrators of sexual crime, not victims, while women and children were viewed as passive targets. In addition to male sexual aggression, psychiatrists imagined the "masculine threat" as the danger posed *to* traditional masculinity by modern technology and socio-political shifts.[20] From this perspective, the sexual deviant was a weakened man. Clinicians studied psychiatric conditions and abnormal sexual behaviour in men that victimized women and children but focused on the perpetrators without much consideration of the victims.[21] This focus meant that the experiences of sexually traumatized children, like residential school survivor Elmer Sinclair (chapter 1 of this book), were not studied. Forensic psychiatrists focused upon masculinity's mutations ignoring cases when it harmed others.

While homosexuality could not be "normal" – it was not heterosexual monogamy after all – it greatly differed from more extreme deviances and crimes studied at the clinic. Homosexuality challenged the binaries of healthy and unhealthy sexuality; while patients seemed sexually "abnormal" they were otherwise mentally healthy. Much to the clinicians' surprise, homosexual relationships were based on consent, mutual desire, and romance echoing healthy heterosexual relationships. And so, clinicians wondered about the contemporary definition of sexual normalcy. Their daily work with patients gradually transformed their perceptions and eventually their ideas about what constituted deviation and normalcy.

The Toronto clinic was a unique component of twentieth-century sexual psychiatry, but many of its decisions were influenced by contemporary codes of behavioural and sexual normalcy. How the clinic initially understood a strict divide between normalcy and abnormality is significant, especially as it related to the modern scientific desire to gain knowledge, and subsequently power, through order. In particular, the Toronto clinicians worked to craft a system of classification that was easily transferable and applicable to other clinics. The labour behind the creation of a systematic catalogue of sex deviations and offenses in the 1950s highlights the Cold War belief in scientific process and an objective "norm."

I. THE CLINIC AND COLD WAR SEXUAL PSYCHIATRY

The Toronto Psychiatric Hospital (TPH) Forensic Clinic was an exceptional facility because of its approach to defining sexual normalcy. The out-patient clinic ran from 1956 to 1967, ending when a larger facility opened in Toronto: the Clarke Institute of Psychiatry.[22] The TPH Forensic Clinic opened at a pivotal point in North American psychiatry. A few years earlier in 1952, the American Psychiatric Association (APA) published its first edition of the *Diagnostic and Statistical Manual of Mental Disorders* (DSM). Initially a compact manual solely used by the APA, the DSM grew over the next few years to become a more comprehensive manual compiled with the intent to standardize clinical diagnoses across North America.[23] The Toronto Forensic Clinic was also established in the wake of the 1954 Royal Commission on the Criminal Law Relating to Criminal Sexual Psychopaths or the McRuer Commission. Both the psychiatric manual and royal commission attempted to provide order and rational solutions for potential disorder in society. The McRuer Commission was especially influential to the TPH clinic, which combined law with psychiatry to solve the apparent crisis of sexual psychopathy in society.

The TPH opened the forensic out-patient clinic in May 1956 with Dr P.G. Thomson as director. Situated close to the University of Toronto's St George campus, the facility was multi-disciplinary from the beginning, providing teaching in the faculty of medicine, school of social work, and department of psychiatry.[24] Before this clinic opened, the Ontario court referred patients to the TPH's ten-bed in-patient clinic.[25] Beginning with a chief social worker and two psychologists, the out-patient clinic grew by the end of the 1950s to include four resident psychiatrists.[26] The Toronto Forensic Clinic's primary objective was to provide psychiatric consultation, diagnosis, and treatment services for adults in Metropolitan Toronto. Psychiatrists like Gray believed that forensic psychiatry should not be restricted to sentencing but be used to help people in prison and on parole.[27] The Toronto clinic provided complete physical and medical examinations of incoming patients with a small battery of ancillary tests (including electroencephalogram and x-rays). Unlike other court-run clinics, such as the facility at Penetanguishene, the TPH Forensic Clinic went beyond providing diagnostic services – it attempted to treat the patients and study the conditions.

Born in the wake of a sex crime panic, the forensic clinic was created to provide knowledge, understanding, and treatment of the sexual offender, while also reassuring the public. Following the murders of three Toronto children in the winter of 1955–56, the *Toronto Star* sponsored a public forum at Massey Hall in downtown Toronto in January 1956. The Parents Action League, concerned members of the public and the press, several psychiatric and forensic professionals, including Toronto's first forensic psychiatrist Dr Kenneth Gray, attended the forum.[28] Edson L. Haines (a QC, past vice president of the Canadian Bar Association, and future Ontario Supreme Court judge) chaired a panel of four experts who claimed that forensic psychiatry, the application of psychiatry to legal problems, would resolve public concerns over the safety of children from sexual predators. Shortly after the public meeting, a provincial committee formed and recommended that a forensic clinic be established in Toronto, something that had been a subject of interest for the TPH since its inception in 1925.[29]

The clinic's progressive purpose was treatment, not punishment, Ed Turner described in 1967: "The Forensic Clinic provides this rational approach to the criminal, his offence and the circumstances in which the violation of the law occurred: already the opportunities of treatment, as contrasted with punishment, are dimly seen for careful testing by social psychiatric techniques."[30] Psychiatrists focused on treating patients as individuals, examining how conditions affected each person differently and grew from unique experiences. The purpose was to overcome ignorance and fear: "Crucial to forensic psychiatric services, and equal to them, is the matter of research to further our knowledge and understanding of emotionally disturbed offenders. Without such research clinical appraisal and recommendation becomes too generalized for meaningful application."[31] The clinic prided its role in researching conditions that were misunderstood and feared, while providing fair treatment of people convicted of various crimes – against property and persons – to reduce rates of recidivism.[32]

El Chenier's *Strangers in Our Midst: Sexual Deviancy in Postwar Ontario* provides an important institutional history of Cold War sexology and Canadian law. Chenier studied how clinical and forensic psychiatrists attempted to control public fears and anxieties about sexual criminals. Chenier's work disrupts the narrative that post-war sexology belonged to Kinsey, highlighting instead a small group of Canadian clinicians. *Strangers in Our Midst* examines gender and systems of power, from the male clinicians to the female advocates who pushed for stronger laws. Concentrating on the psychiatric research and treatment of violent crimes and pedophilia, Chenier dissects the "permissive approach" to dealing with sexual deviancy, a method that was popular among post-war forensic psychiatrists. This method was a positive one to homophile and later gay liberation politics, but it had unintended negative consequences for victims of sexual assault.[33] Rather than addressing the harmful consequences experienced by women and children, these elite male doctors focused on the perpetrators.[34]

As Chenier notes, "sexual deviation" was an ambiguous category that allowed for increased policing and regulation of gay men.[35] The clinic became well-known for its work on sexual deviancy.[36] The majority (60 per cent) of court-ordered cases involved sexual crimes.[37] Kenneth Gray focused his attention on sexual deviation, its causes and how it could be categorized and treated. He sought how best to deal with sexual deviation in a legal capacity and considered society's view of the problem and its influence on psychiatric treatment.[38]

While the public fear of dangerous sexual psychopaths initiated the clinic, this facility focused on less serious sexual offenses. Here clinicians worked with patients who could return to society following non-invasive therapy in lieu of prison time. Sexual offenders were defined as those who were convicted of illegal sexual acts, usually committed in public. During this era, anyone who received sexual gratification from someone or thing other than an adult of the opposite sex or through sexual acts that did not lead to procreation was considered to be "deviant."[39] Notably this category did not include sexual assault or murder.[40] Patients were not necessarily classified as deviants *or* offenders. For instance, exhibitionists were considered deviant because of their desire to sexually expose themselves and were classified as offenders when they *acted* on this desire. The line between offense and deviance was less clear for homosexual patients. Homosexuality had been criminalised since the nineteenth century and, generally, Canadians were not arrested for being gay but for being caught in the act.[41] At the Toronto clinic, however, most homosexual patients were voluntary. While the level of coercion in a patient's search for psychiatric treatment can be unclear, the clinic differed from many in-patient facilities where gay men and women were admitted without their consent for treatment regardless of evidence of homosexual activity.[42]

Throughout the 1950s and 1960s, clinicians and researchers identified forensic clinics as the future of criminology. The Toronto clinic was part of this growing focus on psychopathic care and legislation in North America.[43] McGill University opened a forensic psychiatric clinic through the Allan Memorial Institute's out-patient department in 1955.[44] A 1960 article in the *Canadian Medical Association Journal* stated that since 1957, nearly thirty out-patient clinics and psychiatric "day centres" had opened across Canada. The article proclaimed that these clinics lessened the stigma of mental illness and the fear of psychiatric disorder and mental hospitals.[45] These clinics were symbols of psychiatric modernity, the driving intent to "cure the disease," and a public faith in scientific method and medicine.

Forensic psychiatry promised to define, understand, and at last control what had previously been out of reach: the criminal mind. In Turner's documents, however, this enthusiasm was muted. While he believed in the power of psychiatry to uncover the foundations of mental health, he observed how shame inhibited patients from discussing their sexuality or admitting their deviance to psychiatrists and family doctors.[46] As Turner stated, "Many of my patients have seen their family physician for anxiety, depression, somatic complaints, V.D., etc., yet could not admit to their physician that their main distress was due to homosexuality. Many consider their physician as friend and thereby are ashamed to admit their deviation."[47] Given the treatments of the day it is not surprising that patients sought to hide "abnormal" sexuality.

Despite the rhetoric of scientific progress and modern enlightenment, clinical treatment of homosexuality during the 1950s was typically harmful, painful, and cruel. When the TPH clinic opened in 1956, Gray emphasized its difference from other facilities: "From what has been said it is apparent that surgery, drugs, hormones or other forms of physical treatment are rarely the answer. The cases that belong in mental hospitals will benefit from the improved forms of treatment now available – but they are a small proportion of the total. In many cases, the treatment is psychological, involving a long, painstaking effort."[48] Since homosexuality was first categorized as medically abnormal in the nineteenth century and remained as such until well into the twentieth century, homosexual patients suffered a variety of invasive clinical procedures in addition to psychoanalysis. "Cures" included surgeries on the sexual organs and genitals, chemicals for sexual stimulation or depression, hypnosis, electric shock, and aversion therapy.[49] Methods were often horrific and bizarre – one of the stranger aversion therapies focused on sensitization and encouraged gay patients to imagine pictures of homosexuals and then vomit on them.[50] By contrast, the Toronto Forensic Clinic considered treatments to include *any* interviews with patients after the completion of the assessment period.[51]

The clinic researched the causes of homosexuality and sexually deviant behaviour, reflecting a Cold War public concern about psychological health, family dynamics, and their effects on children.[52] American writer Philip Wylie stoked fears about masculinity, order, and the family in his 1942 book *Generation of Vipers*. He blamed modern America's weakness, which included homosexuality, on the nation's overbearing mothers and absent fathers and coined the term "momism." His pseudo-psychiatric misogynous meanderings were given credibility by psychiatrist Edward Stecher, who wrote extensively about the dangers of "momism" in his studies about parenthood, and grew in popularity through the post-war period.[53] Many patient case-studies from this era emphasized the influence of parents, in particular mothers, on the sexual development of children.

The Toronto clinic aimed to maintain social and psychological norms by returning citizens to their roles within the family and the work force. Its function as an out-patient facility was attractive to those seeking to maintain normalcy and the status quo. Patients would be offered treatment *and* be able to remain within their communities once discharged from the court and placed on probation. In the early 1960s, Gray stressed the importance of male labour on the economy and wider society: "In addition, the head of the family could continue employment and support of his dependents, resulting in a direct economic gain for the community and the indirect social gains from the preservation of an intact family."[54] There were financial incentives to this model: "If treatment can be used successfully as an alternative to imprisonment in a significant number of cases, there would be an immediate saving of the money expended for apprehension, conviction and imprisonment."[55] Regardless of the incentive – the lightened load on the economy, the importance of male labour, or the preservation of the nuclear family – the underlying belief was that sexual deviation could be treated and men, as they were all men, could return to society after receiving therapy at the clinic.

Beyond this attempt to maintain social and gender norms, the clinic researched sexual behaviour itself. Although Turner often referred to the sexual spectrum from the Kinsey studies, he and other Toronto clinicians focused on the normal and abnormal binary in their discussions of healthy and unhealthy sexual activity throughout the 1950s and 1960s.[56] Hungry curiosity for sexual and gendered differences become a callous driving force to "discover" the unknown or hidden at the expense of others. Exhibitions of human sexuality in popular culture and clinical studies during the 1950s and 1960s typically presented gay men, lesbians, and trans people as spectacles, with their "abnormalities" the subject of intense, often insensitive fascination. One example of this was the attention on former GI Christine Jorgensen who, in the early 1950s, transitioned from man to woman. She was the first American widely known for sex reassignment surgery, gaining celebrity status across the country and internationally. A *New York Daily News* article from 1 December 1952 betrayed a sense of awesome incredulity about her transition: "Ex-GI Becomes Blonde Bombshell." The title played with the juxtaposition of the two identities, marvelling in both the bizarreness of human biology and the wonders of modern science. Such publicity fed the public's curiosity for a spectacle of strangeness and exposed the individual to unwanted and sometimes harmful attention.

Pseudo-scientific pulp novels published during the early Cold War featuring stories of gay men and lesbians also fed public imagination and curiosity. Salacious tales of sex, both same-sex and otherwise, were often carefully guised as popularized psychiatric studies similar to the Kinsey reports to avoid censorship.[57] Gay and lesbian pulp fiction could also be powerful and subversive outlets and expressions of same-sex desire and romance. There was, however, a distinct difference between Ann Bannon's *Beebo Brinker* (1962) and Doris Hanson's *Homosexuality: International Disease* (1965). While Bannon's story about a young woman finding true love was unique and empowering in its presentation of lesbian agency, Hanson's pseudo journalistic account satisfied a heterosexual curiosity for tales of peculiar perversions.[58]

The clinic did not exist within a cultural vacuum and psychiatrists similarly pursued a scientific curiosity about abnormal behaviours. Shortly after the Toronto Forensic Clinic opened, however, psychiatrists began to categorize distinct groups of patients, in particular the three most common: exhibitionism, pedophilia, and homosexuality, challenging the simple binary of normal and abnormal behaviour. In October 1956, when the clinic began its group therapy sessions, it started first with a mixed group of patients. The combined group proved unworkable, leading to separate therapy groups for exhibitionism and homosexuality in 1957, and a separate group for pedophiles in 1958. The division between the three most common groups at the clinic was an important decision, not simply for the patients' treatment but for the clinical understanding of the conditions.

The therapy was not without complications. The clinic director P.G. Thomson described the homosexual group as being particularly problematic, stating: "This group, which has largely been experimental, has been beset by certain difficulties."[59] In one instance two of the patients became a couple. When Thomson made it a rule that members of the group should not associate outside of the sessions, one of the men left therapy.[60] Another situation in this group involved a particularly aggressive member who was, as Thomson briefly put it, "sadistic" to the group's "more passive members." He eventually left after the "passive members" retaliated. This situation simply sounds like one patient bullying others, but Thomson presents the group of men as highly emotional and fragile. No similar stories are recorded for the other two therapy groups nor were pedophiles and exhibitionists described as sensitive, unreasonable, or flighty.[61]

Improvement for homosexuals were also measured differently. Whereas for other patients the goal was clear – to end deviant activity and prevent cases of recidivism – homosexual patients were not at the clinic to be "cured" or converted to heterosexuality. While movements "in this direction" were appreciated by some psychiatrists, what constituted for improvement was the patient's greater acceptance of homosexuality, the inhibition of acting out, and the diminution of anxiety.[62]

Turner wanted to properly understand the problem of so-called sexual deviancy: "A great deal more knowledge is required before we shall be able to access problems more accurately ... More understanding of deviant behaviour is necessary before treatment can become effective and extended to more difficult cases."[63] By decoding deviancy, psychiatry promised to help the police and law control the threats to normalcy and order that deeply frightened and disturbed the public. But what is evident in Turner's writings is an apprehension among some psychiatrists about the likelihood of discovering the secret to deviant behaviour.

II. THE PSYCHIATRIST AND PSYCHIATRY

Clinical research cannot be separated from the clinician. Polish philosopher of science Ludwik Fleck wrote on science's social conditioning in the 1930s. Focusing on the treatment and diagnosis of syphilis, prior to Penicillin, Fleck discussed how social perception of a disorder influenced scientific studies. He stressed that science, a study commonly perceived as objective and universal, was structured by subjective views and assumptions; spectators could not be separated from their patients.[64] Fleck was also critical of how truth was dependent on the speaker and their authority: "We are supposedly in possession of 'correct thinking' and 'correct observation,' and therefore what we declare to be true *is* ipso facto *true*. What those others such as the primitives, the old people, the mentally ill, or the children declare to be true *seems to be true only to them*."[65] According to Fleck there was no indisputable truth. Rather, topics and their relevance were dependent on the status of those who presented them, instead of on the quality of the topics in question. Taking this to the context of the psychiatric clinic, diagnosis was not only about the patient and the condition but also about clinicians and the lens through which they observed.

For Ed Turner, maintaining balance was at the heart of his research and commitment to understanding his patients. Turner began many of his talks on forensic psychiatry with the following quotation:

> There is a borderland between crime and insanity, near one boundary of which we meet with something of madness but more of sin, and near the other boundary of which something of sin but more of madness ... With a better knowledge of crime we may not come to the practice of treating criminals as we now treat insane persons, but it is probable that we shall come to other and more tolerant sentiments, and that a less hostile feeling towards them, derived from a better knowledge of defective organization, will beget an indulgence at any rate towards all doubtful cases inhabiting the borderland between insanity and crime.[66]

Judging from Turner's liberal use of Henry Maudsley's 1898 description of the "borderland between insanity and crime," achieving knowledge to combat hostility and fear was foundational to his approach in psychiatry and forensics. In many ways this choice of quotation distils Turner's character as a psychiatrist advocating for his patients. A longtime member of Toronto's St James Anglican Cathedral's congregation and choral society, Turner's use of Maudsley's quotation epitomizes *his* brand of Christianity, which valued compassion over judgment of those condemned and rejected by society. Unfortunately for many patients, this benevolent philosophy was rampant neither among clinicians of this era nor Christians.[67]

While Turner contemplated the borderland between insanity and crime, other therapists wielded their authority in a less benevolent manner. Former patient of the Clarke Institute and novelist Timothy Findley observed this difference. In 1993 Findley published *Headhunter*, a novel set at a familiar clinic in dystopian Toronto and dedicated the novel to his old therapist Turner. He thanked him in the acknowledgments, along with other psychiatrists and staff.[68] In his foreword, Findley wrote: "There are great psychiatric institutions in Toronto, each of which offers excellent care and support to the mentally ill and their families. In part, this novel tells the story of what could happen if the wrong people wielded authority in such institutions."[69] *Headhunter* explores the extremes of sadistic authority, the patient's vulnerability, and the power of fear. Much can be speculated about the influence Turner and Findley had on each other and their careers.[70]

Turner, for instance, did not begin his career an advocate for gay and lesbian rights. His conception of what constituted healthy and unhealthy sexual behaviour evolved over the years and only gradually did he become an ally to Toronto's lesbian and gay communities.[71] Turner's discussions on homosexuality from the mid-1950s through the 1960s reveal a growing discomfort with the classification of homosexuality as akin to other sexual deviations and crimes. As he gained knowledge, he perceived more elements that set homosexuality apart from other conditions at the clinic. He stands out for his reluctance to judge crime or deviancy as well as his dismissal of stark divisions between abnormal and normal behaviours. Turner's understanding of sexuality was laced with his heterosexual monogamous background, but to properly understand his patients he stepped away from his own traditional views, a task he managed more willingly over time.

Turner joined the forensic clinic in late 1958, replacing Thomson as director – a position that he held until 1967 when the clinic closed. Turner, born and raised in Hamilton, received a medical degree from the University of Toronto in 1952. That same year he married a young English-born physician, Gene Ann (Jan) Stewart (1926–2012). Jan had earned her degree in medicine at the University of Toronto in 1951 and after an internship at Vancouver's St Paul's Hospital, she returned to Toronto to marry Ed. Following post-graduate work in England, Ed received his Diploma in Psychiatry in 1957. At the forensic clinic, and later the Clarke Institute of Psychiatry, Ed Turner provided both private and group out-patient therapy. Jan, meanwhile, held a variety of medical positions in Ontario, including Hamilton's first District Health Officer and, for many years, a physician for East York and at the University of Toronto's student health clinic. She later trained and worked as a psychotherapist. Together the couple had four children while pursuing their own careers, defying the stereotype of the Cold War nuclear family with bread-winner father and stay-at-home mother.[72]

Writing the history of psychiatrists, particularly those involved in the medicalization of homosexuality during the 1950s, is a tricky process because of the balance of power between patient and clinician, the assumptions of normalcy, and the dividing lexicon of psychiatry, or medicine, and gender and sexuality. The gay and lesbian community does not necessarily celebrate figures central to the field of psychiatry, and for good reason. The American history of the removal of homosexuality from the DSM, for instance, is from one perspective a history of human rights and from another a history of medical progress. The heroes of these histories are not the same.

Homosexuality was listed as a symptom of mental disorder in 1952 and was the first condition to be removed from the manual. This decision resulted after years of public protest from the lesbian and gay community who staged interventions at the APA annual meetings beginning in 1970, and gained their own panel at the 1971 general meeting.[73] Clinicians like Dr Ronald Bayer, who wrote the often-referenced text *Homosexuality and American Psychiatry: The Politics of Diagnosis* (1981), took the divide between clinician and patient personally. Bayer expressed his feelings of betrayal when gay and lesbian activists challenged the DSM classification of homosexuality as a mental disorder: "Like so many other client populations, homosexuals turned on those formerly perceived as protectors, their sense of self-confidence enhanced by an awareness that they were part of an upsurge of protest directed at every social institution in America."[74]

For gay psychiatrists, the medicalization of homosexuality and the later removal of the so-called condition from the DSM was an especially contradictory and painful story. Caught between their professional association and sexuality, many kept their personal lives private while advocating for the de-classification of homosexuality as a symptom of mental illness.[75] Others were more extreme and hypocritical in their treatment.

In 1975, Michael Riordon wrote an article for the *Body Politic*, the gay and lesbian periodical out of Toronto, about an encounter at a gay dance with his ex-therapist, who had administered traumatic aversion therapies years earlier at the Clarke Institute.[76] His was not the only gay therapist who treated homosexuality as a pathological condition during this period of transitioning psychiatric concepts about normal sexual behaviour. The contradiction that enveloped this encounter highlighted the hierarchy of the patient–doctor relationship, as well as the growing ambiguity around what constituted "healthy" sexual behaviour. Treatment depended on the clinician.

American psychiatrist Dr Robert Spitzer is often credited with removing homosexuality from the DSM in 1973. Although Spitzer made the final decision, the change resulted from the work of activists along with clinicians such as psychiatrist Dr Judd Marmor and psychologist Dr Evelyn Hooker who led a committee to reconsider the pathologization of homosexuality. Spitzer, being head of the APA and central to the re-writing of the DSM in the 1970s, was celebrated for his decision. His view of homosexuality, however, was at best ambivalent. Under his direction, a condition called Ego-dystonic Homosexuality replaced Homosexuality in the manual and Spitzer was rightly criticized for trying to satisfy both sides of the debate.

In 2001, an elderly Spitzer took a more decisive step in the opposite direction of the 1973 decision and authored a study claiming that homosexuality could be "cured" after all.[77] His poorly conducted study countered his colleagues' research from decades earlier.[78] In the spring of 2013, Spitzer, now aged eighty-one, finally retracted his 2001 study on the grounds it was unscientific. This episode exposed Spitzer's obsession with psychiatric nomenclature and control and his belief that homosexuality was *not* normal. Spitzer's insistence that sexuality should be easily classified and understood, if not "cured" exemplified the continued discord between the traditional psychiatric community and the lives of those being studied.

While the APA's DSM was a significant text in mid-twentieth century psychiatry, it was not the only means of determining what constituted for health and illness, normal behaviour and abnormal tendencies. Focus on the DSM debates breaks the story of medicalization into strict paradigms of clinician and patient, heterosexual and homosexual, bypassing the discussions and uncertainties that existed within many different clinics. These are important factors to bear in mind when looking at the history of the TPH Forensic Clinic and Turner's work classifying homosexuality.

In his clinical papers, Turner often exhibited a confidence in contemporary psychiatry to treat homosexuality, but he still doubted the terminology and classification of this so-called condition. Turner redirected his attention to homosexuality's apparent pervasiveness and covertness. His 1959 paper "A Review of Homosexuality" addressed the etiology and the difficulty of pinpointing homosexuality's causes. Countering recent literature suggesting that gay men were easily identifiable, he stated that one "seldom sees the 'typical type' of homosexual."[79] He emphasized the complexity of the condition that went beyond physical traits and psychological characteristics. He believed that research and treatment, therefore, had to address the individual condition and clinicians had to "accept the view that homosexuality is a universal potential that may develop in response to a wide variety of factors."[80] In this early paper Turner identified the problem of defining homosexuality as a condition: "It is confusing when reading the literature and its many attempts at classifying homosexuality and homosexual behaviour. Classifications run into one another and are sometime [*sic*] descriptive, sometimes dynamic and sometimes casual."[81] Homosexuality was not easily contained to a specific category of illness or disorder.

Over the years, Turner travelled across Canada and abroad promoting the clinic's research and encouraging other institutions and associations to consider forensic psychiatry. Throughout the 1960s Turner spoke at conferences on criminology, psychiatry, law, and policing. He presented his research to the John Howard Societies of British Columbia and Alberta, and at the Annual Meeting of the APA in 1965.[82] Turner was excited for the possibilities of forensic psychiatry. But while he saw it as integral to the legal system, he was careful to remind his audience and readership that it was not meant to replace the law. Rather, it was a means to examine problems.[83] And while he looked to the future, Turner was aware of the field's shortcomings in the present.

Turner's enthusiasm for psychiatry and for a clear scientific definition of health and normalcy echoed the Cold War dichotomy between enemy and ally. As conflict progressed through the 1950s and into the 1960s from the war in Korea to the war in Vietnam, from the atomic bomb to the hydrogen bomb, and from bombers to intercontinental ballistic missiles, the principles of "Us" and "Them" disintegrated. In 1960, Dr Thomas Szasz published the now famous *The Myth of Mental Illness*, criticizing modern psychiatry and its focus on mental disorders as diseases akin to physical illness. He also condemned the medicalization of homosexuality, which "legitimized a new kind of witch-hunt where 'the physician has replaced the priest and the patient the witch.'"[84]

Despite claims about scientific method, sexual psychiatry depended on traditional Judeo-Christian codes of morality and homosexual patients were often judged by their doctor's understanding of sin and virtue. Despite his later support of Toronto gay and lesbian communities, in the 1950s and 1960s Turner held traditional views of sexuality and gender.[85]

Reflecting contemporary ideas, Turner blamed men's deviancy – in particular exhibitionism and pedophilia – on domineering mothers and wives.[86] Clinic studies not only ignored lesbianism but also assumed women to be passive partners without independent sexual desire or fantasies of their own. But Turner also willingly acknowledged evidence that disproved his initial assumptions. He later observed that patients with sex deviations differed not in relationships with their mothers but with their fathers, thus challenging the widely held belief in the sexual deviant's Oedipal complex.[87] By the late 1960s, Turner stressed the need to study female homosexuality, thereby acknowledging lesbianism and female sexuality, albeit through the limiting lens of pathology.[88] And decades later he addressed the deeply problematic and pervasive notion that pedophiles were shy deviants, observing that they were sadistic and violent towards children.[89] As will be discussed in the next section, by the late 1960s Turner argued against the very objectivity of sexual normalcy.

A few years after the removal of homosexuality from the DSM, the Ontario Psychiatric Association, under Turner's presidency, passed a resolution to declassify homosexuality as a psychiatric condition in Ontario clinics. Dr Saul Levine, not Turner, led this discussion about whether there was insufficient evidence to continue identifying homosexuality as a diagnostic classification.[90] Levine was vocal in his criticism. He stated that within the Canadian and Ontario Psychiatric Associations there was "still a very strong attitude that homosexuality per se represents a psychopathological disorder when there is no evidence in literature to back that attitude."[91] Despite Turner's writing on the changing perception of homosexuality as a sexual pathology or deviancy, he was not an activist. His significance lies in his questions, his reluctance to assume a connection between homosexuality and extreme pathological conditions, and his focus on the "borderland."

III. THE MOST COMMON DEVIATION

In his 1962 discussion of scientific paradigms, *The Structure of Scientific Revolutions*, American philosopher Thomas Kuhn illustrated how one scientific truth becomes obsolete with the discovery of a newer, better, and more accurate scientific truth.[92] Kuhn described the "paradigm shift" as one that happened when a universally recognized scientific achievement was disrupted by a scientific revolution. The basis of this shift is that two paradigms cannot co-exist, much in the same way that two truths cannot co-exist. Kuhn's description of a shift in scientific facts, presenting fact as something contingent on its society and surrounding knowledge, reflected Cold War divisions as well as the pathologization of sexual behaviour in contemporary psychiatry. The classification of sexuality and behaviour as "well" or "unwell" depended on what was currently seen as scientifically "true," illustrating how science, medicine, and psychiatry were subjective fields and influenced by contemporary social norms and politics. At the same time, as Kuhn noted, "[i]n the sciences, therefore, if perpetual switches accompany paradigm changes, we may not expect scientists to attest to these changes directly."[93] While shifts in reasoning and definition occurred in sexual psychiatry, experts took longer to change their thinking patterns. Over the course of a decade the methods of categorizing homosexuality and sexual deviancy changed at the Toronto forensic clinic. Earlier assumptions about sexual normalcy and mental health became less dependent on sexual acts, or the target of sexual acts, and more focused on the relationship between those involved in the sexual act.[94]

Between 1956 and 1967, the forensic clinic ran a clinical study on sexual offenders, which examined the effects of talk therapy and the rate of recidivism on 123 patients, a total 132 cases.[95] Through this study and a wider examination of the patient population of sexual deviants, Turner and his colleague Hans Mohr reconsidered the classification of homosexuality and the way in which sexual deviancies might be organized. The study began as an overview of the type of sexual offenses studied at the clinic but upon examining the data Mohr soon realised that this was a long-term project and possibly one that would remain open-ended.[96] With a background in etymology and sociology, Mohr, a social worker and psychiatric researcher from Graz, Austria, paid particular attention to how researchers used terms and how they organized psychiatric classifications. Evident in this research was the labour invested in creating a workable nomenclature of sexual deviation and a systematized classification of conditions. Turner, Mohr, and their colleagues confirmed their earlier speculations that homosexuality had little in common with sexual offenses like exhibitionism and pedophilia.

In 1962, Mohr presented their clinical research in an article about the benefits of using psychiatric treatment as an alternative to imprisonment. He identified the researchers' primary issues in this project. The Toronto clinic had a psychologically diverse population that denied easy definition and categorization of sexual deviation.[97] In seeking the causes psychiatrists struggled to find similarities between offenses by categorizing acts and targets. Once the driving force behind an offense was discovered, researchers could recommend treatment, but they could not properly determine the effectiveness of these treatments without significant follow-up. This project revealed that forensic psychiatry's goals were contradictory. Individual sentencing and research standardization both considered the overwhelming diversity of sexual deviancy but from different angles.

After four years, the study was still too small to provide comprehensive results, but Mohr believed it could lead to potential improvements in the field. In his 1962 paper, Mohr considered the future: "We hope we can standardize some of the data of the new study along the lines of the investigations of the Kinsey Institute, which will shortly publish a volume on the sex offender. Dr Pomeroy has kindly extended an invitation to us to discuss this in a workshop."[98] One of the major texts to come from this research was the booklet *Exhibitionism and Pedophilia* (1962) written by Turner, Mohr, and Richard Bell. It is significant that this booklet did not include homosexuality.

The pathologization of homosexuality overlapped with its categorization as illegal activity in Canada but during the 1950s and 1960s these two classifications of homosexuality often ran parallel to one another. The law, set in Canada in the nineteenth century sauntered through the decades with little change in rhetoric. Many, professionals and public alike, saw the medicalization of homosexuality as a step forward; it lifted the blame from an individual's actions and focused instead on the individual's "condition." Once established as a medical condition, homosexuality metamorphosed into a state defined less by action than by character and mentality.[99] These studies offered new information about sexual behaviour but still assumed that homosexuality was "abnormal."

In 1964, lawyer Alex K. Gigeroff presented a paper at the Research Conferences on Delinquency and Criminology in Montreal, which addressed the evolution of Canada's 1892 legislation on homosexuality. Over the decades, aside from slight amendments and two revisions in 1906 and 1927, he noted surprisingly little "real change," considering that social and behaviour sciences had advanced "their knowledge and understanding of human behaviour generally over the last 100 years, and in particular the knowledge and understanding of sexual behaviour over the last 50 years."[100] Gigeroff identified as particularly problematic in the unchanging legislation the archaic and vague terminology used to describe illegal sexual acts and the illogical system of categorization; for instance the association of "buggery" with "bestiality."[101] In addition to using antiquated terms, the legislation focused on criminalizing actions, not sexuality. No differentiation was made between illegal actions committed by a man on another man, a man on a woman, an adult on a child, or a human on an animal. This lack of specification, Gigeroff noted, ignored intent. Forensic psychiatry on the other hand worked to find, define, and categorize the psychological drive.

Prime Minister Pierre Trudeau's cabinet famously amended the Canadian Criminal Code in 1969, effectively decriminalizing homosexuality. But these limited amendments did not equal free sexual expression. Widely misunderstood by Canadians to mean that gay men and women were considered equal to other Canadians, the amendments did little to end everyday oppression. Protestors in the 1970s argued that, "In our daily lives we are still confronted with discrimination, police harassment, exploitation, and pressures to conform which deny our sexuality."[102] Legalized homosexuality was limited to acts committed in private between two consenting adults (aged twenty-one and over), immortalized by Trudeau's 1967 quotation of journalist Martin O'Malley's maxim that there was no place for the state in the bedrooms of the nation.[103] In August 1971, Toronto Gay Action initiated national protests of the limited amendments. Across Canada the gay movement demanded equal rights, an end to job discrimination against gay women and men, and called for "sexual orientation" to be included in the Canadian Bill of Rights as a prohibited ground of discrimination. At this time, homosexuality was *still* officially classified as a mental illness or a symptom of a mental disorder in Canadian mental institutions. Despite clinicians' belief that they were helping the public perception of homosexuality, in an era that glorified heterosexuality as the epitome of normalcy and health, to be classified as sick was to be biologically and socially inferior.

Psychiatrists were not the saviours they had hoped to be. While the forensic clinic's research helped challenge the paradigms of healthy sexuality the clinic's research classified and described what they determined to be sexually and mentally abnormal. The drive to maintain objectivity was evident in the clarification of terms used at the clinic, in particular "deviation" versus "perversion." Psychiatrists at the forensic clinic preferred using the term deviation because it moved away from the legal, moral, and social condemnation implied with the term perversion. In this sense, they considered "deviation" an objective term rather than one infused with a sense of morality. As Gray had stated in 1956, "The role of a psychiatrist is to understand and treat patients, not to judge them."[104] Yet the term "deviation" clearly implied abnormality and inferiority.

As discussed earlier, psychiatrists assessed gay patients according to a medicalized and personal understanding of normalcy regardless of efforts to avoid judgment. Some psychiatrists were extreme in their definitions of deviancy and viewed sexual deviation as a means of repressing violent or sadistic acts. For example, Thomson's view of the sexual offender was that "sadism makes genital sexuality seem so destructive to the deviate person that he falls back on what seem to him less dangerous and harmful forms of sexuality."[105] The harmful belief that minor deviations were merely a starting point or a means of repressing more serious acts partly explains why for years pedophilia was divided into two categories: heterosexual and homosexual. Here deviation was determined not by adult sexual contact with a child but by the perpetrator's preference of gender.[106]

By the early 1960s psychiatrists at the Toronto Forensic Clinic had divided the conditions, or deviations, into two sub-groups. Those in the first group were heterosexual and defined by the *way* in which men expressed their "pathological sexuality" towards adult women.[107] This included conditions such as sadism, masochism, voyeurism, and exhibitionism.[108] The second group included men who directed their sexual drive towards an "abnormal object," such members of their own sex,

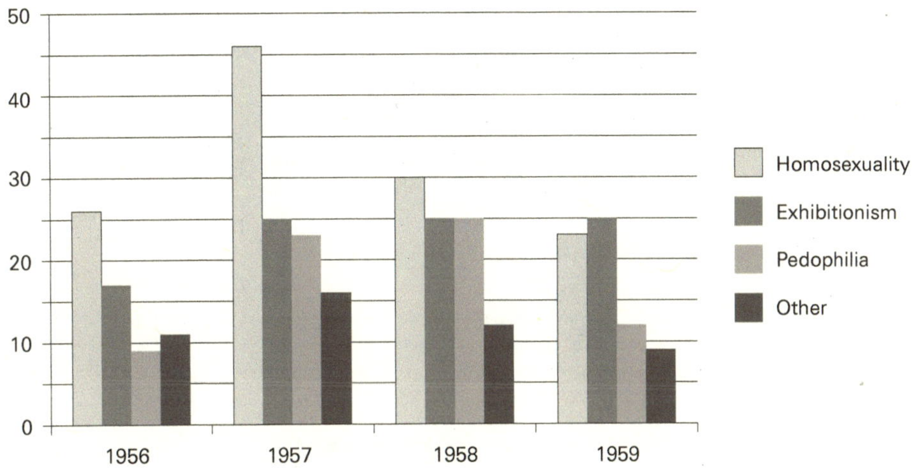

5.1 Bar graph showing the forensic clinic's patient population.

children, or non-human "objects," which could include animals or literally objects.[109] This group's deviancies included homosexuality, pedophilia, transvestism, fetishism, and bestiality.[110] The deviancy of this group was based on to whom they directed their desires.

Turner, Mohr, and their colleagues could not ignore the obvious gaps in the reasoning. The most obvious problem was homosexuality. Unlike other deviancies, it was typically consensual and without victims. Thomson noted in his 1963 paper that homosexuality was also social in a way that other deviancies were not: "There is no public world of exhibitionism, etc. as there is of homosexuality. Homosexuals congregate together in bars and restaurants and often publish their own magazines."[111] According to Thomson, for this reason and what it allowed in terms of self-perception and analysis, homosexuality was a promising subject of sociological study.

Researchers could not ignore more distinct differences between homosexuality and other conditions at the clinic. Homosexual patients consistently made up the largest group at the clinic. A 1960 article analyzed the numbers of the patient population that was "suffering from sexual deviation."[112] Between 1956 and 1959 homosexual patients numbered a total of 125 out of 334 patients, surpassing exhibitionists (92) and pedophiles (69).[113]

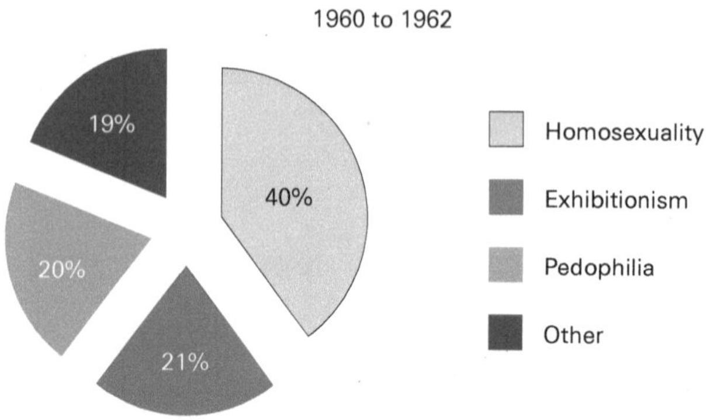

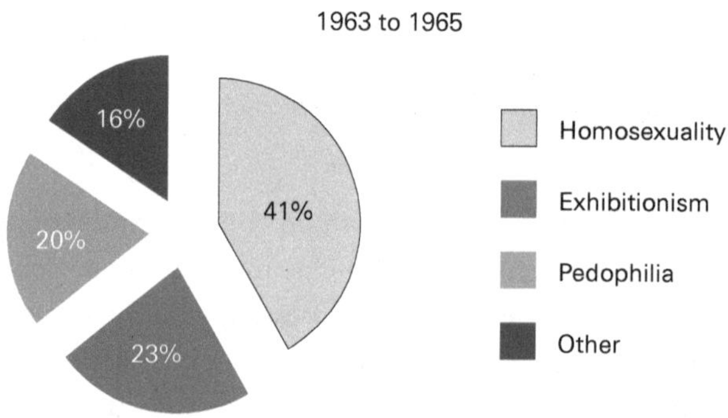

5.2 and 5.3 Two pie charts showing the forensic clinic's patient population.

In a 1967 article, Turner and Mohr presented the numbers of new patient cases at the forensic clinic between 1960 and 1962, and closed cases between 1963 and 1965 prior to the move to the Clarke Institute. Homosexuality again had the highest number of patients among those seeking treatment for sexual deviancy, numbering 156 out of a total of 397 between 1960 and 1962, and 219 out of 526 between 1963 and 1965.[114] This data clearly showed the prevalence of homosexual patients at the clinic.

As clinicians noted since 1956, homosexual patients were primarily voluntary. Those referred to the clinic by court order for having committed an offense, such as "gross indecency," were distinguished as different.[115] While homosexuality was the largest group at the clinic, only

15 per cent of them were referred by court order.[116] This small group was included in the larger study of sexual offenders and recidivism, which examined the cases of fifty-four exhibitionists, fifty-five pedophiles, and twenty-three homosexuals.[117] Turner believed the homosexual cases included in this study – those caught in public – were "promiscuous" cases and unrepresentative of homosexuals in general. Just as the voluntary homosexual patients stood apart from the larger clinic population, these men were distinct among those referred by court order. Turner described the homosexual offenders as having significantly higher IQ than the other court order patients. They were more likely to have attended university, they held white collar jobs, but generally had "poor work records" – perhaps a reference to "character weakness" and likely the result of workforce discrimination. They were more like the clinicians in terms of class and background. Ultimately, they were Others but familiar. These differentiations offered significant social, sexual, and psychological evidence that homosexuality was indeed separate from conditions like exhibitionism and pedophilia. Most significant to the study itself was the conclusion that homosexual offenders were generally the least likely to "re-offend."[118]

By the late 1960s the method of classifying deviations, so that the driving force behind them could be more properly understood, shifted to involve the specific relationship between deviant and victim. By 1965, Turner had developed a different method of categorizing sexual deviancy. He and others, including Mohr, began to look at the relationship between the "object," or victim, the nature of the act, and the agent, or offender. By 1967, they allowed that deviation and "normal" sexual behaviour were dependent on context and existed on a sliding scale.[119] Although the heterosexual married couple remained the sexual norm, so-called deviant sexual acts were now only a problem when perceived as such by the people involved. This method of codifying did not work for all sexual acts, but it was a significant step forward in medical perceptions about homosexuality and understanding it as part of a spectrum of behaviours.

Mohr and Turner acknowledged the importance of categorization and words. The term "disorder" implied that there should be order and "deranged" indicated that there was a range of acceptable behaviour, and both words pointed towards a norm.[120] These researchers expressed both the usefulness and the confusion that resulted from broad categorizations: "every event can be seen and described from an infinite number of positions (and yet not without a position) and that, therefore, a reduction is imperative. Reality is a continuum and terminology implies limits and so understanding and sharing cannot possibly be accomplished in totality."[121] This introspective glimpse into the researchers' process lays bare their awareness of the limitations of their research and of the importance of outside perceptions.

CONCLUSION

Psychiatry, in many cases, was but another form of incarceration and punishment for "abnormal" sexuality. There were, however, psychiatrists like Ed Turner who struggled with changing perceptions and ideas about sexuality and deviation. While these psychiatrists were often *not* activists, they did push for changes in classification, categorization, and definition of deviations based upon their encounters with patients, in particular, for those who were gay.

Debates between clinicians and researchers about the etiology and nature of homosexuality as a condition were at times overt and at other points implicit in their inability to properly determine *how* to treat homosexuality. A booklet in Turner's possession from the British Medical Association's Department Committee on Homosexual Offenses and Prostitution, *The Problem with Homosexuality*, for instance, acknowledged the rudimentary nature of research on the possible treatment methods for homosexual patients.[122] One of the main problems with the experiments, the book stated, was the lack of contact with patients following treatment, which made it difficult to determine whether or not the treatment was successful. According to some of Turner's reports he did keep professional contact with homosexual patients, and several continued their treatment over many years at the TPH Clinic and later at the Clarke Institute.

Psychiatry promoted the belief that modern research would provide objective means for understanding people and enforcing sexual normalcy that aligned with traditional morality. This attitude underlay the pathologization and treatment of homosexuality, sexual deviation, and crime. These modern expressions of moral persecution were subsequently influenced by contemporary politics and social concerns.

Identifying and containing individuals through pathologization were simply old methods dressed up in modern "scientific" garb.

The clinic's drive to treat sexual deviants and criminals pointed to the faith in modern psychiatry to uncover individuals' hidden behaviours and reflected the larger Cold War desire to expose the invisible threat.[123] While the attempts to contain political and sexual deviancy was related to the individual's so-called character weakness, it also stemmed from a desire to define deviance and fears about a homosexual threat to a heterosexual, family-based society. Turner's documents display a mixed sense of confidence, confusion, and persistence in the methods of dealing with homosexuality. He seemed confident that science, namely talk therapy, offered a humane way of treating a population deemed criminal. Gradually, he and others came to question whether homosexuality was a psychiatric condition at all.

Turner's documents from the TPH Forensic Clinic reveal growing doubts about the medicalization and treatment of homosexuality. As illustrated in the first section of this chapter, the contemporary social understanding of a sexual norm greatly influenced the clinic's work and its legacy. Similarly, as discussed in the second section, the psychiatrist's own understanding of sexual norm influenced patient diagnoses. And finally, Turner and Mohr's research and efforts to categorize sexual deviancies exposed absurdities and contradictions causing them to question the inclusion of homosexuality as a disorder. The Toronto clinic was innovative and did not engage in the most brutal treatments of the era. Yet it worked within its society and social norms. The Toronto clinic was a place where white middle-class male professionals categorized mostly white male patients into groups of Others. Psychiatry and its effort to gain clarity and order was rife with uncertainty. Efforts to categorize activities and mentalities into clear camps of "normal" and "abnormal" came to naught as ideas about homosexuality developed and changed. In an era that contained and surveilled Others – scanning for threats to society and national security – the medicalization of homosexuality revealed layers of anxiety about defining and identifying deviancy. Turner's clinical practice created opportunities for study but also revealed the inadequacies of current scientific ideas and methods. In a period seeking clear binaries, sexual forensic psychiatry exemplified the uncomfortable reality that human behaviour defied easy codes of normalcy and abnormality.

NOTES

1 Joan Holloban, "Few Facts are Known: Clinic for Deviates," *Globe and Mail*, 9 May 1961, 7.

2 J.W. Mohr, "The Contribution of Research to the Selection of Appropriate Alternatives for Sexual Offenders," *Psychiatric Treatment as an Alternative to Imprisonment* (Toronto: Canada Law Book Company, 1962), 317, Centre for Addiction and Mental Health Archives (CAMH), Toronto, Ontario. Dr R.E. Turner fonds, box F27, file 6.12.

3 Kenneth G. Gray, "Sexual Deviation: Problem and Thought." Reprinted from *Saturday Night*, 26 November 1956, 3, CAMH, Turner fonds, box F27, file 6.19.

4 This chapter expands research conducted for my PhD dissertation, "Controlling Contagion: Policing and Prescribing Sexual and Political Normalcy in Cold War Canada" (University of Saskatchewan, 2016).

5 For more on Cold War anxiety and the medicalization of citizens, see Andrea Tone, *Age of Anxiety: A History of America's Turbulent Affair with Tranquilizers* (New York: Basic Books, 2009).

6 In 1954, British mathematician and architect of theoretic computer science and artificial intelligence Alan Turing took his own life after undergoing "chemical castration" through the administration of an estrogren medication called DES (Dietheylstilbestrol). Typically used in hormone therapy and cancer treatments, DES was effectively a punishment for Turing's homosexual activity, masquerading as treatment in lieu of prison-time. While the Toronto Forensic Clinic avoided such treatments, other clinics did not. Psychiatrists at the Clarke Institute, which came after the Toronto Forensic Clinic, submitted patients to aversion therapies and the institute was brutal in its treatment of transgendered men and women into the late twentieth century.

7 Mental health experts were predominantly men at this time. Women were more likely to be found in social work. El Chenier, *Strangers in Our Midst: Sexual Deviancy in Postwar Ontario* (Toronto: University of Toronto Press, 2008), 45.

8 It should be noted that these were not necessarily the identifiers used by gay men and women at the time. Valerie Korinek, *Prairie Fairies: A History of Queer Communities and People in Western Canada, 1930–1985* (Toronto: University of Toronto Press, 2018), 17.

9 R.E. Turner, "The Forensic Clinic," *Criminal Law Quarterly* 2, no. 4 (February 1960): 444.

10 A.K. Gigeroff, Johann W. Mohr, and R.E. Turner, *Sex Offenders on Probation: Homosexuality* (1969), CAMH, Turner fonds, box F27, file 6.28.

11 Johann W. Mohr and R.E. Turner, "Sexual Deviations: Part II – Homosexuality," in *Office Management of Psychiatric Problems* (February 1967), CAMH, Dr Donald Blair Coats fonds, box F36, file 8.12.

12 The study of "homosexuality" began with the dawn of modern psychiatry and psychology. Nineteenth-century sexology shifted the view of homosexuality away from the rhetoric of religion and morality and focused instead on apparent causes. Richard von Kraft-Ebing's monumental 1886 text, *Psychopathia Sexualis, with Especial Reference to Contrary Sexual Instinct: A Medico-Forensic Study*, trans. Charles Gilbert Chaddock (Philadelphia & London: The F.A. Davis Co., Publishers, 1892), was foundational to sexologists' interpretation of homosexuality because of its suggestion that sexuality was contingent on environmental and inherited factors.

13 Jennifer Terry, "Anxious Slippages between 'Us' and 'Them': A Brief History of the Scientific Search for Homosexual Bodies," in *Deviant Bodies: Critical Perspectives on Difference in Science and Popular Culture*, ed. Jennifer Terry and Jacqueline Urla (Bloomington: Indiana University Press, 1995), 159–60.

14 While the fear of Soviet spying was based in reality, anti-communism was often a vehicle for police and state surveillance of citizens. Frances Reilly, "Operation Profunc: The Cold War Plan to Intern Canadian Communists," in *The Bridge in the Parks: The Five Eyes and Cold War Counterintelligence*, ed. Dennis Molinaro (Toronto: University of Toronto Press, 2021).

15 See Daniel J. Robinson and David Kimmel, "The Queer Career of Homosexual Security Vetting in Cold War Canada," *Canadian Historical Review* 75, no. 3 (1994): 319–45; Gary Kinsman, "'Character Weakness' and 'Fruit Machines': Towards an Analysis of the Anti-Homosexual Security Campaign in the Canadian Civil Service," *Labour/Le Travail* 35 (1995): 133–61.

16 See Gary Kinsman and Patrizia Gentile, *The Canadian War on Queers: National Security as Sexual Regulation* (Vancouver: UBC Press, 2010); David K. Johnson, *The Lavender Scare: The Cold War Persecution of Gays and Lesbians in the Federal Government* (Chicago: University of Chicago Press, 2004); Robert D. Dean, *Imperial Brotherhood: Gender and the Making of Cold War Diplomacy* (Amherst: University of Massachusetts Press, 2001).

17 More likely it was the gay diplomats that suffered at the hands of the state, rather than the other way around. In 1964, Canadian diplomat John Watkins died while under interrogation by the RCMP for affairs he had had with Russian men.

18 The RCMP for example profiled Canadian historian Frank Underhill as lacking moral courage and of questionable masculinity when he wept while being censured by the police. Steve Hewitt, *Spying 101: The RCMP's Secret Activities at Canadian Universities, 1917–1997* (Toronto: University of Toronto Press, 2002), 62.

19 A small population, 13 per cent, of women patients were sent to the clinic for non-sexual criminal offences such as alcoholism, traffic violations, and assault charges. From interviews with P.J. Thomson, R.E. Turner, and J.W. Mohr, El

Chenier found that the psychiatrists could not think of any women convicted for sex crimes between 1956 and 1966. Chenier, *Strangers in Our Midst*, 119.

20 Doug Owram explores the post-war era's obsessive fear of "de-masculinization." Doug Owram, *Born at the Right Time: A History of the Baby Boom Generation* (Toronto: University of Toronto Press, 1996), 256. Christopher Dummitt examines the perceived threat post-war modernism posed to masculinity. Christopher Dummitt, *The Manly Modern: Masculinity in Postwar Canada* (Vancouver: UBC Press, 2008).

21 Chenier, *Strangers in Our Midst*, 98 and 103.

22 While I did not conduct research for this chapter at the ArQuives (Canada's LGBTQ2+ Archives) I must acknowledge its staff and volunteers – in particular the Community Engagement Committee – who drew my attention to the history of the Clarke Institute and how it is remembered within the Toronto LGBTQ2+ community.

23 Hannah Decker, *The Making of the DSM-III: A Diagnostic Manual's Conquest of American Psychiatry* (New York: Oxford University Press, 2013).

24 R.E. Turner and Erika Steffer, "The Forensic Clinic," in *TPH: History and Memories of the Toronto Psychiatric Hospital, 1925–1966*, ed. Edward Shorter (Toronto: Wall & Emerson, Inc., 1996), 308. R.E. Turner, "The Forensic Clinic of the Toronto Psychiatric Hospital." Given at the Annual Meeting of the John Howard Society of British Columbia (Vancouver, 1965), 2, CAMH, Turner fonds, box F27, file 7.8.

25 K.G. Gray, "Forensic Services in Toronto" (1960 c.), 3, CAMH, Turner fonds, box F27, file 6.19.

26 R.E. Turner, "Forensic Psychiatric Services." Given at Annual Meeting of the John Howard Society of Alberta (Red Deer, 27–28 October 1967), 8, CAMH, Turner fonds, box F27, file 7.9.

27 John P.M. Court, Alexander I.F. Simpson, and Christopher D. Webster, "Contesting Mad versus Bad: The Evolution of Forensic Mental Health Services and Law at Toronto," *Psychiatry, Psychology and Law* 21, no. 6 (2014): 926.

28 Also in attendance were Dr Ralph Brancale (Director of the State of New Jersey's Diagnostic Center for Sex Offenders), Dr Manfred Guttmacher (Chief Medical Officer of the Supreme Bench, Baltimore), and Dr F. Van Nortrand (Chief of Treatment Services, Department of Reform Institutions of Ontario). Turner, "The Forensic Clinic of the Toronto Psychiatric Hospital," 1.

29 Turner and Steffer, "The Forensic Clinic," 307.

30 Turner, "Forensic Psychiatric Services," 11.

31 Ibid., 9.

32 Crimes against property included theft, breaking and entering, alcohol- and traffic-related violations, and breaches of probations. Non-sexual crimes against

people included assault, wounding, and "contributing to juvenile delinquency." The psychological conditions of voluntary patients at the clinic were diverse, including neurosis, psychosis, and character disorder. Turner, "The Forensic Clinic," 445–6.

33 Chenier, *Strangers in Our Midst*, 11.

34 For changing views of sexual assault, see Karen Dubinsky's *Improper Advances: Rape and Heterosexual Conflict in Ontario: 1880–1929* (Chicago: University of Chicago Press, 1993).

35 Chenier, *Strangers in Our Midst*, 165.

36 Herbert Pascoe, "Deviant Sexual Behaviour and the Sex Criminal," *Canadian Medical Association Journal* 84 (1961): 206.

37 Gray, "Forensic Services in Toronto," 8.

38 Turner and Steffer, "The Forensic Clinic," 306.

39 Gray, "Sexual Deviation: Problem and Thought," 1.

40 If the victim was an adult woman, the act was "normal." Chenier, *Strangers in Our Midst*, 166.

41 See Steven Maynard, "Through a Hole in the Lavatory Wall: Homosexual Subcultures, Police Surveillance, and the Dialectics of Discovery, Toronto, 1890–1930," *Journal of the History of Sexuality* 5, no. 2 (1994): 207–42.

42 Many people were sent to mental hospitals for being gay, often against their will, and underwent treatment and aversion therapy at institutions like Manitoba's Selkirk Mental Hospital. Korinek, *Prairie Fairies*, 56–7.

43 Gordon Watson, John Rich, and Kenneth G. Gray, *A Study of Forensic Cases* (Toronto: University of Toronto, Department of Psychiatry, 1957), CAMH, Turner fonds, box F27, file 6.17.

44 The McGill clinics also examined the psychopathy of the criminal but concentrated less on sexual deviancy. R.E. Turner, paper, "Forensic Psychiatry and Criminology in Canada," *Fourth International Congress of Psychiatry* (Madrid, 10 September 1966), 6, CAMH, Turner fonds, box F27, file 6.12.

45 A.L. Jones and M.E. Miller, "Day Centre in Toronto for Psychiatric Patients," *Canadian Medical Association Journal* 83 (1960): 846–8.

46 Turner noted that psychiatrists saw a wide range of psychological issues exhibited by homosexual patients, according to their age and background. R.E. Turner, "Homosexuality," paper (10 March 1972), 9, CAMH, Turner fonds, box F27, file 6.26.

47 Turner, "Homosexuality," 11.

48 Gray, "Sexual Deviation: Problem and Thought," 3.

49 Peter Conrad and Joseph W. Schneider, *Deviance and Medicalization: From Badness to Sickness* (Philadelphia: Temple University Press, 1992 [1980]), 187.

50 Herb Kutchins and Stuart A. Kirk, *Making Us Crazy, DSM: The Psychiatric Bible and the Creation of Mental Disorders* (Toronto: The Free Press, 1997), 59.

51 J.W. Mohr, J.R.B. Ball, R.E. Turner, draft, "A Documentary Follow Up of Sexual Offenders Referred to the Out Patient Forensic Clinic" (1959), 4, CAMH, Turner fonds, box F27, file 7.2.

52 See Mary Louise Adams, *The Trouble with Normal: Postwar Youth and the Making of Heterosexuality* (Toronto: University of Toronto Press, 1997); Deborah Weinstein, *The Psychological Family: Postwar America and the Rise of Family Therapy* (Ithica: Cornell University Press, 2013).

53 Jennifer Terry, *An American Obsession: Science, Medicine, and Homosexuality in Modern Society* (Chicago: University of Chicago Press, 1999), 316.

54 Gray, "Forensic Services in Toronto," 1.

55 Ibid.

56 Turner, "Sex Offender," Course in Criminology and Correction, St Patrick's College, Ottawa (22 March 1961), 1, CAMH, Turner fonds, box F27, file 7.14.

57 These included books such as Richard C. Robertiello's *Voyage from Lesbos: The Psychoanalysis of a Female Homosexual* (New York: Citadel Press, 1959); Benjamin Morse's *The Lesbian: A Frank, Revealing Study of Women who Turn to their Own Sex for Love* (Derby, Connecticut: Monarch Books, 1961); and less seriously Ray Train's erotic parody: *Miss Kinsey's Report* (Cleveland: Chevron Publications, 1967).

58 Neil Richards introduced me to the fascinating subject of pseudo-psychiatric pulp novels through his extensive collection of gay and lesbian pulp literature at the University of Saskatchewan. Neil himself was a wonderful queer history resource and is greatly missed.

59 P.G. Thomson, "The Forensic Clinic at Toronto." Reprinted from *The Journal of Social Therapy* 4, no. 3 (1958): 5. CAMH. Turner fonds, box F27, file 6.12.

60 Thomson, "The Forensic Clinic at Toronto," 5.

61 Pedophiles and exhibitionists were described in positive terms and the members of those groups as well-behaved patients who supported each other.

62 Thomson, "The Forensic Clinic at Toronto," 5.

63 R.E. Turner, "Treatment of the Sex Offender," *Forensic Psychiatry* (Toronto: Canada Law Book Company Ltd., 1961), 470–1, CAMH, Turner fonds, box F27, file 7.13.

64 Ludwik Fleck, *Genesis and Development of a Scientific Fact* (Chicago: University of Chicago Press, 1972 [1935]), 89.

65 Fleck, *Genesis and Development*, 50. Original emphasis.

66 H. Maudsley, *Responsibility in Mental Disease* (New York: D. Appleton and Company, 1898), 36–7. Quoted by R.E. Turner, "The Development of Forensic Clinic," *Manitoba Medical Review* 46, no. 7 (August–September 1966): 453.

67 See Matthew Wiseman's chapter for information on Ewen Cameron, MK-ULTRA, and psychiatric control. In the 1990s one of Cameron's followers, J.S.

Tyhurst (who studied the psychological effects of nuclear war and psychiatric uses of LSD), was found guilty of sexually and psychologically abusing multiple female patients in British Columbia. See Rod Mickleburgh, "Ruling Upheld in 'Deplorable' Case of Abuse by Therapist," *Globe and Mail*, 17 April 2003, updated 18 April 2018; Christopher Hyde, *Abuse of Trust: The Career of Dr James Tyhurst* (Vancouver: Douglas & McIntyre, 1991).

68 Findley also dedicated his short story "Dreams" to Turner.

69 Timothy Findley, *Headhunter* (Toronto: HarperCollins Publishers Ltd., 1993).

70 I am indebted to Sherrill Grace and CAMH archivist John Court for drawing my attention to the connection between Turner and Findley. Grace explores this relationship and Findley's experience as a patient in her book: *TIF: The Life and Works of Timothy Findley* (Waterloo: Wilfrid Laurier University Press, 2020).

71 Chenier, *Strangers in Our Midst*, 11.

72 Indeed, historians of work and gender dispute this stereotype, arguing that women have often worked outside of the home and that the cultural portrayal of the nuclear family was manufactured. See Valerie Korinek, *Roughing it in the Suburbs: Reading* Chatelaine *Magazine in the Fifties and Sixties* (Toronto: University of Toronto Press, 2000).

73 By this point the protestors included Vietnam veterans and other demonstrators. Together they protested inaccurate pathologization (for gays and lesbians) and the lack of medical recognition (for veterans suffering from PTSD). Kutchins and Kirk, *Making Us Crazy*, 66. See also Adam Montgomery, *The Invisible Injured: Psychological Trauma in the Canadian Military from the First World War to Afghanistan* (Montreal and Kingston: McGill-Queen's University Press, 2017).

74 Ronald Bayer, *Homosexuality and American Psychiatry: The Politics of Diagnosis* (New York: Basic Books, 1981), 8.

75 One advocate for gay psychiatrists at the 1972 APA meeting in Dallas, Texas was "Dr Anonymous," who hid his face with a mask, wore a baggy suit to hide his form, and distorted his voice with a microphone. Fryer, who had previously been fired on account of his sexuality, hid his identity to keep his non-tenured position at Temple University. His participation demonstrated both strong support within the psychiatric community for the activists and revealed to the association at large that there were more than 200 other APA members who were gay and that there existed a Gay Psychiatric Association. Kutchins and Kirk, *Making Us Crazy*, 67.

76 Michael Riordon, "Blessed are the Deviants: A Post-Therapy Check-Up on My Ex-Psychiatrist," *The Body Politic* 21 (November/December 1975): 10–11.

77 R.L. Spitzer, "Can Some Gay Men and Lesbians Change their Sexual Orientation? 200 Participants Reporting Change from Homosexual to Heterosexual

Orientation," *Archives of Sexual Behavior* 32, no. 5 (October 2003): 403–17. This journal is the official publication of the International Academy of Sexual Research.

78 Milton Wainburg from Columbia University approached Spitzer regarding the problems of the study and its scientific methodology, or lack thereof, pointing out that the study's participants were primarily advocates for the Ex-Gay Movement and that the questions within the study were biased. The study, published without peer review, received severe criticism from scholars like Wainburg along with sexual advocates who were not only critical of the research but also dismayed at Spitzer's betrayal.

79 R.E. Turner, paper, "A Review of Homosexuality" (20 January 1959), 7, CAMH, Turner fonds, box F27, file 6.12.

80 Ibid., 3–4. Turner referred to Kinsey's heterosexual–homosexual seven-point scale here and several other studies.

81 Ibid., 4.

82 In the late 1960s and 1970s Turner and other psychiatrists at the Clarke Institute educated citizens about psychological and sexual conditions on various local radio and TV programs.

83 "The 'borderland between crime and insanity' is surely becoming better understood. We are in the process of discovering 'natural laws' rather than inventing theories and uttering oracles." R.E. Turner, "Forensic Psychiatry in Canada" (Montreal: 30 August 1965), 10, CAMH, Turner fonds, box F27, file 7.8.

84 Quoted by Andreas De Block and Pieter R. Adriaens, "Pathologizing Sexual Deviance: A History," *Journal of Sex Research* 50, no. 3–4 (2013): 287. Interestingly Szasz later supported the anti-psychiatry movement and joined forces with L. Ron Hubbard to form Citizens Commission on Human Rights that condemned the psychiatric profession. Decker, *The Making of the DSM-III*, 15–17.

85 For instance, Turner's views on abortion were unremarkable for the time. Abortion was criminalized in Canada until 1969. In 1960, rather than arguing whether a woman had a right to an abortion in the case of sexual assault, Turner discussed whether or not sexual assault affected a person's mental health enough to endanger her life, thus working within the acceptable reasons for therapeutic (legal) abortion. Letter, from R.E. Turner to P.G. Thomson, 1960, CAMH, Turner fonds, box F27, file 6.26.

86 R.E. Turner, "The Sexual Offender." Given at Residential Seminar and Research Meeting at Queen's University (Kingston, 24 August 1963), 10–11, CAMH, Turner fonds, box F27, file 7.13. In his commentary, Thomson offered a more Wyliesque description of the feminine threat: "the educated and emancipated modern American female." P.G. Thomson, paper, "Discussion of R.E. Turner's Paper 'The Sexual Offender.'" Given at Residential Seminar and Re-

search Meeting at Queen's University (Kingston, 24 August 1963), 4, CAMH, Turner fonds, box F27, file 6.12.

87 Turner, "Forensic Psychiatry in Canada," 8.

88 Turner, "The Forensic Clinic of the Toronto Psychiatric Hospital," 14.

89 R.E. Turner, "Pedophilia," *Treatment of Psychiatric Disorders* (1989), CAMH, Turner fonds, box F27, file 8.2. Earlier papers referred to the literal and innocuous meaning of "pedophile" as "lover of children." Turner, "The Sexual Offender," 5. Throughout the mid-twentieth century, despite the public fear of pedophiles, psychiatrists considered children resilient and placed responsibility on parents to properly handle their children after an assault to minimize shock and reduce long-term psychological damage. Gray, "Sexual Deviation," 2.

90 Minutes: Ontario Psychiatric Association, "Meeting of Council in the Board Room, Clarke Institute of Psychiatry" (13 June 1975), 12, CAMH, Turner fonds, box, F27, file 4.15.

91 Minutes, 12–13.

92 Thomas S. Kuhn, *The Structure of Scientific Revolutions* (Chicago and London: The University of Chicago Press, 1996 [1962]), 20.

93 Kuhn, *The Structure of Scientific Revolutions*, 114–15.

94 Terms also changed: "object" became "victim," which became dependent on the relationship with the perpetrator of the sexual act.

95 The discrepancy between the number of persons studied and the number of cases was because nine cases fell into two categories.

96 Barbara Moon, "Defining the Sex Offender," *Globe and Mail*, 10 April 1965, A12.

97 Otherwise, the patient population, predominantly white men from the Toronto area, lacked diversity. One document detailed the patients' countries of birth but in the interest of maintaining patients' privacy there was no correlation made between patient demographics and conditions. The majority (77.4 per cent) was Canadian born. Others were born in the United Kingdom, and fewer were born in the United States, Germany, the Netherlands, and Italy. Fewer still were born in Rumania, Hungary, Latvia, and Estonia. R.E. Turner and M. Jerry, paper, "Statutory Referrals to Forensic Clinic, Toronto." Given at Third Research Conference on Criminology and Delinquency (Montreal, 20–24 November 1962), Table 9, CAMH, Turner fonds, box F27, file 7.9.

98 Mohr, "The Contribution of Research to the Selection of Appropriate Alternatives for Sexual Offenders," 326.

99 Allan Bérubé, *Coming Out Under Fire: The History of Gay Men and Women in World War Two* (New York: Free Press, 1990), 146.

100 A.K. Gigeroff, paper, "The Evolution of Canadian Legislation with Respect to Homosexuality, Pedophilia, and Exhibitionism." Given at Fourth Research

Conference on Delinquency and Criminology (Montreal: November 1964), 8–9, CAMH, Turner fonds, box F27, file 7.27.

101 Ibid., 2–3.

102 Kinsman and Gentile, *The Canadian War on Queers*, 260. Quoting the August 28th Gay Day Committee, "We Demand" document.

103 The limited definition of legalized same-sex activity excluded sexual activity with multiple partners, partners younger than twenty-one, or in public places like bathhouses or the outdoors.

104 Gray, "Sexual Deviation," 1.

105 Thomson, "Discussion of R.E. Turner's Paper 'The Sexual Offender,'" 2.

106 J.W. Mohr, paper, "A Short Survey of Sexual Offenders in the Ontario Reform Institutions, Millbrook" (1961 c.), CAMH, Turner fonds, box 6, file 17. As mentioned earlier, "heterosexual pedophiles" were previously seen as childlike and gentle versus the more active and sexual "homosexual pedophiles." Turner, "The Sexual Offender," 5. One of the many problems with this categorization is the unclear definition of an underage boy versus the clear definition of an underage girl. Typically, victims of pedophilia fell between ages six and twelve years, but the difference lay in the peak ages: the oldest girls were generally between ten and eleven, but boys could be as old as sixteen. Most documents do not clarify the age of boy victims, an omission that greatly changes assumptions about the crime.

107 Turner, "Sex Offender," 1.

108 For a time, Turner included cunnilingus in this section, assuming it to be a male heterosexual abnormal desire rather than female homosexual activity. This was later edited out indicating a change in classification and understanding of heterosexual male normalcy. R.E. Turner, paper (draft), "What to do with the Sexual Offender: Treatment of the Sex Offender Without Imprisonment." Given at Canadian Bar Association, Mid-Winter Meeting (Niagara Falls, Ontario, 4 February 1961), CAMH, Turner fonds, box F27, file 7.14.

109 Turner, "Sex Offender," 1.

110 The earlier draft included fellatio under this category, clearly assuming male homosexual activity rather than female heterosexual activity. Turner, "What to do with the Sexual Offender."

111 Thomson, "'The Sexual Offender,'" 3–4.

112 Turner, "The Forensic Clinic," 444.

113 In 1956 homosexual patients numbered twenty-six out of sixty-three, in 1957 they reached a peak of forty-six out of 110, in 1958 there were thirty out of ninety-two, and in 1959 they dropped just below exhibitionists, which numbered twenty-five, to be twenty-three out of a total of sixty-nine. Turner, "The

Forensic Clinic," 444. "Other" included offences like voyeurism, fetishism, transvestivism, incest, sado-masochism, and bestiality.

114 Mohr and Turner, "Sexual Deviation, Part I: Introduction," *Applied Therapeutics* (January 1967), 80, CAMH, Turner fonds, box F27, file 10.4.

115 Turner and Jerry, "Statutory Referrals to Forensic Clinic, Toronto," 7.

116 Mohr, "The Contribution of Research to the Selection of Appropriate Alternatives for Sexual Offenders," 321.

117 Turner, "Sex Offender," 5.

118 Ibid., 6.

119 Mohr and Turner, "Sexual Deviation, Part I: Introduction," 79.

120 Johann W. Mohr and R. Edward Turner, paper, "Empirical Data as a Basis for Model Formation with Special Reference to Sexually Deviant Behaviour." Reprinted from *The International Journal of Social Psychiatry* Congress Issue (1964), 97, CAMH, Turner fonds, box F27, file 7.27.

121 Mohr and Turner, "Empirical Data as a Basis for Model Formation," 99.

122 Edward Glover, ed., *The Problem with Homosexuality* (The Institute for the Study and Treatment of Delinquency, c. 1955), CAMH, Turner fonds, box F27, file 6.17.

123 Gerald Grob, "The Fielding H. Garrison Lecture: Psychiatry and Social Activism: The Politics of a Specialty in Postwar America," *Bulletin of the History of Medicine* 60, no. 4 (Winter 1986): 477.

6

Constructing the Military Career Woman, 1950s–60s

SARAH HOGENBIRK

In the autumn of 1961, National Defence public relations and Canadian newspapers extolled Royal Canadian Air Force (RCAF) Corporal Annie Coutts as "the first airwoman to reach compulsory retirement age."[1] Her service during the Second World War and early Cold War transformed her life in profound ways. Like Elmer Sinclair, whose life story is portrayed in chapter 1, Coutts was promoted to become a non-commissioned officer and enjoyed some status and prestige. She earned the Canadian Volunteers Service Medal with clasp, the British Defence Medal, and Canadian Forces Decoration during her fourteen years of service in the RCAF. Coutts first enlisted in the air force in 1942 and served in the food services branch of the RCAF (WD) until her discharge in 1946. Her Second World War service saw her go overseas to England. After her discharge, Coutts took practical nursing at Dominion School of Nursing in Toronto, Ontario. She then worked as a private nurse until she re-enlisted as a medical assistant in the RCAF in 1951. Coutts became an acting corporal shortly after her return to the air force. During the 1950s, she was posted to several stations within

Canada and went overseas, where she worked with the Fourth Fighter Wing in Germany and the First Fighter Wing in France. Coutts was promoted to corporal during her three years overseas (1955–58). Upon her return to Canada, Coutts was stationed at RCAF Station Clinton, where she served as an assistant ward supervisor in the infirmary until her mandatory retirement at age fifty.[2]

Coutts represented a Cold War military *career woman*.[3] Drawing upon Defence Department press releases, journalists highlighted her promotions, her exciting overseas tours, and her military honours. Reporters reinforced Cold War gender stereotypes by emphasizing Coutts' commitment to nursing, which they portrayed as acceptable and nurturing feminine work. They mentioned that she worked as a civilian nursing assistant before the Second World War but switched to food service during the war because there were no available spots in the related RCAF trade of medical assistant. Reporters then noted that Coutts trained and worked as a practical nurse after the war, before she re-enrolled in the RCAF as a medical assistant.[4] Medical assistants were non-commissioned members who assisted and reported to military nurses and doctors.[5] A staff reporter for the *Stratford Beacon-Herald* explicitly reinforced polarized gender roles and Coutts's femininity by stressing that she "helped feed the famous Sixth Bomber Group in Yorkshire [England]" during the Second World War without mentioning the risks Coutts faced. Reporters left out the German bombing raids of England. While this supportive work formed a milestone in Coutts's career, the articles clearly contrasted it with the more dangerous masculine role of flying bombing raids over enemy-held territory in Europe.[6]

National Defence and Canadian journalists readily presented Coutts's honourable release as a symbol of women's increased acceptance in the traditionally masculine domain of the armed services. Several reporters noted that her retirement coincided with the twentieth anniversary of the creation of the RCAF (Women's Division) [RCAF (WD)] and women's entrance into the Canadian armed services in new non-nursing roles.[7] Women had been limited to service as nurses prior to the Second World War. When the RCAF (WD) and the Canadian Women's Army Corps (CWAC) were formed in 1941, new support roles became open to women who were not trained nurses. The Women's

Royal Canadian Naval Service (WRCNS, often called the Wrens) was created, increasing the numbers and variety of support roles for women. Although prohibited from combat roles, approximately 50,000 women served in medical services as well as in the women's divisions of the army, navy, and air force, with some serving overseas. Despite efforts to retain the women's services, all three were disbanded in 1946 and many women left the forces against their will. Only a small number of women remained in armed services as military nurses, dieticians, and a few other roles. However, by 1951, with the expansion of the forces after the outbreak of war in Korea, the armed services again increased their recruitment of women to fill labour shortages.[8]

Publicity about military career women contradicts popular stereotypes of Cold War domesticity. For many, the 1950s conjures up images of suburbia with stay-at-home mothers, working fathers, and children playing outside. Canadian women's and gender historians have argued that while the nuclear, male breadwinner, family model and the suburban home were powerful ideals, these stereotyped ideals did not capture the full complexity of women's lived experiences. Scholars have documented women's participation in the civilian labour force, women's involvement in professional organizations, and women's activism.[9] Although historians have emphasized the diversity of women's experiences in Cold War Canada, they have paid little attention to servicewomen.[10] Yet some women, such as Corporal Annie Coutts, pursued military service as a career in the 1950s and 1960s.

This chapter will address this scholarly imbalance by exploring the discussions of women's place in the armed services in military publications, internal defence reports, and civilian media. As scholars, such as Lucy Noakes and Cynthia Enloe, have noted, studying images of servicewomen, and especially the military career woman, reveals the negotiation and regulation of gender roles within the armed services and society at large.[11] This chapter will begin with a discussion of the events leading up to the Canadian state's decision to once again enlist women into the army, navy, and air force in non-medical roles. It will then move on to address three topics. First, it will examine how government and military officials constructed the military career women by answering the following questions: What roles were open to women in the armed services? What were the recruitment criteria? And what policies shaped women's labour? Cabinet limited women's roles in the Canadian armed forces. Restrictive recruitment criteria created a narrow pool of women who were eligible to pursue a military career, and policies regarding marriage and pregnancy for those in service further reduced their numbers.

Second, the chapter will address how women were represented in military and civilian publications. This section will analyze the competing messages that stemmed from the tensions between women's gender and military identities. The narrative of military career women challenged polarized gender norms that labelled the armed services as an exclusive masculine domain, and marriage and motherhood as women's ultimate goals. Reassurances that women would maintain their femininity in the masculine domain of the military co-existed with the messages that some women saw a home for themselves in the armed services and that some chose their career over marriage and motherhood. The articles on Coutts, with their blend of her military successes and her commitment to looking after the men who fought, are a case in point. Similar mixed messages were embedded in Second World War depictions of servicewomen including the idea that servicewomen could handle military life alongside reassurances that they remained respectable, feminine women.[12]

Third, the chapter will explore how women negotiated a space for themselves and other women in the armed services. Some women, particularly those who had served before, lobbied to join the forces again. Women had their own reasons for enlisting and their career plans did not always match those of these male dominated institutions. Some misbehaved or left the armed services when military life did not match their expectations. Drawing from the literature on military disobedience, discharges and deliberate misbehaviour are analyzed as an attempt by women to redefine the conditions of their service.[13] Senior servicewomen partly responded to their subordinates' complaints by using them to legitimize their recommendations for policy changes, but their recommendations were constrained by higher level policies and society-wide sexist attitudes that restricted women's employment. The chapter will argue that women, military officers, and government officials all participated in the construction of the military career women, who was typically depicted as a single woman who retained her femininity while accessing some of the benefits and power of the armed services.

WOMEN'S RE-ENTRANCE INTO CANADIAN ARMED SERVICES

Individual women, veterans' organizations, military officers, and government officials all discussed women's place in the armed services in the late 1940s and early 1950s. Journalists, such as the prominent feminist Lotta Dempsey, wrote about individual women's attempts to secure military employment, while raising awareness about women's issues and encouraging women's political activism. In her 1 July 1950 column for *The Globe and Mail*, Dempsey reported that Second World War Wrens visited HMCS *York* hoping to find out when they would be allowed to re-enlist. Similarly, an August 1950 Canadian Press story was entitled, "Girls Want to Go: Ex-Servicewomen, Nurses Seek to Enlist in Canada's Korea Brigade."[14] Sixty army nurses served in the Korean combat theatre and some RCAF nurses served on medical evacuation flights.[15] Civilian media described women's desire to serve.

Military publications also documented veterans' efforts to broaden women's military roles. The RCAF's *The Roundel* carried a regular feature on the activities of veterans' organizations. The September 1950 edition recorded a resolution sent to Air Force Headquarters in Ottawa from the No. 100 (Bluenose) Wing, a Halifax chapter of the RCAF Association. On 18 July 1950, No. 100 (Bluenose) Wing "resolved '[t]hat the Women's Division again be accepted as part of the Permanent and Reserve Forces of the R.C.A.F. to include veterans of the World War II who might wish to re-enlist, as well as new recruits.'"[16] The reference to Permanent Forces hints that some women wanted a military career because career military personnel tended to serve in the permanent or regular forces. Permanent or regular force members served full time, while those in the reserves served part time. Reservists could be mobilized for full-time duty when a crisis or war occurred.[17] Women actively pressured the government to accept their entry into the reserve and regular forces.

While female veterans lobbied the government, some senior military and government officials saw women as a solution to "manpower" problems.[18] Historian Isabel Campbell observes that military policies during the early 1950s were premised on a temporary need for larger numbers of short-term military personnel. Canada had a small, strictly volunteer permanent army, navy, and air forces in 1949–50, which meant it lacked large numbers of "'ready' forces" for quick deployment if combat missions arose. As a result, Canada had to rush to mobilize troops to fight in the Korean War and support its NATO commitments in Europe.[19] Defence spending and the armed services grew exponentially in the early 1950s as the government committed significant resources to Korea and to NATO. The defence budget was $375 million in 1949–50 and $1.45 billion in 1951–52. From 1949 to 1951, the Canadian armed services swelled by 70 per cent and officials repeatedly debated how women fit into mobilization planning.[20] Those government and military officials who favoured the recruitment of women, argued that the armed services, and the country they defended, needed to prepare for emergencies that might include the large-scale mobilization of women. In October 1950, Federal Cabinet ministers noted another strategic benefit: women would take on jobs that were unattractive to men.[21] The increased recruitment of women was tied to a pressing need for more military personnel.

Cabinet officially approved the re-entrance of women into the armed services on 21 March 1951. Only the RCAF enlisted women into its regular and reserve forces in 1951. The army and navy initially only enlisted women into their reserves but both opened their regular forces to women by 1955. Defence officials justified women's re-entrance by referencing manpower shortages and Canadian women's Second World War record. Some officials acknowledged that Canadian women had showed that they were competent military personnel and that "womanpower" helped win the war.[22]

DEFINING WOMEN'S PLACE IN THE ARMED SERVICES

Women had a precarious position in Canadian Cold War armed services. Historian Barbara Dundas aptly characterizes the 1945 to 1965 period as a "time of uncertainty."[23] Women constituted a small fraction of uniformed personnel. For example, they constituted approximately 3 per cent of the Royal Canadian Navy (Reserve) in 1954.[24] In 1965, roughly 900 of the 107,600 personnel in the Canadian armed services were women. Women composed less than 1 per cent of the armed services when military officers once again discussed the future of women in the armed forces in 1965.[25] As this section will show, servicewomen's place in the Canadian armed services was continuously contested in this period. Unlike Elmer Sinclair, whose story appears in chapter 1, servicewomen could never claim equal status with the men.

An exclusively masculine cabinet limited and shaped servicewomen's career paths with a series of restrictions in March 1951. Servicewomen were not allowed in combat roles and were further restricted to trades deemed suitable for women. Civilians cost less than military members as they were paid less and not entitled to uniforms, training, accommodation, and other benefits; servicewomen were not to take civilian jobs either. Their projected numbers were small and kept quiet. They were to be recruited under "the combined ceiling for men and women" and placed "into existing units without any increase in establishment."[26] Each service had a specified maximum number of people, or total establishment, and had to decide whether to fill those spots with men or women. The Defence Council decided that "there would be no special women's units."[27] The council listed an additional condition: servicewomen were not to be clerks at headquarters.[28] Servicemen or civilians remained the preferred employees.

Across the globe, armed forces recruited small numbers of women as an inexpensive[29] source of labour, however in Canada, many Cold War military planners viewed servicewomen as particularly costly employees. In fact, cabinet's restrictions were implemented as cost-cutting measures: the chairman of the Defence Council prefaced the discussion of the restrictions on servicewomen's employment by stating that "Cabinet had approved the recruiting of women, but because it was felt that this was a very expensive way of obtaining womanpower it should be subject to the following conditions."[30] Internal defence documents throughout the 1950s and 1960s frequently contain the arguments that servicewomen cost more to house, train, and administer than servicemen and that the armed services did not see a return on their higher investments because women, it was believed, would serve only for short periods. As will be analyzed more in-depth below, the average regular force servicewoman was defined as a young woman who served during the gap between when she finished her schooling and when she started her family. Servicewomen were also more expensive than civilian employees. The Army Policy Committee observed in January 1952 that civilians were cheaper because they assumed more of the costs of their training and the army did not have to supply civilians with the specialized expensive "housing, clothing, and personnel administration" that servicewomen required. Reflecting a common viewpoint in military planning documents, the Army Policy Committee stated that they only wanted to employ servicewomen when it could not secure enough civilians or in reserved military jobs that were suitable for women. Restrictions on servicewomen's employment were justified as the most cost-efficient way to employ servicewomen.[31]

Ironically, cabinet's limitations contributed to the perceived higher cost of servicewomen for all three services. During the early 1950s, the emphasis was on recruiting single, young, able-bodied male recruits who could fight and not on the retention of regular force members. Since women were prevented from serving in combat-related trades and women counted towards the total establishment, employing a woman meant that the armed services had one less potential male combatant. Military planners in Canada and elsewhere never questioned women's combat restriction in the 1950s and 1960s. Servicewomen only began to be considered for combat roles in the late 1980s. The prohibition against women as combatants contributed to the view that they were less desirable employees and reduced their presence in the Canadian armed services.[32]

Female recruits faced higher standards and had fewer spots available to them than male recruits. The navy promoted a message of exclusivity and informed Canadians that the navy would remain a predominantly masculine space with advertisements that declared that "A Limited Number of Women Will Be Accepted for Part-Time Service in the Women's Royal Canadian Navy Reserve." Officers claimed in newspaper interviews that they could afford to be selective because numerous women competed for a limited number of spots.[33] Like men, women had to meet the medical standards for enlistment. The army allowed all recruits to make a three-year commitment in the early 1950s but restricted women to its reserves. The army favoured single women but allowed married women who were between nineteen and forty-one years old and possessed a "Grade 8 or equivalent education" to enlist in its reserves. In contrast, male recruits entering the army's regular forces could enlist at seventeen years of age if they had their parents' permission and at least twenty-one if they were married. Otherwise, male army recruits had to be between eighteen and forty years of age and many were accepted even if they lacked a grade 8 education.[34]

Recruitment criteria dictated which women could become military career women. Women who sought to enlist in the regular forces also faced more stringent requirements. In the early 1960s, the navy allowed single, male recruits of seventeen to twenty-five years of age with grade 8 education to enlist as a non-commissioned member in its regular forces but required that female recruits be eighteen to thirty years old with a grade 10 education. Female officer applicants had slightly different requirements: they had to be between twenty-one and thirty-five years of age with their "Senior Matriculation (Grade 13)."[35] Initially, women who wanted to serve full-time in the non-commissioned ranks in the RCAF had to be single women "between 18 and 29 years old" with at least a grade 10 education. In contrast, men who wanted to serve full-time in the RCAF had to be between seventeen years and forty years old with a grade 8 education.[36] The RCAF relaxed education requirements to a minimum of grade 9 in the early 1950s because they did not attract as many women as they had predicted.[37] Male and female officers faced additional requirements. For example, women interested in being air force officers had to be at least nineteen years old and have "a university degree or senior matriculation combined with at least two years administrative experience."[38] While the RCAF preferred single men and woman, allowances could be made for an exceptional married woman with no dependent children. Allowances were also made for exceptional men. Patricia Power writes, "men could be married and enrolled if they were an officer, if they had served in the [Second World War] or had served since September 1947." Still the ban of married women remained in place into the late 1960s. The Royal Commission on the Status of Women recommended ending this ban and pregnancy as grounds for discharge when it reported in 1970.[39] Recruitment criteria favoured young, single, physically fit, educated women for full-time service.

These criteria also created space for experienced servicewomen, like Coutts, to continue their military careers. The RCAF and RCN extended the maximum age of enlistment for veterans in 1951. The air force permitted female veterans up to forty years of age to re-enlist as non-commissioned officers and those up to thirty-five years of age to re-enlist as officers, while the naval reserve was opened to veterans of up to thirty-five years of age.[40] Still, only certain veterans qualified. An air force veteran recollected, "The age limit and children prevented most of us originals from rejoining in 1951."[41] A core of Second World War female veterans passed on their knowledge to the new generation of servicewomen. The experienced veteran who reenlisted was one version of the Cold War military career woman.

The numbers of military career women and servicewomen in general shifted as their opportunities in the armed services expanded and contracted. Each service crafted its own employment policy within the general restrictions imposed by cabinet. Only the RCAF enlisted women into its regular (full-time) and reserve (part-time) forces in 1951. The other two services initially only recruited women for their reserves and opened their regular forces to women in the mid-1950s. Cabinet authorized the air force to enlist 5,000 women into the regular force in 1951, the army to enlist 90 women into its regular component in 1954, and the navy 400 in 1955. The RCAF's higher ceiling reflected its requirement for highly skilled women to staff radar lines. Air force women were recruited in 1951 to work as meteorological observers, fighter control operators, clerks, safety equipment technicians, and others. Women also enlisted and subsequently served in the RCAF reserves. About 50 female officers and 330 airwomen were reported in the Auxiliary Reserve at the end of 1960. Female air force personnel in the regular forces were stationed all-across Canada, typically along the Pinetree Line, and some women served in France and Germany.[42]

Airwomen's presence and the trades open to them declined after 1955. The number of women peaked in July 1953, with just over 3,100 women serving in the twenty-eight trades open to them. In 1955, the air council reduced the recruitment ceiling for women from 4,000 to 2,500, stating that the lower ceiling was "most compatible with recruiting capabilities."[43] Women's presence declined as the air force grew.

The RCAF reached its maximum peacetime strength of 55,700 personnel but further limited women's job prospects in 1958. According to a 1965 review of the employment policy of women in the three services, women's "physical limitations" contributed to senior air force officers' decision to restrict women to trades that required at most sixteen weeks of training in 1958. Senior officers also had justified this decision by arguing that women's higher attrition rate, which the 1965 review reported was "in certain trades ... as much as five times that of men," meant the air force lost a return on investment. The RCAF found that the average woman served for thirty months, yet it took military personnel eighteen months to become efficient radar technicians.[44]

Changing technology also contributed to the declining numbers of airwomen. Fewer people were needed in radar units due to the introduction of semi-automated ground environment system (SAGE). Technological innovations resulted in job losses on the Pinetree Line (described in chapter 2) and on the DEW Line (described in chapter 3) adding to the loss of jobs for servicewomen. Approximately 1,800 women were employed in thirteen trades when Air Force headquarters temporarily halted the recruitment of women in 1963. In June 1964, the chief of the air staff (CAS) felt there was no longer a place for women and wanted to "phase [them] out." He wanted to preserve jobs for servicemen. The CAS was reacting to upcoming loss of personnel signalled by Liberal Defence Minister Paul Hellyer's March 1964 *White Paper on Defence*, which proposed to unify and streamline the armed services. Ultimately, a 1965 review of the employment policy of women in the three services led to the overturning of the RCAF decision. The authors recommended that women be permanently made part of the defence forces of Canada and essentially suggested that the services stop asking the question of whether women should or should not be in the Canadian Armed Forces.[45]

Army policy remained relatively steady. Army women enlisted in reserve force anti-aircraft units, signal units, and in clerical roles. The female army reserve component started with roughly 1,000 women but went down to 701 women between 1952 and 1953. By 1954, it had surpassed its initial strength with 1,307 women.[46] Policy shifted slightly in 1954, when the army decided to employ a few women as regular force commissioned officers. These women would work as "Corps Advisors." Another small shift occurred a year later when the posting of men and their families to remote places such as Whitehorse generated jobs for non-commissioned women. The army hired female nursing assistants but stopped recruiting them in August 1963 when the demand dropped.[47]

Women had a relatively larger and more diversified presence in the navy than they did in the army. The naval reserve enlisted 369 women in 1951–52. Women were eligible for employment in various clerical and technical jobs such as radio technicians. The total dropped to 299 women in 1953–54 but grew to 349 naval servicewomen in 1954–55.[48] Women entered into the navy's regular force in 1955. Between 1955 and 1961, the numbers rose from 55 to 140. Senior naval officers debated whether to keep the Wrens in 1961. The naval board decided that there was a place for women of all ranks in communications, supply, medical and operations, but restricted women to the east coast. David Zimmerman notes that the naval personnel called west coast personnel the "Yacht Club" as it was perceived to be a more desirable place to serve. Senior naval officers refused to allow servicewomen's postings to negatively affect men's careers and that meant men were more entitled to the attractive west coast postings than women.[49] Then, in 1962, the navy opened more spots for women as a solution to labour shortages in the communications trades and allowed a few to serve on the west coast. However, the navy created these jobs only after it investigated and then dismissed the question of whether women's involvement would harm naval men's employment rotations.[50]

The situation shifted again in 1964 when the navy re-examined personnel policies. The 1964 review team advised that naval servicewomen were to be used only for postings where the navy had difficulties finding men or civilians. In addition, the review team stated that women were to fill positions only until enough men could be found.[51] Dundas concludes that, though the 1964 review team concluded that women should be retained, the team effectively "reduce[d] RCN servicewomen to near auxiliary status, making them secondary to the men, rather than equal members of their own service."[52] Naval women, like their army and air force counterparts, had a restricted number of career paths and were assumed to be less capable at their work regardless of performance. These overall conditions of service ensured that they were often restricted to postings that few men wanted.

Additional parameters further narrowed the pool of career women. Racial discrimination excluded some women. The RCAF's director of personnel management, Group Captain J.G. Archambault, "ordered in May 1954 that 'coloured female applicants are not be considered for enrolment at this time.'" [53] Air force historian and Canadian Forces member Mathias Joost argues that Archambault's directive lacked support because a junior officer withdrew Archambault's order "less than two weeks later." The policy reverted to March 1942 standards, which dictated that recruiting centres direct the applications from Black Canadians to Air Force Headquarters.[54] The testimony of Indigenous veterans such as Theresa Anderson (née Loyie) reveals that Indigenous women served in the Cold War armed forces but there has been little work analyzing their experience. These policies also reflect civilian labour trends. The labour market was segregated by gender and race. Women, especially women of colour, tended to occupy the lower-paying, lower-status, and part-time jobs. Typically, women worked in the retail, clerical, and service sectors, and some women worked in factories. Teaching, nursing, and social work were among the few professions open to women. For women who met the educational, sexual, racial, and other criteria, the armed forces offered another career prospect.[55]

Defence officials discriminated against women based on sexual orientation as well. Government and military officials labelled homosexual military personnel as security risks and homosexuality was grounds for discharge. Historian Cameron Duder interviewed an RCAF veteran named Cheryl who vividly recalled the time when a "'female officer ... called us all together and vowed to us that if we wanted to be kicked out of the RCAF, then all we had to do was tell them that we were homosexuals.'"[56] Military personnel suspected of being homosexual were closely scrutinized and forced to leave. Sue, who served in the militia in the 1960s, recounts that a colonel threatened her with a court-martial after the military discovered that she was a lesbian. This discovery ended her plans to make the military her "ongoing career."[57]

The forces expected servicewomen to be celibate, single, and devoted to the military despite the conditions of service which ensured that their careers were secondary to men's. Until October 1952, the air force released women because they married, including their numbers in the statistics of those forced to retire "to Promote Economy of Efficiency" and "considered unsuitable for reasons other than misconduct, inefficiency, or medical unfitness." The RCAF classified marriage as separate category of release after 1952.[58] Naval reservists who married in the early 1950s were "automatically released."[59] From 1951 to 1953, marriage led to a discharge for enlisted airwomen. The rule did not apply to women officers. The policy for enlisted women shifted in the mid-1950s, allowing for enlisted servicemen and servicewomen to marry each other. The shift in policies around marriage reflected civilian trends. Married women's labour force participation rose after the Second World War. Historian Joan Sangster argues that the 1950s saw the emergence of the "'two phase' life cycle of wage work." Women ended the first phase of work when they married or had their first child. The second phase began when women re-entered the labour force after their children were old enough to enter school or had grown up.[60] Gradually, the military and society at large reflected acceptance of the idea of married women's paid work.

The shift in marriage policy was also part of broader changes in personnel policy. As Isabel Campbell demonstrates in *Unlikely Diplomats*, military policies discouraged marriage and especially early marriage for men during the 1950s. They also discouraged large families because large families came with housing, education, and additional pay costs. By the 1960s, the forces were much more family friendly – recognizing that highly trained service people were most likely to be married with children.[61]

Yet the forces were only more family friendly when it came to servicemen's families. Pregnancy remained grounds for discharge even after the marriage policy changed. Theresa Anderson (née Loyie), a Metis woman, recalled that she was permitted to stay in after she married her husband but was forced to leave when she became pregnant. Patricia Power argues in her thesis on women in the RCAF that many airwomen left because they felt they could not have the married and family life they wanted while in uniform. Similarly, this author interviewed several RCAF women for her dissertation who stated they left because they married or became pregnant.[62] Unlike their male counterparts by the 1960s, regular force servicewomen had to choose their career or their family.

REPRESENTATIONS OF SERVICEWOMEN

There were competing messages in Cold War depictions of servicewomen. The promotion of military career women coexisted with the nuclear, male breadwinner, family ideal. Recruitment material was one key source of the narrative that women could pursue a career in the armed services. Advertisements promised women an exciting career. The RCAF and RCN constructed this narrative by using the word "career" in its advertisements that ran in Toronto's *The Globe and Mail*. For example, "Help Wanted Female" classifieds for 28 March 1958 carried an RCAF ad that asked, "Do you want a career which offers interesting work, good salary, 30 days holidays a year, opportunity to travel?"[63] In September 1955, the paper ran an ad that triumphantly announced that "[i]nteresting and rewarding careers are now open to capable, energetic young women, who can qualify, in the *Regular* Force of the Royal Canadian Navy."[64] A 24 November 1961 RCN ad informed female readers that there was "A Career Planned For You!" Variations of the announcement appeared in February, March, and April of 1962, and in February 1963.[65] The navy published a pamphlet entitled *Career Opportunities in the Wrens* that outlined the qualifications, responsibilities, and training for a variety of trades.[66] The promise of a career was one tactic used to encourage women to enlist into the Cold War RCAF and RCN.

Recruitment literature depicted the armed services as a stable employer that created space for women to grow professionally. *Career Opportunities in the Wrens* devoted two pages to explaining the "path of advancement and promotion" for non-commissioned members. The pamphlet covered pay, benefits, permanent commissions, and pensions in a two-page section on officers.[67] Similarly, the 1956, 1957, and 1961 editions of *To-day's Airwoman ... in the RCAF* had sections called "Promotion and Advancement" and "A Woman's Career." The RCAF recruitment booklet implied that women could create an advantageous home for themselves in the air force. It informed potential recruits that servicewomen could renew their contracts after they completed their initial one of three to five years. In addition, the booklet stated that the RCAF offered women financial security and independence. It noted that servicewomen paid into a pension plan and that "[a]irwomen who decide to make the Service a lifetime career can look forward to retiring in twenty or thirty years with a guaranteed income for life."[68] Despite unequal conditions of employment, the RCAF presented itself as a liberal employer. The RCAF booklet claimed that servicewomen "enjoy[ed] a status not found in every industry for they have equal pay with men, share equal opportunities, and are given the same opportunities for advancement."[69] Servicewomen were entitled to the same rates of pay as their single male counterparts. The decision was part of larger trends. The Ontario government approved equal pay legislation in 1951. The federal government and most of the provinces followed suit later in the 1950s; Quebec and Newfoundland were the exceptions.[70] The RCN and RCAF repeatedly publicized the military career woman.

However, recruitment material glossed over inequalities. Servicewomen's restriction from combat-related trades negatively influenced their chances at promotion and higher pay. Married men qualified for extra pay and allowances, but marriage was a leading cause of women's discharge. Married women were also largely barred from enlisting. Social attitudes and policy prevented servicewomen from qualifying for higher pay rates.[71]

By the early 1960s, periodicals reinforced the narrative of career servicewomen by profiling women at various points in their service. Some covered women at the start of their careers. In her July 1961 article titled "RCAF Careers: Sault Girls into Wild Blue," *Sault Star* staff reporter Mary Jane Tipton reported that two local women, Maxine Courtney and Marjorie McKinley, had recently left their hometown of Sault Ste Marie, Ontario to start basic training in St Jean, Quebec. Like recruitment material, Tipton publicized the career servicewomen by repeatedly using the word "career." She expanded on this message by quoting Courtney who stated that military service "'is a different career for a girl to enter ... I've wanted to be in the Air Force.'" Tipton also acknowledged that some women might find a long-term home for themselves in the RCAF when she discussed opportunities for promotion, reported that servicewomen can choose to stay in service after they finished their initial contract of three years, and noted that women were "pensioned off" after twenty years of service.[72]

Other newspapers covered successful women with several years of experience. A brief overview of servicewomen's time in the armed forces typically appeared in reports of promotions and overseas postings. The *Port Arthur News Chronicle* implied that Leading Airwoman Joan Turner had chosen military service as her profession when it announced her decision to renew her air force contract and her upcoming overseas posting.[73] Similarly, Tricia Duncan drew upon Flying Officer Viola Savage's service history in a September 1961 article for the *Leader-Post*, a paper based in Regina, Saskatchewan. In a transparent attempt to recruit young women. Savage advised them to "leave home at the age of 18" and pursue one of the "unlimited opportunities for a young girl who wants to get out on her own" in the RCAF. Savage's story exemplified these opportunities. At the time of publication, Savage had served for roughly nine years and had been stationed in Canada and overseas. Duncan revealed Savage's single status by referring to her as "Miss Savage" a couple of times in the article. Savage enlisted as a non-commissioned member in 1952 and successfully applied for her commission in 1956. Savage worked as a women's career counsellor at St Jean and was on a recruiting tour when the article was published.[74]

Some articles featured servicewomen at the end of their careers. This chapter opened with the newspaper coverage of Corporal Annie Coutt's retirement. The retirements of female officers are scattered through Cold War official press releases and newspapers. Newspapers participated in the construction of the career servicewomen with repeated coverage of women who saw a long-term role for themselves in military service.[75]

There were two distinct types of military career women. Savage, Turner, Courtney, and McKinley epitomized a particularly acceptable version of military career women celebrated in Cold War media. All appeared to be young, single woman who had presumably enlisted after they finished their schooling because they desired new opportunities, such as a chance to travel. National Defence and periodicals partly constructed this image by including photographs of these women, who appear to be youthful and well-groomed. These young women had not served in the Second World War but were motivated by service travel. All women used their maiden names and none referred to a spouse or romantic interest, contributing to the impression that these women were single. Some journalists, such as Tipton, specifically reported that the women enlisted after they finished high school, while other reporters let the photograph create the impression of youth.[76] National Defence approved and sought to publicize this type of military career women. These types of profiles which used information supplied by National Defence appeared in newspapers across Canada. Handwritten comments on the write-up on Turner confirm this impression. Squadron Leader Elizabeth Dalton, a senior female RCAF officer, annotated the Directorate of Public Relations (Armed Forces)'s copy of the write-up on Turner as follows: "PR Branch informed by telephone that we are pleased with this type of publicity, it is appreciated and we encourage them to continue in this style with as much emphasis as possible."[77]

Yet there was also the narrative that servicewomen's singlehood status and their military careers were temporary. Reports of servicewomen's engagements are scattered throughout Cold War publications. Squadron Leader Sylvia Evans told an *Ottawa Citizen* reporter in April 1956 that the majority of airwomen entered when they were eighteen or nineteen and "'take off to get married.'"[78] Although *Today's Airwomen...in the RCAF* acknowledged that some women might decide to make "the Service a life time career," it also approvingly stated that marriage "was one career that seems to rate above all others in the eyes of most Canadian girls, and rightly so."[79] Cold War media recognized the military career woman but implied that only a few women would make military service their permanent career.

Coutts offered a more mature and experienced version of a military career woman. She was a Second World War veteran who had reenlisted when the armed services increased its recruitment of women in the early 1950s. Women Second World War veterans had publicly lobbied to rejoin the military and so their re-entry, postings, and promotions were considered newsworthy. Reports of promotion and overseas postings often gave a brief history of various career paths, which for some women included service in the Second World War. For example, the 28 January 1958 edition of the *Edmonton Journal* included a photograph of newly promoted Squadron Leader Laura Johnson. The accompanying caption revealed that she had "first joined the air force in 1942 and re-joined in 1950 as a food services officer."[80] Singlehood was an integral part of the mature women's portrayal, and no mention of a spouse appears in any of the articles on Coutts' retirement. This silence is telling because civilian and military publications both reported that most women left the service to start their families. Women had to choose between a military career and having children. Military and civilian periodicals revealed that some wartime veterans made this choice and in the process helped construct a second version of military career women.

The construction of the military career woman was shaped by longstanding fears surrounding the recruitment of women into the armed forces. Historians Ruth Roach Pierson and Leisa Meyer show in the Second World War context that there were worries women who made the stereotypically masculine decision to enlist in the armed services would soon lose their femininity in an institution designed to turn boys into men. Pierson and Meyer have demonstrated that women's enlistment signalled their potential gender deviance and, in turn, raised the possibility that they were sexually deviant as well. These worries continued in Cold War North America. Alfred Kinsey published *Sexual Behavior in the Human Male* (1948) and *Sexual Behaviour in the Human Female* (1953), which challenged societal notions about sexuality. As Carolyn Herbst Lewis states, Kinsey revealed that many American women were engaging in "sexual behaviors that were outside the parameters of 'normal' (that is, heterosexual, married, vaginal/male-centred)."[81] His findings worried medical, religious, and secular experts who considered the heterosexual, male breadwinner, nuclear family ideal the key to Cold War stability. Lewis shows that experts believed that a woman's "[r]ejection of the feminine gender role – whether in dress, comportment, or employment and familial status – suggested that a woman had not fully matured and that she was not experiencing the healthy sex life that would awaken and reinforce her femininity."[82] Military and government officials, individual women, and journalists had to deal with the perception that women who decided to enlist in the Cold War armed forces and pursue an conventionally "unfeminine" career were "unhealthy," "abnormal," and "immature" women.

Canadian servicewomen faced the perception that only "deviant" women enlisted in the armed services. Historian Cameron Duder interviewed a Cold War RCAF veteran named Billie who stated that her boyfriend ended their relationship because she chose to enlist in the air force in 1956. Billie's boyfriend told her that "'only whores join the armed services.'"[83] Her boyfriend's accusation reflects a continuation of the wartime narratives that servicewomen were sexually promiscuous and that immoral women enlisted to gain access to men. Billie's boyfriend thought she joined to pursue other men or at the very least, he implied that she was sexually loose.[84] Other servicewomen navigated other stereotypes that the armed services attracted homosexual "deviants." Sue, who served in the Canadian militia (the army reserves), remembers that her father, who was an army sergeant, supported her enlistment but warned her to avoid lesbian women.[85] Cold War representations of servicewomen addressed these worries over servicewomen's gender and sexual respectability.

National Defence public relations and Cold War media reassured readers in several ways that servicewomen were not "deviants." One tactic was publicizing the military career women in ways that reinforced traditional gender norms. Press material stressed that women filled conventional female roles, albeit in an unconventional environment. The RCAF adopted this tactic in a January 1956 press release on Wing Commander Margaret St Clair Clark. It announced that she was "one of the 23 women who are home economic specialists making a career as messing officers in the Air Force." The release revealed that Clark had risen to the post of senior messing officer in her approximately twelve years of service and supervised both men and women. RCAF press officials countered potential anxieties about this feminine supervisory role by a description of Clark as "charming and enthusiastic" and comparing mothers with messing officers. The release states, "Just as mother is the expert on food in the home, so are women the majority of food experts in the Air Force." Female messing officers, RCAF press officials implied, remained feminine because they used women's "natural" abilities. The RCAF tried to attract female messing officers by presenting itself as an employer that offered women a chance to use their female expertise in long-term positions of authority.[86]

Civilian and military periodicals also strengthened gender norms by emphasizing that servicewomen were strictly non-combatants. Gender

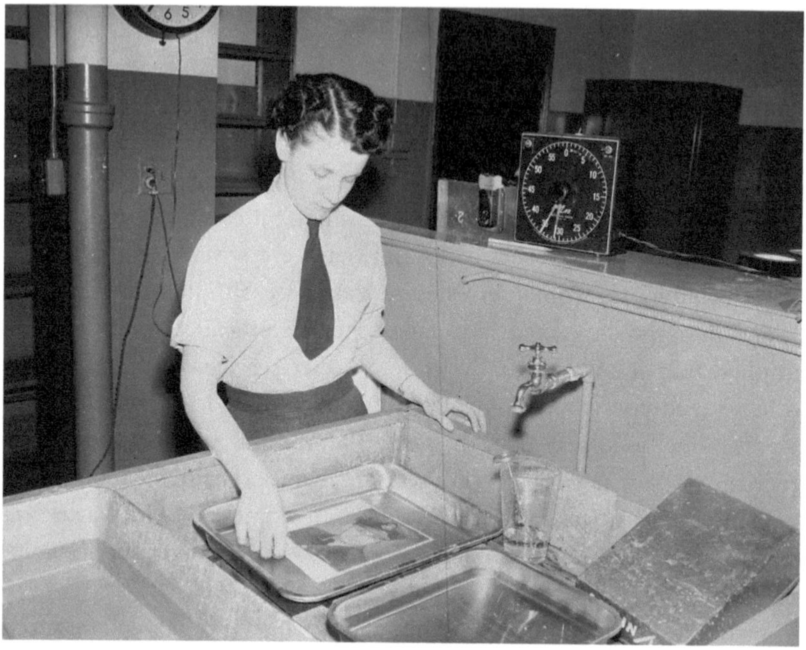

6.1 An airwoman at work.

norms were premised on the binary of male/combatant/protector and female/non-combatant/protected. The *Globe and Mail* reassured its readers in 1956 that "about the only thing CWAC's don't do is train in weapons drill or firearms."[87] Janet Caple noted in her 1955 newspaper article on the entrance of women into the RCN's regular force that naval women would not serve on ships.[88] The youthful airwoman in figure 6.1 is shown to be developing a photograph of a male colleague. A 1958 RCAF ad informed readers that an air force career was open to men and women but stressed that the air force had a clear gender division of labour. It explained, "The flight of an RCAF aircraft is a triumph of teamwork – a study in co-operation between the men who fly the planes and the men and women on the ground who make the flights possible." The explanation was an extended form of the RCAF (WD) motto "We Serve that Men May Fly." Although Canada's first female pilot qualified for her licence in the late 1920s, all RCAF flying roles, including transport, remained limited to men. The ad continued, "It's a challenging life, and one that offers unrivaled opportunities to build a worthwhile career."[89]

Photographs placed in military publications conveyed a similar message. Women personnel were typically shown as well-groomed women placed in front of and not in the aircraft. The one consistent exception is nursing sisters who were sometimes photographed inside an aircraft.[90] *Crowsnest*, the official magazine of the RCN, published a series of photographs of naval women on ships in February 1963. The accompanying caption began, "Occasionally – but only occasionally – women serving in the RCN get a chance to spend a day at sea in a warship."[91] The caption minimized any potential challenge to gender roles by stressing just how rare their presence was and emphasizing masculine control over the presence of women in masculine spaces. The periodical reinforced the armed services as masculine institutions by telling readers that only men had access to the higher status combat and other trades.

Military personnel also addressed potential fears that servicewomen would disrupt gender norms with gender-based stereotypes. In 1961, Mary Jane Tipton reported that Flight Lieutenant Paquette told Maxine Courtney and Marjorie McKinley that women did not serve as pilots "because women are too emotional according to the air force."[92] The RCAF justified the ban on female pilots by invoking a stereotype that labelled women as less rational than men and used women to "police" other women. Military publications bolstered their stereotyped-based arguments by quoting women who agreed that women had emotional issues that prevented them from assuming certain roles. For instance, the women's column for the September 1954 edition of *The Roundel* reproduced a report by Corporal Esther Gardner. Gardner claimed that some female air force personnel also believed that women should not be trained as pilots because the air force would lose money given that "women ... were not emotionally stable enough for flying duties."[93] Military planners limited servicewomen's employment options by emphasizing that servicewomen posed a financial burden; a situation caused by the restricted roles themselves and other conditions of service imposed upon women. Cold War media informed readers that only certain military careers were open to women, presenting these restrictions as reflecting logical masculine decisions made to counter the dangers of feminine weaknesses.

Hints that women disagreed with their limited employment opportunities are embedded in Cold War media. Gardner also revealed that air force women had a range of opinions about whether women should be trained as pilots. Canadian women had been licenced pilots since 1928, and during the Second World War women who served in the American Women's Airforce Service Pilots piloted military aircraft for Ferry Command, helping to transport aircraft to operational areas. Despite these achievements, some servicewomen considered that women had limited piloting capabilities and should not undertake more complex, combat roles. Other women believed that their capabilities in other areas demonstrated sufficient evidence to support training them as pilots. Finally, some considered that piloting might be restricted to those few women who planned to stay in the air force for a long-term career.[94] Cold War media justified servicewomen's limited career opportunities by showing that even servicewomen who sought broader opportunities recognized that these should be available for only a small group of women.

Journalists also reassured readers that women who enlisted in the armed forces were in fact not gender and sexual "deviants" by focusing on servicewomen's appearances. Articles on full-time and part-time servicewomen typically commented on their looks. For instance, Tricia Duncan described Flying Officer Viola Savage "[t]he attractive Women's Career Counsellor" and "a 'Little Mother' to the airwoman recruits."[95] Duncan implied that Savage was both feminine in appearance and manner. Other reporters conveyed that servicewoman remained unaffected by the masculinizing nature of military service. Jack Dobson reported that male officers experienced a shock when they arrived at Camp Shilo, Manitoba and met Captain Lex Swain. He wrote that they were surprised when "[t]he very unmilitary and definitely unmasculine girl at the desk assures them that she is the GSO-2 [General Staff Officer-Grade Two]. It takes time for this to sink in; here in an otherwise, ordinary, common, garden variety male military camp is a female staff officer! CWAC officers are nothing new, but they handle women. There isn't another CWAC for miles."[96] Dobson juxtaposed Swain's feminine (non-masculine, non-military) appearance with her (male) military authority. He tapped into the larger perception that the military environment was not suitable for women. His article suggests the fear of female authority with the implication that female officers are supposed to command women and not men. Dobson painted a picture

6.2 Wholesome off-duty time.

of the limited presence of women in the male-dominated armed forces and hinted at the sexist attitudes they faced. Cold War media insisted that it was possible to be feminine and have a military career.

When taken together, the three photographs that appear in this chapter similarly display the mixed messages surrounding military women since the Second World War. All three images come from a March 1954 RCAF photograph series called "Day in the Life of an Airwoman," which as the title suggests, depicts how an airwoman spends her day.[97] On the one hand, several images, such as figure 6.1, show the airwoman as a competent military member performing her duties. She has a serious expression on her face and appears to be focused on her work. On the other hand, there are reassurances that military women remain feminine and that their military work does not upset hierarchical gender roles. The airwoman is youthful, well-groomed, dressed professionally, and shown intently developing an image of a male, and not female, colleague. Figures 6.2 and 6.3 offer further reassurances. In figure 6.2, the airwoman, now in civilian dress, appears in a mixed-

6.3 Reinforcing gender hierarchies.

gender group surrounding a woman playing piano. The smiling faces, drinks in hands, and mix of uniform and civilian dress presents a narrative of safe wholesome off-duty fun for military personnel. Figure 6.3 overtly illustrates the sexist nature of military service and the RCAF's commitment to upholding gender hierarchies. To a modern audience, the smiling male appears to be crowding the off-duty airwoman who has an uncomfortable expression on her face as they attempt to select a song on the jukebox. It is an overt display of and explicit approval for military male dominance.[98] The three figures and the series as a whole attempt to convince viewers that military women were capable military employees who attracted male sexual/romantic attention in their off-duty hours.

Uniforms frequently appeared in discussions of servicewomen's appearances. Military officials and journalists reminded readers that servicewomen would retain their feminine appearance when they used newly improved uniforms as a selling feature. For example, *The Standard*, a Montreal-based magazine, featured the airwomen's new uniform on the cover and a multipage article entitled "RCAF Fashions" on 23 June 1951. Robert McKeewan opened this article with "The initial group to enter the new RCAF's women's divisions will ... be outfitted with wardrobes modish enough to attract the airmen – and other girls into the services. The new uniforms are more streamlined and fitted than last time."[99] Uniform design also addressed potential anxieties over servicewomen's sexuality. McKeewan offered reassurances that airwomen would remain attractive to men and that airmen might encounter attractive servicewomen in this formerly purely masculine environment. During the Second World War, the armed services tried to dispel concerns that military service created masculine, immoral women by claiming that servicewomen remained feminine and modest in their stylish uniforms and emphasizing improved features. Cold War reporting continued this trend.[100]

The focus on appearance fit in with messages in women's magazines such as *Chatelaine*. Historians Valerie Korinek and Emily Spencer write that articles, fictional pieces, and advertisements provided female workers with fashion tips. Women workers were told that their chances of getting hired, fired, and married depended on maintaining their appearance. Femininity and marriageability were linked: societal expectations for women held that they desired to marry and start a family. *Chatelaine* did create space for readers to question gender stereotypes. Nevertheless, while there was increasing acceptance of coverage of women who worked before marriage and working mothers, the gendered division of male breadwinner and female housewife remained very powerful in *Chatelaine*. Spencer concludes that articles like Mac Reynolds' March 1953 "The Air Force Puts Romance First" piece implied that women entered the armed services and the workforce to find a husband. Reynolds noted the various provisions for heterosexual romance, which ranged from teaching women to make their wedding dresses to lingerie allowances. The idea that women joined to get married might also have contributed to the arguments that servicewomen were expensive because a thought was that the armed forces would spend money training women who would leave to get married. The emphasis on heterosexual romance also served to deflect charges of lesbianism.[101]

Individual servicewomen attempted to negotiate how they were portrayed by the media. *Chatelaine* readers criticized "The Air Force Puts Romance First." One servicewoman grumbled, "The tommyrot you wrote may be true in rare cases, but the majority of us did not join up to rope a man, but to wear Her Majesty's uniform with pride, and to find security, adventure, and most important, a career to be proud of."[102] Decades later, retired Petty Officer 1st Class Rosalee Auger van Stelten similarly rejected the implication that servicewomen placed their familial goals ahead of their careers. She fiercely rebutted a characterization in a mid-1950s newspaper article: "The column said, 'One drawback to permanent service is the stipulation that a girl must finish her term before leaving the Wrens even though she marries. Rosalee wonders if she likes that.' Rosalee didn't wonder at all!" Auger van Stelten left in 1965 after fourteen years of service in the reserve and regular forces of the navy. A self-declared feminist, Auger van Stelten's response mirrors the frustration that many 1960s and 1970s feminists expressed when faced with the expectation that women's sole priorities in life were finding a husband and managing a home. She defended her reputation, feminist credentials, and service by stressing that she was career focused.[103]

The military career woman was one image of Cold War military servicewomen. National Defence and Cold War media informed readers that women could pursue a rewarding career in the armed forces. Through techniques such as profiling women who found a home for themselves, civilian and military periodicals helped craft two versions of military career women. The first was a young, single woman who enlisted after she finished her schooling, and the second was the experienced Second World War veteran who re-enlisted when the services once again began recruiting women. Singlehood was also a key part of this version. Yet, National Defence and media promoted the military career women in ways that attempted to reduce the challenge to gender norms posed by women pursuing careers in a traditionally masculine domain. Reassurances that women did not serve in combat and that they remained feminine co-existed with the promotion of a military career for women. While there was the narrative of the young, single military career woman, there was also an assumption that most of these careers would be short. Senior female officers reassured newspaper readers that servicewomen were respectable, heterosexual, feminine women by stressing that servicewomen were the marrying kind. The average servicewoman was thus portrayed as a young woman who filled the time between when she finished school and her marriage with military service. The military career woman was a popular image, but she represented the minority of servicewomen.

NEGOTIATIONS

Individual women chose to enter and leave military service for their own reasons. Women report a variety of motivations for their enlistment. Some were drawn by the promises of free training and financial security. A Second World War veteran re-enlisted in the RCAF because she was bored and dissatisfied with her civilian job.[104] Recruitment material and servicewomen often cite a chance to travel, meet new people, find community, and try something new as reasons why women enrolled in the armed services. Theresa Anderson states in her contribution to an edited collection about Indigenous women in uniform that a "spirit of adventure" and desire to "do something different" motivated her to join the RCAF.[105] Similarly, Petty Officer 2nd Class Iris Stinson recalls that she enrolled in 1952, "Because the Korean War was on, I felt this was an opportunity to have a new experience outside of the work that I had been doing for 5 years, and I thought there would be new people, new life, and there certainly was that."[106] Retired Petty Officer 1st Class Rosalee Auger van Stelten reminiscences in her memoirs that Lieutenant Carter's "sea sagas, war stories, and tales of high romance" inspired her high school self to become a Wren. She worked with Carter when the navy helped deal with the Great Winnipeg Flood of 1950.[107]

A chance to find like-minded women inspired Yvette to enlist in the RCAF. Yvette remembers, "They needed fighter cops [fighter control operators] for the DEW Lines [*sic*] and the Pine Line [*sic*] for defence, and so they were recruiting women and they were really romanticizing the adventure and all of this. And there were some great-looking women in uniform, and I would see these huge billboards and 'Come and join us,' and somehow I knew that I'd find other lesbians there."[108] Cameron Duder, Gary Kinsman, and Patrizia Gentile argue that for lesbian women, the armed services represented an opportunity to build a community. Kinsman and Gentile state that the military service offered some women, especially those in regions with limited job opportunities, an alternative to heterosexual families.[109]

Servicewomen left the armed services for a variety of reasons. Some women had no choice but to leave early. In 1951 alone, the RCAF enrolled 2,409 airwomen and 115 officers but discharged 184 airwomen and 25 officers.[110] Female officers noted that marriage and the vague, catch-all classification of "unsuitability" were the leading causes of discharges among women.[111] Newspapers suggest that servicewomen negotiated an early discharge when military life did not match their expectations. Much to the chagrin of air force officials, Airwoman Margaret Isabel Burton's negotiations captured the attention of Canadian newspapers. The Directorate of Public Relations (Armed services) gathered more than twenty newspaper clippings from multiple Canadian newspapers that were then stapled together under the handwritten title of "Booklet of Adverse Publicity: 'The Burton Story.'"[112] Journalists wrote that Burton had enlisted because she wanted to escape the confines of her life as a typist for the Department of Veteran Affairs. Burton allegedly deserted for roughly nineteen months because she wanted to travel and came back after she had accomplished that mission. Recruitment criteria frequently mentioned travel as a perk of military service and Burton had reportedly travelled throughout North America.[113] Burton was sentenced to a relatively minor punishment: she spent twenty-one days confined to barracks, was fined $40 and then dismissed "for 'unsatisfactory conduct.'"[114]

Although Burton's case was unusual, the armed services found it difficult to hold onto military personnel. In 1951, "599 men left [the army] each month for every 1,087 recruited."[115] Naval servicewomen's decisions to leave contributed to a policy shift. During 1951–54, female naval reservists could be called out for full-time service on what was called Continuous Naval Duty (CND). Roughly 20 per cent of naval servicewomen called out on CND took advantage of the clause that allowed them to "give 30 days' notice and terminate their service."[116] The clause and servicewomen's willingness to use it meant that the RCN could not fully dictate where servicewomen were posted. A desire for increased control over female personnel partly inspired the RNC's decision to offer women a permanent career in its regular forces. Women's willingness to use the clause also likely fuelled the notion that servicewomen were expensive employees as it showed they would leave after receiving expensive training.[117]

Female officers attempted to address the root causes of servicewomen's discharges. In her 1954 assessment, Flying Officer C.J. Foote blamed some discharges on poor morale and poor discipline. She stated that discipline and morale suffered because many stations were ill-equipped for women. Foote explained that many stations had poor accommodation, under-employment, and inadequate recreational and welfare provisions for women. Discontented women protested these conditions by misbehaving or performing poorly and, as a result, were dismissed. Foote suggested that the RCAF would keep more women if it increased both disciplines and the number of trades open to women both at home and overseas. She noted that many women were coming to the end of their first contract and warned that, unless matters improved, the RCAF would lose many servicewomen and with them its investment.[118]

Commander Isabel Macneill, a Second World War veteran brought back to oversee the entrance of women into the regular force of the navy, also cited poor planning as a reason for personnel problems in her "Report on Wren Organization and Administration" (1954). The chief of naval personnel asked Macneill to review the employment of women over the last three years and "make recommendations" on the full-time engagement of women in the regular forces of the RCN. Her 1954 report concentrated on the first part of the task.[119] Tellingly,

Macneill accepted unequal status and conditions of service for women and sought merely to improve regulations within a system that reinforced assumptions about masculine privilege. Discharges occurred, Macneill explained, because the navy simply applied policies drafted for men without fully thinking through the consequences for women. She reported that from 1951 to 1954, the navy discharged 158 women. Marriage accounted for eighty discharges and thirty-two women on CND used the "30-day notice clause." The remainder (forty-six) were discharged because the navy deemed them "unsuitable." Questioning the significance of the marriage statistics, she reasoned that "[a]lthough it is generally accepted that marriage is the main reason for discharge, these figures show that only 50% are discharged for this reason." She continued, "When over 25% of the total group is discharged as 'unsuitable', there is a definite indication of a selection problem." In her view, attrition rates would be lowered "with a more careful selection" of women.[120] Thus the female recruits themselves were blamed for part of the retention issue.

Macneill promoted the principle that not all regulations and policies for servicemen were suitable for servicewomen. She remarked that the push to recruit those between nineteen and twenty-five years of age ignored the reality that this group was the most likely to get married. Rather than objecting to the practice of dismissing women at marriage, she observed that marriage advanced men's naval careers and ended women's. Her solutions focused upon encouraging the recruitment and retention of single career women. First, she speculated that the navy could lower attrition rates if it offered women "a regular force contract." Second, she advised that the RCN should focus on the recruitment of single women "25 years and over" while still including some younger women. Macneill implied the recruitment of older unmarried women would stabilize the service, and avoid losing women to marriage. The suggestion carved out room for career-oriented professional female administrators like herself.[121]

Macneill's recommendations demonstrate her careful balancing of cabinet's 1951 guidelines for the employment of servicewomen with her assigned task. Women had to be accommodated under the quotas and were to be employed in the few trades deemed suitable for them. She recognized that the prohibition on women serving at sea hurt their careers. Job classifications, or in naval terminology "trades specifications," determined how naval personnel were trained, where they were employed, and the amount they were paid. A specified amount of time at sea was built into the advancement criteria for many trades. Macneill explained that the sea requirement adversely affected women's job choices and advancement opportunities. In fact, the navy did not and in the future would not use resources training women "for duties which they will not be required to perform." Instead of demanding access to sea duty, Macneill argued that the navy should draft and have the proper authorities approve female-specific trade specifications that aligned with women's support roles on land.[122] Although Macneill refused to discuss the advantages and disadvantages "of a peacetime regular force of wrens" in her 1954 report, she repeatedly indicated that she envisioned military career women and concentrated upon arguments that a peacetime nucleus would make future mobilization more efficient.[123]

The March 1955 proposal to establish the Wren component of the RCN reflected Macneill's advice. It included her recommendations for trade specifications and different terms of employment based upon age at recruitment, reflecting consideration of Macneill's arguments about the tendency of younger women to leave the navy for marriage. The length of the first contract was set at two years for women between the ages of nineteen and twenty-two but five years for women between the ages of twenty-three and thirty.[124] On average, Canadian women were twenty-three years old when they entered into their first marriage in the 1950s.[125] Finally, the proposal left room for career military women. For example, the proposal stated that "[o]ne officer born [in] 1917 be enrolled in 1955; this officer would be released in 1967, age 50, served twelve years towards pension." This reference to pension and retirement age indicates that defence officials presumed that at least a few women would have a lengthy naval career.[126]

CONCLUSION

Individual women, journalists and military planners all helped construct the figure of the unmarried Canadian military career women which emerged during the Cold War. Women veterans lobbied the federal government on an individual and group basis for women's return to the Canadian armed services. Civilian and military media brought their readers news of women's efforts to secure military employment. Military planners added another element when they considered how to best use women's labour in their mobilization plans. While some planners and veterans thought women should be employed on a full-time basis, others envisioned a more limited employment. Labour shortages brought on by the Korean War and NATO obligations and publicity about women's contributions to the Second World War effort pushed a reluctant and predominately masculine federal government to authorize an expanded military role for women. Only the RCAF received the government's permission to recruit women into its regular and reserve forces in 1951. The other two services only obtained approval to enlist women into their reserves. By 1955, all three services employed women in regular and reserve roles.

There was limited space for servicewomen and even fewer spots for long term career-oriented servicewomen. The federal cabinet restricted servicewomen's employment. Servicewomen were not allowed to serve in the prestigious combat-related trades and were largely relegated to serve in trades that few men wanted and that were deemed suitable for women. Their very employment hinged on the premise that they did not negatively harm servicemen's careers and did not take jobs away from civilian women who were generally paid much less.

Recruitment criteria and policies that discriminated on the basis on race, gender, and sexual orientation created additional barriers. A woman had to be single and meet strict age criteria. The minimum female educational standards at recruitment were often higher than for males during this period. Although it was quickly cancelled, the RCAF directive that prohibited the recruitment of women of colour hints at underlying, unwritten systematic discrimination. Memoirs and newspaper articles show that some women of colour served in the Cold War Canadian armed forces, but more research is needed. Similarly, more research is needed on Indigenous women and Francophone women in the forces. Marriage, pregnancy, and homosexuality ended women's military careers. Even after the rules around marriage relaxed, many servicewomen were pressured to choose between their families and their service. Military and civilian media contributed to this pressure by painting the average servicewoman as a temporary employee who served until her desire for a family pulled her away from service. The promotion of the career servicewomen co-existed with reassurances that Cold War servicewomen remained feminine.

Although the military career woman was not depicted as the average servicewoman, at least two different versions repeatedly appeared in civilian and military publications. The military career woman was depicted as a single, feminine woman who worked in areas accepted as women's work; she was either a Second World War veteran who re-enlisted or a young woman who entered after she finished high school. Newspapers all across Canada publicized that some women saw a permanent place for themselves in military service. The RCAF and RCN used the promise of a career as a recruitment tactic. Newspapers carried recruitment advertisements that spoke glowingly of the career opportunities for women in the RCAF and RCN. Military recruitment pamphlets expanded on this narrative, highlighting promotion, travel, and pensions as some of the advantages of a military career. Periodicals further constructed the image of the military career women by publicizing the accomplishments of servicewomen at various stages of their career. Women's service histories were woven into reports of promotions and overseas postings. While popular stereotypes focus on stay-at-home mothers, Cold War publications reveal an awareness that some woman created a home for themselves in the Canadian armed services.

NOTES

1 "RCAF Will Retire First Woman," *Ottawa Journal*, 11 November 1961, Directorate of History and Heritage, National Defence Headquarters, Ottawa, Canada (hereafter DHH), 79/208, folder 2; and Directorate of Public Relations (National Defence), "RCAF Retires First Airwoman," Release no 9130, DHH, 79/208, folder 3. The Directorate of Public Relations (Armed Forces) collected multiple newspaper clippings on Corporal Coutts that now reside at DHH. See 79/208.

2 Directorate of Public Relations (National Defence), "RCAF Retires First Airwoman," Release no 9130; "RCAF Will Retire First Woman," *Ottawa Journal*, 11 November 1961; "First Woman Is Retired From RCAF," *Winnipeg Free Press*, 11 November 1961; "Fete Veteran Airwoman At Clinton," *London Free Press*,

11 November 1961; Staff Reporter, "Canada's First Airwoman Released From Service," *Stratford Beacon-Herald*, 25 October 1961; "Canadian Airwoman First to Reach Compulsory Age for Retirement," *Saskatoon Star-Phoenix*, 23 November 1961; Sheila Gormely, "First Airwoman to Retire in Canada: Cpl. Annie Coutts Honored For War, Peacetime Career," Women Today, *The London Free-Press*, 27 October 1961; "Fourteen Years in Service," *The Nanaimo Free Press*, 14 November 1961; and "L'Aviation royale du Canada et la retraite d'un member de sa division feminine," *Le Devoir*, 15 November 1961, DHH, 79/208, folder 2.

3 North American Cold War media used the term "career girl" or "career girls." The author chose to use "career woman" to avoid the patronizing and infantilizing connotations of "career girl." For examples of "career girl" in Canadian and American newspapers see, Classifieds, *The Gazette* (Montreal), 12 January 1965; "For the Career Girl with Limited Space and Time," *Herald-Journal*, 20 September 1949; "Advice for the Career Girl," *Milwaukee Sentinel*, 27 July 1952. For a discussion of women who pursued careers as military nurses, see Nancy Power Shiner, "'In the Best Interest of the Service': RCAF Flight Nurses as the 'New Woman,' 1945–1959" (master's thesis, Dalhousie University, 1998).

4 See the sources cited in endnote 2.

5 Doctors and nurses were both commissioned officers. Nursing schools introduced practical nursing programs in 1938 to address nursing shortages which continued after the Second World War. Practical nurses had shorter programs and less status than registered nurses. Military nurses were registered nurses and as commissioned officers had higher status than medical assistants who were part of the other ranks. The other ranks were the "working class" of the armed forces, even if they were skilled labourers. The officer class reflects a middle or upper class (the white-collar group). For history of nursing and requirements, see *Copy for Nursing Sister Booklet*, n.d., 1–5, DHH, Directorate of Women Personnel Fonds [hereafter DWP], 90/447, file 104; Shiner, "'In the Best Interest of the Service:' RCAF Flight Nurses as the 'New Woman,' 1945–1959"; Cynthia Toman, *An Officer and a Lady: Canadian Military Nursing and the Second World War* (Vancouver: UBC Press, 2007); Nursing History Research Unit, "History of the University of Ottawa School of Nursing," University of Ottawa Nursing History Research Unit, https://www.rpnao.org/about/history http://health.uottawa.ca/nursing-history-research/about/history; and College of Registered Nurses of British Columbia, "Education and Examinations," online source, https://crnbc.ca/crnbc/Documents/Centennial/education-examinations.html (accessed 3 March 2018). For a description of medical assistants, see *Today's Airwoman ... in the RCAF* (Ottawa: Edmond Cloutier, Queen's Printer, 1961), 5.

6 Staff Reporter, "Canada's First Airwoman Released From Service."

7 See sources cited in note 2.

8 Lieutenant Colonel (retired) L.J. Davis, "Employment of Women in Canada's Armed Forces Past and Present," 1966, DHH, DWP, 90/447, file 90; J.M. Hitsman, "'Manpower' Problems of the Women's Services During the Second World War," *Army Headquarters Report*, no. 68, 17 June 1954, DHH, 1–22, http://www.cmp-cpm.forces.gc.ca/dhh-dhp/his/rep-rap/ahqrd-drqga-eng.asp?txtType=3&RfId=257 (accessed 1 October 2014); "She Feeds The Air Force," Release no 8611, January 1956, 1–3, in Biographical File for Margaret St Clair Clark, DHH; "Information re RCAF (WD) in World War II" [n.d.], DHH, DWP Fonds, 90/447, file 104; Ruth Roach Pierson, *"They're Still Women After All": The Second World War and Canadian Womanhood* (Toronto: McClelland & Stewart, 1986), 95–220; and Jeffrey A. Keshen, *Saints, Sinners, and Soldiers: Canada's Second World War* (Vancouver: UBC Press, 2004), 172–93.

9 For a sample of this literature in the American and Canadian context, see Daniel Horowitz, "Rethinking Betty Friedan and *The Feminine Mystique*: Labor Union Radicalism and Feminism in Cold War America," *American Quarterly* 48, no. 1 (March 1996): 1–42; J. Paul Grayson, "The 'Feminine Mystique' and Problems of a Cohort of Female Canadian University Students in the Early 1960s," *The Sixties: A Journal of History, Politics and Culture* 8, no. 1 (2015): 50–74; Joanne Meyerowitz, ed., *Not June Cleaver: Women and Gender in Postwar America, 1945–1960* (Philadelphia: Temple University Press, 1994); Joy Parr, ed., *A Diversity of Women: Ontario, 1945–1980* (Toronto: University of Toronto Press, 1995); Magda Fahrni, *Household Politics: Montreal Families and Postwar Reconstruction* (Toronto: University of Toronto Press, 2005); Judith Fingard and Janet Guildford, eds, *Mothers of the Municipality: Women, Work, and Social Policy in Post-1945 Halifax* (Toronto: University of Toronto Press, 2005); Magda Fahrni and Robert Rutherdale, eds, *Creating Postwar Canada: Community, Diversity, and Dissent, 1945–75* (Vancouver: UBC Press, 2008).

10 There are a few exceptions. The experiences of lesbian servicewomen are discussed in Gary Kinsman and Patrizia Gentile, *The Canadian War on Queers: National Security as Sexual Regulation* (Vancouver: UBC Press, 2010) and Cameron Duder, *Awfully Devoted Women: Lesbian Lives in Canada, 1900–65* (Vancouver: UBC Press, 2010), 52–3, 210, 220–1. For a discussion of air force women, see Patricia A. Power, "'With Their Feet on the Ground': Women's Lives and Work in the Royal Canadian Air Force, 1951–1966" (master's thesis, University of Ottawa, 1998). For a helpful overview see Barbara Dundas, *A History of Women in the Canadian Military* (Montreal: Art Global, 2000). It has little discussion of the concept of the military career women.

11 Lucy Noakes makes a similar point. See Lucy Noakes, *Women in the British Army: War and the Gentle Sex, 1907–1948* (New York: Routledge, 2006), 16; and

Cynthia Enloe, *Globalization and Militarism*, 2nd ed. (New York: Rowman and Littlefield, 2016), chapter 5, Kindle.

12 Pierson, *"They're Still Women After All,"* 95–168; and Keshen, *Saints, Sinners, and Soldiers*, 172–93.

13 Craig Leslie Mantle, ed., *The Unwilling and the Reluctant: Theoretical Perspectives on Disobedience in the Military* (Kingston: Canadian Defence Academy Press, 2006), 1–10; Craig Leslie Mantle, ed., *The Apathetic and the Defiant: Case Studies of Canadian Mutiny and Disobedience, 1812 to 1919* (Kingston: Canadian Defence Academy Press, 2007); and Harold G. Coombs, ed., *The Insubordinate and the Noncompliant: Case Studies of Canadian Mutiny and Disobedience, 1920 to Present* (Kingston: Canadian Defence Academy Press, 2007).

14 Lotta Dempsey, "Person to Person," *Globe and Mail*, 1 July 1950; and Canadian Press, "Girls Want to Go: Ex-Servicewomen, Nurses Seek to Enlist in Canada's Korea Brigade," *Globe and Mail*, 10 August 1950; Valerie Korinek, *Roughing It in the Suburbs: Reading* Chatelaine *Magazine in the Fifties and Sixties* (Toronto: University of Toronto Press, 2000), 44–7, 265–6; Tarah Brookfield, *Cold War Comforts: Canadian Women, Child Safety, and Global Insecurity* (Waterloo: Wilfrid Laurier University Press, 2012), 82–6; W.H. Kesterton, *A History of Journalism in Canada* (Ottawa: Carleton University Press, 1984), 86; Carolyn Davis Fisher, *Lotta Dempsey: The Lady Was a Star* (Toronto: Belsten, 1995), 13–37; Andrew Burtch, *Give Me Shelter: The Failure of Canada's Cold War Civil Defence* (Vancouver: UBC Press, 2012), 37–40; and J.L. Granatstein, *Canada's Army: Waging War and Keeping the Peace*, 2nd ed. (Toronto: University of Toronto Press, 2011), 316–42.

15 Carl Mills, "Canadian Airmen and Airwomen in Korea," Royal Canadian Air Force, 5 June 2017, http://www.rcaf-arc.forces.gc.ca/en/history-heritage/korean-war/airmen-airwomen-in-korea.page#nurses; Veterans Affairs Canada, *Canada's Nursing Sisters* (Ottawa: Veteran Affairs Canada, 2005) (accessed 20 June 2018).

16 "The Royal Canadian Air Force Association," *The Roundel* 2, no. 10 (September 1950): 16. For coverage of the resolution passed by the Dominion Council of Naval Officers' Associations of Canada, see "W.R.C.N.S. Reserve," *The Wren Newsletter* 1, no. 4 (1950): 18.

17 Isabel Campbell, *Unlikely Diplomats: The Canadian Brigade in Germany* (Vancouver: UBC Press, 2013), 120–1.

18 The term "manpower" is used here because it frequently appeared in Cold War planning documents and reveals the gendering of the armed services. Manpower provides a sense of the sexism that existed in the armed services and the attitudes that servicewomen faced in this period. The term "female" also reflects the historic use.

19 Campbell, *Unlikely Diplomats*, 21–62, 120; Granatstein, *Canada's Army*, 316; and Douglas L. Bland, *The Administration of Defence Policy in Canada, 1947 to 1985* (Kingston: R.P. Frye, 1987), 17–18.

20 Enlistment of Women, Cabinet Conclusions, 21 March 1951, LAC, RG2, Privy Council Office, Series A-5-a, vol. 2647, Microfilm reel T-2367, Item Number 10719, http://www.bac-lac.gc.ca/eng/discover/politics-government/cabinet conclusions/Pages/item.aspx?IdNumber=10719 (accessed 13 June 2015); Davis, "Employment of Women in Canada's Armed Forces, Past and Present," 4; Granatstein, *Canada's Army*, 321; Dundas, *A History of Women in the Canadian Military*, 97; Brereton Greenhous and Hugh A. Halliday, *Canada's Air Forces, 1914–1999* (Montreal: Art Global, 1999), 12; and Andrew Richter, *Avoiding Armageddon: Canadian Military Strategy and Nuclear Weapons, 1950–63* (Vancouver: ubc Press, 2002), 166n25. To give a sense of the numbers, the RCAF had 12,200 members in 1947. By 1953, there were 46,100 officers and other ranks. Of those, approximately 3,100 were women. The numbers were taken from the sources cited in this note. For a more detailed discussion of women's re-entrance into the Canadian armed services, see Sarah Hogenbirk, "Women Inside the Canadian Military, 1938–1966" (PhD diss., Carleton University, 2017), 256–304.

21 "Report on Wren Officer Employment," attached to memorandum from Acting/Lieutenant (W) M.W. Fahrig RCN (R) to Staff Officer (Wrens), 29 Nov 1954 to SO (Wrens), Library and Archives Canada (hereafter LAC), RG 112-616-8-E, vol. 34266, file HQ 4360-909/100, pt. 1; Enlistment of women in the Reserve Forces, Cabinet Conclusions, 11 October 1950, LAC, RGrg2, Privy Council Office, Series A-5-a, vol. 2646, Microfilm reel T-2367, Item Number 10242, http://www.bac-lac.gc.ca/eng/discover/politics-government/cabinet-conclusions/Pages/item.aspx?IdNumber=10242 (accessed 13 June 2015).

22 Davis, "Employment of Women in Canada's Armed Forces, Past and Present," 4; Dundas, *A History of Women in the Canadian Military*, 94–8.

23 Dundas, *A History of Women in the Canadian Military*, 91–104.

24 National Defence, Enlistment of Women, Cabinet Conclusions, 21 March 1951, http://www.bac-lac.gc.ca/eng/discover/politics-government/cabinet-conclusions/Pages/item.aspx?IdNumber=10719 (accessed 13 June 2015); Dundas, *A History of Women in the Canadian Military*, 96; Davis, "Employment of Women in Canada's Armed Forces, Past and Present," 4–11; Copy of Lieutenant-General G.S. Simmonds, Chief of the General Staff, to the Minister of National Defence, 29 February 1952, DHH, 112.3S2.003 (D3); "A Limited Number of Women Will Be Accepted for Part-Time Service in the Women's Royal Canadian Navy Reserve," *Globe and Mail*, 14 September 1951; and Marc Milner, *Canada's Navy: The First Century* (Toronto: University of Toronto Press, 1999), 216.

25 The total strength figure dates to March 1965, while the number of women was taken from a September 1965 report. The number of women does not include military nurses. The number of women in each in 1965 was: 40 naval officers and 248 other ranks; 64 officers and 502 other ranks; and 9 army officers and 29 nursing assistants. The numbers for women come from Minister's Manpower Study (Men) [hereafter MMS (M)], "Employment of Women in the Regular Force," para 22–4, Attached to Memorandum to Defence Council From Chief of the Defence Staff, Employment of Women in the Regular Force, dated 2 September 1965, DHH, Raymont Fonds, 73/1223, series 1, box 11, file 19. The total strength figure comes from Phase II (31 March 1965–31 July 1965), attached to file P5800-1 Memorandum from Chief of Defence Staff to Defence Council re Policy with Respect to Redundancy List, DHH, Raymont Fonds, 73/1223, series 1, file 197.

26 Enlistment of Women, Cabinet Conclusions, 21 March 1951. For a discussion of the re-entrance of women into the armed services, see Dundas, *A History of Women in the Canadian Military*, 94–5; and Davis, "Employment of Women in Canada's Armed Forces, Past and Present," 4–5.

27 Extract from Minutes of 53rd Meeting of Defence Council, 29 March 1951, attached to Minute from PMC Meeting 25/323, Item Enlistment of Women, 12 April 1951, DHH, 80/193, box 11, file 236. For a discussion of the conditions which shaped re-entrance, see Dundas, *A History of Women in the Canadian Military*, 94–5; Davis, "Employment of Women in Canada's Armed Forces, Past and Present," 4–5.

28 Extract from Minutes of 53rd Meeting of Defence Council, 29 March 1951.

29 Enloe, *Globalization and Militarism*, chapter 5.

30 Extract from Minutes of 53rd Meeting of Defence Council, 29 March 1951.

31 Copy of Memorandum from Colonel W.S. Murdoch, Director of Staff Duties to Deputy Chief of the General Staff, 31 January 1952, 1–4, DHH, 112.3S2.003 (D3); Hogenbirk, "Women Inside the Canadian Military, 1938–1965," 244–372; and Dundas, *A History of Women in the Canadian Military*, 94–110. The quotation comes from page 4.

32 Dundas, *A History of Women in the Canadian Military*, 97; and Hogenbirk, "Women Inside the Canadian Military, 1938–1965," 244–372.

33 Campbell, *Unlikely Diplomats*, 120–43; "A Limited Number of Women Will Be Accepted for Part-Time Service in the Women's Royal Canadian Navy Reserve"; Jo Carson, "Key Military Jobs Open for Women," *Globe and Mail*, 21 March 1963; and "A Career Planned for You!," *Globe and Mail*, 20 April 1962.

34 "CWAC Appeal Starts at Once"; Jim Senter, "Unit Ready for Mass Recruiting," *Globe and Mail*, 7 December 1955; Canadian Press, "CWAC's Back in Army, Seek

1,500 Recruits," *Globe and Mail*, 23 June 1951; and Campbell, *Unlikely Diplomats*, 127–8.

35 "A Career Planned for You!"; "A Career Opportunity for Young Women, The Royal Canadian Navy Requires Five (5) Wren Officers," *Globe and Mail*, 19 May 1962, Classifieds; "New Opportunities for You in Canada's Navy," *Ottawa Citizen*, 24 April 1962; and *Career Opportunities in the Wrens* (Ottawa: Queen's Printer, n.d.), 3, 40 DHH, 80/82. The quotation comes from "A Career Opportunity for Young Women, The Royal Canadian Navy Requires Five (5) Wren Officers."

36 "Enlist Women Ages 18 to 29 For Air Force," *Globe and Mail*, 31 May 1951; Power, "'With Their Feet on the Ground,'" 28–41.

37 Flying Officer C.J. Foote, "Short History of AW Development in the RCAF since July 1951," 16 March 1954, 1, copy at DHH, DWP, file 104.

38 "Enlist Women Ages 18 to 29 For Air Force"; and Directorate of Public Relations (National Defence) Press Release No. 7882, May 1951, DHH, 71/383. The quotation comes from the press release.

39 Dundas, *A History of Women in the Canadian Military*, 110; Appendix A and Appendix C to "Women in the Royal Canadian Air Force (Regular)," DHH, 90/447, file 104; Power, "'With Their Feet on the Ground,'" 28–41. The quotation comes from Power, 33.

40 "CWAC Appeal Starts at Once"; "A Limited Number of Women Will Be Accepted for Part-Time Service in the Women's Royal Canadian Navy Reserve"; and "Enlist Women Ages 18 to 29 For Air Force," *Globe and Mail*, 31 May 1951.

41 Quoted in Mary Ziegler, *We Serve That Men May Fly* (Hamilton, ON: R.C.A.F. (W.D.) Association, 1973), 171.

42 "Historical Notes – Women in the RCAF – 1941–1960," DHH, 90/447, file 104; National Defence, Enlistment of Women, Cabinet Conclusions, 21 March 1951; Dundas, *A History of Women in the Canadian Military*, 96; Davis, "Employment of Women in Canada's Armed Forces, Past and Present," 4–11; Copy of Lieutenant-General G.S. Simmonds, Chief of the General Staff, to the Minister of National Defence, 29 February 1952, DHH, 112.3S2.003 (D3); and "First R.C.A.F. Women Overseas," *The Roundel* 4, no. 8 (September 1952): 39.

43 Dundas, *A History of Women in the Canadian Military*, 102–4; MMS (M) "Employment of Women in the Regular Force," para 15–20. The quotation comes from MMS (M) para 16.

44 MMS (M) "Employment of Women in the Regular Force," para 15–20; Dundas, *A History of Women in the Canadian Military*, 102–4; Brereton Greenhous and Hugh A. Halliday, *Canada's Air Forces, 1914–1999* (Montreal: Art Global, 1999), 133; and Research Branch of the Library of Parliament, *History of the RCAF*

(Women's Division) 1941–1971 (Ottawa: 26 May 1971), 11–15, copy at DHH, DWP, 90/447, file 104. The quotations come from MMS (M), paragraph 16 and paragraph 44.

45 MMS (M) "Employment of Women in the Regular Force," para 17, 47; *History of the RCAF (Women's Division) 1941–1971*, 11–15; and Power, "'With Their Feet on the Ground,'" 69–84. The quoted phrase comes from MMS (M) para 19.

46 National Defence, Enlistment of Women, Cabinet Conclusions, 21 March 1951; Dundas, *A History of Women in the Canadian Military*, 96; Davis, "Employment of Women in Canada's Armed Forces, Past and Present," 4–11; Copy of Lieutenant-General G.S. Simmonds, Chief of the General Staff, to the Minister of National Defence, 29 February 1952, DHH, 112.3S2.003 (D3); "A Limited Number of Women Will Be Accepted for Part-Time Service in the Women's Royal Canadian Navy Reserve," *Globe and Mail*, 14 September 1951; and Marc Milner, *Canada's Navy: The First Century*, 216.

47 MMS (M), "Employment of Women in the Regular Force," para 11–14; Davis, "Employment of Women in Canada's Armed Forces, Past and Present," 8–9; and Dundas, *A History of Women in the Canadian Military*, 103.

48 Dundas, *A History of Women in the Canadian Military*, 96; Davis, "Employment of Women in Canada's Armed Forces, Past and Present," 4–11; Copy of Lieutenant-General G.S. Simmonds, Chief of the General Staff, to the Minister of National Defence, 29 February 1952, DHH, 112.3S2.003 (D3); "A Limited Number of Women Will Be Accepted for Part-Time Service in the Women's Royal Canadian Navy Reserve," *Globe and Mail*, 14 September 1951; and Marc Milner, *Canada's Navy: The First Century*, 216.

49 MMS (M), "Employment of Women in the Regular Force," para 6–10; David Zimmerman, *Maritime Command Pacific: The Royal Canadian Navy's West Coast Fleet in the Early Cold War* (Vancouver: UBC Press, 2015), 3; and Hogenbirk, "Women Inside the Canadian Military, 1938–1966," 320–65.

50 MMS (M), "Employment of Women in the Regular Force," para 6–9.

51 Ibid., para 9–10, 14, 22–4; and *History of the RCAF (Women's Division) 1941–1971*, 11–15.

52 Dundas, *A History of Women in the Canadian Military*, 102–4. The quotation comes from page 103.

53 Mathias Joost, "Racism and Enlistment: The Second World War Policies of the Royal Canadian Air Force," *Canadian Military History* 21, no. 1 (Winter 2012): 29, 34n92.

54 Letter S304-101 (DPM), 7 May 1954, LAC, RG 24, vol. 298, file 304-117, as quoted in Joost, "Racism and Enlistment," 29.

55 Pearl Bordts, "Pearl Bordts – née Klenman," in *Equal to the Challenge: An Anthology of Women's Experiences During World War II*, ed. Lisa Banister (Ottawa:

Department of National Defence, 2001), 279; Kinsman and Gentile, *The Canadian War on Queers*, 15, 62–3; Theresa Loyie, "Fighter Control Operator Theresa Loyie," in *Our Women in Uniform,* ed. Muriel Stanley Venue (Calgary: Bunker To Bunker Publishing, 2004), 39–46; Joan Sangster, *Transforming Labour*, 16–53; Joan Sangster, "Doing Two Jobs: The Wage-Earning Mother, 1945–1970," in Parr, *A Diversity of Women: Ontario, 1945–1980*, 98–127; and Shiner, "'In the Best Interest of the Service': RCAF Flight Nurses as the 'New Woman,' 1945–1959," 37–45, 52–123.

56 As quoted in Duder, *Awfully Devoted Women*, 255.

57 Kinsman and Gentile, *The Canadian War on Queers*, 15.

58 Foote, "Short History of AW Development in the RCAF since July 1951," 6 (a).

59 Rosalee Auger van Stelten, *Wren: Memories of Navy Days from Royal Yacht to Quonset Hut* (Victoria: self-published, 2010), 2.

60 Sangster, *Transforming Labour*, 16–53; and Sangster, "Doing Two Jobs," 98–127. The term comes from page 18 of *Transforming Labour.*

61 Campbell, *Unlikely Diplomats*, 120–43.

62 "Mountain Climbing is 'Tops' for RCAF's Leading Airwoman," *Ottawa Citizen*, 4 April 1956, clipping, DHH, 79/208, folder 2; Power, "'With Their Feet on the Ground': Women's Lives and Work in the Royal Canadian Air Force, 1951–1966," 62–3, 71–6; Sangster, *Transforming Labor*, 191; Theresa Loyie, "Fighter Control Operator Theresa Loyie," in Venue, *Our Women in Uniform*, 39–46; Dawn Aleknvicus, interview with Sarah Hogenbirk, 12 March 2015; Jennifer Black, interview with Sarah Hogenbirk, 12 March 2015; Jean Olynk (Haché), interview with Sarah Hogenbirk, 17 March 2015; Darlene (Dee) Walmsley, interview with Sarah Hogenbirk, 16 March 2015; and Jacquie Williams, interview with Sarah Hogenbirk, 13 March 2015.

63 "Read This Ad," *Globe and Mail*, 28 March 1958, Classifieds.

64 "Now in the Wrens ... A Navy Career for Women," *Globe and Mail*, 20 September 1955, Classifieds.

65 "A Career Planned for You!," *Globe and Mail*, 24 November 1961, Classifieds; "A Career Planned for You!," *Globe and Mail*, 20 April 1962, Classifieds; "A Career Planned for You!," *Globe and Mail*, 24 February 1962, Classifieds; and "A Career Planned for You!," *Globe and Mail*, 16 February 1963, Classifieds.

66 *Career Opportunities in the Wrens.*

67 Ibid., 36–37, 40–41.

68 *Today's Airwoman ... in the RCAF* (Ottawa: Queen's Printer, 1956), 10–15; *Today's Airwoman ... in the RCAF* (Ottawa: Queen's Printer, 1957), 10–15; *Today's Airwoman ... in the RCAF* (Ottawa: Queen's Printer, 1962), 10–15. The quotation appears on page 14 in all three editions.

69 *Today's Airwoman ... in the RCAF*, 1956, 4.

70 Copy of C.M.D. (initialled) to Mr Sharpe, Chairman, PMC, 22 June 1951, DHH, 80/193, box 11, file 236; *History of the RCAF (Women's Division) 1941–1971*, 12–13; *Today's Airwoman ... in the RCAF*, 1957, 4–14; Dundas, *A History of Women in the Canadian Military*, 95–6; Power, "'With Their Feet on the Ground,'" 28–41; Wendy Cuthbertson, *Labour Goes to War: The CIO and the Construction of a New Social Order, 1939–1945* (Vancouver: UBC Press, 2012), 133–44 and Alison Prentice, Paula Bourne, Gail Cuthbert Brandt, Beth Light, Wendy Mitchinson, and Naomi Black, *Canadian Women: A History,* 2nd ed. (Toronto: Nelson, 2004), 353–4, 362–3. In *Labour Goes to War*, Cuthbertson describes four arguments used by union members in the fight for equal pay. They are: "women's need for equal pay," a recruitment tool that would bring women into the war effort, "to ensure that cheaper female labour did not undercut male wages," and that it was a human right. See Cuthbertson, 133–4.

71 Dundas, *A History of Women in the Canadian Military*, 95–6; and Power, "'With Their Feet on the Ground,'" 28–41. For a discussion of how air force women were recruited and why they joined, see Power, 28–41.

72 Mary Jane Tipton, "RCAF Careers: Sault Girls into Wild Blue," *Sault Star*, 8 July 1961, DHH, 79/208, folder 2.

73 "To France," *Port Arthur News Chronicle*, 25 October 1957, DHH, 79/208, folder 2.

74 Tricia Duncan, "Career Counsellor Tells Girls to Leave Home at 18," *Leader-Post* (Regina), 12 September 1961, DHH, 79/208, folder 2.

75 "Organized RCN Wrens, Cmdr. Macneill to Retire," *Globe and Mail*, 23 July 1957; and Directorate of Public Relations (National Defence) Press Release No. H-1919, Senior Woman Air Force Officer Retires in Biographical File for Evans, Sylvia I, DHH. For the articles on Coutts see sources cited in note 2.

76 Tipton, "RCAF Careers: Sault Girls into Wild Blue." For other examples see "P.E.I. Airwoman Serves in Europe – Also Travels," *Charlottetown Guardian*, 26 June 1957, clipping, DHH, 79/208, folder 2; "Now 3,000 Strong, Steady Enlistment of Women in Air Force," *The Province*, undated clipping, DHH, 79/208, folder 2; clipping on Leading Aircraftswoman Gertrude E. Jordan, *St. John's Telegram*, 12 April 1960, clipping, DHH, 79/208, folder 2; "Law Lilly La Riviere With RCAF in Europe," *Hamilton Spectator*, 28 August 1957, clipping, DHH, 79/208, folder 2, and untitled clipping on Jane Morency, *Port Arthur News Chronicle*, undated clipping, DHH, 79/208, folder 2.

77 Handwritten comments on copy of "To France," *Port Arthur News Chronicle*, 25 October 1957, DHH, 79/208, folder 2.

78 "Mountain Climbing is 'Tops' for RCAF's Leading Airwoman," *Ottawa Citizen*, 4 April 1956, clipping, DHH 79/208, folder 2; untitled clipping on Jane Morency; untitled marriage announcement, *Victoria Colonist*, 24 November 1957,

clipping, DHH, 79/208, folder 2; Power, "'With Their Feet on the Ground,'" 62–3, 71–6; Sangster, *Transforming Labor*, 191.

79 *Today's Airwomen ... in the RCAF* (Ottawa: Queen's Printer, 1956), 14–15.

80 "Promotion," *Edmonton Journal*, 28 January 1958, DHH, 79/208, folder 2.

81 Pierson, *"They're Still Women After All,"* 128–214; Leisa D. Meyer, *Creating GI Jane: Sexuality and Power in the Women's Army Corps During World War II* (New York: Columbia University Press, 1996), 6, 26–7, 43, 143, 150–66, 178; and Carolyn Herbst Lewis, *Prescription for Heterosexuality: Sexual Citizenship in the Cold War Era* (Chapel Hill: University of North Carolina Press, 2010), 37–94, Kindle. The quotation comes from Lewis, 59.

82 Lewis, *Prescription for Heterosexuality*, 42.

83 As quoted in Duder, *Awfully Devoted Women*, 258.

84 Ibid.; Pierson, *"They're Still Women After All,"* 168–86; Leisa D. Meyer, *Creating GI Jane: Sexuality and Power in the Women's Army Corps During World War II* (New York: Columbia University Press, 1996), 6, 26–7, 43, 143, 150–66, 178.

85 Kinsman and Gentile, *The Canadian War on Queers*, 126, 15–16, 27–110, 119, 128–30, 191–3; and Duder, *Awfully Devoted Women*, 220–1, 250–9. Sue tells the story on page 128. For more on Sue, see 15–16, 191–4.

86 "She Feeds the Air Force."

87 Canadian Press, "Women Number 2000 In Canadian Militia," *Globe and Mail*, 6 December 1956.

88 Janet Caple, "Off the Ocean Wave: New Career Open to Women," *Vancouver Herald*, 30 March 1955; Library Archives Canada, Isabel Janet Macneill Fonds, MG 30 E 373 1, folder I.J. Macneill, Press Clippings (Photocopies), n.d.

89 "Above All ... it's Teamwork that Counts!" *Globe and Mail*, 5 September 1958; and Shirley Render, *No Place for a Lady: The Story of Canadian Women Pilots, 1928–1992* (Winnipeg: Portage & Main Press, 1992). The quotations come from "Above All ... it's Teamwork that Counts!"

90 *Today's Airwoman ... in the RCAF* (Ottawa: Edmond Cloutier, Queen's Printer, 1956), 10–15; *Today's Airwoman ... in the RCAF* (Ottawa: Edmond Cloutier, Queen's Printer, 1957), 10–15; *Today's Airwoman ... in the RCAF* (Ottawa: Edmond Cloutier, Queen's Printer, 1962), 10–15. For photographs of flight nurses, see "Para-Nurses," undated magazine clipping in DHH, 79/208, folder 2. For an analysis of flight nurses, see Shiner, "'In the Best Interest of the Service': RCAF Flight Nurses as the 'New Woman,' 1945–1959."

91 "Wren Cruise," *Crowsnest* (February 1963), 21.

92 Tipton, "RCAF Careers: Sault Girls into Wild Blue."

93 "Feminine Gen," *The Roundel* 6, no. 8 (September 1954), 15–16. The quotation comes from page 16.

94 Ibid.; Sarah Byrn Rickman, *WASP of the Ferry Command: Women Pilots, Uncommon Deeds* (Denton: University of North Texas Press, 2016).

95 Duncan, "Career Counsellor Tells Girls to Leave Home at 18."

96 Jack Dobson, "Shilo Visitors Surprised to see Feminine GSO-2," *Globe and Mail*, 13 July 1952.

97 For an example of a photograph in the series, see Government of Canada, Department of National Defence, "Day in the Life of an Airwoman," 23 March 1954, LAC, RE-8097-35, Item no. 3584925, PA-067897, http://central.bac-lac.gc.ca/.redirect?app=fonandcol&id=3584925&lang=eng.

98 See the sources for note 81.

99 Robert McKeewan, "RCAF Fashions," *The Standard*, 23 June 1951, clipping at DHH, 79-208, folder 2. For other examples of the focus on uniform, see "The New Duds," n.d., clipping, DHH, 79/208, folder 2; and *Today's Airwoman … in the RCAF*, 4–14.

100 Deborah Cowen, *Military Workfare: The Soldier and Social Citizenship in Canada* (Toronto: University of Toronto Press, 2008), 89–102. For a discussion of wartime anxieties over female masculinity, see Donna B. Knaff, *Beyond Rosie the Riveter: Women of World War II in American Popular Graphic Art* (Lawrence: University Press of Kansas, 2012).

101 Korinek, *Roughing it in the Suburbs*, 177–85, 194–5, 198–207, 222–54, 296–7, 299–300, 308–9, 230–1; and Emily Spencer, *Lipstick and High Heels: War, Gender, and Popular Culture* (Kingston: Canadian Defence Academy Press, 2007), 100–6, 184–90.

102 D.L. Hayden, *Chatelaine*, May 1953, 3, as quoted in Spencer, *Lipstick and High Heels*, 188–9.

103 Petty Officer 1st Class (retired) Rosalee Auger (van Stelten), "The Good, The Bad, and The Royal: The Challenges and Opportunities of Being a Wren," in *Transforming Traditions: Women, Leadership and the Canadian Navy, 1942–2010*, ed. Stéphanie A.H. Bélanger and Karen D. Davis (Kingston: Canadian Defence Academy Press, 2010), 37–42; and Korinek, *Roughing it in the Suburbs*, 324. Auger van Stelten's quotation comes from page 38.

104 Nellie Ross, "Nellie Ross," in *Equal to the Challenge*, 377–92; and Kinsman and Gentile, *The Canadian War on Queers*, 62–5.

105 Theresa Loyie, "Fighter Control Operator Theresa Loyie," in *Our Women in Uniform*, 40; *Today's Airwomen … in the RCAF* (Ottawa: Queen's Printer, 1956).

106 Petty Officer 2nd Class Iris Stinson, interview by Tony German, interview transcribed 14 January 1985, DHH, 90/292, folder 25.

107 Auger van Stelten, *Wren*, 3.

108 Kinsman and Gentile, *The Canadian War on Queers*, 129.

109 Leisa D. Meyer, *Creating GI Jane*, 6, 26–7, 43, 143, 150–66, 178; Kinsman and Gentile, *The Canadian War on Queers*, 126, 15–16, 27–110, 119, 128–30, 191–3; and Duder, *Awfully Devoted Women*, 220–1, 250–9.

110 Foote, "Short History of AW Development in the RCAF since July 1951," 1–3.

111 Ibid., 1, 6 (a); Commander (W) Isabel Macneill, "Report on Wren Organization and Administration," September 1954, 8, Appendix "C" to "RCN Wren Policy and Planning, August 1954–July 1957, A Review," copy at DHH, 75/533.

112 "Booklet of Adverse Publicity: 'The Burton Story,'" DHH, 79/208, folder 2. Emphasis in text.

113 "'Case of the Missing Fly Girl' She Quit the Air Force So Now It's Firing Her," *Vancouver Sun*, 26 November 1953, clipping in "Booklet of Adverse Publicity: 'The Burton Story'"; and Barry Broadfoot, "Airwoman Faces Trial as Deserter: Girl Missing for 19 Months Held by RCAF," *Vancouver Sun*, 24 November 1953, clipping in "Booklet of Adverse Publicity: 'The Burton Story'"; *Today's Airwoman … in the RCAF*, 13–14.

114 RCAF Approves WD Dismissal," *Sarnia Canadian Observer*, 2 December 1953, clipping included in "Booklet of Adverse Publicity: 'The Burton Story'"; and "'Case of the Missing Fly Girl' She Quit the Air Force So Now It's Firing Her."

115 Campbell, *Unlikely Diplomats*, 127. For the reasons why men left, see Campbell's discussion on 126–31.

116 Dundas, *A History of Women in the Canadian Military*, 98; Commander (W) Isabel Macneill, "Report on Wren Organization and Administration," September 1954, 3–8, Appendix "C" to "RCN Wren Policy and Planning, August 1954–July 1957, A Review," copy at DHH, 75/533. The quotation comes from Dundas, 98. The data has been taken from page 8 of Macneill's report. Macneill states on page 8 that 327 women were called out full time, under Continuous Naval Duty. Of those, 169 were "still serving" at the time of writing and 158 women had been discharged. Of those 158, 80 were discharged due to marriage, 46 deemed "unsuitable, and 32 for "'personal reasons'" (i.e., used "30-day notice clause").

117 Paper on WRNCS, submitted to Naval Board, 23 January 1961 attached to Minute Sheet from [illegible] ACNP (Plans), 8 February 1961, 1–2, LAC, R112-616-8-E, vol. 34266, file 4360-909, pt. 1.

118 Foote, "Short History of AW Development in the RCAF since July 1951," 1–10.

119 "RCN Wren Policy and Planning, August 1954–July 1957, A Review," 1.

120 Macneill, "Report on Wren Organization and Administration," 8–9. All quotations come from page 8.

121 Ibid. The term "regular force contract" comes from page 8.

122 Ibid., 4–7. The quoted phrase comes from page 5.

123 Ibid.

124 "Royal Canadian Navy (Wrens)," 1955, 1–6, Appendix "B" to "RCN Wren Policy and Planning, August 1954–July 1957, A Review."

125 Statistics Canada, "Fertility: Fewer Children, Older Moms," *Canadian Megatrends*, last modified 28 September 2016, http://www.statcan.gc.ca/pub/11-630-x/11-630-x2014002-eng.htm (accessed 10 February 2017).

126 "Royal Canadian Navy (Wrens)," 1955, 1–6, Appendix "B" to "RCN Wren Policy and Planning, August 1954–July 1957, A Review." The quotation comes from page 6.

Conclusion

The Early Cold War and the Sounds of Silence

ISABEL CAMPBELL

Together, the chapters in this collection provide insights into how Cold War masculinized thinking affected privileged workers differently from those who laboured in precarious and sometimes marginalized employment for the state. By defining labour broadly, including service people, construction workers, scientists, and psychiatrists, this volume highlights divergent experiences of Cold War work. The volume analyzes transformations over time, with some chapters reaching back decades before 1945 for contextual understanding and reinforcing the emerging international scholarship that challenges rigid temporal boundaries and simplistic bipolar Cold War comparisons.[1] The lives described here began before and ended after the Cold War, though all these workers, their families, and their communities faced specific challenges as a result of the insecurity and anxiety associated with Cold War super-power competition.[2] As such, these chapters link personal perception with local developments and professional transformations, including increasing doubts about flawed thinking in relationship to race, gender roles, sexuality, mental health, and ethical practices. Chapters 2, 3, and 6 also address the loss of local jobs when radar stations in Canada were completed or closed because of global technological advances that transcended the temporal period between 1945 to 1989.

The first part of this volume especially highlights the linkages between colonization and militarization as Cold War labour transformed Indigenous lives, continuing processes that had begun centuries earlier. While these relentless and sometimes insidious processes threatened Indigenous languages, cultures, and family lives, Cold War job opportunities were often welcomed, even as they exacerbated these threats to traditional ways. Better housing, food and, in the case of Elmer Sinclair, status and the opportunity to excel in technical work, were significant and treasured memories. As a measure of the long-term consequences of these projects, when the North Warning System replaced the DEW Line in the late 1980s, the Canadian Department of National Defence began environmental remediation work on the closed sites.[3] This work was completed in 2007. The North Warning System maintenance contracts contain Inuit employment targets, strict environmental practices, remediation measures, and other local benefits.[4] A majority Inuit owned company, Nasittuq, won the contract for the second time in 2022.[5] These post-Cold War developments highlight the temporal continuum of security projects and the influence of technological advances as one system replaces another. A profound sense of global insecurity and fear still drives security projects. Yet, community activism made a difference in how defence projects were and are managed. While defence facilities created ecological and cultural disruptions, they sometimes benefited communities in ways that were not anticipated. One of those benefits is community activism and engagement in defining the meaning of security and broadening Cold War masculinized definitions of it to include consideration of Indigenous rights, culture, tradition, community, and family life.

Despite these common findings, these chapters also demonstrate that no representative Indigenous service person, let alone Cold War labourer, existed. The first three chapters reveal divergent Indigenous experiences, even as Cold War jobs transformed family and community lives over time. All three primary authors draw upon oral testimony, respecting people's own words and their unique stories. While chapter 1 exposes the importance of a masculinized technological path to equal status, chapters 2 and 3 (and chapter 6) reveal how Indigenous women were generally denied such employment and often relegated to the home. Gender, class, and race intersected. Cold War labour changed individuals, family relationships and community life across Canada.

The biographical approach, which also features in the second part of the volume, brings these stories to life. This approach creates a nuanced challenge to the narrative of progressive improvements that dominated the earlier historiography of this period.[6] The differing methodologies of the first part, which draws upon the lived experiences of those authors as well as from oral testimony, and the second part, which relies upon the scholarly apparatus of the written word, especially professional and official publications, may allow students of history to think about which methodologies are best for the analysis of differing subjects. A comparison between the two parts shows how historical methodologies affect the narrative and the interpretation of the subject itself. The oral testimonies of the first part allow those authors to include consideration of families and communities in their studies of Cold War labour; the documents that support the second part do not generally address family and community life. Thus, the focus of the second part is necessarily more focused upon the labour with relatively little about the personal lives of the workers. The type of documentary evidence creates different possibilities for analysis.

While the authors of the first part do not directly utilize the whole life oral methodology (as practiced at the Concordia University Centre for Oral History and Digital Storytelling) their chapters contain elements of the shared authority that is fundamental to that methodology. The primary authors of the first part draw upon their own life experiences and relationships, even as they are sometimes surprised by their subjects. This transformation of the scholars and their willingness to learn from individuals, families, and communities is based in respect for the perspectives of those being studied.[7] As readers, we experience a vicarious sense of intimacy that is not apparent in the second part. This intertwining of narration, subject, intimacy, and vicarious experience is most evident in the Sinclair story. This family story, complete with treasured photographs and tender recollections, allows readers a deeper understanding of how the silences surrounding the traumatic residential school experiences affected Elmer Sinclair and his family over time. Warren Sinclair's tracking of the historiography and his dad's decision to tell historians about his trauma points to the importance of history in life journeys. By narrating his father's story, Warren is reclaiming this history for their family and their community. Elmer's siblings took their untold stories to the grave, depriving their families of the chance to hear firsthand what their parents had endured. Warren Sinclair has sought to tell his father's story in his own words without the sense of objective distance most academic works impose upon their subjects.

Chapters 2 and 3 also provide the space for authors to draw upon their own observations and sensations, though in these cases the authors are not writing directly about their lives and families. The authors utilize a combination of personal insights derived from lived experiences with academic analysis. When Sue Heffernan mentions how the local people "were dreading the day that they would need to put their teenagers on the train south," readers can imagine how important having the radar station transformed into a local regional high school might be for this community – not least because of the insights readers have gained about the abuse suffered by children, like Elmer Sinclair, who were forcibly removed from their families.

We hope readers will have found that the insights of one chapter build upon the analysis of the next throughout this volume.

In the second part, an academic apparatus inserts itself between the reader and the subject, creating a sense of distance. Yet, if the authors the second part are not obviously drawing upon their own experiences, they nonetheless demonstrate a sensitive understanding of the difficulties their subjects confronted. Matthew Wiseman and Frances Reilly are careful to balance condemnation of harmful medical and scientific practices with contextual explanations and a scholarly analysis of the respective professions and their practices. Sarah Hogenbirk examines the construction of the Cold War servicewomen, how those servicewomen were portrayed by officials, but also how the women negotiated a space for themselves within this masculine institution. These authors provide nuanced insights into how Cold War labour transformed people and professions without becoming part of the story themselves.

The Cold War *was* a war, but as the chapters here demonstrate it was not as monolithic as it has often been depicted. None of the authors in the second part claim to provide a representative experience or archetypal figure. While Sarah Hogenbirk's examination of the single service career woman comes the closest to a representative framing, her chapter highlights how some women experienced military service differently, with a few actively rebelling against the tight discipline and rigid rules of military life. She further highlights how race and sexuality created unequal experiences for some women. Her work supports the idea that feminist progress did not necessarily fit into neat temporal waves.[8] The early Cold War is associated with rigid bipolar gender roles, but feminism progressed by fits and starts, even in a masculinized service environment that defined women as unequal and restricted their roles. This conclusion does not refute Cynthia Enloe's theory that servicewomen supported a patriarchal militarized agenda but adds to her later arguments about how small individual actions modify and disrupt that system. The on-going battle for culture change in the Canadian Armed Forces speaks to the importance of activism in ensuring that security policies include input from diverse sources.[9] Diverse voices change how security is defined and practiced.

This volume demonstrates the value of examining experiences without assuming or seeking out representative or archetypal figures. By comparing the experiences of different types of workers, families, and communities, this volume exposes how race, gender, sexuality, and privilege affected people in diverse and sometimes unpredictable ways. If western masculinized thinking predominated in the early Cold War, the people who worked for the security state, their families, and their communities often challenged that thinking and sought to ensure that their concerns would be heard. As historians, we should do no less. Developments, positive and negative, were not necessarily linear. Attractive employment sometimes led to addictions, environmental issues, the loss of culture and traditions, and other disruptions to family life. In other cases, people and professions struggled, adapted, and transformed, hampered by anxieties and doubts. *Cold War Workers* is about the diversity of experience and the nuanced and contradictory transformations experienced by workers, families, and communities over time.

NOTES

1 Matthew Craven, Sundhya Pahuja, and Gerry Simpson, *Reading and Unreading: A Historiography of Hiatus, in International Law and the Cold War* (Cambridge: Cambridge University Press, 2020), 6–7 deconstructs the idea of the Cold War as an epoch, to demonstrate how it had contrasting effects upon international law extending outside of the temporal boundaries.

2 Edward Jones-Imhotep, *The Unreliable Nation. Hostile Nature and Technological Failure in the Cold War* (Cambridge, MA: MIT Press, 2017) brilliantly examines how global insecurity justified technological invasions of northern territory, including failed defence projects.

3 Defence Construction Limited helped to mitigate the damages of this project in which it took part. Jeffrey Noakes, "Under the Radar. Defence Construction (1951), Limited and Military infrastructure in Canada, 1951–1965" (PhD diss., Carleton University, 2005), 602.

4 National Defence. *Backgrounder – North Warning System In-Service Support*, 31 January 2022, https://www.canada.ca/en/department-national-defence/news/2022/01/backgrounder--north-warning-system-in-service-support.html (accessed 9 August 2023).

5 David Lochead, "Nasittuq Wins $592M Contract to Help Run North Warning System, 2 February 2022, *Nunatsiaq News*, https://nunatsiaq.com/stories/article/nasittuq-wins-592m-contract-to-help-run-north-warning-system/ (accessed 9 August 2023).

6 Brittany Luby, *The Damned*, 10.

7 Elizabeth Miller, Edward Little, and Steven High, *Going Public. The Art of Participatory Practice* (Vancouver: UBC Press, 2017), 5–9; Steven High, *Oral History at the Crossroads. Sharing Life Stories of Struggle and Displacement* (Vancouver: UBC Press, 2013); Concordia University Centre for Oral History and Digital Story Telling Website, https://storytelling.concordia.ca/ (accessed 12 October 2023).

8 Joan Sangster, *Transforming Labour: Women and Work in Post-War Canada* (Toronto: University of Toronto Press, 2010). Kindle, 17.

9 Enloe has spoken about the importance of listening to voices within and outside the military to create moments of discomfort and potential change. "A Feminist Conversation on Military Culture Change," transcript of a public Lecture, TMC Network Annual Symposium, 18 February 2023, Mount Saint Vincent University, Halifax, NS, https://www.msvu.ca/wp-content/uploads/2022/07/Enloe-transcript_Final.pdf (accessed 30 August 2023).

Contributors

ISABEL CAMPBELL, the editor of this volume, is a senior historian at the Directorate of History and Heritage, National Defence Headquarters. They are the lead historian for the postwar official history of the Royal Canadian Navy and a contributing author for the postwar official history of the Royal Canadian Air Force and have published on the Cold War, alliance strategy, nuclear weapons, and gendered aspects of historiography, service families, as well as innovations in archival rules and declassification. They are a co-author for chapter 3 of this volume and wrote the introduction and conclusion. This work represents their own opinions and not those of the Canadian government, but they acknowledge the support of the Directorate of History and Heritage and their colleagues in undertaking this work.

STACEY FRITZ is the primary author of chapter 3, "Voices from the DEW Line." Her contribution draws from her anthropology doctoral dissertation, completed at the University of Alaska Fairbanks in 2010, which traced the legacies of the DEW Line in the western Arctic. As a cultural anthropologist, she worked on public land management in the Arctic from 2010 to 2020 and has published about Nuiqsut's traditional knowledge, fishery habitat, climate change, and about how military developments have affected the northern environment. After working as an anthropologist and project manager at the Fairbanks-based Cold Climate Housing Research Centre, she now co-leads Alaska Adaptable Housing LLC and works on housing insecurity issues, building innovation, remote Arctic logistics, and outreach to communities, environmental justice, and mitigating resource development factors through consultation with Indigenous communities. Her expert analysis is informed by her experiences sailing and paddling the western Arctic coast and Arctic rivers, conducting oral history interviews, and working directly with remote Indigenous communities to ensure that their voices and concerns are heard in interactions with government and industry.

SUE HEFFERNAN earned a bachelor of environmental studies and a master's in regional planning and resource development from the University of Waterloo during the 1970s. She then spent more than thirty years in northern Ontario working for the provincial government before retiring in 2010. The favourite part of Sue's job was working with small towns and infrastructure projects, and it was this experience that encouraged her to study the consequences of placing a Cold War military station beside the community of Moosonee. In 2016 Sue successfully defended her doctoral dissertation "Moosonee, Ontario: A Model of Cold War Change" at Laurentian University (Sudbury). Sue was also a sessional professor in the Geography Department at Laurentian from 2006 to 2017. She taught Northern Canadian Issues and Geographic Perspectives on Urban Systems. She drew upon her doctoral research and her long-term community relationships with Cree elders and leaders in writing chapter 2.

SARAH HOGENBIRK is an independent settler scholar who specializes in the fields of Canadian history, women's history, gender history, and war and society. Her recent publications include chapters in *Women's Experiences of the Second World War: Exile, Occupation, and Everyday Life* (2021) and *Making the Best of It: Women and Girls of Canada and Newfoundland During the Second World War* (2020). Chapter 6 draws from her doctoral work and she gratefully acknowledges the financial support of the Social Sciences and Humanities Research Council of Canada for her doctoral dissertation.

FRANCES REILLY's work focuses on anti-communism, police surveillance, sexual psychiatry, and atomic culture in Cold War Canada. Her recent publications include "Dale and the Bomb: Exploring the Nuclear Future and Cold War Anxiety in 1950s Canadian Children's Literature" in the *Journal of Canadian Studies* (Spring 2019) and "Operation Profunc: The Cold War Plan to Intern Canadian Communists" in Dennis Molinaro's *The Bridge in the Parks: The Five Eyes and Cold War Counter-Intelligence* (University of Toronto Press, 2021). She also contributed to the Graphic History Collective's collaborative project, Remember | Resist | Redraw, with a poster and essay: "Police Surveillance and Democratic Socialism in Cold War Canada" (2021). She undertook new original research and drew upon her doctoral dissertation ("Controlling Contagion: Policing and Prescribing Sexual and Political Normalcy in Cold War Canada") in writing chapter 5. Frances is based in Toronto.

WARREN SINCLAIR, an Indigenous scholar, retired as chief archivist at the Directorate of History and Heritage, National Defence Headquarters in Ottawa in 2021. He received his master's in library and information science from the University of Western Ontario in 1989 and an archives technician diploma from Algonquin College in 1993. After working at Library and Archives Canada from 1994 to 1998, he accepted an archival post at the Directorate in 1999. He became the acting chief archivist in 2003. In addition to his archival work, Warren completed a large Métis genealogical collection between 1994 and 1996 consisting of 910 dependency tables, a body of research which is available online on the University of Calgary website. He authored a chapter on the "Nile Voyageurs" for *A Sketch Account of Aboriginal People in the Canadian Military*. Future projects include research articles on the Cree code-talkers of the Second World War and the St Peter's, Manitoba contingent of the "Nile Voyageurs." His main interests include Métis and Indigenous genealogy and fur trade history in the Canadian northwest. Warren wrote chapter 1, drawing from years of family research, his father's memoirs, testimony, personnel file, and other family documents as well as extensive secondary and primary research.

MATTHEW S. WISEMAN is a Canadian historian whose research concentrates on science, technology, and medical research ethics in the Cold War. He received his doctorate in history from Wilfrid Laurier University in 2017 and held successive postdoctoral fellowships at the University of Toronto (2017–19), Western University (2019–20), and St Jerome's University (2020–22). He is currently a lecturer in the Department of History at the University of Waterloo. He is the author of *Frontier Science: Northern Canada, Military Research, and the Cold War, 1945–1970* (University of Toronto Press, 2024), which examines the social and environmental consequences of military-sponsored research in northern Canada and the Canadian Arctic during the early Cold War. His work on chapter 4 draws from doctoral research as well as original new research. A Social Sciences and Humanities Research Council Doctoral Fellowship funded portions of the research to complete this project.

Index